RESTATING ORIENTALISM

Restating Orientalism

A CRITIQUE OF MODERN KNOWLEDGE

Wael B. Hallaq

Columbia University Press

New York

Columbia University Press
Publishers Since 1893
New York   Chichester, West Sussex
cup.columbia.edu

Cataloging-in-Publication Data available from the Library of Congress
ISBN 978-0-231-18762-6 (cloth)
ISBN 978-0-231-54738-3 (electronic)

Columbia University Press books are printed on permanent and durable acid-free paper.
Printed in the United States of America

Cover design: Martin Hinze

Contents

Preface and Acknowledgments

The arguments of this book have been in the making for more than a decade, particularly since 2009, when they became an almost permanent staple in my course offerings at Columbia University. Throughout these intellectual exercises, I have come to learn that there is no single important aspect of modernity that is not touched, to one degree or another, by the issues that the problem of Orientalism raises. This, then, is a book that is as much about modernity as it is about Orientalism, just as the concerns of my *The Impossible State* were as much about this condition as they were about the state. More importantly, and as this book intends to show, I have learned that Orientalism euphemizes a series of theoretical and substantive inquires that pertain to the constitution of the modern self as much as they are about a supposed "Other," historical or otherwise. Although I am largely unconcerned with the modalities of Europe's self-formation against an Orient, the constitution of the modern self—whose sources certainly transcend the Orient—remains for me a prime concern. In all the colonialisms and genocides that it contributed to, Orientalism emerges as a symptom, rather than the cause or chief culprit, of a psychoepistemic disorder plaguing modern forms of knowledge to the core. I have learned that in the very act of setting up this discipline as an analytical category, Orientalism itself undergoes considerable diminution and expansion, all at once.

The relative demotion of Orientalism complicates rather than simplifies our analytical task. Although this field of discourse is symptomatic of a pervasive psychoepistemic disorder, and as such could be treated like any other field of knowledge, it remains the most obvious corridor through which knowledge about the Other is transmitted. This crucial fact imposes on us a situation in which Orientalism must be recognized as both an accomplice to oppression and violence and, once liberated from its present condition, a necessary bridge to a different conception of the Other. The argument that those parts of academia that stand in the service of modern forms of capitalism, colonialism, and hegemonic power must eventually be made to vanish cannot, and must not, include Orientalism without qualification.

The tension between rejecting and retaining Orientalism requires a set of analytical procedures and resources that must reckon with certain givens. Essential to these givens is Edward Said's important work, most especially his remarkable *Orientalism*. Although my book is not, at the end of the day, about his work as a *terminus ad quem*, and despite the sustained and vigorous—but hopefully fair-minded—critique I direct at it, I record my gratitude to him and to his staying memory, and do so with the full recognition of his influence on my early formation. Without his contributions, I very much doubt that this book would have been possible, just as much as his celebrated book has spun, and thus made possible, an entire field of discourse. On a psychological level, Said provided a model of nearly unmatched intellectual courage that has stayed with me since 1979, when I was first exposed to his work.

I have incurred a large debt to several people whose suggestions helped in sharpening the book's arguments. Gil Anidjar and Sudipta Kaviraj, both of Columbia, read the book with great care and provided detailed critique. Their intellectual companionship has been enriching in more than one way, and beyond the bounds of the present project. Humeira Iqtidar, of King's College, London, subjected the book to a thoroughly constructive critique, from which I derived great benefit. No less generous with his attention to an earlier draft was Omar Farahat, of McGill University's Law School. His warnings, among other things, as to how some of the book's arguments might be misconstrued were invaluable, and will, I hope, minimize the sort of misconceived reactions that befell *The Impossible State*. Dariouche Kechavarzi-Tehrani, one of Columbia's most brilliant students, read two successive drafts of the manuscript, each time providing various insights and extensively engaging me over cognate questions that have arisen in Latin American postcolonial literature. Abed Awad read the manuscript from a jurist's perspective and offered a number of valuable comments. His generous help and support over the years have been inestimable. During the year or two preceding the writing of this book, I benefited from discussions with Sohaib Khan, who was an exemplary and challenging interlocutor. Finally, parts of the last chapter were presented as a lecture at Yale Law School in November 2015. Gerhard Böwering, Owen Fiss, Frank Griffel, Paul Kahn, Anthony Kronman, and Daniel Markovits engaged me in intense, fruitful discussions during the lecture and afterward. To all colleagues named, to Robert Demke for his competent editing, as well as to the anonymous but perspicacious readers of the press, I record my sincere gratitude. Needless to say, any error or weakness that this book may continue to harbor remains mine alone.

A word about the intellectual genealogy of this book. Unlike most commentators addressing the problem of Orientalism and other forms of knowledge, I come to the present project from within the field of Orientalism, having written in it and about it for nearly four decades. In some strong sense, it seems to me that most issues I have written about throughout this period, whether in the legal, historical, or philosophical fields, have been a series of engagements that are woven together around a single thread, despite the sometimes rather dissimilar materials and varied scholarly problems I have studied. While this book is far from being the culmination of my work, it is nonetheless the latest installment in this project, which is to say that it continues much of the work I have produced over the last two decades. What I say here therefore issues from, and often presupposes, earlier deliberations, and by necessity I could only invoke these deliberations with extreme brevity, if not merely gesture to them with citations. Of particular relevance are two books that lay the grounds for the present work, and the reader whose purpose is to *genuinely engage* the present book is strongly advised to read these works before poring over this one. The first of these, offering a fairly comprehensive background, is *Shariʿa: Theory, Practice, Transformations* (Cambridge: Cambridge University Press, 2009), while the second is *The Impossible State* (New York: Columbia University Press, 2013). Indeed, I regard the present book as a sequel to the latter, both together making a particular segment of my larger project more, though by no means entirely, complete. While *The Impossible State* was intended to interrogate the Muslim self and its place in, and exit from, modernity, the present project is about the *place* of the Western self in the modern project, as well as about possible exits from this condition. Yet, to confuse the two Selves, to argue that one *entirely* depends on the other, will amount, by the logic of this book, to denying the particularity and uniqueness, and thus autonomy, of cultures. I shall insist that while the colonized Other and its historical legacies and traditions provide a rich heuristic repertoire for ethicizing the colonizer's self (partly the concern of *The Impossible State*), the ultimate challenge facing Western modernity must be met from within the Western self, whose first act of self-liberation resides in the shedding of sovereignty over all that exists. The two books therefore complement each other and stand within a mutually enhancing dialectic.

Finally, a recommendation about the modality of reading this book is in order. It so happens that the discussions and arguments it proffers gain in expansion and density as the book proceeds. A case in point is the theory of the author, whose full elucidation extends over the introduction and the first three chapters. The same is the case with the concept of sovereignty, to the elaboration of which the whole book is in effect dedicated. There is no complete treatment of any central concept that can be gleaned from a single chapter or part of the book. The reader is therefore urged to suspend judgment of the merits of each argument or concept until the entire book has been perused.

RESTATING ORIENTALISM

Introduction

I

Anyone familiar with debates on Orientalism comes to the realization that there is a profound ambiguity in the meaning of the term that designates this field of scholarship.[1] Essential to this confusion is the matter of classification. Is Orientalism an academic scholarly field or is it an ideological construction, to be treated no different than one would treat any bias-laden discourse? The assumption guiding both the question and the quest for classification is that scholarly discourse is not and should not be ideological, that ideology in fact stands at the other extreme end of dispassionate, objective scholarship.

This is what seems to have driven one author, in his own quest to avoid the "volatility" of the term, to "follow a simple expedient." He decided to employ the "nonpejorative" form "orientalism" to refer to the "ongoing Western tradition of intellectual inquiry into an existential engagement with the ideas, practices and values of the East, particularly in the religious field," whereas capitalized "Orientalism" would be reserved for the "ideologically-motivated 'epistemic construction' and 'corporate institution'" that Anouar Abdel-Malek, A. L. Tibawi, Edward Said, and several others have criticized.[2] Operating on the assumption that there is such a thing as objective and biased Orientalism, this author attempts to show that because there are "orientalists" (mostly Indologists) who seriously engaged the spirituality of the Orient and often condemned colonialism, Said's case was "overstated,"[3] hence the allowance for the nonpejorative form "orientalism." The cause for "overstating" the case is said to have originally been Michel Foucault's problem, which Said replicated, in disallowing individual "agency" in the formation of power discourses. Leaving aside for the moment the issue of misunderstanding Foucault (by both this author and Said himself), nothing more, in effect, is proffered in the way of rendering this confused and confusing designation of "Orientalism" analytically or theoretically intelligible. Once we succeed in subtracting "Orientalism" from "orientalism," which is what our author wants us to do, we are supposed to attain a balance that stands in refutation of Said's sweeping generalization, thereby exonerating "orientalists" from Said's incriminations.

Empirically, this act of subtraction may be legitimate, but the balance sheds not an iota of light on the problematic term itself. It merely makes exceptions to Said's categorical brush, but does not harness the exceptions for further understanding or precision. When all is said and done, and after the subtraction is fully completed, the term in fact gains in substantive ambiguity and diminishes further in theoretical clarity. If there are exceptions, then what are the theoretical parameters that one can employ for distinguishing the norm? And once this operation of distinguishing-cum-classifying has been accomplished, what is the ultimate theoretical significance of it? How do we understand the "Orientalism phenomenon" and the reality that surrounds it? I shall take up the theoretical issues in detail as I proceed, but for now it is the ambiguity of the term in current discourse that interests me.

This author and his otherwise remarkable book nonetheless fare better than the average discussions of the subject. A highly representative and prolific recent scholarly exchange[4] equated the position of Bernard Lewis, on the one hand, and that of the anthropologist Talal Asad and mine, on the other. Scholars whom few would ever associate with what our author above designated as "Orientalism" or for that matter with the faintest "Orientalist" leaning have been charged with "Orientalism," meaning not only that these scholars write within a "Western" scholarly tradition, but that they commit errors that are fundamentally associated with a scholarly discursive tradition that has, since the pioneering writings of the Marxist political scientist Anouar Abdel-Malek, been normatively regarded as pejorative, negative, exoticizing, or otherwise harmful—in some seriously interpretive sense—to Islam and the Orient.

A scholar need not say or write anything pejorative or negative about the "Orient" to invite such charges. Nor does she even need to imply any negativity in the least. An argument, for instance, that the various intellectual traditions in Islam—Shariʿa, Sufism, Kalam, philosophy, or *adab*—stood for discursive moral paradigms or represented a benchmark that insisted on robust ethical foundations that one is hard-pressed to find in modernity may instigate virulent charges of "Orientalist" attitudes, charges as vehement as any leveled against negative stereotypes, political, racist, or otherwise. For, the argument goes, to represent Islam as having an advantage over any major aspect of modernity automatically implies idealizing or exoticizing the Orient, this having the grave consequence of deeming Islam unmodern, antimodern, a mismatch with the modern world, or a Utopia fantasy. To the critics who espouse this position, Islam can be neither good nor bad, and the only way to escape the charge of Orientalism, it would seem, is to construct a vision of Islam and Islamic history consistent with, though perhaps not a replica of, modernity, and most especially its liberalism. This much, it will be my argument, was Said's legacy, although he advanced his case with some subtlety. Thus any scholar who depicts Islam negatively or positively is an Orientalist, the former emerging as a bigot, the latter as an exoticizer. Such criteria, as rudimentary as they are, are furthermore applied to historiographical and historical research, generating questions, for instance, about whether or not Sir William Jones and his likes were "Orientalists," as Edward Said charged, given that these figures in fact valued Indian civilization and were critics of empire and the Enlightenment.[5] Such debates are many; the one regarding the Orientalist Louis Massignon is perhaps the best known.

It would seem that there is a correlation between such charges and the perceived or real ethnic and religious backgrounds of the authors associated or charged with Orientalist leanings. The more distant such backgrounds are from the object of study, the more vulnerable authors are to this charge. Correlatively, the more the authors hail from perceived or real "Oriental" cultures—whatever that may mean—the less they seem to suffer from accusations of Orientalist misconduct. It is more likely for a white Christian scholar from Houston to suffer the charge than for a Muslim scholar teaching in Cairo, or Toronto, for that matter. This is confusion at its best.

It is the argument of this book that both the simple term and the complex concept of Orientalism have been severely misunderstood, that they have in effect been rendered, partly due to Said's writings, into rudimentary political slogans and catchwords that operate extensively in a field of ideological semantics. Labeling a scholar an "Orientalist" has become a mode of condemnation, a negative epithet, whereas the designation "historian," "engineer," "economist," or even "anthropologist" remains predominantly, but falsely, neutral. The politicization of the term and concept has eviscerated its real meaning and denotations, masking its complicity in the deeper structures of thought and action, thereby making it a largely superficial and in fact wholly useless category for serious scholarly, much less intellectual, debate. Confined as it has been to prejudice, condescension, cultural bias, colonialism, and imperial domination, the concept has remained straightjacketed in a strictly political framework that could not transcend its own field of vision, thus leaving it insulated from the very substructures of thought that gave rise to it in the first place. I shall insist that whatever charge the Orientalist may be made to bear, it is one that equally attaches to his or her cognates, be it a scientist, journalist, historian, philosopher, or economist, among academic others.

Defining the world through binaries of the Self and Other, of enemy and friend, the political unconsciously subordinates all other discursive domains to its own imperatives—including pathologies that give it its own raison d'être. To begin and end with politics as a conventional category, as Said has done, is to overlook the premises through which the political itself can be critiqued, premises whose trajectory starts at the genealogical foundations that give rise to it but that finally harness for critique those intellectual positions that stand outside those foundations. Which is to say that a true political critique of Orientalism *must begin with the foundations that gave rise* to a particular conception of nature, liberalism, secularism, secular humanism, anthropocentrism, capitalism, the modern state, and much else that modernity developed as central to its project. Said's critique remained political in the (conventional) sense that it questioned none of these categories of thought and action as *fundamental and foundational* to the construction of the problem that is Orientalism, and to much else that has been left intact. In other words, it continued to plow conventional, if not rudimentary, political terrains because his critical narrative assumed and wholly left in place the same political subject, the modern subject, as the undivided matrix and locus of these categories. To place the subject at the front and center of critique is to inquire, de novo, into the constitution of the subject as a phenomenon whose measure is ethical formation.

That the problem originated in part in the literary approach Said adopted, and that as a result the central problems of Orientalism remained untouched or shallowly addressed, leave us with a simple, if not simplistic, explanation. Foucault had already understood that oppositions and resistances to late modernity make for what he called "'immediate' struggles" because they look not for the "chief enemy" but for the "immediate enemy."[6] I think that Said's work and the various reactions to it, positive as well as "neutral," have been preoccupied with the "immediate enemy." There are, as I shall try to show, deeper reasons why Said (and the vast field of discourse his writings generated) could not undertake a profound investigation, one that would have militated against, if not sharply contradicted, his own positions as a liberal critic and scholar, and no less as a secular humanist. For it is my argument that secular humanism, like liberalism, is not only anthropocentric, *structurally* intertwined with violence, and incapable of sympathy with the nonsecular Other,[7] but it is also anchored, per force, in a structure of thought wholly defined by modes of sovereign domination.[8] Secular humanism is not just a name for a particular type of discourse, of "analyzing" the world; it is the psychoepistemic substantiation of a *particular subject* who articulates the world wholly through disenchanted modern categories that are inherently incapable of appreciating intellectually, and much less sympathizing spiritually with, non-secular-humanist phenomena. *Orientalism*'s canonicity and "popular" reception may thus be attributed to its ability to provide a highly flammable fuel to the fire of what the moral philosopher Alasdair MacIntyre called liberalism's "interminable disagreement,"[9] a discursive strategy whose structure and teleology are intended to bar the definitive (ethical) resolution of perceived problems and crises *within* liberalism and the liberal subject, but that is liberalism nonetheless. The liberal subject, as this book argues, is never the locus or focus of a restructuring critique, however much this subject has been culpable and complicit in contributing to modernity's crises. The problems are always seen to lie elsewhere, threatening and endangering that subject, but are never inextricably and *structurally* linked to that subject's constitution.

Yet, it must be clear that the present book is not about Said's writings on culture, and much less so on literature. Nor is it exclusively or primarily intended to be a critique of Said's writings on Orientalism. The criticisms of his work, fair and unfair, have been legion and *I cannot claim credit for any contribution to that repertoire.* His chief work on the subject, my main focus and concern, has been shown to be replete with problems, however productive these turned out to be. I point only to those problems and contradictions that permit me an entry into their meaning that can serve my purpose in trying to go beyond his, and the current, understanding of the issues that have thus far been construed and constructed. Both Said's critics and his followers remained largely within the boundaries and terms of debate that he set, at times even exacerbating his imprecisions and outright errors. And it is this current state of affairs, *not just* Said's work, that this book aims to interrogate. That Said's work remains relevant for my critique (as evidenced in the frequency with which I invoke it) has precisely to do with the fact that the terms of debate he set have not changed much in almost four decades,[10] and this despite the many brilliant critiques that have been registered against his work. Put differently, his book remains the most learned and sophisticated summa exhibiting the persistent—should I say canonical?—misconceptions regarding Orientalism.

In the process of scapegoating Orientalism, Said and the very discursive field his work has created have left untouched the structural anchors of the sciences, social sciences, and humanities, as well as their political manifestations in the larger modern project. The historical anthropologist James Clifford prudently hints at this absence, unfortunately in passing: Said, he avers, adopted the self-conscious position of "oppositionality" that "writes back" against "imperial discourse from the position of an oriental whose actuality has been distorted and denied." Yet, it is clear that "a wide range of Western humanist assumptions escape Said's oppositional analysis, as do the discursive alliances of knowledge and power produced by anticolonial and particularly nationalist movements."[11] Clifford is ingenious in his assertion that the problem with which *Orientalism* deals "should not be closely identified with the specific tradition of Orientalism. . . . Said abandons the level of cultural criticism proposed by Foucault and relapses into traditional intellectual history. Moreover . . . he does not question anthropological orthodoxies based on mythology of fieldwork encounter and a hermeneutically minded cultural history—orthodoxies he often appears to share."[12] Nonetheless, Clifford's judicious expansion itself remains constrained.

Said's was an indispensable work, timely for the decade or two after its publication, both for the study of Islam in the West and for several other academic fields. He lifted Orientalism from its uninterrogated subterranean normativity to a focus of critique, if not doubt. Yet, Said's problematic framing of Orientalism has invited countless critiques, ranging from the serious to the apologetic. The critiques have mainly been made on the following grounds: (1) *Orientalism* adopts the deterministic Foucauldian theory of discursive formations[13] that does not account for authorial individuality and individualistic contribution; (2) it does not give due credit to predecessors who had leveled weighty critical attacks on the discipline, notably Anouar Abdel-Malek and A. L. Tibawi;[14] (3) it commits the same fallacies of essentializing and totalizing as that which it critiques; (4) it is profoundly lacking in historical and historiographical method, Said himself being a literary critic who had no historical training; (5) it relies on divergent theoretical apparatuses that stem from contradictory epistemological assumptions; (6) it fails to take into account large bodies of writing by the prolific German Orientalists, by women, and by "Orientals" themselves; (7) it does not account for distinguishing features in the various types of Orientalism, again the German component being particularly noted for its formidable output within an alleged context of lack of empire; and (8) it harbors ideological biases against Zionism and Judaism.

I do not intend to engage these criticisms by affirming or negating their thrust; I will have an occasion to discuss the substance of some of them as my argument requires and as I proceed. What is worth noting, however, is their general nature: critiques 1, 3, and 5 take aim at methodology, but do not even come close to providing an alternative, since those who take these stances are a great majority that tends to reject the very premise Said adopts, and since they seem to have made their critiques in the first place exclusively to refute Said's premise. Critique 2 is formal and does not address the substantive issues, for the validity of the critiques proffered by Said's unacknowledged predecessors would remain intact irrespective of their authorial provenance. This, in some sense, is an ad hominem attack. Critique 4 is solid, but as in the cases of critiques 1, 3, and 5, it does not make clear how historiographical or theoretical competence can offer an alternative critical assessment of Orientalism. Critiques 6 and 7 are formal as well, intended to demonstrate absence in Said's work, but they do not articulate how this lack—if we grant it in the case of German Orientalism[15]— can be fertile ground for constructing a vigorous critical appraisal of the discipline. Finally, critique 8 is highly polemical, itself motivated by the same bias that it levels against *Orientalism*.

These critiques, I think, are a comprehensive and accurate representation of the response to Said's work. Much of what they deploy is valuable as scholarly engagement, but some is plainly intended to discredit the work on political grounds. Yet, none attempts to provide an account that improves on or displaces Said's work, much less set new terms for the debate. Indeed, none of these critiques has etched itself in scholarly memory as Said's *Orientalism* did. As problematic as it is, the book remains canonic. But canonicity neither excludes the possibility of the work being transcended or supplanted, nor is it an eternal confirmation of the truth of its propositions. Said's work therefore provides me with the flare, though not the tools, to navigate my seas. If the metaphor is at all apt, I might say that in this work I hijack Said's ship to reequip it for the exploration of oceans that he could see dimly from afar, if at all.

Accordingly, I shall insist that the problems underlying Orientalism are so expansive and profound that the entire discipline, along with the emerging critique and defense of it, has functioned as a discursive mask to cover up serious crises in late-modern epistemology. Surely not to be exonerated in the least, Orientalism has nonetheless been *structurally* and *systemically* scapegoated, a phenomenon that I regard as having the function of emplotment that is aimed at suppressing the real forces that precipitate the actions that it is accused of performing and the attributes that it is accused of having. To anticipate some of my conclusions, it is with the structure and system that have produced and enveloped Orientalism that, I argue, we must begin and end. Which is also to say that it is no less the modern subject and its constitution as the agent underwriting modern structures that must be at the center of our analytical scrutiny. For Orientalism, like any single field of academic discourse, is demonstrably a derivative, and derivatives by definition must have progenitors from which they derive. But if Orientalism must be our point of departure, it is the successive layers of the system and structure undergirding it that we must peel back, the first layer being that which the entire debate has revealed: that Orientalism involves a particular kind or kinds of bias, and that we have thus far failed to develop a proper critical apparatus for the diagnosis of this bias—hence the confusion and arbitrary ascriptions and distribution of the charge. Viewing our subject in this manner therefore explains why chapters 4 and 5—not to mention the thrust of chapter 3—depart from a relatively narrow focus on Orientalism in general and on Said's work in particular, expanding the narrative to virtually the entire range of modern knowledge structures.

The substance and effect of Said's critique were that Orientalism represented a *structured* discourse, one that exhibited a penchant for self-referentiality and a self-enclosed body of knowledge. The method he employed to demonstrate the collusion of Orientalism with power amounted to a series of dissections of individual scholars' writings.[16] These individual dissections always stood in a dialectical relationship to an overarching discourse that gave them unity, but were then corralled back into the overarching discursive tradition. The dialectic, in other words, remained confined to the space between the individual text and the organizing suprastructure. How this suprastructure established well-defined and concrete relationships of power with colonialism and other manifestations of dominance was never made clear. Even less clear was the entire set of forces and formations that undergirded colonialism, which left Said's account largely limited to a critique of the *text as power*. A glance at *Orientalism* reveals an obsession with individual texts, marshaled seriatim and analyzed ad nauseam, without any increase in the thickness and depth of analysis. An author's individual work was for Said a fundamental unit of discourse, through which he presumably uncovered the workings of the structured system. He seems to have believed that the more authors one studied, the more "the historical experience of imperialism" would be uncovered.[17]

The author, I will argue, is indeed a fundamental category but not in the sense that Said understood it. His conception of the author may be said to lie behind most, if not, by implication, all of the problems that engulfed his *Orientalism*. In registering his disagreement with Foucault about the "determining imprint" of individual authors, Said, in a mere two sentences, revealed the limitations of his book in its entirety: "Foucault believes that in general the individual text or author counts for very little. . . . Yet, I do believe in the determining imprint of individual writers upon the otherwise anonymous collective body of texts constituting a discursive formation like Orientalism" (23).[18] This statement amounted to what I call a "genetic slice": it included all the traits, approaches, methodologies, and lines of analysis that were to manifest themselves in full-fledged form in the *body* of the book. Yet, Said's misapprehensions about the author are not, on their own, the reason for my insistence that a robust concept of the author is necessary. Unlike Said, I will argue that Orientalism is not just a structured system but also, and far more crucially, a *systemic* structure, which is to say that it was embedded in, defined by, corralled into, and driven by a larger structure that extended horizontally and vertically throughout the modern project and its Enlightenment (notwithstanding the fact that the latter was neither a single event nor, by any means, a host of consistent narratives).[19] The horizontality and verticality are not only substantive dimensions; they are intrinsically temporal ones. And since so much has been made of who is a ("good") "Orientalist" and who is a ("bad") "orientalist," an undertaking such as the one I am proposing will require attention to the concept of the author. My purpose is not to shed light on the often-shallow controversy that has raged in the field over this issue (obviously a sensitive one, if for no other reason than its having been taken by many as a personal affront). Rather, it is to situate the concept of the author and its potentialities in the systemic structure I have just mentioned.

To do this, I begin in chapter 1 with a critique of Said's choice of the historical and geocultural range from which he selected his subject authors. In my account, the choices do not merely indicate arbitrariness or lack of discrimination (which certainly was the case and for which he was deservedly critiqued heavily),[20] but more importantly, Said does not work with a theory of the author, much less a coherent one, and *this very lack* was in turn not merely a symptom of the problematic critique that he made, but indeed nothing less than a function of the very discursive formation he purported to critique. In other words, it is my contention that Said unwittingly reinforced this formation, and hence reasserted its power at the expense of Orientalism. Scapegoating Orientalism and failing to situate it in its larger epistemological context—that is, systemic thought structure—are not only, through absence, the most defining feature of his work; they also indicate Said's failure to appreciate the full force of Orientalism's destructive power *as a modern form of power.* While situating Orientalism in its proper place within the configurations of the modern project is an important component of my aim here, I do so without attaching central importance to the contributions of individual Orientalists. On my view, the idea of a "bad" or "good" Orientalist is largely, if not entirely, irrelevant. An Orientalist is never "bad" *just because* of what he or she says, teaches, or writes in the way of misrepresenting the Orient. Nor is she "good" *just because* her portrayal of the Orient is positive. *Orientalism hinges not on its discursive appearance as positive or negative, but rather on the quality with which it moors itself in a particular thought structure.*

In order to bring out the full thrust of my argument, I first situate the author, through a reinterpretation of Foucault, within what I call paradigms or central domains, a concept that serves my purposes in at least three ways: First, paradigms enable the specific assignment of the author's location within the larger context of a discursive tradition, and this in turn within a still-larger framework of power systems. Second, paradigms offer a method through which one can speak cogently about two different and even historically and culturally distinct phenomena, each constituting its own paradigmatic structure, in a comparatively instructive way—a "comparativity" that is necessary, among other things, for delimiting the nature and internal dynamics of Orientalism, so that its distinguishing features are methodically identified as disconnected, by virtue of their epistemic location, from what may mistakenly appear to be a forerunner. And third, this sort of handling of such temporally and spatially different paradigmatic domains prevents false analogies and uneven comparisons, where a secondary feature of a peripheral domain or an exception in a central domain is compared to a principal or dominant feature in that domain or, alternatively, to one belonging to another central paradigm, say, in another culture. (This feature is furthermore pregnant with significance for a proper interpretation and assessment of the very arguments I marshal here in constructing a theory of paradigms, a theory that insists on a conception of reality that sharply distinguishes between driving—and therefore paradigmatic—forces and what might be called exceptions. Characterizing modernity as materialist or capitalist, to take a starkly illustrative example, tends to invoke the usual objection that exceptions abound, represented as they are by noncapitalist social and political movements or by outright antimaterialist thinkers. The theory of paradigms does not deny but fully acknowledges the existence of these exceptions, arguing that the very exception is precisely that which proves the dominance of central domains, however much exceptions remain integral to the power dynamics within these domains. Claims made in this book about Buddhism, Islam, or Hinduism—that they acted "paradigmatically" in ways that provide sharp contrasts to modernity—cannot be in the least invalidated by noting cognate or similar voices from within modernity, voices that otherwise constitute exceptions. For instance, there is no philosopher's anticapitalist philosophy, or a social or political antimaterialist movement, however vigorous, that can affect the validity of the proposition that capitalism is a central paradigm of modernity.)

This last feature of paradigms raises yet additional questions specific to our inquiry. One of the widespread legacies of Said's *Orientalism* is that one cannot speak of "Islam" as having one quality or another, or as acting in one manner or another, without this constituting reductionism, essentialism, and thus an egregious form of misrepresentation. While it is a truism that no single macrophenomenon can be reduced to a single quality or form, it is also true that cultures and even so-called civilizations do operate through central domains (in fact, they have no way of avoiding such domains, since they are *constituted by them*), so one can say, for instance, that a central domain of Euro-American modernity is capitalism. Reacting to vicious misrepresentations of Islam in the West, Said, with a traumatized edge, argued in effect that even equivalent statements such as I made about Euro-American capitalism (being a central domain and thus a defining feature of Western modernity) would, in the case of Islam, constitute reductionism, because such characterizations have a tendency to create difference, which he diagnosed to be a cause for Orientalism's misguided performance. I will argue that this is an issue that created multiple problems in Said's narrative, because Said *did not develop an understanding of his own about the Orient*, wavering between the Orientalists' "different" Orient that, precisely because it is different, gave rise to their prejudice and a modern and liberal Orient that would give rise to the charge of "reconstituting" the Orient in the image of the West, no less a prejudice. The theory of paradigm will thus allow us to continue to speak of difference without committing the fallacy of reductionism.[21] In fact, on this theory difference militates against Orientalist discourse as well as against its prejudices and its domination.

In chapter 1, I argue that a proper understanding of Orientalist discourse requires a particular understanding of performativity, for if there is any performative power to Orientalist discourse, it is so only by virtue of the so-called conditions of felicity that undergird it. Unlike advocates of radical forms of performativity, however, I subscribe to the view that language generates effective power to mold subjects only by virtue of underlying, often masked structures whose force is constituted by the dynamics of central paradigms. Which is to say that in my conception of performativity, representation qua representation *is less a constitutive operation of the object represented and more a linguistic function of actual remaking, reordering, destruction, and intervention*. Thus, an account of language's conditions of felicity is in turn intended to reconnect Orientalist discourse with the larger structures of modernity that Said overlooked,[22] with the attendant implication that an exclusively literary analysis of texts is both a partial and a distorting exercise. Indeed, I argue that Said's preoccupation with the text as a well-nigh self-enclosed structure of (mis)representation is in effect itself a misrepresentation of the phenomenon he studied.

This is said bearing in mind the caveat that if *Orientalism*, along with *Culture and Imperialism*, is evaluated within the exclusive boundaries of the modalities through which Europe constructed itself against the Other, then Said's explorations remain monumental,[23] though these modalities are not immediately germane to the concerns of my work. In some strong sense, this book could not care less about Europe's self-formation insofar as it is Europe's nontransgressive business. For it is one of my conjectures (which cannot be anything more than that) that even if the "Orient" has never existed, Europe would have found other "realities" against which it would elaborate a "self," as have most premodern cultures, however dramatically different these were. But this project of construction-by-opposition cannot, according to the general argument of this book, be taken too far, for Europe's choices and internal realities during the "long seventeenth century" and the century after remain its own choices, based in good part on *its own* realities, however much an Orient or an "Occident" may have been present in its imagination. It is this assumption that governs this book, an assumption that forces us to confront not so much texts and textual strategies as the actual destructive violence on the modern ground (or is it the ground of modernity?).

By resorting to a concept of performativity, I intended to bring Said to the reality of modernity, or modern reality, one that involved and could not have evolved outside certain deep structures of thought, epistemic sovereignty, segregation, fragmentation, cultural engineering, colonialism, and especially genocide, in all of its forms. Said seems to have overlooked Foucault's important insistence that it is "necessary" to "distinguish power relations from relationships of communication that transmit information by means of a language, a system of signs, or any other symbolic medium. No doubt, communicating is always a certain way of acting upon another person or persons," but the effects of power "are not simply an aspect" of communication. "Power relations [and] relationships of communication . . . should not therefore be confused."[24]

The title of the first chapter could have been "The Place of Orientalism," a counterpoint to *Orientalism*'s first chapter, "The Scope of Orientalism."

The present title, "Putting Orientalism in Its Place," reflects the intensity of the correction to Said's "Scope." For Said, the scope was far and wide: it travels to classical Greece and to the far end of the colonialist globe, but lacks a vertical dimension that delves into the depths of a particular structure of thought that is more than a generalized or transhistorical phenomenon. "The Place of Orientalism" would have been a mild-sounding revision that nudges Orientalism into a delimited space within the modern period as a temporality that has its own problems, including colonialism and the "occasional" genocide, generally seen as an exception to modernity. "Putting Orientalism in its Place" is a deliberately transgressive title that attempts to *position* this discipline and its discourse in nothing less than the deep structures of the modern project, thereby according the verticality otherwise missing from Said's narrative a structure of its own. If, as I will argue, Orientalism is a microcosm of the macrocosmic modern structure, and if modernity *and its human subject* demand—and could not be sustained without—colonialism and genocide in all its forms, then Orientalism and many more forms of knowledge are embedded in terrains that Said and other commentators on Orientalism never cared to plough.

I begin delineating this structure in chapter 2, but not before discussing the place of the author in central paradigms. This is not just an introspective exercise, locating my own critique within these conceptions. It is additionally, and no less importantly, an essential component of the repertoire of methodological tools necessary for a proper evaluation of Orientalism in its larger context, which is itself equally subject to the terms of this critique. One way in which this critique can be deployed consists in exploring the intricate interdependencies between knowledge and power. While it is true that this is an old theme, worn out by clichés and nauseating formulaic repetition, its meanings and implications have become obfuscated in academic and intellectual debates. I maintain that the obfuscation of the unique relationship between knowledge and power in modernity is itself a function of the discursive formations and not just intellectual shallowness.[25] In order to better convey the force of this relationship, I begin with a problematic in Said's conception of it, showing its unidirectionality. I argue that the relationship is not only dialectical, but that this dialectic proceeds in a circular fashion, amounting to what I have called in another context a dialectical wheel. This leads me to ask the fundamental question as to why modern knowledge should be so dialectically woven into power at all, a question that in turn compels questions as to why Orientalism—or for that matter modern science, anthropology, economics, business schools, journalism, engineering, and many disciplines besides—came into existence at all.

The acuity of this relationship still seems difficult to expound, for no phenomenon can be truly appreciated if it is the only thing one knows. I will never know what compassion means or feels like if I have never experienced mean-spiritedness, nor will I ever understand the true meaning of quenching if I have never known real thirst. Contrast, and not just comparison, is a remarkably efficient epistemological tool. Without contrast, one can spend a lifetime studying that sphere of reality that exhibits the intersection of knowledge and power without ever understanding its full force and power, much less its structure, exceptionality, uniqueness, or genealogy. This absence of perspective, contrast, comparison is a debilitating dead weight for understanding. Even when Foucault energetically analyzed the emergence of the modern European phenomena of power, knowledge, surveillance, health, and so forth, his comparativist framework, far from being consistent or systematic, was in the preceding *European* contexts, whose striking and dramatic impact can be seen, for instance, in the transformations of punitive forms and torture (with Foucault presenting, for instance, Damien's ordeal when he was guilty of regicide before suddenly leaping to its modern contrast) or in the Christian origins of telling the truth as a practice through which modern forms of power have been reenacted.[26] Foucault's points of contrast, however illustrative, are always European, save for the occasional invocations of Greek or Roman forms (which admittedly increased during the last few years of his life). According to the theory of paradigms, contrasts are most useful when they are crisp, sharp, and—especially—*alien* to the tradition being investigated.

The absence of perspective and its attendant effects permit an easy universalizing of phenomena, projecting them onto history at large, European and non-European, modern and nonmodern.[27] Since the central problem of Orientalism (as well as of most academic fields) is its location within this relationship, it is important to ask what makes the organic association of power and knowledge possible in the first place. Or, to pose the question differently, what makes this relationship systemically dialectical, strong, weak, awkward, tentative, and tenuous, or, most importantly, what renders it altogether impossible? Answering such questions is indispensable, hence the requirement in my discussion of introducing a contrast, a starkly comparative dimension. I therefore dwell at some length on a case study that serves this purpose, namely, the relationship between knowledge and power in the Islamic tradition of premodernity.[28] Through this case study, I argue that certain kinds of knowledge intrinsically do not lend themselves to the use of power, and, conversely, that power—as biopolitical concept of hegemony and force—is useless to them (not to say inimical). This formulation, however, assumes that power has one meaning or structure, which it in fact does not. A modified understanding of power, which is to say, a conception of power from which sovereignty and knowledge-based *force* are subtracted, would eo ipso dissolve the problem of "power" as modernity conceived it, and thus entirely change the meaning and connotations of the term. This is the case because it is conceptually impossible to view power in the modern and Foucauldian senses as anything other than being organically tied to knowledge. Logically and ontologically, there is no modern power without knowledge, and if this is accepted, as it should be, then our language, in this context at least, is highly redundant. All we need to say is the word "power," and knowledge is automatically included in the very term, just as the word "mother" must include an unadulterated reference to "daughter," "son," or "child," without whom "mother" is inconceivable.

An equally important question arises here: Is modern knowledge subject to the same rules I have outlined with regard to power? To answer this question, I present a narrative of the Enlightenment that sheds light on the nature of modern knowledge and its structure. I argue that the seventeenth and eighteenth centuries gradually produced particular and unprecedented kinds of knowledge that indeed *made themselves substantively and inherently amenable to the manipulation of power*, giving the latter its distinctive and complex meaning.[29] Once it constituted itself as sovereign and above nature, this form of knowledge opened the flood gates for the state to embark on the colossal nineteenth-century project of forming its subjects as citizens, and this by means of creating a number of "engineering" institutions that brought out their potential. Of all these institutions, juridicality and the modern educational apparatus acquire immediate relevance to my narrative, for they were the means through which a *new human subject*, the object of modern forms of power, was constituted.

What I have just outlined remains preparatory for my engagement with colonialism as a concrete manifestation of the knowledge that Europe produced, a knowledge of a distinctive category. In chapter 2, I attempt to show that this knowledge did not just reproduce the Orient in the Orientalist text, as Said supposed, nor was the text an aftereffect of political and economic power and colonialism. Rather, the text was embedded in a larger subtext that both prescribed and described engineering projects *on the colonized ground*. In other words, the Orientalist text was not really just about misrepresentation, though misrepresent it did. Nor was it really about scholarly biases, a sense of superiority, and such things as a discursive "style of domination," to cite Said (3). The Orientalist text was the blueprint or a road map for an effective, and not just textual, re-creation of the Orient. This claim must be framed within a larger argument in which I insist on two fundamental points: first, that the Orientalist text was in no way unique or alone in this project, for there were several other "texts" operating on various aspects of the "Orient's" reality; and, second, that the "Orient" also includes the "Occident"—the west of Europe, as well as the Americas,[30] not to mention the "Oriental" enclaves within Euro-America itself. In the process of *putting Orientalism in the place in which it belongs*, this larger picture about other "texts" and other "Occidental Orients" will, I hope, become clearer.

Yet, to unravel the full meaning and significance of the textual "power over the Orient," it will not do to begin with the texts, for that would amount to no more than scratching the surface.[31] In contrast, locating the beginning of research and critique *in* the colonialist project on the ground at least keeps that promise viable. But a promise is never more than a potentiality, hence the need to connect the colonialist practices on the ground with the structure of Enlightenment thought expounded in chapter 2. This is precisely what the rest of the chapter does: it offers a specific account of the engineering projects of colonialism in the Ottoman Empire, Algeria, India, and the Indonesian Archipelago.

The choice of these four regions is anything but arbitrary, nor is it accidental that the Ottoman Empire, a formally sovereign entity, is included in the list of colonized countries. The list is rather intended to underscore the point that colonialism, engaged in an extensive, intensive, and circular dialectic with a single-minded formation of Orientalist knowledge in particular and academic knowledge in general, produces, mutatis mutandis, the same structural effects, which are accurate reflections of the constitution of one and the same thought structure that modern Europe cultivated, and which defined it in every step of its *concrete* modern manifestations. Put more precisely, the effects, paradigmatically speaking,[32] are *structurally* similar, if not nearly identical, whether colonialism was direct or indirect or took a genocidal-settler form. The four regions chosen are, first of all, far flung across the globe, stretching across the entire range of the Old World, which is also to say that they each have their own demographic, topographic, geopolitical, ethnic, cultural, legal, economic, material, social, and spiritual-intellectual constitution, which is often unique. Second, three of the four were colonized by three presumably different European powers: the British, the Dutch, and the French. The fourth region, the Ottoman Empire, was subject to multiple forms of imperial power, which is to say that it was in effect colonized by a European common denominator. Third, this latter empire was not colonized in the conventional sense of the term. But it is my argument—as I will articulate it in chapter 4—that colonialism does not have to be directly and physically present on the ground in order to bring about the effects of its sovereign power. Arguably, such a case of what one might call a remote-control colonialism not only exhibits the same colonial effects as the other regions but in some respects exceeds them, both in terms of the rapidity of transformations and in terms of their magnitude. Yet, the quality of these remains the same, as evidenced in the culmination of colonial effects that one can observe today around the world.

Because Said was almost exclusively interested in the Orientalist text, and only in quite specific and limited ways, the relationship between the text and its actual realization on the colonial ground was passed over in silence.[33] This is why he deemed the juridical (which he called "law") to have but a "symbolic significance for the history of Orientalism" (78).[34] And it is striking that he makes this statement in no other context than the colossal British overtaking of India. Juridicality—the legal and political concept of sovereignty, education, the formation of the subject, the modern state, and a host of other concepts and institutions—is not up for analysis in his work. For a thinker who advocated the necessity of reading the text with a due consideration for "worldliness," these absences are stunning. In my four colonial case studies, I bring the Orientalist text and the

Orientalist himself as a performative presence into conversation with colonizing spheres, in an attempt to show that in the dialectic of forces operating on the Oriental subject, the text cannot be privileged as an exclusive analytical site, however important it may be; and what is more, the text's analytical value remains entwined with and thus dependent on that dialectic, thereby requiring, if not presupposing, the marshaling of concepts and institutions of coloniality into an analytical framework in which the thought structure of the Enlightenment is an integral part.

In light of the four case studies I propose to discuss, I wish to dispense, once and for all, with a possible critique that might be leveled at the dichotomization of modern Europe and the rest of the world. It is argued, often by political economists, that to attribute the emerging forces of modernity to Europe (or the West) reenacts and perpetuates, while attempting to subvert, the very European discourse that installs Europe as the birthplace of the modern project, thereby provincializing the rest of the world as subsidiaries to, and followers of, the European model.[35] The evidence for this argument is usually drawn from the colonial experience and experimentation on the ground, such as on sugar plantations and in other modes of structured exploitation. The main point of this argument is that it was these colonialist experiences that allowed Europeans to construct modes of production and methods of governmentality that they would in turn bring back home, cultivate further, refine, and then export again to the colonies. The modern project thus becomes a story of interaction between Europe and its colonies, *both of which are seen to contribute to the production of modernity*, however much in unequal fashion. My position is that this is a fundamentally erroneous argument, one that privileges economic-materialist interpretation to the exclusion of crucial others.[36]

While I will not explicitly address this argument beyond this introduction, my various discussions about the thought structure of instrumentalism and its logic of instruments will amount to an ongoing critique of it. Here, I briefly offer the following additional counterarguments: The modern project did not evolve through a series of economic and material developments that required an attendant system of coercion and discipline, one that *presupposed* these developments. As I shall insist throughout this book, non-European cultures—as illustrated in the case study I offer in chapter 2—have upheld benchmarks within their central domains, benchmarks that set limits on what can and cannot be done.[37] I use the example of the corporation to argue my case, and the logic of that example will serve me here as well. For the European colonists to be able to exploit the Haitians, the Amerindians, and untold others in the manner that they did, to subjugate them as machines rather than as humans (or, for that matter, as human labor), to subject them to unprecedented forms of slavery and to merciless conceptions of property, to develop these experiments into a system of coercion and discipline in a Foucauldian fashion, and to turn all this around and further colonize the world with a view to enriching their coffers and in the process reengineer them as new subjects (which will be one of the main arguments of this book), to cultivate genocide as a new weapon when all else fails, to do all this, they must have *already* been in possession of, or in the process of possessing,[38] a worldview that did away with that benchmark. Had that benchmark been eliminated in Qing Dynasty's China, China would have most likely evolved a "project" similar or nearly identical to that of European modernity.[39] Similarly, had material, scientific, and economic developments been a sufficient initial condition for the rise of a modernity, Islam too, with its colossal premodern economy and advanced sciences, would have become *modern* before Europe did, especially between the tenth and fifteenth centuries.[40]

None of these phenomena—not the economy, science, or discipline— nor their cumulative and dialectical effect can explain the rise of modernity and its genocidal nature *without the prior conditions* that made all of them thinkable and indeed feasible. In other words, to make colonialism qua colonialism *the* prerequisite for the rise of modernity necessarily entails a circular argument. Whatever vaccine, technology, or scientific method Europeans appropriated from the colonies or, earlier, from Islamic lands[41] were, like imported Chinese gunpowder and Indian medicine, put to uses and purposes considerably and *qualitatively* different from those that their inventors ostensibly intended for them. Like free labor, these technologies existed for centuries in Asia and the West Indies before Europe encroached upon the world. The extraordinarily violent nature of rehabilitating these technologies at the hands of Europeans can be explained only with reference to a worldview and a structure of thought that were uniquely European. Free labor, something that could have been found anywhere, including in Europe itself (think of feudalism), is not an explicans, not even a poor one. Furthermore, the geographical location of the various colonial experiments is nothing more than a contingent, situational feature; the thought structure and frame of mind behind them were uniquely and *exclusively* European. In terms of "agency," design, thinking, contrivance, manipulation, and overall conception, the indigenous peoples had nothing to do with these experiments other than being victims of European ingenuity.

Although highly critical of colonialism, and despite its rejection of the theology of progress, my approach may nonetheless be regarded as Eurocentric. If my reader should insist upon this charge, then this is a Eurocentrism that deprivileges Europe, one that methodically argues for unmasking a universalist vice that was touted as global virtue. From this ethically critical position, there would be little ground for the argument that in the very process of condemning Eurocentrism, it reenacts and reasserts itself. That colonialism is not merely a derivative of modernity but one that constitutes modernity's very structures, resting squarely on what the semiotician Walter Mignolo called "colonial difference," is a proposition that I take for granted. But it will not do to argue (as certain Latin American transmodernists have) that because modernity's self-reproduction rests on the fabrication of its own exteriority *through the process* of dehumanizing the Other, the experience of the Other *as a production of colonialism and Orientalism* should become the axis for modernity's critique. For such an argument is in effect tautological: colonialism and Orientalism, being processually productive of the Other par excellence, structure modernity because modernity is structured by colonialism and Orientalism! My overall interrogation is then this: the uniqueness in world history of the modern forms of colonialism and imperialism, and of their handmaiden Orientalism, brings up the question of where *this particular form* of imperialism, colonialism, and Orientalism came from. The "Oriental" Other cannot be granted an active agency, for to do so is in effect to argue for the Other's colonizability. Subtracting this agency from our calculation would then have to lead us back to the forces that underlie colonialism and Orientalism, forces embedded in the European structures of thought that cannot be allowed to conscript the Other in its genealogy and narrative. None of this, however, should imply that by centering our critique on Europe we erase the Others or flatten their experiences as victims. If anything, this book insists, just as *The Impossible State* did, that a heuristic moral retrieval of the Others' traditions and histories, as well as their dehumanization by modernity, provides fertile grounds for modernity's critique.

IV

The analyses of the four colonized regions I proffer are thus not affected by this or similar arguments in the least. My account of colonialism as sovereign knowledge generated by Orientalism with the support of European academic learning in general is situated within a larger dialectic in which the political projects of conquest and modern knowledge stand within still larger formations whose foundations are firmly anchored in a particular view of nature. Because it is performative, this view can easily lead us to the same conclusion as Said reached, namely, that there is something all too powerful that would corral all Orientalists into a routine practice of misrepresentation. Exceptions simply cannot be made, however much one might allow for the "determining imprint" of certain authors or individual attempts to maneuver the constraints of "national ambience" (271), whatever this means. The distinctly political commitment to a blanket condemnation of all Orientalists leads to a major theoretical difficulty, one that, carried to its logical conclusion, would have adverse effects on our conception of power, and hence on our understanding of modernity, on our ways of living in it, and more importantly on the possibilities of escaping its hegemonic grip.

Despite his rhetorical allowance for the author's "determining imprint," Said, in every important and substantive way, effectively subscribed to a theory of discursive formations that gave performativity a metaphysical power. But performativity, today taken to extremes in academic discourse, and used in confusingly different ways, is not a license to accord language an absolute power. As I argue in chapter 3, the totalization in Said's narrative is made possible only at a theoretical price. I attempt to sort through the problem of this totalization by offering a further refinement of the theory of the author while giving an account of René Guénon, a credentialed Orientalist who—as a case study—subverts Said's narrative in almost every way. On the basic level, the very ideas and writings of this Orientalist falsify Said's totalizing discourse. What matters to my argument is the *quality* of this Orientalist's *positional* work and its potential for framing the entire debate on Orientalism and modernity in more serious ways than we have thus far seen. This Orientalist's critique of Orientalism goes into the depths of the phenomenon, transcending by leaps Said's liberal and secularist, and thus excessively limited and insulated, account.[42] It is not without an undiluted sense of irony that this critique has the all-too-ready potential to put Said's discourse in the same place where Said put Orientalist discourse. In harnessing this systemic critique, I try in chapter 3 to theorize the role of what I will call the subversive author within central paradigms, and in the process I attempt to locate Said himself in this theoretical configuration.

It will become increasingly clear as I proceed that a theory of the author is not only relevant for constructing a discriminating typology of Orientalists, a basic yet important undertaking. The theory is also crucial, and indeed has a larger role to play, in redefining the dynamics of power and knowledge in terms of the exit strategies it provides in and out of this configuration. Without such a theory, the narrative of power/knowledge and discursive formations would remain locked in a hopelessly ahistorical framing, a fallacy that is fatal to a proper critique of modernity. Yet, it must be clear that the construction of typologies for the various fields of academic inquiry is in no way separate from, or independent of, the theoretical narrative that locates such exit strategies. Which is to say that Said's totalizing account of Orientalists, however unwarranted, is not truly relevant to the shallow debate over his failings to account for certain Orientalists who are otherwise innocent of the charge. The totalizing, as I take it here, is nothing short of a theoretical predicament of the first order, having grave implications for everything we say about the modern condition and its material and thought structures.

Said's targeting of Orientalism and his narration of it as a totality have had the effect of not only insulating it from its academic surrounds, despite repeated vague reference to the general "culture" from which Orientalism received support. It has also had the powerful effect, due to its liberal entrenchment, of inoculating the discipline, allowing it to refortify and thus regenerate itself without changing its traditional dispositions. The connections drawn between Orientalism and the surrounding culture emerge as political in nature, in the rudimentary and conventional senses, with a peppered reference to economic interests and material greed. There is no clear vision that liberal academia is overwhelmingly and *structurally* involved in the very same domineering and sovereign project for which Said attacked Orientalism. There is even less of a clear sense that science, the "high" humanities, secularism, and secular critique are as much implicated as was Orientalism. And it is these ideological narratives that frame Said's critique and give it its defining character. Yet, whatever references we find in his work to the location of Orientalism in its larger academic context are distinctly cast in terms of Orientalism's singularity, its "backward" methodology in comparison with the general humanities and the social sciences.

Taking seriously Said's own counsel that all things in the world are "linked" (xxiii), chapters 3 and 4, among other parts of the book, embark on the argument that all academic units of the central domain are as involved as in, if not more implicated than, Orientalism in the very project for which this latter stood charged.[43] Beginning with science and philosophy, and moving to departments of economics and business schools, I attempt to show that these and other academic units of the central domain undertake a division of epistemological labor in the creation of sovereign knowledge and practice.[44] That their overall effect dwarfs that of Orientalism will emerge as a given. That this book remains in good measure about Orientalism is not just the function of my academic expertise (which it is); there is much more to commend the retention. If the way *into* the Orient *required* Orientalism as the most obvious and direct bridge, the way out of the Orient, and back to a reformed self, requires a bridge as well. Structurally reformed and ethicized, Orientalism continues to have an important function, as the final chapter will argue.

Through the prism of the company and corporation, and more generally of corporate institutions (a constant and persistent theme in this book), I argue not only that academic units partake in an underlying structure of thought that is inherently colonialist but also that they are enmeshed, like all corporate bodies, within a larger condition of collective sociopathology. Having offered a general typology of academia in terms of central and peripheral domains, I will argue that the academic units of the central domain are connected, however unconsciously, in structural and structured ways to the colonialist project of Western modernity (now proliferating to the rest of the world). I then contend that there exists an equally structured relationship between modern colonialism and genocide, an argument that, in the final analysis, amounts to an explication of the relationship between knowledge, including its paramount academic variety, and genocide. Dwelling at some length in chapter 4 on the concept of genocide, I maintain, along with certain genocide scholars, that collective elimination takes on a variety of forms, all of which are pertinent to my narrative. Unlike those who emphasize material and economic motives for colonialism and its inherent genocidal tendencies, this book offers a continuous critique of conventional notions of instrumentalism, placing genocide and the knowledge that enables it squarely within a structure of thought wholly made up of epistemological sovereignty.

Consistent with my reformulation of the theory of the author as a discursive exit strategy, chapter 5 argues that it is possible to transform Orientalism, as a prototype of specialized academic knowledge, into a field of humane inquiry once it has shed secular humanism, anthropocentrism, colonialist potency, and a sovereign epistemology. I do not propose an institutional approach, but rather one that begins with an ethical formation of the subject, which is constitutive of the institutional. In the course of this argument, I dwell on a liberal philosophical predicament that is intended to show the impasse that liberalism encounters when it thinks about such a formation, and the impossibility of undertaking any operations on the Self within the prescriptions of such a formation. Since it is my argument throughout the book that establishment Orientalism is nothing more than that "department" of modern academia that specializes in the study of the Orient, and that other "departments" perform the same work but through their own specializations, Orientalism appears as the most obvious discipline to stand in the position of dealing with the Other. Of course, this is a deceptive appearance, one for which Said fell. Instead, I take Orientalism as an illustrative example (particularly because I have studied it for four decades), but not as a target in and of itself. However, the same or similar approach may be adopted, and to no lesser effect, toward any other academic unit in the central domain, be it anthropology, sociology, or history, not to mention economics, business, journalism, philosophy, and science. The intention here is to open up critical space for a scrutiny of the entire range of modern academia, leaving no escape route for even the fine arts and other aesthetic endeavors, however less incriminated these are in the violent and destructive projects of modernity.

Finally, a word about the place of this book in the landscape of academia. Although my point of departure is Said's *Orientalism*, I continue to expand my circle of inquiry around it, adding historical and philosophical texture, and culminating in obviating his narrative and its conventionally political underpinnings. In other words, although my book starts with politics as a site of critique, it ends up in an entirely different domain of thought, which is precisely the point. This, therefore, is an essay on foundational moral principles and ethical structures that stand in a complex set of relationships with modernity, mostly as a matrix of denials and negations, but also as the loci of regenerative critique. In an epistemological system whose very existence has been grounded in an ab initio exclusion of certain views and modes of thought, it might seem that any such advocacy would be doomed from the start. Yet, as this book will argue energetically, performativity, discursive formations, knowledge, and structures of power are dynamic things that always leave—by virtue of their very dynamism—openings, cracks, fissures, and fractures *antithetical to the paradigmatic structures*.[45] The modern project is replete with such fissures, precisely because it denies them, and to believe that they cannot provide for what I call regenerative critique is not only a paradoxical proposition, but one that merely perpetuates the metaphorical deadness of Foucault's dead author. To think through openings and fissures, to give exclusions and silences an active presence, to resuscitate what the central domains have rendered marginal and irrelevant—these are ultimately the only true meanings of critique. Most obviously, a critique that sanctions the death of the author is no less dead than the author herself. It had better not be made, for its *deadly* effects are what this book attempts to describe.

CHAPTER I

Putting Orientalism in Its Place

I

The jacket blurb of Said's *Orientalism* (2003 edition) announces that the author "traces the origins of 'orientalism' to the centuries-long period during which Europe dominated the Middle and Near East." To any historian of the modern Islamic world, this is a puzzling pronouncement, since students of Dutch, British, and French colonialism in such regions as the Malay Archipelago, India, and North Africa would know that these European powers could not widely control, much less effectively or systematically colonize, these vast domains until the middle, if not the later parts, of the nineteenth century. It would be hard to say that modern colonialism became effective (which is to say, performative) earlier than two centuries ago, and thus the unqualified use of "centuries" in the blurb must be traced back to the body of the book where it receives ample clarification.

The first piece of evidence pointing to Said's fuzzy conception of chronology is the nearly infinite historical roots and geographic scope he assigns to what he regards as the discursive activity of Orientalism. Early in the book, he seems to suggest that Orientalism started a "thousand years" ago (17).[1] A few pages later, Orientalism is taken as far back as the Greek tragedian Aeschylus, a supposedly "non-Oriental" who flourished in the fifth century BC (21). Thirty pages later, Orientalism is claimed to have "commenced its formal existence" in 1312, when the Church Council of Vienna of that year established a series of Chairs in Arabic, Greek, Hebrew, and Syriac, in cities as far-flung as Paris, Oxford, Bologna, Avignon, and Salamanca (49). Thus Orientalism, plotting "Oriental history, character, and destiny for hundreds of years" (95), represented Islam to medieval Christianity (60), although its "schematization began . . . in classical Greece" (68). What the difference is between "formal existence" and "schematization" we are not told; nor are we told how these two phenomena, separated by more than one and a half millennia, relate to each other. Thus, there are for Said "modern Orientalists" (18, 22, 42), "renaissance Orientalists" (50), ancient Greek and Christian Latin Orientalists (68).[2]

Orientalists can be found everywhere and in every period, *in the West*. About how an Orientalist of the fifth century BC differs from a medieval or a nineteenth-century one we get not a single word from Said in the way of an explanation, except that they all spoke on behalf of, and thus *misrepresented*, the Orient. What the performative means and discursive technologies available to Aeschylus to "transform" the Orient (21) are we are not told. Nor are we privy to the qualitative differentials or cognates between an Aeschylus and a Dante, or a Dante and a Bernard Lewis. What is striking especially in the case of "classical Greece," to which Said attributes a "schematization of Orientalism," is that Said himself, in another writing in the context of the debate over *Black Athena*, made so much, and rightly so, of Europe's relatively recent appropriation of Greece as "Western."[3] Said's citation of Aeschylus (apart from its anachronistic nature) necessarily leads to the absurd conclusion that knowledge is determined by geographical location qua location, not by a specific culture, a specific ideology, or a specific structure of thought.

The absence of historical distinctions in Said's understanding of Orientalism (from the evidence presented earlier alone) is intimately coupled with gross geographical indistinctions. Aeschylus, Homer, scholastic scholars, Dante, Renan, Massignon, and Lewis are viewed in the same vein. The only commonality, which we infer as existing in Said's mind, is that, again, they write from a geographical location identified as the "West" about the Orient, at times tagged as "East." There is no single "Easterner" or "Oriental" in Said's definition who engaged with the "Orient." Thus, for a while, it may seem to the reader that Said's criterion for one to qualify as an Orientalist is simply to belong to a certain place called the West, although the West may be in the East. This is not surprising in view of Said's first definition of Orientalism: "Anyone who teaches, writes about, or researches the Orient, . . . either in its specific or its general aspects, is an Orientalist" (2). Of course, this definition does not resolve, or dissolve, any problem, for it does not account for Greece, Aeschylus, or Émile Tyan, a twentieth-century French-educated and French-writing Maronite-Lebanese scholar, who wrote on the legal history of Islam in a vein that would probably have instigated Said's sting more than Bernard Lewis did.[4] Nor does it account for the likes of the French "orientalist" René Guénon, the subject of chapter 3. Nor, still, does it account for the same—indeed identical—structure of discourse that was directed westward, at Amerindia. That Said appears not to have read Tyan or to have known of Guénon, or, still, to have cared in the least about legal Orientalism, or westward Orientalism, is a matter whose significance is to be discussed later. What is of immediate interest here is that historical myopia stands concomitant with geographical and ethnic indistinctions: geography meshes with history to create an absurdity. My aim in pointing out these historical and geographical confusions is to show not that Said's critique of Orientalism is invalid, but rather that its critical edge is incoherent and dull. In other words, it lacked sharp boundary-definition of target area, all due, I think, to analytical instruments partly grounded in, and partly the function of, a set of ideological assumptions. Nor is this, in the final analysis, about Said the individual scholar and intellectual. Rather, it is about the category of academia's Saids, a category, however exemplary, that remains bounded by what I will call, in chapter 3, dissenting authorship.

On page 204, having by that point already conveyed much of what his book was intended to accomplish, Said reaches this stunning conclusion: "It is therefore correct that every European, in what he could say about the Orient, was consequently a racist, an imperialist, and almost totally ethnocentric." Nowhere is there a qualification of any sort to limit this to a particular contingent of scholars, to a historical period, to a certain formation of power that gave such a phenomenon its conditions of possibility.[5] The statement is sweeping and massive, again lumping together in it, so it seems to the careful reader of *Orientalism*, every figure who pronounced on the Orient, stretching back to Aeschylus and reaching down to the deserving Bernard Lewis and his likes. Needless to say, given the historically and culturally specific notion of discursive formations elaborated by

Foucault (which generally do not travel back beyond the seventeenth century),[6] and considering Said's own admission of the influence Foucault exercised on him (23), Said's wanderings into classical Greece and early-fourteenth-century Vienna suggest a questionable understanding of what Foucault meant by discursive formation. The misapprehension extends, in very specific ways, to that part of discursive formation which has to do with the author, which Said seems to have misconstrued no less.

Nor do Said's critics fare any better. It has been repeatedly pointed out, often in highly politicized and polemical tones, that Said, deliberately or not, overlooked the many "good Orientalists" who were influential in the field and who were otherwise "credible," who allow "the native voice to speak and who suggest little evidence of cultural superiority." These include Julius Wellhausen (d. 1918), Theodor Nöldeke (d. 1930), Carl Heinrich Becker (d. 1933), Christiaan Snouck Hurgronje (d. 1936), Giorgio Levi Della Vida (d. 1967), Henri Laoust (d. 1983), Shelomo Dov Goitein (d. 1985), Noel J. Coulson (d. 1986), Robert Brunschvig (d. 1990), Claude Cahen (d. 1991), Franz Rosenthal (d. 2003), William Chittick, Michael Gilsenan, and many others.[7] The list's author is as indiscriminate as Said is in his categorical generalizations and lack of historical acumen. Some of these scholars can easily be subjected to the same critique that Said has of the others to whom he attended, if not a more cutting one. The problem with Said's approach to this issue is not that he was aiming in the wrong direction, but rather that his unwarranted geographical and temporal sweep masked, even suppressed, the deeper structures that would have allowed him to be more discriminate. Both Said and his critics (who equally deny these structures) were preoccupied with what I call horizontality (and its politics), not verticality, the archaeological depth of the epistemology and philosophy on which Orientalism and most other academic disciplines were founded.

In his assault, Said did not carefully attend to the concept of author, misconstruing Foucault on this score,[8] and furthermore failing to distinguish between thought structure, discursive formation, force fields, subversivity, and paradigm, among others, and how individual authors operate, function, and are put to—and out of—use in these domains. A theory of the author is a crucial part of any conception of discursive formation, and one would be terribly amiss without it. The study of the problem of Orientalism rides on it, and not only because of the methodological and theoretical errors Said committed in this regard. I shall now attend to this and to what I have called the theory of paradigms, before proceeding with the central body of my argument about Orientalism, although I shall take up the theory of the author once again, much later on.[9]

II

I begin with another problematic in Said's work, the concept of representation. The question at this point of my inquiry is not how the Orientalists represented the Orient, but how we might represent the Orientalists. In a striking and oft-quoted statement, Said says, "Unlike Michel Foucault, to whose work I am greatly indebted, I do believe in the determining imprint of individual writers upon the otherwise anonymous collective body of texts constituting a discursive formation like Orientalism" (23).[10] Yet, nowhere in his *Orientalism* does Said proffer an instance of a writer whose work left a "determining imprint," not even in the cases of H. A. R. Gibb and L. Massignon, who receive, in relative terms, perhaps the most favorable treatment from his scathing pen. Nor is this imprint—assuming "otherwise" in Said's language to be intelligible—more than a veneer under which the author, in practical terms, suffers death, for *Orientalism* is peppered with statements confirming that authors, no matter how much they try, inevitably succumb to the imperatives of national "ambience" or the "guild" rules of their discipline (271). In Said's narrative, all Orientalists, including Gibb and Massignon, stand squarely within the Orientalist tradition, and nowhere does he allow for textual space that shows, in genuine ways, their "determining imprint." All one gets out of his otherwise brilliant analysis of their writings is that they had a *generic* imprint, one that characterizes any scholar by virtue of being a "guild" scholar, but one that is hardly "determining." For what is meant by "determining," as Said used it in explicit reference to Foucault, is the ability to change, or markedly contribute to a change (what Foucault called an "analogy" and "difference") in, the paradigmatic structure of a particular discursive formation, just as Foucault himself and others before him—including Kant, Marx, and Freud—have had their definitive "determining imprint." For Said, Orientalism has a definite, transhistorical character, "a corporate identity" (202), and since all those who wrote on the Orient were Orientalists, they necessarily and squarely belonged to that paradigmatic identity.

In both his general narrative throughout the book and his treatments of various individual authors, Said has no place whatever for any Orientalist with a "determining imprint." In a typical fashion, in what I shall refer to in Said's case as his "touch-and-go" style of expressing his positions, he takes one step forward and one step backward when dealing with Massignon, the single figure in the book that could have achieved the supreme state of "determining imprint" but did not. This, Said tells us, is due to the fact that

> no scholar, not even a Massignon, can resist the pressures on him of his nation or of the scholarly tradition in which he works. . . . We must allow, however, that the refinements, the personal style, the individual genius, may finally supersede the political restraints operating impersonally through tradition and through the national ambience. Even so, in Massignon's case [as if for Said there was another case] . . . his ideas about the Orient remained thoroughly traditional and Orientalist. (271)

A few lines after he makes his statement about the determining imprint of authors (23), Said remarks that "Foucault believes that in general the individual text or author counts for very little." Apart from the correctness or incorrectness of this attribution to, or of this understanding of, Foucault, and setting aside for the moment the momentous significance of this issue to Foucault's ideas and to a proper analysis of Orientalism, we note how, toward the end of the book, Said comes to contradict the very statement he made earlier with regard to the "determining imprint" of authors. Paying lip service to the notion that originality and talent "can leap beyond the confines" of their own "time and place in order to put before the world a new work," Said diminishes the force of this notion, which he calls "a mythology of creation," by saying that "such ideas as these carry *some* truth" (202, emphasis mine). This is further chipped away at by another passage that seems to negate the very possibility of a "determining imprint." The "possibilities" available

> to a great and original mind are never unlimited, just as it is also true that a great talent has a very healthy respect for what others have done before it and for what the field already contains. The work of predecessors, the institutional life of a scholarly field, the collective nature of any learned enterprise; these, to say nothing of economic and social circumstances, tend to diminish the effects of the individual scholar's production. (202)[11]

Thus the theoretical exception of the author's determining imprint paradoxically proves the substantive and effective rule of nonexception. Which leaves us wondering what determining imprint Said considered himself to have as the author of *Orientalism*, "writing" as he did within a "scholarly field" and under the purview of particular "economic and social circumstances."[12] Although he simply has not offered a theory of the author and does not seem to understand Foucault on this score, Said, most likely against his own aspirations, was prophetic as to his own critique of Orientalism, a point I shall argue in detail in chapter 3. Furthermore, allowing for even a single Orientalist to have a "determining imprint" would have required of Said at least an explanation. Indeed, since the problem of the author constitutes a phenomenon rather than just an empirically given individual instance or a particular occurrence, or for that matter a collection of instances, such an allowance would have in effect required nothing short of a theory that can handle and account for distinctions, exceptions, variations, and the like all within an articulate conception of discursive formation. It was perhaps easier for Said to lump together all those who wrote on the Orient, needlessly including figures such as Aeschylus and Dante, and simply castigate them as Orientalists. But how in theory and where in practice did the "determining imprint" manifest itself?

One way of resolving Said's problematics as they relate to the issues commanding our attention is to think of human reality as consisting of structures that are governed by paradigms, which in turn establish divisions between central and peripheral domains and determine a set of relationships between and among them. A theory of paradigms[13] not only informs the assignment and determination of the author's location within a domain, but also offers a meaningful way to speak of two phenomena in a *relevantly* analogical[14] and comparatively instructive way (what I call "comparativity," amounting to the full weight of foregrounding perspective, an essential epistemological tool). This comparativist function, as will become evident in due course, is no less necessary in delimiting the nature and structure of Orientalism, that is to say, what makes it a uniquely modern phenomenon, with remarkably distinguishing features, and not merely a replica, continuation, or reenactment of an undistinguishable, preceding human experience.

The theory then assumes that phenomena are structured paradigmatically and that certain ideas, material structures, "ideological" positions, and institutions stand in them as paradigms or in relation to paradigms. Authors, like all participants in paradigms and domains, stand, or are made to stand, in a particular relationship to them, for paradigms are possible only through common will, or a driving force that may substitute for such will. Paradigms and domains allow us to identify parallel systemic features the comparison of which makes for a rationally valid undertaking. They serve, then, the important function of identifying, within systems, relations and sets of relations, and furthermore identifying conceptual and material structures of what might be called "driving forces" that give systems and central domains a particular "order of things," to borrow one of Foucault's expressions.[15]

A starting point toward a definition of paradigm is Carl Schmitt's notion of "central domain." If a domain becomes central, "then the problems of other domains are solved in terms of the central domain—they are considered secondary problems, whose solution follows as a matter of course only if the problems of the central domain are solved."[16] In illustration of this notion, Schmitt offers the example of European technical progress during the nineteenth century, an arena of progress that, to use our term, was paradigmatic. The massive upsurge of "technical progress" affected all "moral, political, social and economic situations." Its overpowering effect gave it the status of "a religion of technical progress which promised [that] all other problems would be solved by technological progress." It became "a religion of technical miracles, human achievements, and the domination of nature."[17] Whereas in an age of traditional religion the central domain upholds a benchmark[18] of moral upbringing and of moral education and worldly moral desiderata, in the "technical age" what counts as progress, as a true achievement, is "economic and technical progress." Similarly, in "an economic age, one needs only solve adequately the problem of the production and distribution of goods in order to make superfluous all moral and social questions."[19] Hence, all concepts, including "God, freedom, progress, anthropological conceptions of human nature, the public domain, rationality and rationalization, and finally the concept of nature and culture itself, derive their concrete historical content from the situation of the central domains and can only be grasped therefrom."[20]

As an example of paradigm in modernity, capitalism not only possesses a crucially determining effect upon modern life, but holds the force of constituting, shaping, and coloring other spheres, including what Schmitt called peripheral domains. Capitalism forged a system of moralism, a structure of ideas, and a materialist worldview that inform and determine a particular concept of profit and financial operations. It dictated and continues to dictate a particular set of relationships between and among institutions and, to no lesser extent, between and among individuals, thus forming a particular meaning of the self. It reestablished, at least as early as the Industrial Revolution, a new way of viewing and dealing with ecology and nature, one that gave the concept of domination the new and added meaning of internal transformation, which is to say that capitalism is *performativity* in its full force. The paradigm that defines the central domain of capitalism affects and transforms all lesser domains, particularly those standing in its periphery. Aesthetics of the fine arts, in modernity a peripheral domain, often gives way to the forces of capitalism, rendering these arts "commercial" or at least easily susceptible to material and commodified valuation.[21] It is a tacit rule that to be regarded as a painter, one must have exhibited *and sold* her paintings; the latter is essential to what it means to be a "real" artist. Likewise, a Picasso in 1905 in Picasso's Paris studio may be said to express the aesthetics of the artist, a pure form of artistic pleasure and production, but the same Picasso on a billionaire's yacht can be said to have significantly lost its "aesthetic location."[22] The monetization of a Picasso, a Renoir, or a Bacon has relegated the domain of aesthetics to a secondary status, making it peripheral, which is to say, subordinate. The quality of charity and philanthropy has likewise been transformed by the same driving forces of capitalism, taking the concept and thus practice and institution of charity out of the realm of psychological ethics and moral technologies of the self and putting them into considerations of profit, prestige, and public relations.[23] The inner psychologies of private piety, spirituality, and ethical constitution have given way, almost entirely, to the externally abstract and corporate material interest.

This is not to eviscerate modernity of all authentic and sincere practices of aesthetics and charity, but rather to insist that central domains transform the structure, meaning, and even appearance of peripheral domains.[24] As I will show in the equivalent case of the author, such essential exceptions as we find in sincere, authentic, even "pious" acts of charity are just that, *essential*, and hence indispensable, notwithstanding their peripheral position within the system in which they happen to be found. When a central domain assigns profit premium place, as the highest, unequaled, and unrivaled desideratum, the peripheral domain must follow suit, for its internal structure and relations are measured by the ethos and modus vivendi of the central domain. And since a central domain must, by absolute necessity, have its own defining mental, ideational, and material culture, this culture in turn respectively transforms the peripheral domains that stand in its vicinity. It is not to be taken for granted that inasmuch as we admire a Picasso as aesthetic, its "price" hangs over it like its own frame. The most common and almost singular piece of news about Gerhard Richter, for instance, has very little to do with aesthetics but rather with the hard fact that he is the most expensive *living* artist. What gives Richter a "determining imprint" on modern art is thus as instructive a question as that of the imprint of certain Orientalists. Although Richter's foot is firmly planted in the peripheral domain of the fine arts, his other foot is as firmly anchored in the central domain of capitalism. As the philosopher and literary critic Kojin Karatani has perceptively remarked, "ever since" in modernity "*art came to be art*, it has been connected to commodification."[25] That artists have often resisted, and continue to resist, these malevolent tendencies is not as much a weakening of this argument as it is a confirmation of the power of commodification.

The Enlightenment, highly relevant to our concerns here, provides yet another example of a paradigm. There is no doubt that this project encompassed intellectual and political movements that ranged across a wide spectrum of intellectual difference. Suffice it here to cite the philosophical divergences of, and dramatically opposing Weltanschauung between, Voltaire, Diderot, Herder, Berkeley, Fichte, Rousseau, Hume, Spinoza, and Kant, to mention only a few of Enlightenment's major names. It would thus seem impossible to lump them—and many others—together, much less to lump together the thought systems and movements they generated, under any single, identifiable category. Yet, it is eminently arguable that the Enlightenment in its totality—and despite its Kierkegaards and Herders, for example—exhibits a paradigm, featuring a shared substrate of assumptions and presuppositions that bestows on it a certain unity, despite its internal multiplicity. As the political philosopher John Gray aptly argued, the core project of the Enlightenment "was the displacement of local, customary or traditional moralities, and all forms of transcendental faith, by a critical or rational morality, which was projected as the basis of a universal civilization."[26] This new morality, dominantly secular and humanist, and "binding on all human beings, . . . would set universal standards for the assessment of human institutions." Under the command of human reason finally divorced of traditional principles of morality, the project would aim to create a universal civilization, one premised upon a particular notion of rationality, materiality, individualism, autonomy, and, crucial for us, domination of nature. "This is the project that animated Marxism and Liberalism in all their varieties, which underpins both the new liberalism and new-conservatism. . . . [And it] is this core project that is shared by all Enlightenment thinkers, however pessimistic or dystopic they may sometimes be as to its historical prospects."[27]

This core Enlightenment project constituted a central domain, one by which all major and central problems were solved and which gave and continues to give direction, for better or worse, to our ways of life.[28] Seen as a far-flung central domain that distributes itself over a range of other, well-defined central domains—such as the modern state, capitalism, and Schmitt's technical progress outlined earlier—the Enlightenment, like its handmaiden Orientalism, was articulated by authors and philosophers that present us with the same issues of "determining imprints." Kant and Herder, for instance, both claim a prominent presence in the Enlightenment's landscape, but no one doubts that Kant had a determining imprint that Herder (and several other accomplished philosophers like him) did not manage to achieve.[29] Again, Kant's brilliant presence in the relatively limited domain of the "humanities" is never in doubt, but his most influential presence is to be found imperceptibly permeating the entire range of central domains, including the culture industry of late-modern capitalism. In this sense, Kant's feet were planted no differently than Richter's were.

But central domains as paradigms have more to them than Schmitt's account allows for. Calling, after Schmitt's own linguistic usage, the non-central domains "peripheral," we must acknowledge a dialectical relationship between the central and peripheral domains. The "solutions" provided for the latter do not just "follow as a matter of course" and only "if the problems of the central domain are solved." In our account of paradigm, what is involved is a system of knowledge and practice whose constituent domains share in common a particular structure of concepts that qualitatively distinguishes them from equivalent domains in other systems. While it is undeniable that the problems in the central domain acquire priority, and thus subordinate the other domains to said priority, all these domains function within a system of knowledge, or a regime of truth, that shapes the *priorities* within the peripheral domains, but does not displace or eliminate the values that make the peripheral domain what it is, however much suppressed or vitiated these values may be. If I understand Schmitt correctly, his account seems somewhat linear, because his concept of the political[30] requires marshaling and single-mindedly subordinating all forces within the modern structures of power in favor of privileging his neo-Hobbesian concept. In our account of paradigm, the peripheral domains are as subsidiary and supportive as they are peripheral, their relegation to this status being *not the function of logical or ontological precedence* of the central domain, but rather the entrenchment and anchoring of this domain within a system constituted no less by the subsidiary domains. The privileging within a culture of a particular domain is therefore a perspectivist act, one that is a function of the culture's placement of a particular value (or set of values) that appears more prominent in that domain than in others. But that value must, per force, pervade the subsidiary domains, which at once partake in producing, and are produced by, it.

While Schmitt is right in insisting on the central domain as a driving force, my account of paradigm emphasizes the centrality of the values adopted in the central domain as ideal values that remain the distinctive desiderata and the locus of purposive action and thought, even *when their application and realization are not always achieved*, and even when the competing forces within the domains constituting the paradigm undermine such application and realization. Yet, in this very account of hegemony, the differential between the premium values and forces of the central domain, on the one hand, and the incomplete "application and realization," on the other, is precisely the gray area in which the entire regime of truth and its system experiences a continuum of dynamics that either threatens its collapse or reinforces its power; but either way, it is the arena that makes inertia impossible. For paradigms embody fields of "force relations," encompassing opposing and competing discourses and strategies. This is what led Foucault to observe that these discourses of power, in their oppositional trajectories, are inseparable, for discourses "are tactical elements or blocks operating in a field of force relations; there can exist different and even contradictory discourses within the same strategy; they can, on the contrary, circulate without changing their form from one strategy to another, opposing strategy."[31] The full materialization of power's effects amounts to the production of a central domain, but within the very confluence of the various components of power there reside opposing and subversive strategies, those that inhabit no other than the gray area.[32] This is perhaps why Foucault, in proposing a "new" diagnosis for the "economy of power relations" governing "our present situation," suggests that we take "the forms of resistance against different forms of power as a starting point." For resistance amounts to a "chemical catalyst" that brings to light power relations, locating their position and finding their "point of application and the methods used. . . . Rather than analyzing power from the point of view of its internal rationality, it consists of analyzing power relations through the antagonism of strategies. . . . [that is,] we should investigate the forms of resistance and attempts made to dissociate these relations."[33]

Thus, while the supreme values reigning in the central domain might operate against competing and subversive strategies within this domain itself, as well as those within the subsidiary domains, a central domain remains central as long as the balance of force relations allows for those values to dictate the rules of play and relations of power within the system. An author's imprint is determined within and by such a system; it can be "determining" only through, and by virtue of what has been called, after J. L. Austin, the conditions of felicity[34] that the system provides; or, irrespective of "brilliance" (a favorite descriptive of Said), the imprint may be waived out of existence or diminished in the extreme. It is not in the least trite to say that Said's association of "originality" and "brilliance" with "determining imprint" betrays a credulous, if not romantic, understanding that does not transcend into the realm of power structures. Originality, as chapter 3 will in part show, is *always* subject to the perspectivism of discursive formation, in which it must necessarily find itself, and by which it is assessed. Originality is evidenced in the manner it is ineluctably sliced up within any given discursive formation, which then assigns some slices to certain of its authors and buries the rest deep under. Which is to say that there does not exist and has never existed an objective standard of originality and that a construct of it is always determined by its own conditions of felicity that are necessarily both relative and mutative. (In this connection, it is worth noting in passing that for an Aeschylus to have any role to play in Said's narrative, his work must have an appeal or relevance within the discursive traditions connected to Orientalism. The only way he can be shown to have relevance is through, say, a Renan's reliance on his ideas or writings. Otherwise, to invoke an Aeschylus within the tradition of Orientalism is tantamount to invoking a Zou Yan as a voice integral to Enlightenment philosophy.)[35]

So far I have been speaking about central and peripheral domains as they stand in a dialectic with each other. Equally important, however, is the recognition that *within* both domains there always exist subversive discourses and resisting strategies that constantly challenge the paradigmatic discourses, that is, the discourses that constitute, reflect, and advocate the central domain and its values. To obviate the importance of such discourses, or, worse, to ignore them altogether because they may not sufficiently challenge the central domain, is to miss the significance of the dynamics of power structures and how—often through unpredictable modalities—they can mutate and generate new forms of power. On its own, "determining imprint" is thus a misleading category of analysis, for to make any useful analytical sense, it must always be viewed within, and in relation to, the various constitutive elements of the larger context of central and peripheral domains in which it locates itself.

Our account of paradigm then allows for diversity within unity, for exceptions and violations, and for irregularity and "abnormality." But if these are subversive forces, as they are by definition, then they are so precisely because they are not *positively* determinative of the central domain, although they may *negatively* be so by virtue of the responses the central domain provides to meet their challenge. However, once any of these forces is able to subvert the existing paradigm, replacing it as the locus of supreme value(s), what has now become a former paradigm, or former central domain, will join the ranks of the subversive forces or just vanish altogether. For every instance of change in the central domains must by definition start with an "undetermining imprint" of one power element or another (that is, discursive or otherwise) since this imprint is the qualitative differential that is necessary for the very concept of change. When modernity in Europe superseded[36] the central domains dictated by Church and monarch, it started with a multiplicity of "undetermining imprints," which grew in time into subversive and, still later, dominating discourses, creating their own discursive formations and, in some strong sense, their own central domains.[37]

This paradigm shift (and my account here must be seen as exceeding in qualitative and quantitative coverage that of the science historian Thomas Kuhn) finds attestation in nearly all modern phenomena, beginning with the creation of a distinction between fact and value and Is and Ought, and ending with the modern state, modern bureaucracy, law, modern capitalism, and nationalism.[38] All these (clearly evolving gradually yet aggregately constituting a break with previous forms) signaled the rise of modernity, and if this was ever possible, it was by virtue of the rise of central domains partly *out of peripheral domains*. Although many authors will never have any effect whatsoever, there are others whose work begins in obscurity although it gains initial traction for, and gradually constitutes, a process of power formation in which the ideational stands in constant dialectic with the material. Without such a theory, for instance, we might find it difficult, if not impossible, to explain the rise of modernity out of Europe's premodern self, or that of Greece or Islam out of the civilizational constellations that they replaced.

As I intimated earlier, the theory of paradigms and central domains serves us in more ways than one: first, it frames the discussion about the location of the author within power relations; and second, it explains and, as I hope to show, comparatively expands the concept of dialectic between knowledge and power, this clearly being a mainstay in the writings of both Foucault and Said. I first turn to the author.

III

Simply put, Said lacked the theoretical tools—Foucauldian or not—to handle the concept and practice of the author. This lack is not a mere register of critique against Said, as many Orientalists have understood it; for us, it is an additional index of the failure to identify the true nature of Orientalism, to pin its malevolent effects on a group of scholars and their "guild's" intimate association with a vague and perhaps incoherent concept of power, domination, and coloniality. It is my argument here that Said at once made too much and too little of the author. On the one hand, and as a theoretical claim, the author in the tradition of Orientalism—and, he seems to argue, at large—possesses a "determining imprint," while, on the other hand, the Orientalist author has effectively been declared "dead," for in that discursive formation he appears as an "effaced" entity, to use Foucault's term. The contradiction aside, his declaration that "Foucault believes that in general the individual text or author counts for very little" is highly problematic, especially in the way Foucault's position, which might have been extremely useful for Said's analysis, was dismissed immediately. If authors have "imprints" (to stay for the sake of clarity with Said's own designations for the moment), and some do possess "determining imprints," then one must be able to show not only their distinctive contributions to the field but also how such contributions changed aspects of the field, segments thereof, or the entirety of its course. The presence of "imprints" also entails the presence of individual and unique authorial contributions, and the manner in which they are conducive to discursivity. But none of this seems to have been on Said's agenda. In his reply to the historian Albert Hourani, who charged that Said did not consider the "achievements" of such Orientalists as Marshall Hodgson and Claude Cahen, Said pays lip service to these accomplishments and insists, in a persistent fashion, that such claims as these "do not conflict with what I say in *Orientalism*, with the difference that I do insist on the prevalence in the discourse itself of a structure of attitudes that cannot simply be waved away or discounted" (341). But if this is the case, and if, as we have already seen, every European (or is it every Orientalist?) is a racist and imperialist because no one can "resist the pressure" of one's "nation" or one's "scholarly tradition" (204, 271), then the author in Said's thinking appears to resemble Foucault's dead author. One then wonders why Said felt obliged to register his disagreement with Foucault on this crucial point.

Nonetheless, Foucault's theory of the author has left much that remains unresolved, and to some extent (at least in his "What Is an Author?") it created problems where none exists.[39] Yet, what Foucault argues remains relevant to our account, and should have been so for Said as well, for it is through this account that Said could have avoided falling into contradiction. In his account of the "author-function," Foucault articulates a category in which the author is very much alive, having not only averted death but rather flourished as the very engine of discursive tradition. For without such an author, discursivity itself—as expression and as an integral part of power—would be rendered impossible, for there cannot be discursivity without a collection or collectivity of discourses, despite the fact that a "theory of the work does not exist."[40] Indeed, it appears that it is *because* such a theory does not exist that "founders of discursivity" are at all possible.[41] And it is no coincidence that Foucault pinpoints the nineteenth century as the period in which these "founders" came into being, no coincidence in view of Said's repeated reference to this time period, in which Orientalism gained in power, prestige, and, for Said, "quantity" (a point to which we shall return in a different context).[42] Yet, the appearance of these "founders" coincides, in Foucault, with the disappearance of the author as individual, a disappearance that must command attention, for, Foucault continues, "we must locate the space left empty" by this absence, must trace down "the distribution of gaps and breaches, and watch for the openings that this disappearance uncovers."[43] Although the transition into the author of discursivity culminated in the nineteenth century, the "reversal" seems to have gradually taken place during the two centuries before, with the appearance of "the anonymity of an established or always redemonstrable truth" that does not make reference "to the individual who produced them" a necessity (149). (This is Said's governing principle, when he speaks of Orientalist doctrine as self-referential, virtually transhistorical, and needing no demonstration. However, the principle is neither solitary nor, as I will show, sufficient on its own.)

"Founders of discursivity," Foucault argues, are "unique," since they are not only authors of their own texts but also the agents and producers of the very "possibilities and the rules for the formation of other texts."[44] What is more important about these founders—Marx and Freud being Foucault's "most important cases"—is that their work made possible not only "a certain number of analogies" but also "a certain number of differences," "something other than their discourse, yet something belonging to what they founded." "In other words . . . the initiation of a discursive practice does not participate in its later transformations"; it only constitutes the "primary coordinates" to which discursivity, or the "science of discursivity," refers. However, this reference to the "origin . . . is not an ornament . . . [for it] never stops modifying it" and in the process "transforms" the "discursive practice itself."[45]

Equally important for our purposes is Foucault's insistence that a proper analysis of discourse cannot be constructed "solely from the grammatical features, formal structures, and objects of discourse: more likely there exist properties or relationships" that are "not reducible to the rules of grammar and logic."[46] Note the relationship in Foucault's thinking here between the moment of "initiation" and (its?) "later transformation." That moment is a "primary coordinate" to which the discursive practice refers or, indeed, must refer. It is not, in other words, nonexistent, absent, or irrelevant; it, in fact, *has* a role to play, however much quantitatively or qualitatively that role is superseded, diminished, exaggerated, amplified, transformed, contorted, or even eviscerated by the force of its discursive reincarnation. What makes that moment of initiation the site of "primary coordinates," and thus very alive, is that discursivity never stops modifying it, which implies, indeed entails, that in the very process of "reference" there is an affirmation or denial of a point of departure, a progenitor, a point of reference. It may be puzzling then to read that the "initiation of a discursive practice does not participate in its later transformations." This, I think, would have to mean only one thing, which is trite: that the moment of initiation can never maintain the same identity or the same hermeneutical stability as existed between the author himself and his text. But without a referential acknowledgment of the moment of origin, which unceasingly continues to modify it, there would be neither a discursive formation nor a constant mutation of the "discursive practice itself." Taken altogether, this line of thinking cannot dispose of the author, who indeed suffered a common death, but left an elite whose identity was wholly defined by notions of author. As we will see in chapter 3, the death of the author is never total, even for Foucault, rendering the metaphor of death (originally coined by Ronald Barthes) an altogether powerful word for easy circulation but hardly adequate for rigorous analysis. For at least the later Foucault, critique of or by the author is never marginal, and certainly not easily susceptible to a common death.

As one Foucault scholar has noted, Foucault's entire project has itself challenged "point by point the grounds of an unacceptable pastoral government: biblical theology, the juridical theory of natural right, and the pursuit of the means of certainty in the face of authority."[47] Foucault himself asserts that if government is "a social practice of subjecting individuals by mechanisms of power which lay claim to truth," *critique* will be "the movement by which the subject assumes the right to question truth on its effects of power, and power on its effects on truth," for the "*art of voluntary nonservitude [is] considered nondocility.*"[48] There is no critique without the author, whose docility is neither total nor assured. If anything, the author, as a post-Kantian subject, is entrusted with the task "not to [just?] discover what we are but to refuse what we are." The task "nowadays," Foucault insists, is to "build up what we could be" in order "to get rid of this kind of political 'double-bind,' which is the simultaneous individualization and totalization of modern power structures."[49] "Building up what we could be," "critique," and "nondocility" are nothing if they are not ideational and authorial, keeping in mind the nonliteral meanings of the "work" as Foucault himself expounded them.

This interpretation of Foucault not only is evident in his own language, but receives further support from his understanding and theory of the history of epistemic regimes, what he called *épistémè*, on the latest *cycle* of which he pours his analytical energies. Being trapped in this regime is not the end of history, for both the author and critique, and with them the human agent as the subject and predicate of history, would then entirely cease to matter. But that is not an absurdity of which Foucault could be accused. It is therefore difficult to avoid the suspicion that Said, like many others, took

Foucault's overly dramatic metaphor too seriously, and at face value, treating it as an analytically categorical statement of fact.

In line with J. L. Austin's theory of performativity, Foucault calls for studying discourses not in terms of their "expressive value" as communicative speech but rather "according to their mode of existence."[50] In a revealing and quite pertinent statement for the study of Orientalism, and contra Said, Foucault says: "The manner in which [discourses] are articulated according to social relationships can be more readily understood . . . in the activity of the author-function and its modifications, than in the themes or concepts that discourses set in motion."[51] If Foucault's individual author had indeed died, he would have died an ideological death, one that *also* performed the double function of resurrection. If generation and corruption are not a structure of dialectic, then they are nothing. Discursivity, however impersonal and supra-authorial it may be, remains an impossibility without a notion of the author resurrected, but an author nonetheless. It is therefore a grave error to cite Foucault's proclamation of the death of the author without the concomitant rise of what he called the author as an "ideological figure,"[52] an author who has emerged to contain the proliferation of meaning and in fact to create silences as much as elucidate the "truth." Yet, in all of this there is the "critique," the emblem of resistance and refusal of power's individualization and totalization.[53]

Foucault's historicizing of the author problem, consistent with his concept of the rise (and, by implication, displacements and breaks) of *épistémès*, is crucial, especially in light of what is for us an important statement, that the "modes of circulation, valorization, attribution, and appropriation of discourses *vary with each culture* and are modified within each."[54] The rise, through suppression, of the ideological author at the expense of the individual author, as well as the ineluctable disappearance and death of the former in favor of an as yet unidentified newcomer, belies any claim for a perpetual, much less eternal, regime of truth, certainly not one in modernity that an Aeschylus or a Dante—or for that matter an Aristotle or a Protagoras—could have advocated. The historicizing for us is thus pregnant with significance in terms of how the death and rise of authors fit within a theory of paradigms.

I do not take the fact that Foucault was as much a historian as he was a philosopher lightly, nor do I overlook the other crucial fact that Said was a consummate literary critic who lacked, it must be said, any historical sense.[55] These are critical givens in any discussion such as ours, as well as every other. Theory without a proper historical perspective[56] will remain incomplete, defective, and certainly myopic, lodged in the biases of the present, just as the doctrine of progress is.[57] Every moment of the present obviously stems from a prior moment, to which yet another moment gives rise, and so on. There cannot be then a theory of paradigms or a theory of the author outside a historical outlook, no matter how involved the theory may be or may become. A perennial rule for central paradigms is that, by the very fact of being paradigms, they rise and fall, that, in the nature of their constitution as historical and human constructions, they necessarily undergo change, one for which we must account on both the theoretical and the "factual-historical" levels. While the latter is the business of the empirical historian, the former, historically informed, must be the guiding matrix, since it is with this theoretical construction—and it is after all a construction—that an intelligible picture of change in regimes of truth and their ramifications becomes possible.

Yet, it is impossible to proceed with an adequate explication of Foucault's positions on the matters at hand without noting that Foucault insists throughout his writing that his explanation of the author-function is "schematic," which I take to mean an outline generalization that aims to cross a point as unequivocally as possible, without delving into the details of exceptions and exclusions, which tend to vitiate both the main argument and the larger picture. Foucault's schematization focuses on the "transition *into* modernity" as opposed to the "transition *from* pre-modernity." Depriving Foucault of the benefit of the doubt and taking his words at face value would be all too easy an exercise, one that would leave us with a Foucault that is replete with unjustifiably attributed contradictions. For if Foucault was clear, as he was, about the historical origins of the death of the author, then a logical explanation would be to say that his concern with discursivity and discursive formations has abducted all of his attention, that he simply is not very interested in the dynamics of the rise and fall of discursivities *as such* but in their ontological status and modes of operation roughly between the eighteenth century and late modernity. Nonetheless, Foucault's "schematic" exposition leaves too much between the cracks, too much that is relevant to our concerns, but not to his.

What is equally interesting and important for our concerns are the origins of the "founders of discursivity," namely, why and how they arose in the first place. Foucault spoke of their ontological modalities of the way they operated and the truth regimes they generated or partly were born into; but I think he overlooked, to put it mildly, the historical causes (that is, premodern structures) within Europe that precipitated such a change. I will not address the issue of causality directly, although an explanation will unfold as this writing proceeds.

It must be explicitly stated that the reincarnation of the individual author in the form of the discursive or ideological counterpart should not mean, even in Foucault, that the author is irrelevant to (that is, does not have "a determining imprint" on) the existing discursive formations or discursivity within a given context. For such a claim would leave us with either a mysterious conception of history, where things suddenly and inexplicably appear out of nowhere, or a crude form of end-of-history theology, assuming that there ever are secular theologies of the end of history that are not crude. Or, and very likely, we will be left with both misfortunes.

Foucault's choice of Marx and Freud as the exemplars of founders of discursivity is intended to make the fundamental point that the discursive traditions have both generated and defined our modern intellectual, political, psychoanalytical, and cultural landscapes, that, in the spheres of their contributions, they have unintentionally birthed, and in some important sense lost control over, the theories they advocated in their various writings, writings, we might stress, that may originate with highly individualized potential. What must be of immediate concern here is the potential *passage* (which I think both Foucault and Said, in particular, neglected) of the work from one stage to another, from individuality to canonization, and from singularity to discursivity. Foucault's "death of the author"—a theatrical pronouncement (not unlike the provocative others he made throughout his extraordinarily rich intellectual career) intended to stress the schematization he was drawing—cannot account for the first years after the publication of the *Studies on Hysteria* or the *Communist Manifesto* in any terms other than individual writings *by individual authors*. Neither of these works, at the moment of initiation, was the fruit of an ideological authorship in Foucault's sense. The transition of Marx from an individual author to a founder of discursivity is most illustrative, at least for our purposes, since his oeuvre has become the cornerstone and, more accurately, flagship of central domains in the former Soviet Union, not to mention of several other "second-world" countries and movements across the globe. It is in this context that Foucault's argument finds the most eloquent manifestation, namely, that Marx's "work" not only made possible a host of "analogies" but also enabled, beyond Marx's original intentions, "a certain number of differences," something different and divergent from his discourse, "yet something belonging to what [he and surely Engels] founded." Marx's authorship is illustrative for two important reasons: first, his emergence into discursivity was inextricably tied to the rise of economic and political formations, which is to say, the rise of such formations constituted the conditions of possibility for the transition into discursivity; and second, important for us, is that the transition both signaled and represented a profound departure—in terms of philosophy, political practice, and Weltanschauung—from the theory and practice of liberalism and its capitalism, which was already dominating in Western Europe.

It is, I think, pointless to engage in the question of whether ideas precipitate and bring forth material realities, or the other way around. It is more fruitful to view this question in terms of a dialectic: it is in the nature of systems of power to produce within them opposing strategies, what we may commonly call strategies of subversiveness (or "subversivity," a term that resonates with discursivity). We might then say that while central domains are defined by the discursive formations they produce, these very formations in turn per force produce discursive subversivity. No one, I think, can reasonably think that a Marx, for all that a Marx can represent, could have been possible without an industrial revolution or without a laissez-faire system of capitalism. Nor could Foucault himself, no doubt now a founder of discursivity, have been conceivable, much less possible, without the emergence of particular systems of political, economic, and cultural power that are unprecedented in human history. We might be tempted therefore to add Foucault to Foucault's chosen duo, Marx and Freud.

The fact that Foucault's well-known disinterest in colonialism and coloniality opened a gap not only for Said's project but also for a host of fields with such labels as "postmodernism" and "postcoloniality" is testimonial to the predominance of departures and differences over analogies in his work as a founder of discursivity. It is then reasonable to argue that only the Austinian conditions of felicity residing within and dominating central domains make Foucault's ideological author possible. This view of conditions does not bank on a particular logic of power or a predictable outcome of power's constructions, but can include even chance as a possible factor.[58] Thus, it is not as reasonable to argue that, because such authors are the product of the central domain and its conditions of felicity, their work, their discursivity, must obey the logic of power within either the domain or the discursive formation. I therefore attach a great deal of importance to Foucault's notion of "difference" in the effects ("unintentionally") produced by the founders of discursivity, for without giving full weight and justifiably expansive and elaborate meaning to the concept of difference, Foucault himself, as well as Marx and Freud, can never be intelligible either as a phenomenon or as an author/founder of discursivity. Yet, in all of this, the ideological author begins—must begin—as an individual author, for there is no other place from which discursivity can begin. The individual author, I should put it emphatically, is the ontological precondition of both the founder of discursivity and that of subversivity. And if we must exercise further discrimination in the concept, then we would be compelled to recognize the "author" as a homonymous or polysemic concept.

Said's author, who is charged with a "determining imprint," at times resembles a revived version of Foucault's individual author, who has, under an expansive and even somewhat metaphorical interpretation, met his death, while, on the other hand, Said's author seems to be a stunted version of Foucault's ideological author. Strictly speaking, however, his author is neither, for it is a confused category. The collection of Orientalist authors Said chooses to dwell on can hardly be described as founders of discursivity, a fact that diminishes the truth-value of Said's response to Hourani, namely, that he studied Orientalism as a "structure of attitudes." It may have been a more legitimate claim of his had he given an expansive and textured treatment (in the manner he gave, for instance, Massignon) to the mostly German and Austrian Orientalists writing between the mid-nineteenth century and mid-twentieth, notably, figures like Ignaz Goldziher and Joseph Schacht, among others, whose absence from his work (especially in the case of Schacht and the entire field of "Islamic law") not only is striking but also, as we will see in due course, bears tremendous significance for what Orientalism is and what it must mean.

IV

It is not trite at this point to schematically recall Said's arguments about Orientalism, however well known they are by now, for it might be a worthwhile exercise to employ history and the theories of author and paradigms to check their veracity. If discourse about Orientalism, as Said has made it into a common academic topic, is to have any meaning or significance, it must be something that is neither commonplace nor ordinary. In other words, for the discourse on Orientalism to be worthy of any special attention, much less the locus of vehement controversies, Orientalism must be a singularly important phenomenon that can be isolated and identified as having particularly distinctive or unique characteristics. For if Orientalism turns out to be just another scholarly tradition or just another field of study, one among many like it, and with more or less the same performative and destructive effects, then we might find it unwarranted that it should have been segregated for the kind of analytical and political attention that it has thus far received.[59] What then is so distinctive about Orientalism?

Said's characterization of this discipline can be summarized, schematically, as follows: First, a central feature of Orientalism is represented in the distance it created between the West and the Orient. "Thus all Orientalism stands forth and away from the Orient" (21–22). For Said, distance is not just the ontological matrix in which Orientalism found itself, or that it established for itself in dealing with the Orient or, for that matter, it would seem, with any Other. Distance appears to emerge in *Orientalism* as an epistemological category that constructed the particular facts of ontology. Said's complaint, which runs throughout his book, is captured in the summational statement that an essential condition for Orientalism, and one on which it "depended," was "the almost total absence in contemporary Western culture of the Orient as a genuinely felt and experienced force" (208). (Of course one cannot make sense of this proposition in light of the "noncontemporary" "Orientalists" in Europe's premodern history; the Latin West and "classical Greece," Said told us earlier in the book [49], did after all have their own Orientalists. If these also failed to garner this knowledge of the Orient as a "genuinely felt and experienced force," why not include them? Nor does the contradiction engendered by the specification of "contemporaneity" diminish when Said also says that the "absolute demarcation between East and West . . . has been years, even centuries, in the making" [39]. And if the "demarcation" has been in the making for centuries, then how many centuries, and how do "Orientalists" such as Dante and Aeschylus fit within the Foucauldian discursive formation that Foucault clearly dated no earlier than the eighteenth century? And if Said was drawing on Gramsci more than he did on Foucault, then is the hegemonic power recognized by Gramsci a transhistorical phenomenon?)

Be that as it may, the first and foremost of the "facts" generated by distance is the silent nature of the Orient, which calls upon the Orientalists to represent it *in their own way*. It is not a mere coincidence that Said begins his book with what he thinks is a telling encounter between Flaubert and an Egyptian courtesan, where Flaubert "spoke for and represented her . . . [but] she never spoke of herself, she never represented her emotions, presence, or history." This is "not an isolated instance," but a structural feature that Said regards as a demonstrative "pattern of relative strength between East and West" (6).

Distance generates other "facts" that inextricably stand connected to silence. Placing itself "outside the Orient," Orientalism's province and self-perceived function are to "make the Orient speak" through "describing" it. But in this description, a fundamental feature emerges as constitutive of the Orient, namely, "that the Orient was the Orient, that it was different" (277).[60] With this difference as an indubitable given, Orientalism "renders [the Orient's] mysteries plain for and to the West" (20–21). But in explaining these mysteries, much malevolent discourse ensues. As accurately and poignantly represented in Comte de Volney's voyage to the East, Orientalism is antagonistic and aggressive, if not "canonically hostile" (81). And Said admirably shows this hostility in the writings of a nearly infinite list of Orientalists. As the philosopher Akeel Bilgrami puts it in summing up Said's thesis, Orientalism adopted "attitudes of civilizational condescension," where Orientals stood "inferior and underdeveloped."[61] The negative stereotypes are virtually countless, including the attributes of "monolithic caricatures," laziness, biological inferiority, lack of cultural refinement, and so on. Thus Orientalist logic progresses clearly: distance breeds difference and difference in turn breeds contempt and a host of trenchantly negative images and stereotypes. (This context may also provide fertile grounds for theorizing the Anglo-Saxon notion of familiarity and of proximity as equally prolific sources for breeding contempt, a notion that I shall take up later in the context of shame of nature and self-hate.)

Difference, however, appears to gain its own ontological and epistemological momentum, especially in the second half of *Orientalism*. So important was it to Said, and so crucial for my considerations of the author as well as the theory of paradigms, that we would do poorly not to regard it as a structural feature of *Orientalism*. It is not, I think, without good reason that in his resume of Said's work, Bilgrami lists it as the third of the five "features" of Orientalism,[62] although he does not specifically locate it, as I do, within an epistemology and ontology of difference. Accordingly, when the Orientalists did not engage in the discursive activity and attitudes expounded under the first structural feature, and even when they "made the effort to find the Orient's civilizational glories," their attitude "was that of wondrous awe, only this time it reduced [the Orient] to an exotic rather than an inferior or monolithic object."[63] Even for a "genius" and a highly ethical scholar and human being, as Massignon was, and irrespective of his ceaseless efforts on behalf of the Palestinians and their cause in particular and Islam in general, exoticizing the East and thus Orientalizing it would remain a charge against him. The strong point to be taken from this is not that Said erred in his judgment of Massignon (that requires a separate investigation); it is that for Said no Orientalist can avoid the pitfalls of the effects of ontological and epistemological distance and difference. Said's position seems to be this: that anyone who says or writes anything about the Orient in a way that constructs the Orient as either inferior or superior to the West (that is, as either a "bad" or a "good" Orient) is an Orientalist and thus guilty as charged.

The third structural feature, for which Said's *Orientalism* deservedly gained notoriety and which influenced postcolonial studies immediately after its publication, is the complicity of Orientalism as a scholarly discipline and tradition in the structures of political and economic power. Possessing a "highly articulated set of relationships to the dominant culture surrounding it," Orientalism "borrowed and was frequently informed by 'strong' ideas, doctrines, and trends ruling the culture" (22). It is important to notice the directionality of the relationship between Orientalism and colonialism in Said. The "growing systematic knowledge" of Orientalism is said to have been "reinforced by the colonial encounter," an encounter (just in case it is not clear) in which "Europe was always in a position of strength, not to say domination" (39–40).

I will attend to a critique of this feature at some length later, but it is worthwhile for now to stress that the directionality in Said travels from the "colonial encounter" to the Orientalist "guild" and its scholarly texts. The Orientalist's Orient is "a system of representations framed by a whole set of forces that brought the Orient into Western learning" (202–3). These representations, the core of Said's interest, are seen as problematic *within* Europe, because they turn out, upon analysis, to have genealogical associations with power, thus betraying the "objectivity" or, if you will, the purity of the quest for knowledge (this point being no less integral to Said's interest).

Orientalism's association with power is thus a European or Western problem: "Indeed, *my real argument* is that Orientalism *is*—and does not *simply represent*—a considerable dimension of modern political-intellectual culture, and as such *has less to do with the Orient* than it does with 'our' world" (12, emphasis mine). What, one might ask, is the exact relationship between Orientalism as a representation and Orientalism as an ontological reality of the Orient, and how does one make the epistemological leap between the two? Is there an "is" that is outside of representation? And if Orientalism *is* a considerable dimension of modern political-intellectual culture, how can it do less with the Orient than it does with our Western world? Is modernity limited to the West? And if Orientalism is implicated with colonialism (which Said intimates but never articulates in any detail), isn't colonialism, whose locale is by definition the "Orient," modern? Is difference, the function of distance, so great that Orientalism is "really" just about "us"? Is the destination of Orientalism and its "learned texts" limited to the West, having *to do less with the Orient*, the real place of colonialism and genocide? Indeed, the Orientalist's text is "specifically designed to be read not by the Orientals but by other Westerners. This is an important point. . . . None of the Orientalists I write about seems ever to have intended an Oriental as a reader" (335–36). Or is it, as we will see, that these texts were describing a fait accompli, one having to do with the Orient and its reengineering *before* the Western reader came into consideration?[64] Or, still, is it that the first reader of these "texts" (or "works," to use Foucault's more apt descriptive) was in effect the Oriental himself, and only secondarily the Westerner?

The unidirectionality from Orient to Occident, or at best a dialectic that ends, in term of effect and manifestation, in Europe, more than finds adequate attention in Said's *Culture and Imperialism*, a work that the author deemed to continue the investigations he started in *Orientalism*.[65] In other words, Said's concerns begin and end in the metropolitan centers of Western Empire, in their cultural and political constitutions and manifestations, centers that produced "estimable and admirable works of art and learning," from which he derived aesthetic "pleasure" and "profit."[66] And so like Orientalist works, which he on the whole appears to find less aesthetically appealing, if not downright objectionable, his preoccupation is, at the end of the day, the West's metropolitan cultural and scholarly production, the world that Said in reality knew and the world that in effect formed him in almost every important way, despite any articulation of his identity as a Palestinian. Whatever dialectic between power and knowledge one may detect in *Orientalism* (39, 94), it is one that is judged by a chronological causality, not by a mutually dependent production of knowledge *as* power. That all paradigmatic modern knowledge is power and that its converse is equally true amount to a proposition that Said does not seem likely to accept: that if modernity with all its knowledge forms is inextricably predicated on colonialism, then colonialism defines modernity par excellence, for they are one and the same.

The comparative literature scholar Emily Apter insightfully makes the point that in his preface to the reissue of Auerbach's *Mimesis* from 2003, Said "demonstrates his obvious passion for the great works of Western literature . . . but there is a noticeable lack of attention to Auerbach's Eurocentrism. . . . There is nothing obviously 'Saidian' about the preface, and if the reader covers up the signature, he or she might never guess that it corresponds to that of the author of *Orientalism*. Perhaps this was a text in the spirit of confirming the critic's freedom to address his interests in any way he sees fit, an example of the pure intellectual pleasure Said has always taken in certain forms of traditional humanist scholarship."[67] Later on in her essay, Apter explains Said's silence over Auerbach's Eurocentrism as a way for Said to focus on fashioning a new humanism, one that is less concerned with aesthetic pleasure than with Said's "belief that humanism provides futural parameters for defining secular criticism in a world increasingly governed by a sense of identitarian ethnic destiny and competing sacred tongues."[68] That this "new humanism" is, like Auerbach's, profoundly Eurocentric and in fact unconscious of its origins and biases—that is, of its own Eurocentrism—Apter, like many others, does not seem to find problematic. Nor is the secularism of Said's "critical secularism" less secular and secularizing because he saw "the mandate of humanism" to be the definition of "a critical secularism that seeks to reconcile the competing claims of theodicy, relativism, ontogenesis, and antiimperialism." There is nothing here that removes the adjudicative power and monopoly of secularism over everything else, just as the "secular" liberal state's "mandate" to regulate religion does little but subjugate the latter to the former. Both Apter and Said take too much for granted, even when Apter, going beyond Said, carves out a wider domain for critical secularism by connecting the "'renewal of liberal disciplines with subjective consciousness' within the broader context of colonial history, imperialism, and the critique of nationalism."[69] To systematically avoid the definition and use of secularism as oppositional to the religious, and to harness it for a critique of nationalist theology and other secular forms, is, as this book vehemently argues, no longer sufficient and, moreover, leads to incoherence. For however much secularism is free of the secular, it will not do as a critical apparatus of the very system that gave it its own form and structure. Involving far too much collusion and *interdependence* with racism, colonialism, imperialism, and the fabrication of "religion" as an enemy and straw man, critical secularism of the secular will, as typical of modern solutions to modern problems, solves one problem only to fall into another, as repeatedly evidenced in the social, economic, and medical fields.

Apter also significantly notes Said's alleged "flirtation" with matters of God just before his untimely death in 2003. She says: "Almost seeming at times to be flirting with the temptations of paradise himself, Said identifies the godly within humanism with a logic of extension."[70] Yet this mere "extension," seemingly born in the last year or two of Said's life, does not save his analysis of Massignon or of any appreciation of the "spiritual" Orient, which always seemed to him to do nothing but pit the Orient, as the Other, against the "secular" Occident. Genealogically, furthermore, we will do well to take seriously the religious studies scholar Gil Anidjar's assertion that "Christianity made itself increasingly forgettable by foregrounding religion as a generic category and a target of criticism, . . . doing so at the same time it was arguing for the end of religion in its own practice, often pushing its colonial endeavor explicitly as a kind of critical secularism, a secular science."[71]

Said's critique then amounts to a one-sided philosophy of secular rationality and to a significantly diminished quality and quantity of the dialectic between modern power and dominant forms of knowledge, thereby leaving his account with a strong texture of unidirectionality, one that begins with what appears to be external political and cultural forces from which Orientalism "*borrowed* and [that it] was frequently informed *by*" (22, emphasis mine). The passive voice is of course unmistakable: Orientalism is the recipient and beneficiary of these forces, their object, and perhaps, we have every reason to conclude, their *terminus ad quem*. Misrepresenting the Orient, the major theme of Said's work, is an effect of the forces working on Orientalism, by virtue of having this discipline "reinforced by the colonial encounter" (39–40). I shall discuss this matter at length later, but wish here to make the point that the suppression of a strong dialectic between colonialism and Orientalism, and, more importantly, between Orientalism and the "surrounding culture," is not mere inattention to the analytics of power's dynamics, a scholarly failure, so to speak. This is no scholarly failure at all, for, as I argue throughout, this type of discourse *is the function* of what Foucault called a "discursive strategy" whose ontological mode *requires* keeping the dialectic either suppressed, silent, or at bay. Changing this element in the discursive strategy would have entailed changing everything else, including the *partial* reservations about the otherwise totalizing and imperial liberalism, secularism, and ideological others.

A less obvious structural feature of Said's *Orientalism*, though no less significant, is that Orientalism itself is represented as a "text." In his otherwise incisive analysis of one Orientalist writing after another, the Orient is shown to be (mis)represented and thus re-created *in these texts*. The colossal project of the incomparable William Jones in India, which changed the life of that subcontinent *and* its history forever, remained for Said a matter reducible merely to law, "an occupation with *symbolic significance* for the history of Orientalism" (78, emphasis mine). Receiving a little more than a page in Said's work, Jones's project emerges in the final analysis as no more than a textual exercise, "grounding . . . European languages in a distant, harmless, Oriental source" (78).[72] Likewise, Renan, who deservedly receives Said's wrath, "believed that he had re-created the Orient, as it really was, *in his work*" (88, emphasis mine). Since Said deliberately made it his business not to engage with any question as to what the Orient truly is or was—for this would involve representation and, as we will see, every representation for Said in effect constitutes a misrepresentation—there was nothing for him to say about the Orient itself, having been left with an Orientalism that seems to be wholly defined by texts, "*because* the texts made that Orient possible" (94, his emphasis). Nor does the epistemic location of the Orientalist and Orientalism travel beyond the West, so it seems. The "specialists . . . do their work, so to speak, because in time their profession as Orientalists requires that they present *their society* with images of the Orient, knowledge about it, insight into it. *And to a very large extent* the Orientalist provides *his own society* with representations of the Orient" (273, emphases mine). Note here the cumulative effect of the unidirectionality I have just discussed: the Orient is re-created in the Orientalist text, which is why it "*has less to do with the Orient* than it does with 'our' world." Orientalism emerges as our "text" that "our" world "reads" about "our Orient," the text being all that "our" world knows, but it is a text that is "reinforced by the colonial encounter." The text then not only defines "our" knowledge but also keeps this knowledge internal to it.

Reengineering the Orient thus emerges as a textual product: "After Napoleon, then, the very language of Orientalism changed radically. . . . The Orient was reconstructed, reassembled, crafted, in short, *born* out of the Orientalist's efforts" (87, his emphasis). The laboring of the Orient under the weight of company Orientalism, colonialism, and structural genocide never looms large in Said's account.[73] They remain not only unarticulated; they are effectively left to occupy a capacious space for a host of silences. What, other than the politics of empire, lay behind, and beneath, de Lesseps's statement, which Said quotes, that "nothing . . . could stop us, nothing was impossible, nothing mattered finally except the realization of '*le résultat final, le grand but*'" (90)? How is the *résultat final*, the Suez project that amounted to splitting apart no less than two continents, different from the other engineering project of *solution finale* or *die Endlösung*? Is there a structural link between them that goes beyond politics and political explanation?

James Clifford aptly argues that Said frequently suggests that an Orientalist text "distorts, dominates, or ignores some real or authentic feature of the Orient. Elsewhere, however, he denies the existence of any 'real Orient.' . . . Said's concept of 'discourse' still vacillates between, on the one hand, the status of an ideological distortion of lives and cultures that are never concretized and, on the other, the condition of a persistent structure of signifiers that, like some extreme example of experimental writing, refers solely and endlessly to itself. Said is thus forced to rely on nearly tautological statements."[74] While Clifford may be right that the denial of any "real Orient" is a "significant methodological choice," it is likely (and this is integral to my argument) that Said perhaps knew that acknowledging any such reality would have led him to two difficulties: first, condemning the Orientalists' depictions of the Orient would then require him to offer his corrections, which he elected not to do; and second, he would then have to reckon with his own finding about *that* "real Orient," which is nonsecular, traditional,[75] and perhaps offensive to modern liberal sensibilities, Said's included.

V

If we turn to a consideration of the first structural feature outlined earlier, we find that Said spends most of *Orientalism* discussing and finely elaborating on this feature. Indeed, the emphasis on the malevolent effects of distance preoccupies his text to such an extent that the theme of Orientalist misrepresentations turns into a never-ceasing and exhausting repetition that cuts across chapters and their sections and subsections. (In my estimate, the book would have averted some criticism and been more effective had it been streamlined into a little more than half of its published size.) The point about this technical deficiency is substantive, however, not merely formal; it is to say that the inordinate attention that this feature received from the author makes the book (at least) appear as a continuous register of various forms and styles of portraying the Orient in negative terms. But what about the sources and true significance of these (mis)representations?

My argument is that while this feature can be neither naively overlooked nor intentionally omitted, it can largely be assumed to exist in all cultures viewing the "Other," and that it is thus not—as a general category—particular to Orientalism. If the plural form "cultures" exists, then the "Other" exists along with it both ontologically and epistemologically, which is to say that the very concept of "culture" (now in the singular) is ontologically and epistemologically impossible without the *existence* of the "Other." Because "culture" and "Other" are modern categories, an interlocutor might argue that if the former did not exist in the past, then the latter could not have arisen; but this argument is rendered partially invalid by virtue of the historical presence of other forms of self-identification (religious, tribal, ethnic) that made the "Other" (or its equivalent) an equally ontological and epistemological necessity, although modernity admittedly constructed a particularly thick meaning of the term. The presence of Self/Other in all cultures of all times makes of epistemological distance a genus whose latest species is the modern form, and it is within a comparative study of the various species that the special characteristics of Orientalism can be properly understood. Lest this paragraph insinuate any agreement with Said's view of all "advanced cultures" as racist and oppressive (204), it is precisely the *systemic* destructive and intolerant[76] edge of modern culture that is being distinguished here.

One advantage of such assumptions as I have proposed is that if distance and its resultant stereotypes are to be taken for granted, then one of the issues that proved confusing to Said and just as confusing to many commentators on Orientalism writing today will be averted. More precisely put, if this feature is not deemed a condition of possibility but an accidental attribute that, by definition, may or may not exist, then one would not confuse Aeschylus or Dante with a von Grunebaum or Lewis. The advantage thus allows a sharper edge in engaging a theory of falsifiability, however simplified it may be. Said, for one, would not have erred on Aeschylus, Dante, and their likes had he proceeded with such assumptions, although there remain several other conditions that needed to be met, as chapter 2 will attempt to show in due course.

Another advantage is the analytical clarity made available when speaking of distance and power, for the entailment between them, *strictly speaking*, does not exist, which is to say that while they may appear to stand in a relationship of concomitance, they in fact logically do not. Thus while Flaubert's representation of the courtesan *happened* to be associated with a "pattern of relative strength between East and West," such a representation is plausibly conceivable within a different balance of power, say, among distant equals. A Tang Chinese merchant visiting Abbasid Baghdad in its imperial heyday could easily have represented a Baghdadian courtesan in very similar terms.[77] This is not to exonerate Flaubert, but rather to make clear the point that the effects of distance must be analyzed on their own, within a specifically modern setting, for there is no *necessary entailment*—if I am allowed the redundancy—between distance and its effects, on the one hand, and relationships embedded in power, on the other.

My third, and more fundamental, point about the first structural feature of Said's *Orientalism* has to do with his notion of representation, a notion that emerges as "canonical" within the work, and that is captured by statements that declare outright that "Islam" and its whole Orient were "fundamentally misrepresented in the West" (272). I here return to the central question that concerns this feature: What is so particular about Orientalism? It seems that Said himself answered the question, with what amounts to a resounding "nothing." But the answer does not come without its own problems.

Speaking untypically like a philosopher, Said, in the later parts of his work, makes the revealing statement that the

> real issue is whether indeed there can be a true representation of anything, or whether any and all representations, because they are representations, are embedded first in the language and then in the culture, institutions, and political ambience of the representer. If the latter alternative is the correct one (as I believe it is), then we must be prepared to accept the fact that a representation is *eo ipso* implicated, intertwined, embedded, interwoven with a great many

other things besides the "truth," which is itself a representation. What this must lead us to methodologically is to view representations (or misrepresentations—the distinction is at best a matter of degree) as inhabiting a common field of play defined for them, not by some inherent common subject matter alone, but by some common history, tradition, universe of discourse. (272–73)

In the next paragraph, Said makes it even clearer that Orientalist (mis)representations are nothing more than what we, as humans, commonly do with language, that they are what representations do as a matter of course. Said goes as far as to say:

My whole point about this [Orientalist] system is not that it is a misrepresentation of some Oriental essence . . . but that it operates as representations usually do, for a purpose, according to a tendency, in a specific historical, intellectual, and even economic setting. In other words, representations have purposes, *they are effective much of the time,* they accomplish one or many tasks. Representations are formations, or as Roland Barthes has said of all operations of language, they are deformations. (273, emphasis mine)

This is puzzling, to say the least. If representation operates in the manner Said himself describes—a matter, I think, now generally agreed upon—then why should a substantial part of the book be dedicated to a repetitive detailing of the Orientalists' negative depictions of the Orient and Islam, including the reduction of the object of study (Orient, Islam, Arabs, and so on) into essences, which Said—in opposition to what he says in the quoted paragraph—spends a good deal of time detailing?

I believe Said's drifting into and out of critiquing negative depictions stems from having taken too seriously the literary and linguistic effects of these representations. And his legacy continues to flourish until the present. In the paragraph quoted earlier, he comes close to a beginning, however rough and simplistic, toward expressing something profoundly important about language and representation, but a beginning that quickly meets a crib death. When he says that "representations have purposes, they are effective much of the time, they accomplish one or many tasks," he is touching on the fundamentals of Austinian performatives, yet without taking them seriously. There are questions that needed to be asked in this context: What typology of purposes do representations have? Which of these types are pertinent to a study of Orientalism? Which are not? When are representations effective? "Most of the time" tells us nothing about the *quality* of those representations that *do* produce effects. When and under what conditions do they accomplish one task, multiple tasks, or none at all?

To attend to these issues in the study of Orientalist discourse is to delve into the heart of the question of Orientalist representation, to understand what matters and what does not, what one needs to take seriously and what to dismiss as no more than babble—in other words, what types of discourses are performative and in what way exactly they are so. Take, for instance, premodern Islamic travelogues and travel writings, ranging from those of Ibn Fadlan (tenth century) to Ibn Jubayr (d. 1217) and Ibn Battuta (d. 1369).[78] Or for that matter consider such works as Biruni's *India* (mid-eleventh century),[79] or the Islamic or Chinese historical annals in which the Other is represented. Such works are replete with references and extensive discourses that portray other peoples, other cultures, and other religions in less than favorable, indeed often pejorative, terms.[80] And since many of these happened to be speaking about peoples east of them, the question we face is this: Are *these* "Orientalist" writings? And whether the answer is affirmative or negative, there remains the necessity, in order to answer the question, of defining and understanding what Orientalism really is. Defining it in terms of misrepresentations will not do.

Before we take up this matter in detail, a topic that is more appropriately discussed in our later analysis of the structural feature of knowledge and its association with power, we will do well first to say a few things about the Austinian performatives and their theoretical implications for our context, without which the issue of representation and representationalism cannot be satisfactorily resolved.

As is well known, J. L. Austin's theory of performatives was a response to the positivist philosophical doctrine that propositions or, less technically, utterances lend themselves only to the test of truth-valuation, since their function is to describe, report, or constate something, making them either true or false. This, Austin argues, excluded an expansive type of propositions that logically do not, and, in fact, cannot, fulfill this function; what they rather do is to construct action. Since they perform action, create a reality, or produce a "material reality," in part or in whole, he called them performatives. Austin gives numerous examples of such propositions, the most illustrative of which is the statement "I do" in a marriage ceremony. Strictly speaking, "I do" does not lend itself to being true or false, but in effect constitutes a new creation, that of the marriage as a legal and social act. The most important "leading incident in the performance of the act . . . is the utterance of the words" whose object is the act itself.[81]

What is of interest to us here is what Austin calls the "appropriateness" of the circumstances in which such performative words are uttered. The lack of appropriate conditions will result in the thwarting of the act, in turn creating an "unhappy" or infelicitous result. Accordingly, for an utterance to lead to an act or, properly speaking, to *constitute* an act, the condition of the existence—or presence—of felicitous conditions, or conditions of felicity, must obtain. "I do," for instance, is empowered by the legal norms of juridicality. The source of its effective force does not reside within the utterance, but derives from the fact that someone with great force and power has decreed that saying it has force. But this requirement cannot stand alone, for to be effective, it must operate within and upon an environment. Among the possible conditions necessary for utterances to engender action are that they should be intelligible to the hearer as complete and coherent language, that the speaker as a derivative must carry a certain kind of authority, that their proper setting must be within an agreed-upon convention, and—partly associated with this last condition—that their intended consequences are revealed by the speaker and generally accepted by the hearer.

Austin's performative utterances and their conditions of felicity challenged the formal analysis of propositions and brought to our attention a new and valuable aspect of the power of language. However, the theory of felicity itself remained relatively framed by formalism, until Foucault adapted it to his theory of power, an adaptation from which other philosophers, such as Judith Butler, Bruno Latour, and Karen Barad, derived great benefit in their own work, expanding on and refining Foucault. Wholly pertinent to our concerns, Butler's seminal diagnosis within the context of gender formations sums up a central feature of performativity, taking her cue from Foucault. Foucault insists that "juridical systems of power *produce* the subjects they subsequently come to represent" since, by virtue of being subjected to such structures, the subjects become "formed, defined, and reproduced in accordance with the requirements of those structures." The "juridical formation of language and politics . . . is itself a discursive formation *and effect*," where the subject is "discursively constituted" by the very system that is "supposed to facilitate its emancipation."[82]

What is worth emphasizing in Austin's conditions of felicity and Foucault's concept of juridicality is neither linguistic propositions nor discourses themselves—a common misconception—but rather the force or power that gives discourses their constituting effects, that is, their power to enact reality.[83] In some sense, the entirety of Said's *Orientalism* rehearses the theme that what the Orientalists said about the Orient was their own creation, that it was as much a misrepresentation as it was a representation, which is to say that discourse for Said remained bound by the dichotomy of truth and falsity,[84] the very position against which Austin militated. It also remained, in the final analysis, bound by its formalistic, nonperformative structures. For Said, language is "a highly organized and encoded system, which employs many devices to *express, indicate, exchange messages* and information, *represent*, and so forth" (21, emphasis mine). Note that none of these qualifiers is performative, and all belong to language as constatives. Attaching undue importance to language as a representationalist tool, Said engaged Orientalist discourses as false representations of the Orient.

It is my argument that the most profound problem in Said's *Orientalism* and in the ensuing common understanding of what Orientalism is begins with the representationalist approach taken toward Orientalist discourse and the discursive tradition that this field stood for. The feminist theorist Karen Barad writes that a

> *performative* understanding of discursive practices challenges the representationalist belief in the power of words to represent preexisting things. Performativity, properly construed, is not an invitation to turn everything (including material bodies) into words; on the contrary, performativity is precisely a contestation of the excessive power granted to language to determine what is real. Hence, in ironic contrast to the misconception that would equate performativity with a form of linguistic monism that takes language to be the stuff of reality, performativity is actually a contestation of the habits of mind that grant language and other forms of representation more power in determining our ontologies than they deserve.[85]

In the following chapters, I will try to bring out the problematic implications of representationalism for our current conception of Orientalism and propose a performative conception that aims to place Orientalism in a different—though no less damning—light as well as in its proper larger context. The next chapter aims at fleshing out the performativity of Orientalist discourse not in the West-grounded Orientalist text, in the metropolis that gave it its formal existence, but rather in the location in which it was meant to apply and the destination to which it was meant to be deployed.

CHAPTER II

Knowledge, Power, and Colonial Sovereignty

Part 1

I

In the previous chapter, I elaborated on the problematics of distance and difference, but largely left out of the discussion the third and perhaps most remarkable feature of Orientalism, namely, its complicity with power. Treating this aspect of a scholarly discipline, which pretended for a long time to be dissociated from modernity's ideological narrative, was Said's true accomplishment in *Orientalism*; and if we now take the collusion of Orientalism's corporate discourse with power for granted, it is by virtue of the fact that Said's important work has become canonized. After *Orientalism*, no serious scholar or thinker could assume or write that Orientalist discourse is "scholarly" knowledge that can, despite its own presumption to the contrary,[1] tell us what the Orient "objectively" is or was; rather, Orientalism has emerged as a product of the specific cultural and intellectual formations of colonialist Europe, which are essentially saturated with prejudice and its attendant misrepresentation.

Yet, this understanding remains constrained. It is my argument that this limited understanding is not merely a shortcoming or narrowness of vision, a lack of analytical insightfulness, or something similar; Said was a talented scholar who could often make the best out of any empirical and informational repertoire available to him. And this is precisely my point. The limitation, which the post-Saidian discourse continues to internalize, remains the function of a discursive strategy that could do nothing else, because it could not, by virtue of its own nature, *conceive* of anything else. The limitation, in other words, is built into the very structure of thought that allows this critique to emerge. And every critique, like every tool, comes with its own structure, intended to accomplish the specific task for which it is intended. There always exists a relationship between the tool and its intended object, however distant or seemingly unrelated the genealogies of the tool and the object may appear. Tools and instruments deriving from a central domain, that is, from the very structures through which the domain itself was constituted, cannot be of service in reconstituting that domain. By virtue of their structure, such instruments can function as correctives and enhancements, but cannot perform tasks qualitatively at variance with the teleology of the domain itself. A *paradigmatic* critique of capitalism, for instance, cannot issue from within capitalism itself as a central domain, just as a structural critique of "liberal environmentalism" cannot derive from within liberal thought itself.[2]

This concept of critique is fundamental to at least two of my concerns, the first of which consists of two parts. It is often argued (in what has become received wisdom among university students and most scholars) that a critique of modernity is ineluctably bound with modernity and cannot escape or transcend its epistemological framework. Every critique is thus destined to reenact or at best revise an aspect of modernity, but modernity nonetheless. Of course, the ramifications of such a view are serious, not only because of the sense of epistemological resignation that it signifies, but also because it is profoundly erroneous. It is also serious, if not dangerous, because it fortifies the ideological discourse of modernity, validating the status quo, the desideratum of the modernists. The second part of this concern, which attends to an answer to the claims in the first part, is that this concept of critique is fundamental to the theory of the author I have been discussing and to which I will return in chapter 3, a theory that is in turn integral to the concept of paradigms and its dynamics of power and force fields. If every system of power is temporally bound, being necessarily a contingent creation, then it takes nothing more than a historical common sense to realize that *épistémès*, to use Foucault's concept, are changeable, mutative, and ultimately replaceable. Furthermore, every *épistémè*, and consequently every system of power, has its own different logic and structure (even when the system has no predictable logic of power). Yet, every such system emerged directly out of a different, at times radically different, preceding system, modernity itself being an example of a phenomenon entirely at variance with its "medieval" predecessor, however much it replicated its theological forms. Second, this concept of critique demonstrates the need to examine Orientalist discourse as colonialist discourse and the latter as structural and material genocidal discourse and practice, aided by Orientalism and abated no less by what I will call paradigmatic domain's academia. At this stage, I limit my discussion to colonialism showing its reliance on Orientalism from the Western side of the map and its performative effects from the Eastern side, thus tying academic discourse with this performativity as an essential step toward genocidal conduct (the subject of chapter 4).

II

Orientalism was developed largely in Europe and by Europe, but it was not just for Europe. It was not therefore only "a style of thought" based on a "distinction" between Orient and Occident (2),[3] and it played to the internal satisfaction and pleasure of Europe, in the way the style of the European novel is written and analyzed. Orientalism *was performative, and not representationalist* in any serious sense of this term. In other words, *Orientalism as an institutional and thought structure was, contra Said, more about the Orient itself and the material, physical, and psychoepistemic reproduction of it* than it was a distortion and a *textually* reconstructive form of "knowledge and scholarship," naively idealized by the initiate sophomore in academia. That it was complicit with power is beyond doubt, but this is only half of the story, a weaker half, that, when seen alone, politicizes (and in effect *has* politicized) Orientalism to the degree that we ceased to see it in its larger global involvement.

First, let us dispose of any doubt that Said's concept of Orientalism was almost wholly framed in conventional political terms. In the entirety of the book, and invariably in all discourses on Orientalism after the book appeared in print, the reference to Orientalism was couched almost wholly in political, if not politicized, terms. Orientalism and charges of Orientalism and Orientalizing remained prisoner to representationalism, descriptivism, and the political and even ethnic, nationalist, and religious position or affiliation of the writer. But in all of this, the core conditions of felicity and their real underpinnings were entirely absent from the scene. Orientalism is often reduced to what you do not like about another scholar's work, and it made the charge all the more easy if that scholar was not an Oriental or a Muslim.

Furthermore, Orientalism was reduced to a rudimentary political concept and political enterprise,[4] because Said himself, after all, was heavily inclined to this view of reality; and his book is replete with statements that amply attest to this fact. When speaking of Orientalism as "a system of representations" produced "by a whole set of [European] forces," Said says, "If this definition of Orientalism seems more political than not, that is simply because I think Orientalism was itself a product of certain political forces and activities" (202–3). Note here how the European "whole set of forces," a categorical attribution, is elided into and reduced to "political forces and activities," not the political as an epistemic formation. But elision and reduction have a short traveling span. "My contention is that Orientalism is fundamentally a political doctrine willed over the Orient because the Orient was weaker than the West, which elided the Orient's difference with its weakness" (204). Note also that the explanation does not transcend the balance of power in international relations or beyond *their* discursive manifestations. Nor does colonialism appear as a distinct category of analysis; nor still do genocide, other forms of collective atrocity, social and cultural engineering, and totalistic transformation of indigenous traditions. If anything, Said is not sure that the narrative of colonialist destruction of native lands and peoples is wholly accurate, standing without a good measure of "mythmaking."[5]

The political sting of Orientalism derives, both genealogically and phenomenologically, from nothing deeper than political relations and political strength. The vertical traveling span of this explanation is even shorter (complicated, furthermore, by the incommensurability of this claim with the purported existence of Orientalism when weak Europe was for centuries under the threat of a massive Islamic conquest). But a more pertinent question here is this: Why did Europe and its Orientalism elide difference with weakness specifically? The premodern Chinese dynasties, for instance, equated cultural difference with barbarity or lack of refinement, but they did not see this as a justification for developing an army of scholars or for staffing whole departments in their educational institutions for the sole purpose of "studying" the "barbarians." Nor did any of the Islamic or Indian empires.[6] To limit the answer of such questions to a metaphysic of weakness and difference is not to see beyond conventional forms of politics, and a constrained notion of politics at that.

In order to go beyond Said's explanations—which have dominated all discourse on Orientalism for too long and in fact until this day—we must begin with the basic yet most crucial question of all, a question that, to my knowledge, is not frequently asked, if at all: Why Orientalism in the first place? Why, in other words, do we have a phenomenon we call Orientalism, a major constellation of scholars, departments, institutes, entire institutions and foundations, specialized periodicals, book series, students, fellowships, budgets, and so on, all of which amount to an integral part of the modern Western academia (now increasingly present in other parts of the—shall we say Orientalized—world as well)? There should not be any doubt whatsoever that no other culture or civilization in world history has produced such a phenomenon, not even the exquisitely bookish and erudite Islamic civilization that—as I will show—came to an effective end upon Europe's colonial encounter in the nineteenth century. Nor did the great Chinese dynasties during the episodic heights of their power, when, for instance, during the early fifteenth century AD, their notorious imperial fleet navigated the oceans down to Madagascar, if not much farther, and returned home, having annihilated pirate ships and carried back exotic flora and foreign emissaries, only to be left to rot in China's ports.[7] Neither on the fleet nor in the home country were there scholars studying the Indian Ocean and the coasts of Africa—much less their surrounds and even less the entire hemisphere—who constituted an organized contingent, a discursive discipline, an academic institution, or something similar. It is no surprise then that 'Abd al-Rahman al-Jabarti, the distinguished Egyptian historian, was thoroughly baffled when encountering Napoleon's army of scholars who constituted an integral part of the French military campaign to conquer Egypt. And this was a scholar who was familiar with the tradition of Sultans and emirs often embarking on military campaigns accompanied by some jurists.[8] But *it is* surprising that Said notes Jabarti's bewilderment but makes very little of it (82). It did not occur to him to ask: Why was this historian so baffled, so "impressed"? Why Orientalism in the first place? But of course this most obvious yet most profound question was not to be entertained, nor could a whiff of it have been possible, because asking such a question would instantaneously lead to the next: Why anthropology, a close kin to Orientalism? Why sociology? Why economics? Why business and law schools? But then this line of questioning might become even more expansive and alarming. If anthropology, sociology, economics, journalism, and their likes are included, then why not also science or the deceptively innocuous history? Why did Western academia arise in the way it did, in its entirety?

Of course this is a tall order of investigative liability, whose detailed critique requires multiple volumes. While the rest of the book will outline some answers, I begin here by trying to eliminate the anachronisms and ahistoricizing that pervade both Said's book and the writings that his work has spun. As earlier noted, Said's concept of Orientalism stretches back to classical Greece, and travels through Dante and the Catholic Church of the early fourteenth century down to the living scholars working in Western academia. It did not provoke Said's interest to inquire as to why the Church Council of Vienna in 1311–12 decided to establish chairs in Arabic that would sit along chairs in Syriac, a politically irrelevant language, and Greek, which is not, by Said's own measure, Oriental. Could these have been established, apart from the goal of conversion (shared by Islam as well), for the scholastic purpose of acquiring philosophical knowledge of Greece, seen to have been "transmitted" by the Arabs—an act that did not much differ from the Abbasid initiative for Bayt al-Hikma ("House of Wisdom"; fl. ca. 800–950)[9] and similar projects of translation? And if the Abbasid initiative is charged with misrepresentation and a host of manipulations as much as Orientalism is, then how does Said explain the total absence of "Orientalist" ("Occidentalist"?) tendencies, or anything like, or even parallel to, them, from Islamic civilization? Or from the Chinese and the Indian? And if conversion to Christianity was behind the establishment of chairs in Arabic, as Said seems to suggest (355n18), then does this policy constitute a *ratio legis* for Orientalism, a goal absent from "secular" Orientalism of the nineteenth and twentieth centuries and noticeably present in Islam, which had neither Orientalists nor "Occidentalists"? And if secularist conversion was at stake (a point, to my knowledge, never raised by Said), then how would Said's own secularism—which amounted to a processual act of "divination"[10]—cope with the problematics of Orientalism's sovereign domination?

Said does not stop here, however. His notion of representation and his (un)limited historical imagination become so sweeping and overwhelming that every "advanced culture" in world history has acted in a fashion similar to Europe's colonialism and its Orientalism. When condemning "every European" as "a racist, an imperialist, and almost totally ethnocentric," Said attempts to mitigate his outrageous categorical reproof by saying this: "Some of the immediate sting will be taken out of these labels if we recall additionally that human societies, at least the more advanced cultures, have rarely offered the individual anything but imperialism, racism, and ethnocentrism for dealing with 'other' cultures" (204). Several questions arise from this wildly categorical statement: If what Said describes is true, then are we to conclude that racism and its "scientific" theories did not originate in modern Europe but rather were universal phenomena? And if the nature of human societies is as Said says, then why single out Orientalism and the West for critique? Unless Islam, India, and China do not qualify as "more advanced societies," they must, by Said's logic, qualify as imperialist, racist, and ethnocentric? And if he *had* to study Orientalism (because it stood to him in close proximity as a literary scholar and because it engaged his interest as a Palestinian with intimate familiarity with oppressive prejudice and outright discrimination), then why not at least point out cognates elsewhere in the modern world, in the world in which he lived (such as China in Tibet, the Soviets in their spheres of interest during the Cold War, or Israel in Palestine, this latter being, as we will see, an equally flagrant case of academia's entrenchment not only in politics but in the heart of colonialism and its atrocious violence)? If the phenomenon is so widespread and so transhistorical, then why not at least point out the equal presence of such racism and ethnocentrism in other academic disciplines? Said's wanderings into "other civilizations" are emblematic not only of his extraordinarily confused "scope" of Orientalism, but also, and this is my point, of greater confusion regarding the qualitative meaning of Orientalism, its organic location in modern Western culture, and its inner dynamics and outer academic connectivity. His was a typical, though remarkably sophisticated, position of a liberal who could not see the world outside of liberal values, however critical of them he and other liberals are.

In Said's sweeping and anachronistic narrative, "modern Orientalism" (22) could not be justified except in terms of quantitative distension, for the quality—apparently possessing a rudimentary structure—seems to have been ever present. The difference between eighteenth-century Orientalist discourse and its nineteenth-century manifestation, Said tells us, was a matter of "range . . . [which] expanded enormously in the later period" (22). Just to make sure that the phenomenon is not made to appear confined to modernity, Said paints with a wide brush for ultimate clarity: Having "plotted history for hundreds of years," Orientalism during "the nineteenth and twentieth centuries . . . became a more serious *quantity*" (95, emphasis mine). It is my argument then that the absence in Said's *Orientalism* of *qualitative* distinctions has led to a blurred vision not only of Orientalism as a particular phenomenon, but also of modernity at large and, importantly, of the organic and comfortable location of the former in the latter. In other words, Said's isolation of Orientalism for critical attention was made for the wrong reasons, hence his inaccurate and partial diagnosis. It is my argument that while Orientalism is unique in human history, it exhibits the common and quite ordinary common denominator of modern knowledge.

Since Said's singular accomplishment in *Orientalism* is the links he made between Orientalism as a scholarly discipline and political power, I wish to ask why knowledge and power, both of which have existed since time immemorial, have never produced such an intricate and inextricable association in any other place or time in the world. My purpose in engaging this question is to try to demonstrate the qualitatively singular structure and thus special meaning of Orientalism *as a modern standard*. To do so, I turn—in a conscious move against dominant postcolonial and poststructuralist critique—to a comparative case study of substantial magnitude, in geographical, cultural, intellectual, literary, pedagogical, political, legal, and military terms, to name only a few. I will focus on Islam before the eighteenth century, a civilization that once extended its dominions, much as modern Europe did, over a large surface of the world known then (by military force in the beginning, of course, but mostly through missionary activity in later centuries). Much like Europe, it also conquered and ruled; it had its scholars, intellectuals, educational practices and institutions, not to mention a massive mercantile and agricultural economy that made it one of the richest constellations of empires in the world. Yet, like its Indian and Chinese counterparts, it did not develop anything like Orientalism. Why?

Although I will delve into a detailed account of Islam insofar as it is relevant for my discussion, it must be clear that the point I am making is not to single out Islam and its cultures as having possessed any unique quality. In fact, it is my hypothesis that, being no more than a case study, Islam in premodernity acted more or less like any other civilization, leaving modern Europe as the exception. My goal in discussing this case study is therefore to show the singularity and exceptionality of that Europe which produced Orientalism.[11] For without such an exercise, which has thus far been absent from any discussion of the subject, Orientalism cannot be isolated for an analysis of its qualitative structure, which made it, like modernity itself, a new phenomenon embodying an unprecedented and unique structure and therefore teleology.

III

In line with the theory of paradigms I set forth earlier, it will be said that Islamic cultures were defined by an ethos, by a particular range of attitudes to the world, and by a group of discursive and highly dialectical traditions that attempted to fashion, and often produced, certain kinds of subjects. To see in this characterization a tendency to essentialism or to reductionism is to misunderstand the theory of paradigms that I have advanced in the previous chapter. It is to misunderstand how paradigmatic systems drive cultures and "civilizations," for, as I have noted, there are undeniable central domains that characterize every society. The cultures of Islam varied in their ethnic, demographic, geographical, material, economic, and indigenous customary laws, variations easily observed across the Islamic landscapes from Morocco and Muslim Spain in the West to China and the Malay Archipelago in the East. Many of the lands cordoned off by Italy, Poland, and Russia in the North and Sub-Saharan Africa and the Indian Ocean in the South were inhabited by Islamic cultures most of the time, this being sufficient reason to speak of wide variation in social habits, social structures, customs, tastes, sensibilities, and the like. Yet, all these regions, when inhabited by Islam to any noticeable length of time, shared very similar educational practices and social institutions and were ruled, most of the time, by very similar forms of governance. One therefore can speak not only of education as the accurate embodiment of the civilization's central domains, but also of its political governance and political constitution.

The scholars, thinkers, and intellectuals, from East to West of Islamdom, were those whom we call *ulama*, jurists, judges, professors, Sufi Shaykhs, Quran specialists, hadith experts, *adab* writers, linguists, historians, biographers, traveler-scholars, *kalam*-theologians, philosophers, astronomers, Tasawwuf philosophers, chemists, vision scientists, logicians, mathematicians, scholars of instruments ("technology specialists"), and a host of subsidiary others. Unlike modern education, where "expertise" tends to segregate fields of specialization (resulting, in late modernity, in the pervasive call for interdisciplinarity), Islamic learning was generally *constituted* by cross-fertilization through what may be called dialectical traditions.[12] Whereas a modern historian typically studies and writes about history, and may perform a scholarly incursion into another subject when her field intersects with that subject, a typical Muslim historian normally undertook his basic and main training in other fields, nowadays considered outside of history. Thus, a Muslim historian was usually at once an expert, or at least proficiently educated, in Quran, hadith, history, *adab*, "law," biographical sciences, and, not unusually, theology, Sufism, and mathematics. The same can be said of a jurist or a scholastic theologian, who would have engaged, and produced works, in poetry, *adab*, logic, *usul al-fiqh*, disputation theory, philosophy, linguistics, Sufism, history, and so on. This trenchantly "interdisciplinary"—or indeed *predisciplinary*—education also explains certain modes of academic training and learning: it was often the case that a professor (*shaykh*) of hadith might sit as a student in the study circle (*halqa*, somewhat like a classroom)[13] of a professor, at times his junior in age, who taught, say, logic, or that a logician might attend, as a student, the teaching circle of a law professor or a linguist.[14] Such practices were not just external forms; rather, they were indicative of profound dialectical relationships between the various fields of knowledge.

This system of scholarship produced yet another interesting phenomenon. Whereas in modern education scholars tend to author, throughout the entirety of their career, books and articles within a single discipline, occasionally drawing on one or another field outside their own, a Muslim scholar was more often than not productive in a wide variety of different fields. It is usual to find individual writers producing long and short works in fields as different as Quranic studies, history, poetry and *adab*, law, logic, disputation theory, theology, mathematics, and even philosophy and mysticism, in one variety or another (since each of these last two fields, among some others, offered a number of different, at times divergent, intellectual orientations).

The close proximity between the fields of classical Islamic education is not a formal matter, however. Nor does it necessarily mean that these fields shared a common subject matter. Nor, still, should the proximity be explained by just an intense scholarly interest. Rather, the entire system's telos made such a proximity both necessary and inevitable, and stood behind the underlying ethos of moral instruction. The cultivation of knowledge, however professionalized it became after the tenth century, remained anchored in a tendency that eventually connected abstract thought to modes of ethical conduct.[15] The central domain of the Shariʿa in its theoretical underpinning, theology in all its forms, most philosophical strands, and the entire range of mysticism were all geared toward articulating the theoretical and discursive methods that aided in the pursuit of ethical or spiritual life, these being connected and interconnected at various junctures but often differing in their approach to achieving their goals. Most commonly, the Shariʿa had its various approaches to the technologies of the self and the production of the moral subject,[16] while Sufism, a highly individualized philosophical spirituality, navigated at a higher level of pious formation, and at times argued for the dispensability of the Shariʿa for the true Sufi.[17] However different the approach and even the subject matter, the desideratum constituted a common denominator, namely, the cultivation of the individual as a moral subject. This cultivation, far from being an *externally* imposed system of "training the subject," was designed to operate *internally*, through deliberate and self-conscious choices of conduct and belief that the autonomous subject exercises upon his or her body and soul.[18]

The educational and intellectual disciplines were textually oriented, which is to say that the genealogies of their bodies of knowledge were governed by the practice of commentary and study of texts. Yet, before reaching the level of writing—a largely physical act—the entire mechanism of learning rested on direct intellectual and spiritual contact between master and "searcher,"[19] between teacher and student. The master did not just impart "theoretical" knowledge, but as a rule represented in his own way of living in the world an ethical exemplar.[20] Writing then was the formal expression of a prior nonformal activity that represented an intensely intellectual and spiritual interaction between teacher and student, between "guide" and disciple, and between one scholar and another (in scholarly "circles" as well as in disputation sessions, among other forms of intellectual interaction).

The founding text across all Islamic traditions and subtraditions was of course the Quran (invariably seen as an ethical message), but within one or two generations after the Text acquired a vulgate, individual scholars began to elaborate on the significance of the Quranic language in a variety of ways, resulting in the numerous fields of study I have just mentioned, including the sciences. Education and scholarship were not only driven by an ethical thrust, but they also were highly individualized phenomena, generating intense interest in literary as much as purely scientific fields.[21] This is also to say that education, along with the vast intellectual activity surrounding it, was neither the province nor the jurisdiction of any political power, although rulers did engage heavily in endowing *waqf*s (charitable trusts) for the benefit of education, which involved the alienation of the property endowed, thus rendering it largely, if not entirely, autonomous. Of course by establishing these charitable educational foundations some rulers aimed at garnering political support and the acquisition of legitimacy, which depended on the cooperation of the scholars and their willingness to mediate between these rulers and the "civic" population, but this never, under any circumstance, meant that these rulers, as rulers, could decide on the substance of educational material,[22] who is to fashion it, and how to teach it, all of which always remained in the hands of the private scholars.[23] This fact is of monumental importance for us, as we will see in due course.

But I must make sense of these generalizations in specific ways; and here the theory of paradigms is immediately relevant and helpful. The subjects and fields of Islamic learning, in their divisions and subdivisions, were countless and nearly inexhaustible. Yet, they stood in a particular relationship to one another, one that could be said to have had a cohesive structure in which cross-fertilization was routine. Leading components in this structure were the Shariʿa and Sufism, two discursively dialectical traditions and paradigmatic domains that permeated the educational, legal, social, and spiritual practices of Islam, and influenced much in the economic and mercantile spheres. In point of fact, the Shariʿa governed "urban" mercantile and country-side agricultural economy, and its maritime law often regulated commerce in the Mediterranean, the Indian Ocean, the South China Sea, and elsewhere, and was at times followed even by non-Muslims navigating these high seas.[24] Furthermore, Shariʿa's "law" was the dominant form of practice in city markets, and the Sufi guilds and orders were no less active, as specifically Sufi entities, in the mercantile life of these cities.[25] Sufism infused society in comprehensive ways, having created countless orders around which much of social life revolved. Nearly every scholar of the law was a Sufi of some sort, and so were nonscholars and quasi-scholars (such as merchants, princes, princesses, and emirs, who often dabbled in one form of learning or another, holding scholarly and literary circles in their homes and palaces). It could be said that while the Shariʿa was effective in regulating society somewhat in the way modern law does, Sufism constituted a performative field that functioned in regulating and organizing the spiritual and often material life of society. From around the eleventh century, Sufi teachings began to be heavily intermeshed with "legal" doctrine, bestowing on the latter further layers of spirituality.[26] But what distinguished both from any modern discursive tradition was their extraordinary emphasis on the production of moral technologies of the self, a private, psychoepistemic, and introspective technology that no state could engender, regulate, or impose.

The Shariʿa represented, and was constituted by, a moral "law."[27] Its paradigmatic status lies in the very fact of its being a moral system in which so-called law was a tool and technique that was *subordinated to* and enmeshed in the overarching moral apparatus, but not an end in itself. In the Shariʿa, the legal was the instrument of the moral, not the other way around.[28] As a central domain, the Shariʿa was the measure against which the subsidiary domains were judged, and its solutions largely determined the solutions of those domains. In the pedagogical spheres, the structure of Muslim education was determined by priorities laid down in the Shariʿa, and was run entirely by private specialists. Such fields as language, linguistics, hermeneutics, rhetoric, dialectic, science, and logic (which included epistemology) were created, developed, and refined within the purview of the *sharʿi* domain, however much they embarked on speculative and abstract inquiries that lay outside of any juristically oriented engagement. Even mathematics and astronomy—which became the foundations of early modern European science[29]—evolved to impressive degrees as responses to *sharʿi* stimulae, where science, viewing the Is and Ought as one, unraveled the secrets of God's creation. (And unlike Catholic Europe, science threatened neither "religion" nor the ulama.) In whatever field a scholar or an intellectual ultimately specialized, his or her basic "undergraduate" training was nearly always *sharʿi*. Those fields that prepared the student for the study of *sharʿi* subfields also prepared other students for nearly every other field, be it theology, *adab*, astronomy, or mathematics. The peripheral domains, on the other hand, catered to the demands and priorities of the Shariʿa, and were often designed and organized to serve its needs.[30] Yet, one should not draw from this picture the conclusion that subsidiary and peripheral domains stood apart from the Shariʿa and its intellectual and educational interests (as, for example, poetry stands apart from engineering or law in the modern academia),[31] for, as we have seen, individual scholars engaged, over the range of their career, several disciplines at once, navigating between fields that we nowadays consider wholly unrelated.

In the practical sphere, economic life, however messy, was regulated not only by technical *shaʿi* rules but also by a pervasive *shaʿi* ethic. Violations and occasional evasions of the system no doubt existed, but these never amounted to anything regular that could be installed as norms. They were relatively irregular and sporadic, having failed to constitute even a peripheral domain.[32] The economic domain was *shaʿi*-minded because society, the subject, object, and predicate of Shariʿa, was *shaʿi*. And political governance, while being somewhat less organic to the social-communal domain than it was connected to the economic realm, was constrained by a culture and society that by and large knew and accepted as normative the Shariʿa and its paradigmatic ethical stature (*a structure whose warp was always inextricably woven into the woof of mild mysticism, among others*). In its most expansive sense, legitimacy then lay in and with this multilayered Shariʿa, but not in any political form.

As I emphasized earlier, paradigms or central domains are not only supported by subsidiary domains; together with the latter domains, they embody exceptions, irregularities, and violations, all of which amount to subversive discourses, often contingent and ephemeral, but at times not. The Shariʿa was no exception, in that it had to *live in* a society that was, like any other, messy and in constant need of certain forms of order and organization. That society no doubt witnessed the overtaxed peasant, the oppressive ruler,[33] the criminal, the insolvent debtor, and the abused wife, not to mention the occasional loud, if not influential, poet advocating "unconventional" sexual mores (homosexuality having often been at the top layers of poetic expression). Nor were all segments of the population inclined toward Shariʿa norms: the Bedouins in particular had their own powerful customs, often conflicting with these norms. Like any social groupings, Muslim society from North Africa and Muslim Spain to Java and Samarkand had its share of misery. It obviously had its own invaders and conquerors, its rebels, larcenists, petty thieves, and highway robbers, and even the occasional corrupt judge.[34] Nonetheless, the Shariʿa was the normative system and the law of the land, its paradigmatic discourses and practices persisting in the continual re-creation of a particular order and, more importantly, a particular subject. With their military might and often unmatched power, sultans in Islam, the heads of the executive, came and went, one after the other, without as little as a murmur about an ambition to challenge the Shariʿa. This was the unchallenged "law," and every sultan accepted it as de facto as well as de jure.

Both Shariʿa and Sufism, being constituted by an ethical and moral subject matter (down from their epistemological foundations and up to their social dispensations), strove toward the realization of moral ends. Being central paradigms and performative discourses, they may be characterized by what I call a persistent moral benchmark. Benchmarks do not always fully succeed in implementing their desiderata in the real world; rather, they stand as reminders and standards against which reality is not only measured but pressured. A persistent benchmark is one whose pressure is greater than the pressure possessed by other benchmarks, especially if its matrix and source of authority stem from a central domain. To flesh out this claim in substantive terms, two fundamental examples may be in order; the first is solely relevant to the idea of benchmarks while the second pertains, additionally, to the larger issue we are dealing with here, namely, the relationship between knowledge and power.

The first example is juristic personality. In its long life of about twelve centuries before Western colonization, the Shariʿa encountered numerous issues that required it to treat certain concepts and institutions in terms more abstract than the concept of private legal person. Perhaps the most noteworthy and important context in which a type of juristic personality came to be recognized existed within the juristic elaboration of charitable endowments, known in Arabic as *waqf*s.[35]

As a legal institution and instrument, the *waqf* acquired an abstract juristic personality, acting as such in judicial claims and litigation. Thus a *waqf*, qua *waqf*, may sue for damages or recovery of rent of its own property (which was often the income that sustained the operation and maintenance of the *waqf* itself). Yet, when economic developments imposed requirements on the legal system, the Shariʿa, even though it succeeded in developing complex forms of trade, investment, and commercial partnerships (complex by any standard, including the modern), refused to grant commercial and financial enterprises the same concepts of juristic personality, stopping, as it did, at the limits of individual responsibility and personal liability. In other words, despite the complexity of legal instruments it had developed, the Shariʿa held itself short of developing any concept of limited liability. And it is easy to see why it did so. One of the central benchmarks of the Shariʿa was the notion of *shariʿ* subject, one constituted by moral technologies of the self, technologies in which ethical and moral liability of the *individual believer*, the subject, stood supreme. This benchmark was not only operative but performative, which is to say not only that it was applied without reticence, but that in the process of its operation it *produced* subjects. The premium value in this configuration was moral accountability, not profit. Money and wealth were of such secondary status (despite the great importance Islam and its Shariʿa placed on business, profit, and material wealth)[36] that they could hardly compete with the fundamental, if not constitutive, concept of ethical duty, moral responsibility, and general accountability of the private, individual person. There was no financial or material consideration in the world, however tempting and important, that could alter or mitigate the *benchmark* of individual and personal accountability, responsibility and liability.[37] This type of accountability and responsibility was irreducible and constituted the most stubborn feature of the entire culture. The implications of this feature for our inquiry are inestimable, as I will try to show.

Compare this picture with the beginning and rise of the concept and practice of limited liability in modernity, to be found nowhere other than in England and at no other time than during its initial imperialist and colonialist ventures (roughly around 1600). In spite of the fact that the early modern British government recognized the moral repugnancy of the limited-liability company shortly after Parliament approved it, and although it had outlawed it on the grounds that it subverted personal moral responsibility by allowing investors to absolve themselves of any liability for their companies going bankrupt (just as the Shariʿa's logic of the benchmark operated, but without wavering), Parliament, a few years later, nonetheless went back on its own previous decision and legalized it again, only this time the reenactment came with an enhanced juristic personality, the very quality that initially outraged the government's moral sense.[38] Apparently, the British government's ethical benchmark was uncertain, to say the least, and differed in significant ways from what I have just called Shariʿa's persistent moral benchmark.[39] I shall pursue the implications of this European development in due course.

The second example of a benchmark that is additionally relevant to the question of the relationship between knowledge and power pertains to the concept of the rule of law in premodern Islam, one that brings into focus the competence and jurisdiction of legal scholars, who stood at the helm of the learning institutions. The concept is significant for us not just because it was at once a legal and political concept, as modernity has developed it, but mainly because it was a foundationalist epistemological doctrine, determining in originary ways the meaning and scope of the legal and political understanding of constitutionalism in Islam.

Yet, the rationality of this epistemology was framed within an ethical conception of the world, conceived as woven by a moral fiber. The presumptive basis of this rationality is that humans live *in* the world, not above it, just as anyone or anything else, sentient or not, does, except that humans are exceptionally charged with the burden of custodianship, a concept that is in turn heavily saturated with, if not made of, moral and ethical duty, not right. Put in another way, classical Islam's conception of the world, which directly effected the juridico-political structures,[40] is nonanthropocentric. It refuses, on strict principle, to accept the modern premise of man's domination over nature[41] (a central notion in the larger analysis of Orientalism as a modern phenomenon). In this picture, God stands as the Sovereign because he literally owns everything.[42] Human ownership of any kind, including the absolutely unencumbered ownership of property, is merely metaphorical and ultimately unreal. It is at best derivative of the original state of sovereign ownership. This explains, for instance, why care for the poor in Islam is explicitly legislated in the Quran as "their right"[43] against the wealth of the well-to-do, since the wealth of the latter is God's; and God's compassion is *first and foremost* bestowed on the poor, the orphans, and the wretched of the earth. *The poor's right was nothing short of God's right; violate the rights of the poor and you have violated the rights of God.*[44] This was a *posited* doctrine, a priori accepted as the rational foundation of moral behavior that governed all aspects of life, social, legal, and, no less, political. Many things can and do change in the world, but whatever the change, this principle governed.

If the physical world in its entirety is derivative, then human ownership cannot have any real form of original possession, including possession of an autonomous law or, much less, a cosmic/universal moral code. It is God therefore who is the sole Legislator, and it is with him *and him alone* that sovereignty and sovereign will lie. It is, in other words, with Him that the grand moral laws originate.[45] If the modern state's sovereign will is represented in the law, so is God's sovereign will, determined in the Shariʿa, significantly, by "*the best interests of the social order.*"[46] The Shariʿa is then *the moral code, an earthly, sociologically contextualized representation of divine moral will.* The temporal and spatial expression of God's Law and Will, the Shariʿa precedes all other forms of rule, both logically and in time. The law, being an expression of *collective* and *mass-produced* "legal" interpretation over time and space, stands above all, especially above all political structures and any form of political organization.[47] This was not just another persistent benchmark, but perhaps the benchmark of all benchmarks. As will become all too obvious in due course, this unwavering benchmark precluded political power not only from commanding the law and its legislation (as the modern state does), but also from interfering in the performative educational and intellectual formations that produced the Muslim subject. Unlike the modern citizen, largely a product of the state, the Muslim subject was produced by nonstate socioethical formations. Fully grounded in social communal structures, and performative in the first degree, these formations are no less potent than Foucault's discursive formations and biopower, however radically different in their ethical constitution they were.

The Shari'a, a hermeneutical, educational, jurisprudential, and cultural system, was a colossal project of building a moral-legal society whose foundational and structural impulse was summed up in the ever-continuing attempt to discover God's moral desideratum, without God having provided anything except the faintest outlines of his moral law. "To be good," "to do good," was the dominant prescription in the Quran, the foundationalist text.[48] The discovery of the law was the learned's business, who stood as the interpretive mediators, the epistemological link, between God and the rest of the world. Realism about the world was an ever-present consideration, but it was always placed in a metaphysical context, just as this metaphysics was constantly teased out from the realism of mundane existence. To run through the gamut of the spectrum ranging from metaphysics and cosmology, on the one hand, to the core of reality, on the other, was a logic that not only structured legal theory (*usul al-fiqh*)—the interpretive methodology that determined hermeneutical legal principles and their modes of application—but also framed the totality of Shari'a as a system of juridico-moral, even mildly mystical, practice.[49]

As a representation of a higher value, one seen to stand above the arbitrariness of ever-changing human predilections, the Shari'a regulated the entire range of the human order, either directly (through its jurists) or by means of a well-defined and limited delegation (through the executive). Whereas the modern state rules over and regulates its religious institutions, rendering them subservient to its legal will,[50] the Shari'a ruled over and regulated "secular" institutions. Accordingly, any political form or political (or social or economic) institution was ultimately subordinate to the

Shari'a and a derivative thereof, including the executive and judicial powers. The Shari'a itself, on the other hand, was the "legislative power" par excellence, and legislation was both a cumulative and a collective process, which is to say that "law," in the moral and technical legal senses, was the result of a corporate-like entity, a collectivity of juristic voices over time and space, and not subject to the will or whim of any single jurist, any single ruler, or even any contemporaneous group of jurists. Being the law of the land, the Shari'a was unrivaled; no power other than it could truly legislate. *Siyasa Shar'iyya*, the "legislative" competence of the ruler in administrative spheres, was not only a Shari'a-delegated power but also significantly constrained by the higher precepts imposed by the law of the land.[51] And since judicial review was unknown, the judiciary could never directly contribute to "legislation."[52] The executive power was mandated by the Shari'a to legislate in limited and restricted spheres, but this right was derivative and subsidiary and its practical manifestations—compared to the modern state[53]—were thin.

Like modern legal systems, the Shari'a developed a certain distrust toward executive political power, distrust that attested to its ability to command loyalty to and by the society and morality in which it functioned and lived.[54] It mediated between the ruler and the masses, always tilting its preference distinctly toward the latter.

Sufism, on the other hand, came to permeate society at large as a spiritual and sociopolitical force, creating its own orders and circles, practices and rituals, and, importantly, a philosophical tradition that reflected various grades of mystical understanding of the world. From monism to pantheism to mild mysticism, the tradition was ultimately about reaching a particular station or state in or with the divine, with great differences among Sufi maters as to the means to accomplish this spiritual-moral "annihilation." Needless to say, the intersections between Shari'a and Sufism were many, as evidenced in the earlier-mentioned fact that almost every "legal" scholar was a Sufi. The larger point, however, is that the driving ideas, methodologies, doctrines, and constitution of these two central domains were thickly ethical, and while many rulers established religious foundations in the service of the Shari'a and Sufism, there was little in these— other than garnering legitimacy—that was useful for political power.[55]

If politics and the state, as modernity came to define them, produce their subjects in the form of national citizens, it was the Shari'a and Sufism, together with the associated discourses I enumerated earlier, that *performed* the Muslim subject, producing a different concept of human—a human who was not given to a specifically political understanding of power. The Muslim subject, who was the subject, object, and predicate in the operation of the moral technologies of the self, understood legitimate power in terms of moral authority and virtue ethics, even when he or she did not rise up to the standards of the benchmark. But the benchmark was a constant reminder in life and in the art of living. A power that was not sanctioned by the concepts and philosophies of Shariʿa and Sufism—and their peripheral performative and discursive traditions—was not legitimate, and thus remained nonperformative, however mighty it was in military or material terms. It might not be too much of an exaggeration to say that virtue ethics, moral technologies of the self, piety, and simply a life guided by the positive freedom from material needs—as well as other varieties of such ethical considerations—were not exactly useful stuff for politics and political power. In such an environment, neither the national subject (the citizen) nor biopower could ever be conceivable.

IV

Thus far, the Islamic case study has shown why an educational-intellectual system consisting of moral subject matter and constituted by ethical precepts cannot be useful for politics, especially when such precepts stand, as a constitutional and legal matter, above the will of that power.[56] In one crucial sense, knowledge in premodern Islam ab initio precluded itself from substantive, though not formal,[57] association with political power, thus preventing the latter's rise in a Foucauldian or Gramscian sense. The differentials, as Foucault himself realized, are represented in the two exemplars of Aristotle and Nietzsche, themselves capturing the "transmutation" from the premodern to the modern forms of knowledge. In Aristotle's *Metaphysics*, knowledge is innate to human beings and thus the search for it—being the result of an interactive harmony between sensation, pleasure, and truth—constitutes one of the essences of humanity. Yet, this search, however much it is precipitated by pleasure, is never utilitarian or hedonistic but one that is wholly geared toward moral contemplation. Representing a stark contrast to this ethical vision, Nietzsche's *Gay Science*, on the other hand, draws a picture of knowledge as an invention whose ultimate desideratum is to occlude base instincts, malicious striving, and fears within a conflictual and disharmonious world. Rather than being a natural faculty for ethical construction, Nietzsche's concept of knowledge is one geared toward, and stands in the service of, struggle, domination, and subjugation,[58] a conception shared by numerous twentieth-century successors. In line with these differentials, the Islamic case study (of a piece with the Aristotelian exemplar) illustrates why such a system can never genuinely lend itself to a meaningful Foucauldian analysis of power/knowledge, leaving us with the by-product and conclusion that Foucault's theory is obviously not for every culture, time, or place (as I think he himself realized).[59] But there remains the question as to why such association of power and knowledge and therefore the ensuing Foucauldian analysis have become possible in modernity, specifically a modernity in which the state as we know it rules without a significant rival.

There are, I think, two necessary conditions that combined to create the sufficient condition for this phenomenon. The first is the rise of the modern state, which has updated and refined to a state of art modes of rule that existed in obvious and crude forms under monarchical absolutism but especially under the Catholic Church; the second is the doctrine and practice of domination over nature (in its widest meaning), represented by the distinction between fact and value and expounded philosophically in the respective divorce between Is and Ought.[60] I begin with the second condition, employing as may be necessary the term "Distinction" to refer to the two forms of separation I have just noted.[61]

There is reason to believe that domination over nature has its primitive origins in *European* Christian dogma that was transformed in modernity, as often is the case, into secularized forms. I say "primitive origins" for at least three main reasons: First, it is true that Christian Europe as a social and political tradition developed, for centuries before the Renaissance, a complex form of what the philosopher Murray Bookchin, among others, has called domination of man over man,[62] which Feudalism, the Church, and, later, absolute monarchism made effectively possible. Yet, if European Christianity as an intellectual tradition and doctrine were to be held as the common or exclusive source of this domination, as the technology historian Lynn White has famously maintained,[63] then several phenomena occurring only in the seventeenth, eighteenth, and nineteenth centuries would have had to happen at an earlier stage, the eleventh or fourteenth century being as auspicious a context for such developments as any later time. That domination in the eighteenth and nineteenth centuries *qualitatively* exceeded any earlier bounds calls for an explanation that transcends Christian doctrine and practice. Second, and by virtue of the religious and political domination that did take place in Europe, it is eminently arguable that the seed of the concept was Christian and it was that very seed which the mechanical philosophers, the deists, and the early Enlightenment thinkers cultivated, not to say complicated,[64] in their drive to construct a virulently secularized counterpart. Third, Europe's very transformations into the domain of the secular stand for an index of the perceived need to liberate the European Self from the constrictions that Christianity imposed—as evidenced in the death of the Salamanca School,[65] the rise of the company/corporation, the introduction of the Distinction, the rise of the modern state, and much else. If Christianity was too constricting for such ambitions, and was thus *reinvented and expanded* as secularism, it is because it did not possess all the right and necessary conditions.[66]

This sovereign "deficit" in Christianity problematizes the "long sixteenth century" as the spatiotemporal birthplace of modern colonialism and genocide. The philosopher Enrique Dussel has argued that the *ego conquiro* was the condition of possibility for Descartes *ego cogito*, that "I conquer, therefore I am" became the foundation of "I think, therefore I am," a modus vivendi that characterizes a subject who perceives himself as the center of the world because he has *already* conquered the world. This foundation is mediated, Dussel tells us, through the *ego extermino*: "I exterminate, therefore I am." A series of four genocides in the "long sixteenth century" is posited as constituting the sociohistorical conditions of possibility for this transformation. The first of these was the "genocide" against the Muslims and Jews of Andalusia, who were forced to convert under the doctrine of "purity of blood." Yet, Dussel acknowledges that by virtue of the very possibility of conversion, the Castillian project was not yet racial, for integration was still a viable, if not desirable, option. "The humanity of the victims was not in question."[67] The second "genocide" of the Americas turned on the question of "people without religion," for Christian dogma of the time paradigmatically rested on a syllogism: Beings without religion are entities bereft of God; beings without a God cannot possess a soul; therefore, beings without religion are entities without soul. Central to the dominant discourse of the first half of the sixteenth century, the question bore the crucial implication that if the Amerindians were without a soul, then enslaving and killing them as animals would be justified.

The controversy culminated in 1552, in the Valladolid Trial, whose chief protagonists were Gines Sepúlveda and Las Casas. Accepting the latter's argument, the Spanish monarchy decided in favor of the position that the Amerindians do have a soul, although they were deemed barbarians in need of Christianization. It was only after this trial that the third and fourth genocides, against Africans and European "witches," began in earnest, having intensified in the seventeenth century.[68]

Arguably, however, by the beginning of the seventeenth century, the Christian Church's capabilities for rationalizing mass atrocities and subjugation were exhausted, thereby opening the space for the rise of the deist movement, of Descartes, Hobbes, Galileo, Newton, Locke, and a host of transformations[69] that defined what we should call the first long modern century. The processes of secularization brought about by this century heralded the need to break away from the ethical constraints that Christianity seems to have wanted to escape but could not *fully* accommodate. This is by no means to dismiss Dussel's valuable narrative, but only to incorporate it into a larger process narrative that accounts for yet another reason for considering European Christian dogma deficient. Nowhere in Dussel's account do we find a convincing solution to the challenge he posed: if the *ego conquiro* mediated the *ego extermino in* European Christianity, then why did the former never "succeed" in yielding the same effects in Chinese, Indian, Muslim, and other contexts? Why did the *ego conquiro* of Islam, which fully shared the concept and practice of conversion with Christianity, never lead to *ego extermino*? As importantly, why did it take Christianity a whole millennium in Europe to cultivate this *ego*, having lacked this feature in its crusading and brutal conquests in the so-called Holy Land, crusades that were launched in as late as the end of the fourteenth century? And if the Church underwent a development in the fifteenth century or sixteenth that allowed such an *ego* to emerge *in it*, then what is that development, and why would it give way to a secularizing deluge so soon after the sixteenth century?

European Christianity may then be said to have made for one necessary but insufficient condition. The following account of modernity's domination (which I will argue in due course to be an inadequate term of description) must therefore be understood to have been a reaction to, and simultaneously and paradoxically a transformation and enhancement of, its premodern forms as Christian Europe—with its noblemen, clergy, and kings—articulated them at least in rudimentary practice.

Which is to say that the other necessary conditions that not only made the phenomenon possible but also brought it to a state of near perfection were Enlightenment-based. It is my argument that domination over nature was not an event but a structure and a systematic process of thought that made domination a way of living in and seeing the world, an attitude, which explains why the destructiveness of nature and subjection of human beings to its forces were thoroughgoing and commensurately systematic. The historians Lewis Moncrief and Richard Grove make the familiar but ill-thought argument that non-Christian and premodern peoples have often destroyed or degraded their natural environments, such as "the periodic flooding of the Nile River basin and the fire-drive method of hunting by prehistoric man," both of which "probably wrought significant 'unnatural' changes in man's environment."[70] Similarly, Grove cites the "rapid deforestation" of the Ganges basin in precolonial Northern India during the sixteenth century as an example of environmental degradation.[71]

While these phenomena may have indeed occurred, the authors fail to consider the larger context of the modern European and the premodern forms of degradation. First, the latter are obviously extremely limited in scope, dealing with specific and localized situations and contingencies; in other words, they were not extendable to either the expanse of the empires in which they were undertaken or to the world at large, for once the problem for which they (and others like them) were created was solved, the method and structure of the phenomenon disappeared with them. Second, it is not clear that the quality of these premodern projects was the same as that of its modern counterpart. Occasional flooding of certain basins or burning forests on an extremely limited scale (relative to earth surface) is unlike systematic deforestation, waste and toxic dumping, massive air pollution, and hundreds of such large-scale, *structural*, destructive practices. The comparison borders on the absurd. And third, it is clear that the advocates of such views have not identified a particular system of thought akin to that which stood and continues to stand behind modern attitudes. But we should not take these arguments as merely misguided. It is this very narrative of "distributing" the burden of destructiveness that is itself part of the very theology of progress which in turn requires, for its success and survival, the conversion of its destructiveness into a paradigm of exceptions (as the Holocaust, for example, was made to be), on the one hand, and generalization and exaggeration of premodern "problems," on the other. Progress always emerges as the winner, even when it loses.[72]

Yet, it cannot escape us that there are at least two conceptions in European Christianity that seem to loom large in contributing to the development of a modern matrix for domination. In a remarkable attempt to formulate a theory of evil, the Yale philosopher Paul Kahn has argued that the Christian conception of genesis continues to haunt the secular modern West, a conception that provides the basis for understanding the horrors of the twentieth century. Kahn forcefully argues that the myth of the Fall captures the conceptual boundaries that have defined the very genesis of evil itself. The first element of this myth locates the beginnings of creation in the series of equivalences between God, man, and nature, where man is created in the image of God, for he is "after our likeness." It quickly follows that this man is bestowed with "dominion over . . . all the earth, and over every creeping thing that creeps upon the earth. . . . And God said: 'Behold, I have given you every plant . . . and every tree.'" The replication of the image is of course not physical, but one that pertains to "dominion," in effect delegating to man God's authority within the created world. The idea of the exercise of this authority was simply maintenance: God created "a very good" world, a simple extension of himself, and all man has to do is to continue the venture of goodness.

It has been argued, mostly by environmentalists and environmental ethicists,[73] that this biblical understanding must be held (at least partly) responsible for the modern attitudes toward nature, for when the deists and, later, secularists embarked on their modern projects, they thought that they—now having "dominion" as managers of a world that was made by God to run by itself—will be the arbiters of what goodness is, a project that, by the evidence of the havoc wrought upon the environment and twentieth-century humanity, has clearly failed. But this, according to Kahn, does not truly account for the evils of domination, whether over nature or man over man. This is merely part of the story. The evil of domination thus comes from the complex of shame that the Fall has generated. For to be created in the image of God means to partake in the divine purpose, in which creation, knowledge, and goodness are various aspects of the same order of things. To know is simply to realize the goodness of creation, to realize that even knowledge itself is good, for evil simply does not exist— not yet, at any rate. The Fall thus constitutes a rupture in knowledge, for creation and goodness no longer maintain a natural continuity. The Fall is the very embodiment of a failure of comprehension, the failure of man to be a true image of God. Kahn poignantly argues that this failure is "a substitution of appearance for reality. . . . There is a long history of this form of theodicy in the West. If all creation is good, then the appearance of the bad—misfortune, natural disaster, and even evil behavior [and Kahn might have added genocide]—must be a false appearance."[74]

The Fall, symbolized by the act of eating from the tree of knowledge, amounts to man's attempt at seizing God's knowledge. It is not a matter of ignorance. Yet the failing initiative causes rupture, for to eat of that tree is to discover the truth of the self, to know oneself. It is to know that one must die: "You shall die," God announced, for "You are dust, and to dust you shall return." After the Fall, to bring out the good—an endless quest of man—is to be condemned to a commensurately endless need for labor. "Apart from God, knowledge of the good is only possible for a temporally conscious being: one who can look to the future and ask: 'What should I do?' This effort at self-government, however, inevitably results in knowledge of death. For when man looks to the future, he sees his own death."[75] There is nothing that man can do or say to overcome this existential fact. But mortality, the existential condition of shame, is an expression of the earthly and base nature of the human, who, by gaining, rather than losing, knowledge, discovers that shameful fact. Christ comes to redeem man "from the shame of Adam—the shame of endless labor, moral failure, naked bodies, and death."[76]

The attempt at redemption continues in modernity, albeit in secularized forms. Shame of nature and dominion over the earth are entwined, making the latter the means for the conquest of the former. If labor, nakedness, and death are the moral failures of natural man, then dominion over the self is the solution, an endless quest of denial. One might say that inasmuch as this redemption is an attempt to conquer and dominate nature, it is also a denial of the inevitability of nature. In chapter 4, I will continue this line of thought and attempt to show its relevance to colonialism and genocide, but for now I wish to stress that in this tradition it is the very nature of man himself, of man's very self, that is the starting point of domination and conquest.

Being sentenced to a life of labor precisely means labor against the self, against what man is. The finitude of life, inescapable nakedness, and moral failure are enmeshed with endless labor, the labor of hating the self. And the more hatred there is, the more domination is exercised upon that self, or on a substitute for it. In the deist and secular continuum of the Western tradition, issuing from a biblical seed, there is no knowledge without domination. Always clothed with politics and the political, knowing the self is the summation of knowing the enemy. The Schmittian adage "tell me who your enemy is, and I will tell you who [what?] you are" eviscerates any Christian concept of love, relegating it at best to the simplified individual and private act.[77] Collective identity is thus an identity of bellicosity and hate, for by Schmitt's own logic (the implications of which he does not seem to realize) the "love" of the self is structurally grounded in the hate of the other, always the enemy.[78] There are no other grounds on which love can stand.[79]

V

Max Scheler has effectively argued that modern man, by which he meant Western man, possesses an a priori will, an inherent "struggle for knowledge" that "grows out of an innate drive impulse."[80] What was seen as a disenchanted world by Weber was taken by Scheler as proof that this "innate drive"[81] culminated in an all-inclusive "thought structure which has been the basis of all realistic thinking since the Renaissance," one that "sprung from an underlying, *a priori* will- and value-structure centered upon the desire to dominate the material world."[82] Compared with Eastern thought structures, Scheler argued (and this is rather relevant for us in light of our case study earlier), Western "metaphysics rests on an entirely different consciousness of self and entirely different interpretation of man himself, viz. as sovereign being *above* all of nature."[83] Having become "the decisive *axiological* element," a "*systematic*," "not only occasional,"[84] phenomenon, and a "*central value attitude*," this inhering attribute of domination was the basis "from which the study of reality was undertaken."[85] Put differently, this "attitude" or "innate drive impulse" became constitutive of modernity's central domains, having been meshed with their warp and woof.

However penetrating Scheler was in his insights, I shall argue that his conception does not capture the entire range and depth of the modern European conception of sovereignty, since "man" did not stand above it, but was subject to its purview like everything else. Nietzsche may have been right on target in viewing the will to power as being much more than mere human willing. It has become in modernity *the* mode of Being par excellence, ruling over everything, man being no more than the modality, the instrument, of its accomplishment in history. Writing within

a Eurocentric environment, Scheler's concept of "man" was insuffi-
ciently inclusivist.[86] Indeed, my argument is that what was involved in the
conception of domination is nothing short of an ontological sovereignty[87]
as conceived to be a first order of existence. Its capaciousness, in other
words, was made to range from the mildest form of domination to the
decision over life and death, and anything in between. Unlike Schmitt's
limited *political* concept of life and death, domination exercised this right
over the entirety of sentient and insentient life.

In the study of reality, philosophy played a crucial function, but philosophy's conditions of felicity are to be squarely located within the context of the early rise of capitalism and its accommodation within the
Enlightenment.[88] In philosophy, the Distinction, especially in its Is/Ought
form, was perhaps the dominating problem in moral thought. As the philosopher Charles Taylor has asserted, "the fact/value split" has become "a
dominant theme in our [twentieth] century" and has undergirded "a new
understanding and valuation of freedom and dignity."[89] What needs to be
said in addition is that it determined the entirety of our conception of reality, which Taylor appears to subsume under "freedom and dignity." Powerfully expressed in the Kantian notion of autonomy,[90] freedom ceases to
denote God's omnipotence and becomes instead an expression of man's
own natural powers of reasoning. Human reason becomes the sole arbiter
in the project of objectifying the world, of submitting it to its own
demands and will, which now have turned relentlessly instrumentalist.
The pursuit of happiness, utility, and much else that is subservient to
these imperatives—such as preservation of life and protection of private
property—become natural rights derivable from the natural order by what
is/was seen as far-sighted, calculating reason. Formerly restricted by the
power of revelation as defined by the Catholic Church, reason now
becomes, like a free market, free and unbound by any restricting consideration or enduring moral principle. It is reason on the loose. Yet, in the
very outburst of Enlightenment reason against the absolutism of Church
and monarch, precisely in its mighty reaction against such powers that had
ruled over it with utterly *free* absolutism, Enlightenment reason's distension and extension went the full circle of replicating the very tyranny that
caused its rise in the first place, but this time it was not just people who
were its subject of rule, but also nature and indeed the world in its entirety.

In this transformation, the sources of reason, of obligation, of duty, and
of such notions as the Kantian Categorical Imperative[91] now descend from

within the self, an inner human power,[92] whence freedom, much like reason, breached its relations with an external world to become part of the Self, originating and operating entirely within its confines. Human dignity now also attaches to the notion of sovereign reason, for dignity can be attained only by the realization of this sovereignty in the regulation of human affairs and no less vis-à-vis the world as a human and insentient existence.

The Is/Ought dichotomization is representative of the conflict between the instrumentalist manifestations of reason and, to a great extent, the instrumentalist manifestations of the remnants of the Christian legacy of morality and virtue. This is precisely why the philosopher E. M. Anscombe rightly made the grave charge against Kant's notion of duty that it is nothing but a Christian intrusion wearing an Enlightenment garb of reason.[93] What Anscombe argued in philosophy, Carl Schmitt had famously argued in politics, that all central political concepts of modernity are essentially secularized forms of Christian concepts. The gist of Anscombe's and Schmitt's critiques are enormously important for us, as I will try to show, since the Foucauldian/Saidian power/knowledge problem can be traced back to European Christian values and epistemology, which provided the seeds that were to be cultivated in modernity's soil.

An outcome of particular historical circumstances, of a certain economic and later philosophical development that has given new meaning to the notions of dignity, freedom, and reason,[94] the Distinction has gained the status of a metaethic but one that, as MacIntyre argues, "does not stand as a timeless truth. . . . It makes sense only within certain ethical outlooks."[95] Like much else in modernity, it was made to be a sort of timeless and, moreover, universal truth designed to "outrageously fix the rules of discourse in the interests of one outlook, forcing rival views into incoherence."[96] Both Taylor and MacIntyre have advocated the contingent, contextual nature of the split, arguing for the possibility not only that the Distinction may be false in the first place but also that—even if it has any validity—no moral reasoning can "do without modes of thinking which the split rules out."[97] This in effect amounts to saying that moral thinking and the fixing of moral values and ethical considerations in our modes of thought and practice cannot be achieved while maintaining the Distinction.

The culmination of the philosophical distinction in real terms is tantamount to a justification to dominate nature, including, as Scheler and the early Frankfurt School[98] have argued, human nature and the Self. Together with nature, Scheler argued, the self is *"conceived* as being controllable and manipulable . . . through politics, education, instruction, and organizations."[99] Domination thus was the paradigmatic attitude not only toward "brute" and "inert" matter but also toward the self, the human subject. Scheler argued, furthermore, that "the more recent history of the west and its independently developing cultural annexes (America, etc.) exhibits a systematic, increasingly one-sided and almost exclusive propensity to cultivate knowledge which aims at a possible practical transformation of the world. Cultural and religious knowledge has been pushed more and more into the background. . . . Internal life- and soul-techniques, that is to say the task of extending the power and domination of the will . . . over these processes of the psycho-physical organism, . . . [have] undergone a far-reaching involution."[100] It is not clear what Scheler meant by "cultural knowledge," but if "culture" is shaped and defined by what he himself described as an a priori propensity of the will to garner knowledge for the sake of domination, then it could not have been "pushed into the background." That is, unless he meant by "culture" what I will call here the fields of artistic and aesthetic endeavor that were relegated to the peripheral domains (see chapter 1, section 2).

If Scheler—along with Bacon, Vico, Nietzsche, Foucault, and the Frankfurt School thinkers, among others—is right that the modern system of Western knowledge is programmatically geared to the service of power, discipline, domination, and transformation of the world, then to know, *stricto sensu*, is to engage in power and in transforming the world.[101] It was not a coincidence that in the early seventeenth century a host of discourses emerged in different languages and forms but with the identical message to the effect that man now commandeers the world. With his revolutionary and influential idea of the body politic, Hobbes grounded his thought in the secularized assumption of a divine creation in which the Lord made the world for Man to run, having abdicated any supervision over the world; and Bacon, the first to diagnose the connection between power and knowledge, departed from a similar position, in the process identifying what is in effect a distinctively European reality.[102] In Catholic Christianity, knowledge resided in the wisdom of God and was exhibited in his creation, but the deists believed that God's creation must be limited to the act of creation, the act of designing and installing a self-regulated world. Paul Kahn states the matter pointedly when he says that once the world is conceived in this manner, "then there is no reason to refer to God at all. If God is done with us, then we can be done with him. There is no need to think about the author as long as we have the text."[103]

Knowledge, having displaced God, becomes equally omnipotent—with a difference, however. God was bound to be and do good, and while man's duty, however interpreted, was to follow his example, his omnipotence was constrained by this goodness. God, in other words, remained bound by his own rules and principles, notwithstanding the miraculous state of exception in the way of earthquakes, volcanoes, and the like. Man, on the other hand, was restrained by no permanent laws or principles, making them up at will as he proceeded, reflecting his own freedom and sovereignty. Man's omnipotence could destroy the Earth on which he stands, but God cannot and will not permit himself to do the same.

The inextricable connection between this thought structure of unbounded desire for domination, on the one hand, and morality and values, on the other, is of immediate relevance to Said's mild and glossing statement that Orientalism is "a Western *style*" of domination (3, emphasis mine). There is little appreciation in such a statement of the defining force represented by such movements as the mechanical philosophers, Boyle and Newton included, who laid the foundations for, and dialectically reflected, a new attitude to the world. Effectively ousted from the world, God has now lost not only his privilege as the creator of an *anima mundi* but also any credit he had for an ex nihilo creation of the world.

In this new vision, nature just exists, is what it is, and is separated from actual creation, which is to say that the direct traditional connection between creator and created had been erased along with any connection between matter and spirit. But the mechanical philosophers went far beyond this position, arguing that matter is "brute," "inert," and even "stupid,"[104] qualities that had parallels and equivalents in describing soon-to-be colonized Afro-Asians and West Indies. All spiritual agencies, or the *anima*, had been banished from the universe, rendering matter spiritually meaningless, but still relevant in an anthropocentric, materialistic sense, that is, to be dominated, manipulated, changed, re-created, reengineered, all to the satisfaction of this vision. If matter exists in a "brute" and "inert" form, then the only reason for its existence must be that of its service to man, not to any man, but only to those who have the power to *know*. When Robert Boyle stated that "man was created to possess and to rule over nature,"[105] he surely did not mean any man but the European, for non-Europeans, in Boyle and even in the "freedom philosopher" John Locke, did not unconditionally belong to the category of humanity, at least not *this* one. Locke's advocacy of freedom and constitutional guarantees to protect freedom applied to the White Man, affecting no part of his own business as a substantial investor in slave trade.[106]

Having come to structure the central domains of modern Europe, domination over nature was canonized through various conceptual tools, "natural resources" being a "natural fact" of pedagogy. Highly exploitative and violent in the extreme, this taken-for-granted pedagogical instrument necessarily follows from denuding nature of all value. If nature is "brute" and "inert," then one can deal with it without any moral restraint, subjecting any subclassification of it to the will to power. And if matter is, in itself, devoid of value, then we can treat it as an object. We can study it and subject it to the entire range of our analytical apparatus, without it making any moral demands on us.[107] This separation allowed for the emergence of what has been called objective and detached scientific thought, represented across the academic fields of natural science, engineering, economics, business, law, history, and the like—all of which pretend to some sort of objectivity. "Detachment" is converted into virtue, because any lack of it permits the intrusion of man's evil nature. In all these disciplines, the scholar can study the Other (who is an integral part of nature) dispassionately, without it making any value-laden or moral demands on him. For to allow such demands to be made would contradict the Weltanschauung, that is, the thought structure of domination, in the first place.[108]

If this much is true, then our language—my language—must aspire to further accuracy. It is no longer accurate in this context to employ the term *domination*, for it underrepresents the force of modern Europe's structure of thought and its performativity. Domination is merely control and influence exercised over someone or something else, a characteristic that may be attributed to all complex societies and empires of the past, since the dawn of "civilizational" time.[109] The term, I think, might be adequate to describe the way empires ruled over subjects, especially the conquered; and it is certainly too strong to describe premodern domination over nature in the material, physical sense. However much the environment and ecology were exploited, and to a limited extent they undoubtedly were, the conception and understanding embedded in domination did not extend to a consciousness of control-for-the-sake-of-transformation to one's will, if not one's pleasure. Nor did premodern domination over conquered subjects involve conscious or even semiconscious designs that began with the assumption that they were an extension of a controllable and—as Scheler put it—manipulable nature and thus subject to domination that integrates the power to *transform*.

It is therefore linguistically and substantively more accurate to employ the term "sovereignty." Linguistically, this is the case because this form of European domination possessed *in addition* a supreme power that articulates the conception of free will in the manner that domination was exercised and in the quality of that domination. The term "domination" does not articulate the meaning of unbounded will to control and influence someone or something else, *nor does it exclude external restraints or higher moral or ethical considerations that define the field of play and its range*. Domination can still obtain when ruling a subject population while being restrained by political and even moral principles. Islamic empires and kingdoms are a case in point: they *dominated* the subject populations, but under the constraints of a "law" that was not, as we saw, of their own making and that constrained them in multiple ways.[110] Sovereignty, however, *does not only rule over principles, but makes them, as it goes, at will*. Even when it decides to adopt a principle or a set of principles, the decision is the result and, indeed, manifestation of sovereign will. Substantively, and this is my main argument, mere domination would be egregiously out of sync with the real effects of environmental destruction resulting from this attitude, and, importantly, with the concomitant political phenomena that the *very same* developments in Europe produced.[111] Just to make the connection—which I shall pursue later—clear enough for now, environmental degradation, the modern state, colonialism, modern power, genocide, and much else of the same are inseparable from one another. Or, put schematically, to speak of genocide and the destruction of the environment as if they are separate or less than organically entwined phenomena is to misunderstand.

Nor, strictly speaking, is the term "power" adequate as an account of the Foucauldian diagnosis of modern systems of control and management, for while it accurately reflects the modalities and dynamics of these systems, it falls short in delineating the *sources* from which this type of power ensues. Again, and as happened with the short supply of theory regarding the author, Foucault's characteristic work was more often than not preoccupied with the modalities and operations of modern power as it has yielded certain performative effects, but the sources of this power remain understood only by implication. Yet, Foucault made it clear enough that this power does not have any particular logic, that its logic is not linear, consistent, or predictable, and that it is not governed by any fixed rules that control its operations. From this plausible diagnosis, one can infer that power *begins* from no predetermined point or source, and that, lacking dictates from any other source or authority, it is sovereign in both its origins and its modalities of operation. This, I think, is crucial for understanding colonialism and sovereign knowledge, not least because it constituted a regime that was a subset and an offshoot of that particular form of power that gave Europe its modernity. Because the pre-Foucauldian, conventional associations and connotations of the term "power" remain present with us today, and perhaps also because Foucault did not interest himself in colonial forms of power, the term seems to be inadequate in accounting for colonialism, hence the recourse made to the term "domination." The utterance "power over nature" seems rather banal, failing to indicate the intensity conveyed by the term "domination" (although a consistent application of Foucault's theory should, but did not, endow the term with a much denser meaning that reflects the full implications of sovereign power). In either case, and formally speaking, both "power" and "domination," for different reasons, do not readily lend themselves to a complete description of what is involved, leaving the term "sovereignty" as the winning contender. Just as there is political sovereignty, so is there epistemic sovereignty, a parent of all other forms of sovereignty.

It is this sovereignty that defined the concept of nature in the Enlightenment, a concept inclusive of all existence. It is no coincidence in the least that an overwhelming number of thinkers, political philosophers, scientists, and the like have individually and aggregately advocated a common conception of "man" and "nature." In its collective and cumulative effect, this was the governing understanding in the central domains whose roots were in turn embedded in the central domains and central paradigms of the Enlightenment (however varied and divergent at times their voices may appear at first sight). The political philosophers, for instance, beginning with Hobbes in particular, were leading to a conception of politics and state that tallied well with the mechanical philosophers, and these in turn with the new moral philosophers who came to clothe the new material reality with a philosophical garb. The rise of sovereignty over nature, together with its residue of non-European humanity, was a *structural concomitant, and did not merely coincide,* with the rise of the modern state and its integral feature of sovereignty. For sovereignty, like Foucauldian power, was every-where, and in many important senses, they were one and the same.

It is not just the modern state as a totalistic entity[112] that constitutes the second necessary condition I have insisted on, but rather its sovereignty and the effects ensuing from *this* sovereignty in particular. As a point of entry, I think we should take seriously Foucault's concept of pastoral power, for it provides the matrix for a proper understanding of sovereignty. The modern state, which began to take a preliminary form in the sixteenth cen-tury, has integrated into a new political shape the old power techniques of Christian institutions. Foucault thinks, and I believe he is right, that "Christianity is the only religion that has organized itself as a Church," which I take to mean an institutional structure of governance equipped with a particular form of performative epistemological power, one that forms subjects internally *and*, as an institution, externally. As a "Church," it postulated that in principle individuals, because of their religious quality, serve others not as princes, magistrates, or prophets, but as pastors. Fou-cault enumerates various attributes of this "very special form of power," but two of these are of immediate relevance. First, it is "a form of power that looks after not just the whole community but each individual in par-ticular, during his entire life"; and second, it is a form of power that "can-not be exercised without knowing the inside of people's minds, without exploring their souls, without making them reveal their innermost secrets. It implies a knowledge of the conscience and an ability to direct it." Being "coextensive and continuous with life," this form of power "is linked with a production of truth—the truth of the individual himself."[113] Although this form disappeared as an ecclesiastical institution in the eighteenth century, its function has spread and multiplied, within a new configuration, in modern secularized forms. The state is thus "a modern matrix of individualiza-tion"[114] that has worked, through various institutions, on the whole social body. What Foucault implies, and as Nietzsche constantly reminded us, this is a theological, though secularized, godly power.

True sovereignty, whose most exemplary, and readily identifiable, mani-festation is to be found in the modern state, gives birth to law, which in turn constitutes the expression of sovereign will. This will is the paradig-matic feature in the practice of government, for it is the tool that defines the quality, range, modus operandi, and modus vivendi of the state. With-out total command of the law, in principle and in overwhelming practice, a state can never be recognized as a state. Likewise, a state that does not possess the ability or mechanisms necessary for legislating and making exceptions to so-called normative law cannot be deemed a state. The entailment between sovereign will and the capacity and prerogative to legislate and suspend legislation explains why a state must claim ownership of its law in the sense that what it adopts becomes *its own law*, even when it is suspended, and even if that law was originally "transplanted" from another state. This, as I have stated, is most integral to the concept of sovereignty: deeming a law binding as a practical or formal matter becomes possible precisely because the sovereign will *itself* decided to be bound by it, not because of any inherent force in the law (or in a principle) that binds. The exception to the law is as legal as the law itself, an exception that defines the very concept of sovereignty on which the state stands. Sovereign will therefore has enshrined the state as the new god, precisely the same status and position to which "man" was elevated by the Enlightenment as a sovereign over nature ("Man" here being of course used to the exclusion of the Afro-Asians, native Americans, tribal societies, Irish, Basques, women, children, the poor, and their "inferior" likes).

A monumental effect of the state's sovereign will is modern education, a phenomenon as recent as the nineteenth century, precisely, and not coincidentally, when Europe's colonial ventures *and their effectiveness* increased by manifolds. The causes for the rise of this form of education were largely internal to Europe, related as they were to the Industrial Revolution, which replicated and intensified earlier forms of exploitations that had prevailed during the preindustrial and premodern periods. Appalling social and economic conditions and monarchical rule, barely emerging out of the stage of raw absolutism, gave rise to mob violence, especially among the urban populations, thereby inducing the state to create an organized police apparatus that extended its sway into the countryside as well. By the third quarter of the nineteenth century, no village, town, or city could escape the watchful eye of this apparatus, giving surveillance a new yet thick layer of meaning. And in order to reinforce the policing apparatus, an unprecedented, vast prison system was created.[115] But crude physical force was not enough, and this the European rulers understood well enough. The population had to be educated in the ways of good conduct, and good conduct meant social order and, in a thoroughly capitalist system, an ability to work and produce. This was governmentality, elevated from a household term to a state-managed project.

In effect, all this meant reengineering society and its individual members, be it man, woman, or child. The engineering would not have been possible without the capacious power of legislation, which not only regulated academic and social forms of knowledge, but integrated into social production a particular conception of materialism and economy (not to mention specific forms of capitalism and consumerism of the liberal state). Sustained discipline, legislated to a detail, was the method by which the subject was corralled into a system of order that was intended to transform; and this system—a regulative mechanism of first order—was the school, which began to spring up everywhere. *Systemically concomitant* with the consolidation of the police apparatus, the school became a standard social institution by the end of the nineteenth century. The laws of education coerced parents to send their children to schools on pain of imprisonment. Primary education forced the great majority of Europe's children into a regimented system, mostly stern and punitive, where certain ideas and ideals were inculcated.[116] This was the culmination of the moment in which the citizen was formed, the child of the state, the loyal subject, the lover of the homeland and the nation. And this subject was as unprecedented as the conditions that gave rise to it. Europe was indeed exceptional.

Epistemologically speaking, the various institutions of coercive surveillance, education, and health (the famous Foucauldian trio of prisons, schools, and hospitals) were not distinct from one another but were formed, thanks to a supporting and increasingly trenchant bureaucratic machinery, into a cohesive system of doing and ordering things,[117] all of which culminated in the production of new identities and subjects, a new regime of truth. Extensive regulations, shaped by empirical, calculated, and calculating methods, were applied to these institutions for the purpose of disciplining the operations of the body, producing submission to regulating and systematic training techniques that engendered docility and obedience. The body, the site of both empirical analysis and intelligibility, had entered "a machinery of power that explores it, breaks it down and rearranges it."[118] It has become *colonizable*, capable of being manipulated into, and shaped according to, the will of the sovereign, who has now become constituted not by the will of a king or a pope, but by the very diffused and bureaucratized subject that was newly engineered. Colonization did not begin in the distant colonies, but right at home.

All this was not just control but training for the sake of the remolding, refashioning, and, in short, re-creation of subjectivities through sovereign power. With the maturation of educational, bureaucratic, and discipline-based institutions, the formation of the state subject was now complete. But the subjectivity of the subject, far from being individual or unique, was common and diffused; for after all, subjectivity was the product of one and the same interdependent and intersecting system. One can now count on relatively unified syllabi and textbooks, on integrated nation-wide programs in education, economy, and politics. The unity of the subject embodied and expressed the unity of the nation, for nearly every subject was a microcosm of the nation. But I should be clearer here. Nationalism is not just a political formation; it is both an ontological and an epistemological formation in the first order. True, it creates the national subject, but it does so *only after* creating the subject as a particular identity, and creating it as a knowing, thinking entity, *with a particular mode of rationality.* There is no citizen, student, scholar—Orientalist or not—who can entirely escape this ontological and epistemological formation and, importantly for our concerns later, the occasional loosening of the grip and shaking off of the dogmas of this formation cannot occur except *post eventum,* which is to say that the freeing, or partial freeing, of the subject from this status happens within the givens of this status. There is no modern subject who can exist in a state originally free of this ontological and epistemological status; and when one frees oneself from it, it is, ipso facto, against this very status that one must struggle. This is precisely what central paradigms mean: to be against or outside of them is to resist them; it is not to be able to conceive or operate in the world, whether in harmony or contrariety, without first *presupposing them.* All this is to say that the modern state produces the paradigmatic citizen and vice versa, that for the individual to be *in* and *of* the state, which the citizen almost wholly is,[119] calls for a totalizing subjectivity, reflecting in turn several essential features of the state. *It means the introduction of a subjectivity in the human individual in which power and knowledge are entwined, inextricably.*

Enter academia and its scholars, an establishment that was, like everything else, brought under the state's sovereign will during the nineteenth century. As an institution, academia is a state entity in at least four senses. First, despite by-laws and internal regulations, the university, as just intimated, is ultimately regulated by, and thus subject to, state law, largely subsidized by state and corporate funds that often come attached to political and other conditions (think of the Title VI phenomenon in the United States, or the creation of so-called area studies during the Cold War).[120]

The second is its nearly unqualified and unquestioning adoption of the positivism of the state;[121] indeed, the scholarly thrust of academia remains thoroughly, if not entirely, positivist, reflecting, as we have seen, the unqualified adoption of the Distinction in its full effects. The third is the overwhelming acceptance within academia of the state as a taken-for-granted phenomenon, this having overshadowed and continuing to govern mainstream discourses in the social sciences and the humanities. On the whole, academia thinks the state, and the world, through the state.[122] The fourth is the role academia plays in state governance, and this does not mean just its direct and obvious involvement in the production of research with military and political implications, if not research overtly dedicated to state violence.[123] As chapter 4 will detail, even the torture of political prisoners has become an area in which the medical profession and medical schools routinely provide support. The educator of the nation and its elite, academia exercises upon itself a particular discipline that seeks, among other things, to develop expertise in fields relevant to the interests of the state, although the porosity of state and society often clothes these interests in the garb of social and societal concerns. Governing, a business divided between countless departments and institutions, presupposes that the sphere under the purview of each of these units is capable of representation, that each sphere is known or at least knowable, and therefore can be subjected to deliberative political calculation. Accordingly, "theories of the social sciences, of economics, of sociology and of psychology, thus provide a kind of intellectual machinery for government, in the form of procedures for rendering the world thinkable, taming its intractable reality by subjecting it to the disciplined analyses of thought."[124] But these "theories," as we will see in due course, do much more than that.

Furthermore, the university has increasingly been transmuting itself into what might be termed a corporate modality, not only in the sense of structuring itself on the lines of the business corporation but also in functioning within the parameters of profit and technicalism.[125] The trend has been for boards of trustees to hire business leaders with a view to restructuring universities in the image of the marketplace. "For-profit universities offer up a future image of the new model of higher education, characterized by huge salaries for management."[126] Colleges and universities are opening their curricula and teaching to corporate interests, standardizing the curriculum, and offering courses that cultivate "entrepreneurial values unfettered by social concerns or ethical consequences. . . . Rather than enlarge the moral imagination and critical capacities of students, too many universities are now encouraged to produce would-be hedge fund managers, depoliticized students, and modes of education that promote a 'technically trained docility.' . . . Corporate gifts flood into universities making more and more demands regarding what should be taught."[127] In emulating the corporate world, and being embedded within state structures of education, the university is the institution that cultivates the national-cum-economic subject who internalizes and reproduces modes of existence governed by sovereign domination and exploitation.

VI

There are, I think, no conditions of felicity that lie outside our considerations as outlined in the previous section; any subversiveness against, or extrication from them can only, as I have argued, presuppose them while acting against them. If academia and its Orientalists are to make any sense, then they must be seen as domesticated structures of learning within the two necessary conditions of sovereignty over nature—including that over man—and of the rise and operation of the modern state, both standing in a continuous dialectical relationship with each other. Neither could acquire its identity or operate in the world without the other. In their unity, they were not meant to live in the world but rather reproduce it, perpetually, without a teleology in sight; and in the process of production, they manufactured the European subject, who was in turn integrated into, and thus became, the machinery that was to extend and transpose the *structure and act* of sovereign knowledge—of power, that is—to the rest of the world.

For the concept and idea of sovereignty over nature to have any extramental and actual effect—that is, to be more than just an idea—it needed the machinery of the modern state, and for the state to engage in anything beyond what rulers, kings, and emperors have done since time immemorial, it needed the concept of sovereignty, a concept that gave it its modern status, its *modernity*. In all of this, it shall not be forgotten that an ethical training of the self, that which requires a set of operations on one's body, soul, thoughts, and conduct, amounting to a highly deliberative and psychological state of being in the world, produces precisely that kind of subject who is utterly useless for the modern state and for any type of such political power, even in its rudimentary form. Before the modern European subject was formed as a deployable colonist, he was already colonized as an epistemological subject who could think the world as a generic Orientalist. It is in this context that I should make the point that a European did not need to say or write or even think anything about the Orient to be an Orientalist. All of Europe, especially in the eighteenth and nineteenth centuries—and not much earlier—exhibited Orientalist structures of thought that spurted over the Americas as much as over Africa and Asia. Orientalism's Orient is as much the Americas as the Orient itself. Notwithstanding its subversive authors, Orientalism *was* Europe and became another name for modernity, for it is, like any other discourse of the central domain, a microcosm that has concentrated in it all the *paradigmatic* features of the modern project. If this much is plausible, then to speak from modernity's governing systems of thought is to speak from Orientalism. Which is to say that to assume any central domain of modernity as a point of foundational reference—be it secularism, secular humanism, capitalism, instrumental rationality, the modern state, progress, anthropocentrism, or anything similar—is to engage in Orientalism, whether one is by profession an Orientalist or not, whether one "says" or "writes" anything about the Orient or not.[128]

Like all academic fields and specializations, Orientalism was raised on and thus imbibed the Distinction, mostly unconsciously, to be sure, but thorough imbibing it did. For the Distinction was the foundation of the modern regime of truth. Orientalism was saturated with the Distinction under the shadow of the state, under the wings of which it flourished, and which it served in countless ways. Orientalists produced other Orientalists, serving in academia itself but in society at large, operating within and cooperating with, by necessity and as a matter of course, society—a society that has been and continued to be produced by the state as much as it produced the state. But some Orientalists were also civil servants and as such served as counselors and advisors to the government as well as semigovernmental agencies and institutions. Some, as is well known, functioned as colonial officers and on-site experts who greatly influenced colonial policies. None of these colonial advisors, to my knowledge, questioned the originary rationale of the colonialist enterprise, although some surely did criticize certain colonialist practices (William Jones being one prominent case in point). None of them questioned the Distinction, much less did they articulate its malevolent effects on what they were doing (assuming that they were always aware of it); and none of them interrogated the state either as a project or on principle. If there was any questioning, it was about incidentals, mostly colonial practices, even the situational justifiability of colonizing a country. But colonization itself as an epistemological and ontological phenomenon, and as a uniquely modern form of subjugation and sovereignty, no paradigmatic "voice" seems to have questioned. Of course we could not in good conscience ask them to be aware of or understand the ontological and epistemological depth of the projects in which they participated and at times very effectively helped; but this is precisely the point. Given that they believed (and continued to believe) in the glory of their civilizing and "advanced" mission, they were enmeshed in their societies and states as *wholly formed subjects* and to such an extent that no one could reasonably expect them to know any better. And this is precisely where the latent potency of Orientalism lies: it did not and still does not understand what it is really doing, in what context, for what purpose, and exactly to what effects, despite the crises of late modernity (as the final chapter will argue).

Nor do I think Said could appreciate the full force and dimension of Orientalism. His conception of it, as we saw, was largely political, limited to its discourse as a malevolent representation of the Orient; and whenever he came close to diagnosing it as an effective reengineering force *in the Orient itself*, he typically retreated into the inner boundaries of the Orientalists' texts (as I showed earlier). He does say (as he said of the author's "determining imprint," which finds no support whatever in the substance of his argument from beginning to end) that Orientalism is "a Western style of dominating, restructuring, and having authority over the Orient" (3) but this turns out to be an enigmatic, and argumentatively unsupported, statement in light of the overall thrust of his work, a thrust undergirded by the omnipresent notion that Orientalism "has less to do with the Orient than it does with 'our' world" (12). There is nothing in *Orientalism* to show what that "structuring" consisted of, and the use of "style" to qualify "dominating" betrays an almost literary, and certainly textual, liminality. When he dedicates a meager two paragraphs to the extraordinarily influential William Jones, he never speaks of the real engineering projects that this scholar/administrator/politician engaged in, devised, and pioneered. Said's total silence over the law, the single mechanism that made colonialism possible, not only is stunning, to say the least, but also betrays his inability to see what really mattered. To miss the juridicality of

Orientalism—which defined the essence of the modern state and its formed subject—is to miss in an engineering analysis the crucial fact that an automobile has an engine. But this is not surprising, for Said missed the entire Enlightenment's weight in producing Orientalism. This, indeed, is too much to miss.

For Said, Jones was a linguist, a man of letters, one who lived with and in the text and its language, not a ferocious colonialist whose knowledge of Orientalism (including—as Kojin Karatani might as well have said[129]— his admiration of the "superior" Indian civilization) was the weapon of sovereign domination over the Orient. In effect, and not in mere claim, Orientalism for Said was by the West, for the West, and colonialism "gave force" to it as a misrepresentation of the Orient. It is my argument here that establishment Orientalism *primarily* constituted a part—and only a part—[130] of the indispensable but all-pervasive machinery that *effectively* remade the Orient in the mirror image of Europe, and only secondarily a domestic Euro-American discursive formation.[131] To confine analysis to the latter is to utterly fail to see the forest for the trees.

In defense of Said, one can say that he wrote about what he knew best— literary texts—and that most of the time he did not pretend to be a historian (and when he did try on extremely rare occasions, it was not a pretty outcome [58–60, 74–75, and passim]).[132] But what Said knew best should not and cannot define our understanding. Nor should it lead anyone either to deny or to minimize the effective and sovereign practices of colonialism and the role Orientalism *and other fields of academic knowledge* played in it—and continue to play. Of course some scholars engage in such minimization for crude political purposes, but many others, if not a majority, do so under the unconscious influence of the theology of progress and of modernization. When combined, and mostly they were, these theories lead to distortions of history, and as a consequence unwittingly partake in the further entrenchment of sovereign domination and its designs. For ideological discourse, especially in modernity, is a key element of any form of domination, particularly the sovereign type. When the theology of progress is universalized, as it is inherently made to be, historians, however unconsciously, begin to see the world as moving on a linear trajectory, one that *progresses* from an earlier and less developed stage to civilization, always dictated by Western terms.[133]

It is striking, for instance, that in earlier (and a majority of current) accounts of so-called legal reform in the Muslim world, the narratives are dominated by a modernization theory that almost never refers to colonialism, but to "indigenous" will and desire to reform. (Recently, however, colonialism has begun to be insinuated into certain reform narratives.) This was, consciously or not, a discursive strategy to avert responsibility and accountability for imperial and colonialist ventures, but it also seemed consistent with "good scholarship" to attribute agency to the "native" populations and their leadership. Arguably, the theory of agency itself is ideologically charged, for it posits, as a modus vivendi, a certain set of conditions as given and in which the agent operates willfully, and with desire and capacity. But the theory never seems to account for the historical processes that lead to the conditions that constitute these processes and that place and constrain the "agent" within these conditions. Because the processes are seen as having been predetermined by an inevitable course of unilinear historical trajectory, the course itself dominates the field of vision, excluding any other possibility. It means very little to say that a person sentenced to death has agency just because he happened to be given the absolute choice to die by hanging or by a bullet. For once the processes that led to this sentence are fully revealed and *taken into account*—that, for instance, he was entirely innocent of the charge against him—the entire theory collapses, since his choice of the method of execution is rendered irrelevant to the overall facts of his life and its tragic end. The theory of agency here is of no use. It does not tell us that the mere encounter between the victim and victimizer ab initio sealed the fate of the victim, that, whatever resistance the latter showed, it was within the foregone sovereign predetermination and decision of the victimizer to terminate the victim.

The theory has so far utterly failed, and will continue to fail, to produce one instance in which the agency of the non-European succeeded in rebuffing the colonialists' assault. To be intelligible, even possible, agency must always be presumed to operate only within the very system of power in which the agent operates. Conversely, there can be no agency from outside power, whatever form that exteriority may take. If we accept the fact of profound and structural transformations on the colonized grounds (against which massive resistance utterly failed) then we must be ready to accept that attributions of agency to the oppressed natives are tantamount to inscribing onto them and their history a modernization theory of progress, the very theory, the very theology, that subjugated them in the first place. The "room for negotiation or change" that such scholars as Homi Bhabha[134] ascribe to the colonized natives can be possible only when the natives have been permitted into the power system of the colonizer, when they have already been systemically and culturally converted, when it is already too late to recover who and *what* these natives once were. "Room for negotiation and change" may be possible and can indeed be enabled, but only *after* conscription, *after* conversion, for this is the entry ticket to modernity's power systems.[135] Agency, then, begins here, in such deliberations as to how the master's house can be brought down, with master's tools or with others in some neglected shed.

The history of the Muslim world, determined and written by Orientalism, and now normalized by the Orientals, has been a story dictated by modernization theory and the theory of agency, the latter applied to one degree of sophistication or another, and the former always propped by an invidious theology of progress. Had Said attempted to recover the history of colonialism in the Islamic world, and the role Orientalism played in it, he would have probably failed in his effort, precisely because of the camouflaging discursive effects that left much hidden from view. And Said is not the only victim of modernization theory and of the theology of progress. Consider what one critic has to say about European colonization in response to Said's definition of Orientalism as "a style of domination":

The further assumption implied in Said's third definition poses more problems. European cultures, of which America becomes an extension by default, are said to have both managed and produced the Orient. With no specification of what qualifies as either managing or producing, we are left only with the obvious historical fact that Britain and France managed to gain a colonial foothold in parts of the region. From a strict political view it would be nonsensical to speak of the actual history over the past few centuries as well managed. Up until the end of the Ottoman empire, it can hardly be said that this region was controlled on puppet strings by European powers. British and French encroachments [were] at the margins, as [befits] empires built on naval supremacy. Both imperial powers were adept at negotiating with indigenous leaders in order to further the economic interests of empire without always having to suffer the bruises of direct colonial control. . . . Here was virtually no on-the-ground management of most people in the Middle East, China, Japan, or large chunks of India. Islam, far from being replaced or even dented by Christianity, . . . spread dramatically in Asia and Africa during this same period of European colonial expansion. The fact that all these colonies were dismantled after World War II is a sign of the ultimate failure of imperialist Orientalist discourse in empire-molding.[136]

The only correct observation in this long passage is that Said indeed did not specify what constitutes "domination" or "management" of the Orient, nor did he appear interested, as I already noted, in transcending the inner boundaries of the European text by engaging the full meaning of domination, much less sovereignty. As I will try to show, Said's own apprehensions about religion,[137] coupled with his liberalism, secular humanism, and the attendant anthropocentrism, precluded a true engagement with such themes. Indeed, my real argument is that Said did not grasp the true nature of modernity as a project, as a phenomenon, or as a unique occurrence in human history.

The rest of the quoted passage, however, is stupendously ignorant of the history of colonialism and its true meaning, and the place of Orientalism in it. It is strikingly superficial, not to say highly misinformed. The understanding typified by such explanations as found in this passage is standard fare, and reflects the backbone of much discourse, even when colonialism, imperialism, and Orientalism are assigned a more serious role in "dominating" and "managing" the Orient than this author allows. This is because the driving principles of modern historical thinking, which by necessity always seeks legitimacy and attempts to avoid the charge of demagoguery at any cost, are embedded within a larger structure of thought systematically conceived to engender domination, not to mention supremacist attitudes to the world, including its human Others. As Amy Allen has competently shown in a recent work, even the pioneering and leading figures of Critical Theory remain caught in such Eurocentric conceptions of progress while at the same time trying to free themselves of the very shackles of power that Enlightenment thought produced precisely *because* of these conceptions.[138]

Endowed with a new structure by the Enlightenment, history ceased to be a narrative of moral instruction and became a structure of thought that encompasses all human experience. The infinitely varied experiences of countless societies and cultures of the past began to represent a collective monolith driven by a *Geist* on a linear trajectory toward the goal of progressive improvement, what Walter Benjamin called "the infinite perfectibility of mankind."[139] Founded on the assumption that time has a homogenous teleological structure, this theory has internalized the conception that all earlier phases of history and human experience are preparatory for what is to come, which always is better than what has gone before. And what is to come is always European or European-inspired. As Adorno observed, this structure of time effectively justified and validated the events and developments of the present, because these latter were regarded as *predetermined* and therefore *inevitable*.[140]

The normativity of the theology of progress effectively wrote the history of the world, including that of the Orient. An absolute standard by which to judge the past, the present becomes a predetermined movement toward progress that culminates in the present state of things.[141] Once this is taken for granted and thus normalized, the appearance of colonialism and the modern state in the Orient is seen no longer as an imposition but as a logical step in the march of history. The doctrine of progress itself is self-sanctioned as integral to this process; to adopt it and live by it is likewise inevitable. For to view this doctrine as unnecessary or an intrusion is self-negating in the first place. Once it foregrounds all historical thought, as it did, the theology of progress allows for no imposition that can continue to be seen as domination, intrusion, or manipulation. Hence the meaning of the passage I have just quoted at length, a meaning that is normatively *structured* so as to give the appearance of regularity of forward march on a course of development. In this picture, colonialism can hardly be charged with anything more than scratching the surface of Oriental societies. It is nothing more than "furthering the economic interests of empire," a casual practice of empires of all time, whose "encroachment was at the margins," and a practice that could not have been possible without "negotiating with indigenous leaders."

Once we extract the doctrine of progress out of our thinking, the history of the Orient, especially after the eighteenth century, ceases to have the normalcy and normativity that have been assigned to it, and by which it has been thoroughly clothed. Being the exception in world history, modern Europe's hypothetical absence from the scene of life leaves us with an Orient, a world, entirely different from the legacy it has in fact bequeathed. This is not wishful thinking, but an epistemological stand of the first order; it is to normativize a conception of history in which the full effect of European colonialism is *understood*, and not merely assumed or posited, to exist in a linear, teleological conception of history. It is, in other words, to argue that our historical narratives, including the postcolonial,

Subaltern, and all their likes, would necessarily be entirely different had this doctrine been nonexistent. This is also to insist that "wherever there is a charge of nostalgia" or of historical romanticism, "there is a virulent presence of a doctrine of modern progress."[142]

Part 2

As I have argued in *The Impossible State*, the Orient, including and especially its Islamic part, did not know anything like the modern state. Put more precisely, the Islamic world (our case study here) developed a form of governance that, until its encounter with modern European colonialism, did not know the concept of political sovereignty that modernity introduced. Political organization and constitutional arrangements were driven not by politics, since, like the state, politics, in the normative meaning we have come to know, did not exist either. Rather, it was the moral law of Islam, the so-called Islamic law that determined the meaning of sovereignty, and this law was a temporal-spatial phenomenon, as I earlier explained. This law stood resilient against political manipulation and could not be placed under the willful command of any single branch of government,[143] not even under the command of all of them (legislative, judicial, and executive) had they decided, inconceivably, to collude against it or subject it to a state of exception. The moral law, a dispersed doctrinal and sociolegal phenomenon over time and space, was beyond political reach, depriving any branch, including the executive, of the right to sovereignty.[144] This was possible by virtue of the stark fact that the "law" was the work of a collectivity of grassroots jurists, whose learning and piety combined gave them the authority to engage in atomistic contributions to the law. No single jurist, not even a founder of a school, could claim ownership of the law.[145] In other words, there was no unified agency that produced or managed the law. And since the source of all moral-legal authority was an anthropological-hermeneutical engagement with authorized texts by a countless, unidentifiable number of men of piety, across regions, decades, and centuries, the law not only was beyond political reach but also stood above all human institutions (notwithstanding its built-in structures of legal change).[146]

This is the meaning of the distinction between the rule of law and the rule of the state,[147] a distinction unknown to modernity. Comparatively speaking, modernity has produced a rule of law *within* the state, managed by the state, and subordinated to its imperatives; Islam's conception and practice were one in which "law"—constituted by a *shariʿi-sufi* regulating structure—ruled *over* any concept or practice of governance or body politic. One of the most crucial implications of this account is that there was no one individual, no one authority, agency, or institution, who could even attempt to decide on the Schmittian Exception. In premodern Islam, there was no Exception. Law was not, and could never be, suspended.

In colluding with colonialist administration, the Orientalist text—which in turn consorted with Europe's scientific, cultural, and administrative knowledge—stood in a dialectical relationship with effective power on the Orient's ground. Said, the author of the passage quoted above, and nearly every Orientalist and twentieth-century Muslim writer have taken the phenomenon of the modern state for granted, assuming it to be a timeless truth, when in fact the modern state is a particular political and politico-cultural arrangement that is distinctly European in origin,[148] one that was the result of a particular set of circumstances and transformations that Europe underwent in the seventeenth, eighteenth, and nineteenth centuries, transformations that were occasioned by rapid shifts in its own colonialist economies, unprecedented military technologies, social and political structures, and, indeed, epistemologies. Of particular importance for us is this last category, not only because new forms of governmentality have emerged, but also because the massive intellectual movement of the Enlightenment exercised tremendous influence on political conceptions and political practices, the same movement that produced and articulated the Distinction and within whose bosom philosophers, historians, scientists, and Orientalists were reared, for without the Distinction the modern European state and its subject, the nation and the state-reared citizen, would have been no more conceivable than Europe's unprecedented forms of colonialism.

It should not surprise then that the Distinction contributed directly to the ideological formation of the state, continuing to lend it legitimation and a normative status that stood dialectically intermeshed with the theology of progress and a particular conception of rationalism.[149] The state rested in part on the conviction that civilized human beings lived in and were nourished by state systems, while those who did not and were not were assigned a primitive "tribal" status or worse, and, being "stupid" like nature, were thereby deemed for all purposes and intents to be "scarcely human."[150] This ideological formation not only sustained the practices and discourses of the colonial state, but also, needless to say, rested squarely, as Europe's theories of race to no lesser extent did, upon the Distinction. From this "original position," from this constructed formation, most everything else followed.

The direct and indirect imposition of the state on the Muslim world has largely gone unnoticed as a field of inquiry. Like its Western parent, the Muslim state (that is, the state in the Muslim world) was deeply embedded within latent assumptions of "natural" progress, and was therefore seen as a natural and timeless phenomenon. This is in part due to the ideological formations to which the Western state itself was subject, but it was also because it developed through various stages of imposition over a century. In other words, both in British India and especially in the Ottoman Empire, the modern state arose by virtue of its institutions, together with the ideological props that cushioned and legitimized them by necessity. Conversely put, it was the so-called reforms of the nineteenth century that created the state structure, not the other way around. The reforms, rarely if at all seen to produce such effects (precisely because the modern state lives in an ideological web), were far more potent and effective than even the critical historian has accredited them. They were not a series of acts that just changed the law, education, administration, and similar spheres (however important these are); they had the effect of *raising* a state, which, as it was evolving, designed and implemented them. The process was clearly dialectical, which explains why the first reforms in the Ottoman Empire were what one might call ordinary reforms, but reforms that strengthened the physical might of the protostate, a precondition for developing the status of a legitimate monopoly over violence and the threat to use it.

It was not a mere chance that the culmination of the Ottoman military reforms in 1826 coincided with an act unprecedented in the entirety of Islamic legal, social, and political history, an act whose monumental importance was to be unraveled only with time, and then only partially. Once the traditional army units were eliminated, the Istanbul government decreed that the major *waqf*s of the empire were to be placed under the control of a new Imperial Ministry of Endowments, which meant, within a few years from that act, that the incomes of all these *waqf*s were seized. The same ministry also seized the Water Works Administration, since public fountains and the public water supply were largely constituted as *waqf* endowments.[151] Having been effectively owned by the public for centuries, water and its distribution have now become subject to the will of government.

Before proceeding, it is important to understand the magnitude of this phenomenon. The institution of *waqf* in Muslim lands had over centuries effectively cemented the relationships between the human, physical, educational, and economic elements within society and, to some extent, the polity. A thoroughly pious institution, it formed the substrate and matrix of philanthropy in Islam, playing an important role in the redistribution of wealth. One gave up one's property "for the sake of God," a charitable act that meant offering aid and support to the needy (this latter defined in a broad sense and ordained by the Quran as integral to the ethical formation and constitution of the individual). It also provided for the distribution of wealth within the family, affording care for its members and preventing the fragmentation of family property.

The promotion of education through *waqf* represented one of the best forms of engaging in good works, essential for Islam's social welfare and ethos of cultivating the moral technologies of the self. A considerable proportion of charitable trusts were thus directed at *madrasa*s (colleges), although *waqf* provided significant contributions toward building mosques, colleges, Sufi orders, hospitals, public fountains, soup kitchens, travelers' lodges, street lighting, and a variety of public works, notably bridges.[152] The list of social services provided for by *waqf* is expansive. A substantial part of the budget intended for such philanthropies was dedicated to the maintenance, daily operational costs, and renovation of *waqf* properties. A typical *waqf* consisted of a mosque and rental property (for example, shops), the rent from which supported the operation and maintenance of the mosque. A striking fact about the *waqf* was the volume of property dedicated to it across Islamic regions. By the eighteenth century, it is estimated, more than half of the real property in the empire was consecrated as *waqf*. Depending on the region, an estimated 40 to 60 percent of all real property across the Islamic world was constituted as *waqf* by the time Europe began its colonialist encroachments.[153]

The Ottoman government's economic and political gains were thus enormous. An increasingly centralized government had become the "middleman" who secured considerable profits in the process of collecting the revenues of the endowments and then, back from the center, dwindling salaries were paid for the minimal upkeep and operation of the *waqf* foundations. The back payments to the educational sector progressively declined, reaching a near zero point by the middle of the 1850s. *Waqf* money—formerly, and for centuries, belonging to the autonomous *waqfs*, which used them for their own operations and the fulfillment of their mission—were now diverted to military and other state-building projects, such as railways, through which the grip of the central government over the periphery was enhanced (this being a replica of what happened in Europe, except that the process in the Ottoman Empire and other Islamic regions was condensed). *Waqf* property, and the institutions it supported, including those of the Shari'a, began to fall seriously into ruin. This process was not unique, however; nearly all Islamic regions suffered a similar fate. In due course, it will become clear that the French campaign against Algerian *waqfs* was the model that the Ottomans were forced to emulate, a campaign that was designed, justified, and rationalized through French Orientalism.

The salarization of *waqf* administration constituted the first step toward the salarization of the entire legal profession, which was to take effect in the wake of the decree from 1839. There also was a series of minor but important judicial reforms that aimed at instituting new policies for judicial appointments, including entry exams, and the regulation of court practices. A series of laws were replaced by European codes, and new European-style institutions were raised to replace their *shar'i* equivalent. Which is to say that these fundamental changes were made to be concomitant with institutional restructuring, within a policy of demolish-and-replace. We will see that this policy, implemented in a detailed way in the formally sovereign Ottoman Empire, was the hallmark of colonialism in general and settler colonialism in particular (chapter 4).

New European courts, new European schools, and new European-style administrative and other institutions came to displace almost every sphere that the Shari'a and its related institutions had occupied.[154] The effect of these "reforms" was not merely to displace the Shari'a and the "traditional" institutions of Islam or just to secularize them, but to create a new subject, the citizen, who sees the world through the eyes of the modern state.

The "reforms" constituted the effective means to accomplish "order," "regularity," and "law," all of which stood in opposition to the steadily diminishing Shari'a culture that was perceived as lacking on these counts. They imposed a regimenting practice, and reflected highly modern notions of discipline, law, inspection, and incarceration. Indeed, these notions found expression not only in the evolving judicial structures and codes (as well as reporting, statistics, centralized supervision, and surveillance) but also in the significant fact that they generated an unprecedented and colossal prison system, one that was unknown to Islamic—or any other—civilization since its inception.

Amid these foundational and structural changes, European pressures on Istanbul continued to increase dramatically, a pressure that was designed by politicians on the basis of knowledge that European scholars articulated. Deeply in debt after the Crimean wars of 1853–56, the Ottomans secured substantial loans from Britain, loans that came with political strings attached, but what is most important for us are the *other* strings that were unequivocal. As if the capitulations and concessions in favor of foreign nationals were not enough, the British demanded and secured further allowances pertaining to the purchase of real property in the empire. The introduction of land codes, which had essentially privatized real property, was one step in this direction. But they also demanded, and received the promise, that the *waqf* system—which barred real property from entering the open market—would be abolished. Over the next two decades, more specifically between 1860 and 1880, the pressure was intensified by *both* the British and the French, whose scholars—doubling as colonialist officers—were already propounding the idea, in academia and outside it, that *waqfs* reflected a primitive mode, that they belonged to the age of decadence when the "Church" controlled much wealth, and that they stood in the way of economic development, which is to say, progress. All this amounted to a campaign, in Europe, in French Algeria, and in the Ottoman Empire, to the effect that *waqf* was a cause of cultural malaise and material decline. As a result, the so-called reformers moved aggressively against the *waqf*, thus sustaining the drive that eventually led to its abolition in the new Turkish Republic and elsewhere.

These policies that changed the structure and face of Ottoman societies were part of a series of major acts toward the end of the nineteenth century that aimed at a further consolidation of the Ottoman state's legal and thus sovereign powers. A Ministry of Justice, which was to bring under its wings the Shari'a and the European-style Nizamiyya courts, was established in 1879, thus not only unifying a hitherto fairly heterogonous system but also having the latter absorb the former. Several codes pertaining to the competence of tribunals, judicial salaries, public prosecution, and civil and criminal procedure came into existence. The courts were also instructed to expand their documentary range and to refuse orality as standard procedural evidence. By this point, oral testimony and the traditional procedural laws that were predicated on it became largely obsolete, producing serious effects on conceptions of personal integrity, trust, moral standing in society, and much else. Through these and similar displacements, the subject was given a new formation, a new epistemology for living and for dealing with social others. The Muslim subject was being steadily transplanted out of a technology of care of the self and its inner psychological operations into an internally disciplined but externally formed citizen. The new state technologies of training, discipline, and control came to seize the body and to create for it a new identity, a new human, and a new way of being in the world. This was the colonized subject, a replica of his European forerunner I discussed earlier.[155]

If we were to judge the Foucauldian diagnosis of surveillance and discipline by its colonialist effects nearly everywhere, including in non-French colonies, we would be compelled to conclude that Foucault embarked on a more important project than he himself thought. The French model reigned supreme nearly everywhere, even in the British colonies, and perhaps possessed even a greater power than the scope Foucault assigned to it, at least from the perspective that interests us. This model brings to the fore and epitomizes the structured and structural involvement of scholars—mainly Orientalists—in reengineering and, quite concretely, re-creating the Muslim world. Occupying Algeria in July 1830, they embarked on an extraordinarily brutal occupation of the country, one that was to last for thirteen decades. As happened in the Ottoman Empire and British India, juridicality was the means through which the Oriental was refashioned.

In a sustained effort to convert Algeria into a capitalist creature, the French engaged in direct appropriation and exploitation of the agricultural and mineral resources of the country. The problem, as the French saw it, was that too many Muslims lived in the country and that these "natives" were in control of the lands necessary for commercial exploitation and capitalist economy. As genocide involving a population of over two million natives was—at least at the time—not a practical option for the colonial authorities, freeing the land from the grip of the natives by other means dominated all considerations, in the legal field no less than in the political. This option would also afford the opportunity to exploit cheap labor, which would be lost if genocide were to be carried out.

Nearly half the land, as expected, was *waqf*, known to the Algerians as *hubus* (Fr. *habous*). Mostly by force, the French settlers gained control of a good deal of property in the *waqf* domain, causing the beneficiaries of the endowments to sue for the restoration of the sequestered property. In response, the French declared all property in the hands of the *colons*, whether acquired lawfully or not, to be lawfully owned by its colonial usurpers. And as if this was not enough arbitrary sovereign power, new laws of property came to displace those of Shari'a, facilitating further the settlers' commercial ambitions. As I will show in chapter 4, these colonialist policies find their source in what I have called "the state of extraordinarity" that was integral to a Europe-based political arrangement whose foundations in turn resided in the concept of sovereignty over nature.

Enter the Orientalists. In a forceful bid to corral the *waqf* properties into the open market, the French government enlisted the aid of scholars, historians, and nonhistorians alike.[156] French lawyers, jurists, and academicians who knew anything useful about North Africa (and some who knew near to nothing) began to discourse on matters legal and nonlegal in the Muslim tradition. Many of them were *colons* who were both scholars and civil servants, and who were involved in the colonialist administration. After the middle of the nineteenth century, they began to produce a massive bulk of legal literature about Islamic law in its North African context, especially about the theory and practice of the dominant Maliki school. The literature was to become an integral part of Western scholarship on, and therefore Western knowledge of, Islam. Certain of these writings acquired an academic form while others were effectively pieces of legislation, the so-called Code Morand being a prominent case in point. This scholarly, juridical, and legislative discourse came to constitute the infamous *droit musulman-algérien*, which found parallel, but to a less aggressive degree, in the Anglo-Muhammadan Law that the British produced in India. The methods of the two forms of colonialism may have differed, but the aim of re-creating the Muslim world and the Muslim subject was the same.[157]

The French Orientalists, like their British and Dutch counterparts who cofounded the very discipline of Orientalism, proved themselves to be more than instrumental in their government's colonial designs.[158] In the government's bid to seize control of *waqf* properties, on which countless religious institutions were founded, France's heavyweight Orientalists not only helped in matters pertaining to legislation, but also effectively "campaigned," in the words of an American Orientalist, to "discredit the institution [of *waqf*] among the Algerians themselves."[159] Intended to "conquer the minds," this campaign was as central to the project of colonialism as economic gain, for the project, as I have been arguing, was not confined to capitalism, however important it was to Europe. The project heavily invested in the production of cultural and academic discourse, in the creation of new subjectivities and European-like subjects. When the intellectually unremarkable Thomas Babington Macaulay famously said that the British in India need to create a "class of persons Indian in blood and colour, but English in tastes, in opinions, in morals and in intellect,"[160] he was not speaking on behalf of the British alone. His statement captured Europe's colonial project in its entirety and, in light of my discussion earlier, Europe's own internal history over the two preceding centuries. Algeria, like India and everything else, including Europe itself, had to be refashioned.

It might not be trite to observe how the French Orientalists went about their mission, since their story is merely a crude microcosm of the entire Orientalist project, which at times seems so complex, involved, and serpentine that the underlying forces behind the political, colonialist, and imperialist agenda are masked by a thick "scholarly" cloud, an essential feature of discursive formations.[161] To accomplish their goal, the French legal specialists produced a flood of argument to the effect that a fundamental distinction existed between family and public *waqf*s—a distinction that had never acquired the same meaning, or a sharp separation, in the Shari'a. Capitalizing on the centrality of the Quran to Muslim belief and practice, they vehemently insisted that the family *waqf* was a later innovation (*bid'a*) in Islam, also playing on this latter concept as a topic that had received some attention in the Muslim legal tradition itself, in which some jurists had rejected certain legal rules as unwarranted creations. On these grounds, they concluded, through the best scholarly method they could muster, that family endowments circumvented the Quranic law of inheritance that operates by the principle of shares. It was not relevant to their argument to clarify that Muslims had a good reason to develop *waqf*s in the service of inheritance law within the family, because the Quranic shares' system tended to fragment family property. Nor was it relevant to note, as scholarship is supposed to do in the interest of balance, that the *waqf* not only was a space for property devolution but had the much larger function of redistribution of wealth, a mechanism that reflected Islam's great emphasis on egalitarian "economics." Nor yet was it relevant, if it was understood at all, that this institution was crucial for the formation of a civil society the likes of which modernity has never known. That such a venue of investigation was out of the question and that the focus of scholars was limited to certain kinds of questions speak volumes about the directions of Orientalist research and its extraordinary selectivity,[162] all of which were the function of the single-minded obsession with the project of reengineering the colonial subject.

Consistent with this project, family *habous* and Quranic inheritance were declared—on behalf of Muslims—mutually exclusive; and since the raison d'être of the former was the skirting of dictates of the latter, family endowments were deemed both immoral and illegal. But the French Orientalists, who drove colonialist policy, did not stop here: family endowments were said to have tied down, by their very nature, valuable property and to have prevented it from "efficient" exploitation, a fact that ineluctably led to economic stagnation. From here, it was a short and easy step to link this "stagnation" with cultural malaise and, indeed, a stunted civilizational progress (an argument that was, as I have already noted, imported and circulated by the Ottomans, under European hegemonic terms, in justification of their assault on the *waqf*). The Algerian Muslims, the French Orientalists decided (or concluded as a matter of scholarship and, in effect, of legislation), should therefore get rid of them, once and for all. This aspect of the French Orientalist discourse moved toward reforming the Muslim subject economically, although the real argument was clothed with culture talk. What the French saw as "cultural malaise" was in fact the cornerstone of an economic system that tied, in precolonial times, economics to a particular ethical formation of the self, a technology of inner introspection in which the agent operates on his own soul as a means of reaching a particular state of spiritual existence. This state would then dialectically reconnect back with material acts in the real world, producing ethical and moral effects in social realia, without particular regard to efficiency as the means to strictly material profit. "Cultural malaise" then was a French cultural translation of ethical thought and moral action, two "Oughts" that needed to be separated from the "Is" of economics. The Distinction is never far from any modern colonialist project.

To conclude that the socially and economically central family *waqf* was to be eliminated, as well as to legislate accordingly, is the very definition of sovereignty over the Other as a "civilizational" collectivity. It is to decide not only a matter of the law but a way of living and a host of socioeconomic relationships that this law created within Islamic society at large. It is to change the way Muslims themselves perceived and lived in the world, and with one another; differently put, it is to change what and who they are, their very "nature" as social beings, whether as individuals or as communities, and their very being in the world. These were laws driven with a potent performative effect, with a discursive formation generated and manned by nothing short of the best and most prestigious academic and state institutions in the world. Yet, with all its performative power, this was neither the full project nor the only one.

Targeting family endowments went hand in hand with an unusually liberal strategy to centralize the Shariʿa institutions, with the disingenuously declared purpose of building Algeria's religious unity. This was no contradiction at all. Advocating the Quran's integrity, which appeared to maintain the "true" form of Islam, and simultaneously attacking the family *waqf* constituted a two-pronged weapon: the first allowed for the fragmentation of property and precluded it from entering the *waqf* domain, and the second broke up property held in joint ownership. Either way the French would defeat the "natives" into submission. This strategy had another advantage: maintaining a semblance of solidarity with, and insisting on, the Islamic tradition (by promoting the Quran's injunctions) forestalled the much detested assimilation that, were it to run its full course, would prompt the Algerian Muslims to demand political rights, even rights equal to the French themselves.[163]

It cannot escape us that sovereignty over the colonized—as over anything else—does not, in its full meaning, obey any particular rules or principles. That economic and material exploitation contradicted the spirit of the declared *mission civilisatrice* suggests the real meaning of sovereignty: the colonized can be used, abused, exploited, enslaved, freed, civilized, or not; but in the process, and if they survive the whims of subjection, the purpose is to transform them, to re-create them, continually, perpetually, just as progress itself is a never-ending process. Nothing in all of this is contradictory, and everything remains within the realm of the possible. This was real sovereignty.

The French two-in-one policy served several ends at one and the same time. The Islamic legal system, or at least an expedient rendering of it, was asserted but simultaneously centralized and bureaucratized, thereby imposing on it a form of instrumental rationality that rearranged it, reorganized it, and in effect reconstituted it. This was not all, however. Having secured enormous areas of cultivable land, thereby achieving their immediate target, the French now no longer needed to maintain the argument for the Quran's integrity. The premise that the Quranic law of inheritance was fragmentary was adopted with zeal, reversing their earlier position with a view to paving the ideological grounds for another assault on the Shariʿa, this time nothing short of the law of succession, the single area in the law so extensively regulated by the otherwise "nonlegal" Quran. As often was the case, the lines of separation between the Orientalist text and legislation were thin, even porous; the text frequently was a prelude to legislation, serving as an exercise, a test, and a study of feasibility, but more importantly as ideological conditioning and mental preparation preceding the actual campaign to reengineer the Shariʿa. Accordingly, in the project of writing scholarly treatises on the law of inheritance, themselves performative discourses, the Orientalists enlisted "native" Arab students who had come, mostly from Ottoman regions, to study with the French Orientalists.[164] Under the supervision of such influential Orientalists as M. Morand, these students wrote on and advocated anything from reforming the Quranic law of inheritance to eliminating it altogether. This campaign against the interrelated areas of *waqf* and inheritance, among others, had a substantial traveling span. It not only operated on the Algerians, and later on a new generation of Arab lawyers, intellectuals, and scholars who acquired the culture and mentality of colonialist Orientalism; it also was exported to the lands of the Ottomans, who were inculcated, under French pressure, into French cultural models, including the Revolution's ideas of *liberté and égalité*.

Typical of nearly all colonialist projects, the imposition of laws pertaining to property and commercial activity came hand in hand with the imposition of penal laws, which were designed to regulate and discipline the colonized populations as a first step toward further domination and ultimately transformation of identity. The Loi Warnier from 1873 decreed that all land in Algeria would henceforth be regulated by French law and that Shariʿa courts would be restricted to adjudicating cases of inheritance and personal status. The high point in the imposition of criminal law came less than a decade later, with the promulgation of the highly and infamously repressive Code de l'indigénat, a law that did not recognize due process and gave free hand to civil administrators to inflict excessively harsh punishments against Muslim subjects at will. Sovereign European power, reflected in the Schmittian state of exception (or, as I shall argue later, along with Agamben, the state of extraordinarity), becomes normative law.

By the last quarter of the century, the French managed to break up the Algerian legal class and its system of law and legal education, in near-exact parallel with the Ottoman scene. Deprived of their resources due to the expropriation and centralization of *waqfs* and to various French administrative and educational reforms that changed the structure of the Shari'a, the *ulama* were subjected to a qualitative diminishment in the very pedagogy and hermeneutical practice that defined their functions. As happened in other colonial contexts, the socioepistemic mechanisms that reproduced the legal profession largely ceased to exist, and in its place a European system of legal reproduction was installed, with new courts, new types of jurists, lawyers, and European codes of every type and shape.

With this new system in place, the new generation of "native" lawyers was equally subjected to the inculcation of a procolonialist reading of reality, in which the "progressive" European law was pitted against a "backward" Shari'a. (Even as late as the 1990s, many judges and lawyers from North Africa and the Middle East could be heard speaking, when the Shari'a was discussed, ad nauseam and in a most pejorative manner of its "arcane," "disorganized," and "primitive" nature.)[165] By the time the French were done with Algeria in 1962, the Shari'a was reduced in competence to the adjudication of personal status (and of course to the "innocuous" "ritual laws" of prayer, fasting, and so on), having lost its reproductive hermeneutical command over every other sphere of the law. A central paradigm that had defined so much of Islamic culture and civilization, the Shari'a and along with it the Muslim subject were changed and largely eviscerated. It may not be a detail, or without irony, that much of the fray over Algerian land, and the consequent campaign against the *waqf*, had to do with coveting chunks of Algerian territory for cultivating vineyards for the production of the much-beloved French wines, an intoxicant prohibited by *shar'i* precepts. As genocides will become relevant for us later, it is no detail that by 1962, close to a million Algerians lost their lives to French colonialism, most having been unarmed civilians, including a large proportion of women and children. Sovereignty, I have been insisting, commands the right over life and death, even for the sake of a luxurious triviality. Indeed, sovereignty does not have to operate by reasons, at least not ones normally associated with common standards of rationality or ethics.

French colonialism and its Orientalists epitomize an acute form of brutality and cruelty, which is to say that the policies and practices determined by their sovereignty were less discriminating and more arbitrary than those of other colonialists. Nonetheless, as chapter 4 will show further, sovereignty and nothing but sovereignty remained the shared denominator of all European colonialist projects. Another example of sovereign knowledge and practice is Dutch colonialism in Indonesia, an example that is particularly instructive because of its long duration. Their occupation of Java, beginning in 1596, was, at the time of conquest, a fairly ordinary one, little different from hundreds like it throughout human history. And it would have continued to be ordinary had Europe not undergone the transformations during the seventeenth and eighteenth centuries. During roughly the first two centuries of this occupation, the Dutch did nothing more than exploit the region economically, as most occupations have done for millennia, except for the added dose of extraordinary greed. No Orientalists were involved, for they had not come into existence yet. And, as had been the habit of occupations for a long time, they did not interfere in "native" affairs. When Daniel Lev, a leading expert on Indonesian history and politics, said that the Dutch during that early period "resolved to respect local law, . . . [which is] another way of saying that, by and large, they could not have cared less,"[166] it was not a sense of respect for native traditions that precipitated this seemingly tolerant attitude. It was because Europe had not yet developed the Distinction to a state of art, nor had it yet teased out its implications in detail. Sovereign knowledge was still being born. By the middle of the nineteenth century, Europe's intellectual arsenal, coupled with a new technology of military weapons (also the result of *this* intellectual-scientific development), was ready to subject the world to its will, and the Dutch were more than prepared for the task.

But before turning to Dutch colonialism and its Orientalists, something must be said of my observation in the previous paragraph about the new European military technology, for it is the common belief (almost invariably so among too many in academia) that colonialism, genocides, and other mass killings are merely the function of this sophisticated weaponry, that, *because* this technology was available, colonialism and mass elimination became possible. This understanding in effect structurally replicates the substance of the position (one of whose offshoots is the way Islamic history itself was written in modernity) that assumes and takes for granted modern phenomena as an inevitable course of human development, treating them as "natural" stages in man's experience and *progress* in the world. But this is to engage in history as metaphysics, where historical processes begin at some inexplicable pregiven, or as a matrix of assumptions that need not be demonstrated. Such an argument ignores the crucial fact that, like everything else, military technological development is not a predetermined historical process that moves linearly by virtue of a predetermining *Geist*, integral to and parallel to the "inevitable" forces of progress. Rather, this new technology is integral to a contingent and particular set of circumstances that made modern Europe the way it is. It was, in other words, a by-product of regimes of knowledge, and particular ways of thinking the world, that evolved in the wake of the Distinction.

This structure of thought had established with society and with early technological science an extensive and, one might say, an organic dialectic. Early- as well as late-modern military technology, including Holocaust-like uses of technology, was all symptoms and tools, not causes of sovereign violence, the kind that routinely produced horrific, unprecedented holocausts, genocides, and colonialisms in the twentieth century. A strong penchant for violence was the lot of humanity since time immemorial, and to this extent the moderns, Nazis included, have not distinguished themselves over their predecessors. What is new is an added layer of cataclysmic violence that created a new quality. Modern sovereign will, including will to violence, is an epistemology and a way of seeing the world that commensurately created the new atrocious weapons. To argue that such weapons are incidental to this emerging European reality and that they are, because they "happened to be available," responsible for genocides and atrocities is to ignore this contingency with a view to universalizing, in typical European discursive fashion, the burden of sovereign, genocide-inducing violence. It is therefore my argument—to which I shall return later—that such military technology may not, on its own, be deemed accountable for any of the considerations I have been raising.

To return to the Dutch then. By about the last third of the nineteenth century, the major regions of today's Indonesian Archipelago had been taken. In good fashion, "law and order" constituted the backbone of colonial administration, demonstrated in the promulgation of a penal code for the "natives." All criminal cases and major offenses were tried at the exclusively Dutch-staffed Landraden courts, which also handled important civil cases pertaining to the natives.[167] It cannot surprise by now that all matters of *waqf* and the all-important inheritance law fell within the jurisdiction of these courts. Furthermore, in 1882, the Dutch reorganized the Islamic courts, now calling them, not coincidentally, "priest-courts," *priesterraden*, perhaps a psychological projection of the oppressive Catholic Church in Medieval Europe on the inculpable peoples of the Archipelago.

As the French did in Algeria and the British in India, the Dutch colonists of Indonesia called upon the Orientalists for assistance. If India had its Sir William Jones, Indonesia could boast Cornelius van Vollenhoven, an influential Dutch Orientalist specializing in "*adat*-law"—or what was called "*adatrecht*." "Pioneered" by the even more stellar Orientalist Christian Snouck Hurgronje, this field of study confirmed the legal duality that had been "discovered" by the Dutch. There is no indication that this duality was construed by the Malay peoples in oppositional terms; nor was the relationship between one and the other problematized. Rather, before the end of the nineteenth century, *adat* and Shari'a appear to have been viewed as complementary and entwined. But Snouck's "discovery" of *adat*, and van Vollenhoven's elevation of the study of this discovery into a "science," in effect opened a Pandora's box within the political and legal life of Indonesia that has not been closed to this day.

We tend to take it for granted that a scholar is free to make the distinctions he or she sees fit about any topic of study, and to some extent this is wholly justifiable. But this is not the case with the Dutch van Vollenhoven, Snouck, and their peers. Theirs was not scholarship in the common sense of the term, something akin, say, to studying the history of American elections with a view to understanding their pattern, structure, and variables or to predicting future results. Rather, the overall impact of these scholars' "contributions" is tantamount to a policy report, all too readily adoptable by government, to the effect that both parties cannot run together in elections, that Americans can vote only for one party, the other being less congruent with the "nature" of Americans. Theirs was indeed *adat* scholarship, but one endowed with sovereign decision, as history has proven in matter of fact. To bring out the full weight of this scholarship and its enduring effects on Indonesia, one must introduce a contrast and ask: How would such "a study" of American elections fare in terms of actual effect?

"*Adat* law" had always existed in an oral form, and despite the fact that certain elements of it were written down, orality remained its defining characteristic, for orality had a function: It required communal participation in the construal and application of this "law," what might be termed local knowledge. It additionally constituted a state of affairs, a practice, a state of mind, a moral code, and a way of seeing the world, but it can scarcely be reduced to our modern notions of law, operating in whole or in part as a legal organ of a coercive state.

Knowledge of the "*adat* law" and of its localized implementation precluded the need for a specialized class of people, such as Islamic legal specialists or modern lawyers. It was knowledge of common behavior, individual and communal, and perceived as such in relative terms by those upon whom it is incumbent to conduct themselves in a particular way. In other words, this knowledge did not reside in an elite but was rather diffused in the community, although the elders tended to be particularly regarded as repositories of it. And since it did not require writing, or therefore any "scholarly" commentaries or glosses, no jurists or lawyers could become the locus of either legal or epistemic authority. The preclusion of writing therefore entailed the exclusion of codification, an essential tool of a centralized state authority, and a modern one at that. The *adat*, therefore, in its natural form and traditional historical evolution depended on the crucial fact of remaining in a state of orality, a state of fluidity and thus malleability.

Much like Shari'a's substantive principles (*fiqh*), *adat* was not intended to apply in letter, but in effect constituted a guide to proper conduct or a maximal limit to what can and cannot be tolerated by a particular, local community. The writing down by the Malay people of a fraction of *adat* practices before colonial intrusion did not considerably affect their fluidity, for the record remained both partial, unofficial, and a matter of reference. It could not have, at any rate, represented more of an official law than any of Shari'a's *fiqh* manuals. But the Dutch codification of *adat* changed their nature forever, and gave them different and unprecedented structure and meaning. A crucial effect of codification was an elision into rigidity.[168] Yet, it is not difficult to understand why the Dutch insisted on capturing *adat* in written form. Coming from the continental legal tradition, they could not conceive of any unwritten law as law properly speaking, as a code of conduct interpreted and practiced by the individual and the autonomous, self-ruling local community; hence, for *adat* to have any force, suitable to a coercive state, it had to be endorsed by a written jurisprudential form. Thus, to be so sanctioned, *adat* law had first to be identified and set down in writing.

None of this, again, should be taken for granted, as if it were no more than a "natural," predetermined progression of history. To think that the Dutch policies were "natural" because this mode of conduct has always been the habitual conduct of colonialist regimes is not only to engage in anachronism but also to confuse cause and effect; it is not to understand that European colonial *effects* are unique because their *causes* are embedded in a unique structure of thought. Our Islamic case study provides a contrast, yet again. When Muslims occupied new territories, only "public law" applied to the conquered populations, such as tax law, criminal law, land law, and the like. The new subjects were to live by their own denominational laws, and more importantly, there were no further "campaigns" or programs to integrate them into the occupiers' legal system and force them into an educational apparatus with a view to remold them into new subjects, that is, national citizens.[169] Even the Muslim civic population, as we saw, was not subjected to such an educational technology since education was both denominational and free of the state's interference (because there was no Muslim state in the first place). Yet, although Islamic conquests and rule over non-Muslim populations involved "domination,"[170] this mode of rule can be comfortably described as one "at arm's length."[171] By contrast, European colonialism, the Dutch included, was intrusive and penetrating to a degree that aimed to, and did, change the very constitution of the colonized subject, to fashion it in new ways, to act on its body through a system of juridicality, to discipline it, to subjugate it into docility, just as European governmentality had performed its own subjects at home. But to implement this project, the entire social order, moral communities, customary practices, traditions, modes of material transactions, and every major traditional concept had to be destroyed or eviscerated, and then replaced. Long-standing cultures, *continuously* evolving over centuries, if not millennia, are ecosystems that maintain webs of intricate and intertwined relationships between the human and the environmental, between the communal and the cosmological. The infliction of "progress" on such cultures yielded and continues to yield the same results that this theology has produced in the natural environment and its ecology.[172]

Colonialism and its Orientalist handmaiden played the most crucial role in this assault. Hailing from a pedigree of Dutch scholars who viewed Islam as a menace (very similarly to how the French saw this religion and its law in Algeria), van Vollenhoven vehemently espoused the position that *adat*, not the Shariʿa, should be held to govern the pluralistic societies of the Netherlands Indies. This was a reaction to various other scholars, such as L. W. C. van den Berg, whose scholarly project essentially declared enthusiastic support for the position that the Shariʿa, not *adat*, was the sustainable law of the islands. Criticizing the proponents of Shariʿa, Vollenhoven argued that *adat* exercised such a wide sway over the archipelago's population that Islamic law stood in comparison as both thin on the ground and virtually irrelevant.[173] Remarkably, all this knowledge he managed to garner from two rather brief visits to the colony. Vollenhoven espoused the view that any attempt at weakening *adat* was nothing less than an invitation to open the floodgates to Islam, a religion seen by Vollenhoven and many of his compatriots not only as a native political tool of unification, but as the very religion that had threatened Christendom for centuries. Furthermore, to side with *adat*—which did not have a semblance of "religious" constitution—was to promote secularism. Among other initiatives, he compiled an extensive work in which he committed to writing the otherwise oral *adat*, identifying eighteen versions of it, when in fact the archipelago consisted of over a thousand islands, each with its own version (or versions) of *adat*. The writing down of *adat* "violated a primary principle of *adat* law theory, that the *adat* lived in local tradition. Now, written, it lived in books, which Dutch judges, and Indonesian judges half a century later, used as if they were codes."[174]

In the wake of the Dutch government's formal declaration in 1927 that *adat*, not the Shariʿa, was the normative law, institutional changes began to take effect, and further scholarship aiming at systematizing *adat* (especially by Bernard Ter Haar) came to bolster that policy with renewed vigor. Henceforth, Dutch scholars and their native students—who hailed mainly from a coopted Javanese aristocracy—as well as colonialist advisors and administrators were officially trained in *adatrecht* as the paradigmatic law. The Shariʿa sunk to a distant secondary position, where it would be accepted only insofar as it was provisionally allowed to modify *adat* under particular circumstances. This change was formally sanctioned by yet another academic and policy discourse and was assigned the appellation "reception theory." But the project did not stop here. In a typical colonialist fashion, a new educational system was introduced to enhance the hegemony of the colonial project. Dutch schools at all levels numbered more than a thousand by the first decade of the twentieth century,[175] giving the Javanese and other elites the means of education that prepared them to pursue their legal studies in Western institutions, whether these were located in Batavia or Leiden. It was from among this elite that students of the *adatrecht*, many of whom advocated the divisive and fragmenting reception theory, emerged. Indonesia, now reengineered into an institution and virtually into a subject, continues to struggle with the effect until this day.

The situation in India was not much different. "Local" law was even more "disorderly" and "confused" to British taste, and like every other colonialist administration, the Orientalists were brought in. The British did not gain effective military control of India until 1757, when they embarked on a systematic campaign to draw out the resources of the country through the cheaper method of legal control, rather than military control, which had been used up to that point. The immediate purpose was of course profit, set within a larger vision of bringing India into the open market. Yet, as Macaulay's "Minute" testifies,[176] the ultimate goal was to refashion Indians in the image of their colonizers, to civilize them short of changing their "blood" and brownness. The legal system was, and continued to be, the performative sphere that determined and set the tone of domination and re-creation. A serious "legal" plan was called for, and it was the British governor of the Bengal, the corrupt Warren Hastings, who initiated it in earnest. What has become known as the Hastings Plan conceived a multitiered system that required exclusively British administrators at the top, seconded by a tier of British judges who would consult with on-the-ground Muslim legal experts with regard to issues governed by the Shari'a. At the lowest rung of judicial administration stood the run-of-the-mill Muslim judges who administered law in the civil courts of Bengal, Madras, and Bombay. The plan was designed to absorb local customs and norms into a British institutional structure of justice and to streamline them in accordance with "universal" ideals of justice.

The British magistrates found it difficult to make sense of the staggering variety of opinion and the pliability of Islamic and Hindu "law," a situation they often described as a chaotic, uncontrollable, and corrupted mass of individual juristic opinion.[177] To deal with this "chaos"—a mess exhibiting "disorder" and "primitive existence"—the classicist and foremost Orientalist Sir William Jones (1746–94) was marshaled from Oxford.[178] There seems to have been no question in Jones's mind as to what he should do to solve the "Indian problem." He decisively proposed to Hastings the creation of codes or what he termed a "complete digest of Hindu and Mussulman law,"[179] what amounted in the long run to nothing short of a structural revolution in India's laws and society. The justification for the creation of such an alien system within Islamic and Hindu juridico-moral systems rested on the claim that these "laws" were arbitrary, inconsistent, and disorderly, and only through the recovery of the great texts of the tradition could the country be brought back to its former glory.[180] Sovereign domination did not allow for the possibility, in reality the only one, that Hastings and Jones did not understand or did not want to understand what they were dealing with and that they needed better education before they declared their audacious plans, or that they did understand but their understanding was irrelevant and thus set aside without a second thought. If sovereign domination can decide that the object of knowledge possesses no complexity beyond the mind of the subject, its subset, then sovereign knowledge can decide that the exception is indeed the rule.

Yet, this step of textual reengineering was only half of the plan. Rewriting and restructuring the two legal systems were to be further accompanied (as it indeed turned out they were) by another project of engineering the sociology of legal knowledge itself, this time as it existed in the mind of *living* human beings. Jones constructed a system that offered "a complete check on the native interpreters of the several codes,"[181] a project that subjected the Indian's mind to new modes of interpretation: disciplined, deductive, objective, orderly, and in line with "universal" conceptions of justice, equity, and fairness.

The first step in Jones's project resulted in the translation of a few classical Islamic legal texts into English (Hindu law was subjected to the same strategy). The immediate purpose of these translations was to make Islamic law directly accessible to British judges who deeply mistrusted the Muslim jurists advising them on points of law. As happened in Dutch Indonesia, the texts primarily functioned as codes, and codes they became. (In point of fact, in this respect the Dutch emulated the British, not the other way around.) It may be said that the very fact of translation *was* and effectively constituted codification, a phenomenon foreign, nay antithetical, to the makeup and structure of the Shari'a, as much as it was to *adat*. The magnitude of this change, which opened the floodgates to codification, is inestimable.

Codification is the nation-state's modus vivendi, a method that entails a conscious harnessing of a particular tool of sovereign power. It is a deliberate choice in the exercise of legal and political power, a choice that at once accomplishes a multitude of tasks. The most essential feature of the code is the *production* of order, clarity, concision, and of course authority.[182] Modern codes are said, even by noncolonial experts, to replace "all previous inconsistent customs, mores, and law,"[183] a testimony to the fact that "colonialism" is everywhere, including in Europe itself. This replacement is also totalistic, since codes must also fulfill the requirement of complete-ness and exclusivity. They must comprehensively cover the area they claim to regulate, an act that perforce precludes any competing law. Should any other law be allowed to remain operative in a jurisdiction, it would be so allowed by virtue of the code's permission,[184] which always has exclusive and superior authority over and above all previous law.

Codes must also be "systematic and clear," arranged rationally and log-ically, and rendered easily accessible to lawyers and judges,[185] the presump-tion always being that "traditional law" does not possess these rational and logical qualities. Codes are not only declaratory and enunciative of their own authority but also universal in the statement of rules, hence their con-cision. They pay direct attention neither to the particular case nor to the human individual as individual. They are always abstract, "to the point," and deliberately preclusive of the concrete. It was considered a virtue that the "French and German Civil Codes could be held within the boards of a volume while the common law required a full library" to house it.[186] Con-siderations of instrumentalized economy, as always, are paramount. But the primary attribute of the code is its capacity to create uniformity, an attribute in keeping with the homogenizing and universalizing ethic of modernity. The sway of the code's authority therefore extends beyond its own legal, administrative, and regulatory power: the code possesses a per-formative power that, through the law, *constitutes and reconstitutes subjects.*[187]

The national subject not only was far from Shari'a's desideratum but in fact plainly contradicted the very raison d'être of that system, whose per-formative thrust was the production of the *individual* and local-communal moral subject.[188] The Shari'a ran counter to the great majority of the code's attributes. First, in both theory and practice, the Shari'a depended on the cooperation of custom and customary laws.[189] Nowhere did the Shari'a operate exclusively, and everywhere customary law was in principle rec-ognized as essential to the formulation of precepts and rules within the Shari'a, a fact that gave a deep meaning to local practice and even local cultural uniqueness. Self-rule, a robust premodern concept of autonomous existence, was not only allowed to exist within Shari'a's hands-off mode of governance; it in fact flourished and thrived[190] (which in part explains the autonomous private status of conquered populations integrated under Shari'a governance).

By its hermeneutical and highly individualistic nature, the Shari'a may not have been systematic according to the European perception of the world, although an expert in it will see it as systematic in a different way. While the code is by any standard more accessible than most *fiqh* treatises, the argument of clarity is no more than a relative one. For an expert in Shari'a, the *fiqh* is as clear as the modern lawyer finds the code. It is, however, true that the *fiqh* cannot be said to have internal uniformity, or the intellectual simplicity of the code, since plurality of opinion is its defining feature par excellence. It is on the diversity of its own character that it thrived (and insisted), and it is *in* this diversity that it found the flexibility to accommodate, through variant legal norms, different situations, different societies, and culturally divergent regions. Plurality of opinion not only answered the multiplicity of particular and special situations but also served the exigencies of legal change, which were accommodated through built-in dynamics in the structures of legal reasoning.[191] Its plurality ran counter to the spirit of uniformity, since homogenization was largely absent from its agenda. And since its interest lay in the individual as a singular, rationally autonomous worshiper of God, there was no need for an abstract and universalizing language. Most importantly, however, it is the declaratory nature of the code as well as its uniformity of substance and legal effect that betrayed a will to power that emanated from the higher offices of the nation-state; by contrast, in the Shari'a, such a will to power did not exist because law and the legal system worked from the bottom upward, from the individual and local community first, moving up to larger governing ("political") mechanisms, which Shari'a itself also largely regulated.[192]

Jones's project of translation and, effectively, codification severed the legal text from its Arabicate interpretive and commentarial tradition,[193] which had been defined by a certain epistemology and a morally anchored system of hermeneutic, meaning that the text ceased to function in the way it had done for a millennium, since the text was not an "event" but rather an *interpretive process and a habitus*. This is still not to imply that the text was central or indispensable to *shar'i* hermeneutics, legal reasoning, or general practice. In a complex oral culture, as Islam was, orality constituted the measure of ethical formation in the transmission of knowledge, legal or otherwise, which is to say that the spoken or transmitted word held a force of authenticity that a text could not ensure. A text can always be forged, and the culprit is not always guaranteed to be caught, but oral knowledge transmitted directly from one person to another made the source and every link in the transmission identifiable and knowable, with all the attendant moral and ethical accountability this made possible. Orality, in other words, meant a particular technology of knowledge that shaped its human operators—by virtue of its own content, teleology, and modes of operation—into ethical subjects. Orality qua orality was then performative, not just a "way" of transmitting information. But most important of all, in ethical and moral terms, it certainly cannot be associated with the "primitive," which is how the British and almost every other European saw it.

Furthermore, the suppression of customary law, having tremendous effects on its own, also meant the obliteration of the communal ways in which the Shariʿa operated. In other words, the *very act* of translation uprooted Islamic law from its interpretive-linguistic soil and, at one and the same time, from the native social matrix in which it was embedded and on which its successful operation depended.[194] This is not all. The new legal configuration allowed the British to oust Shariʿa's jurists and replace them with lawyers trained in the British ways of doing law, thereby initiating the transformation of "Islam law" into a state law. This also meant that the autonomous and socially grounded Islamic legal profession was displaced by the corporate and ultrasocial agency of the state. The overall result was reengineering the Shariʿa (as well as Hindu "law"), rendering it a sort of replica of English law, what became known as "Anglo-Muhammadan Law." And with this transformation, the new state institutions and methods of governance broke up the communal structures as a first step toward fashioning the nation. European to the core, the nation and nationalism literally reengineered Asia, as much as they re-created and reinvented the rest of the world.

In this colossal engineering project William Jones's intervention was not an expression of an individual effort; it represented the full force of the institutional and epistemic weight of Europe that gave it its conditions of felicity. Jones was perhaps the best talent available at that time and place, but it also was one that embodied and gave full expression to the potency of the performative power of British knowledge and its resultant colonialism. His other discourses, translations, and poetry and all the discursive versatility of his fertile intellectual and artistic life amounted to very little in the conquest of India or of any other territory[195] (as was the case with his equivalents, or even the much sharper and encyclopedic minds within the Islamic tradition who happened to accompany the great conquerors, including, coincidentally, those of India). If Jones played this transformative role, it was by virtue of the *kind* of knowledge he seized upon, a kind that not just was unique in human history but also was located within a

Europe-based discursive formation and power system that gave it an equally particular potency, all of which amounted to sovereignty, sovereign disposition, and a sovereign disposal of reality that made a particular form of knowledge of the world its engine.

The *driving engine* of colonialism was not, as most military and other historians think, the Maxim machine gun, the steamship, or even a new form of bureaucratic and administrative management. The driving engine was the structure of thought that made all these and many others like them possible. To focus on the machine gun and its massively destructive power is to miss the point altogether. To focus on the Euro-American Orientalist text as an epitome of misrepresentation and on its collusion with political and economic power—as Said and others believe—is merely tantamount to saying that the Europeans and Americans invented the destructive machine gun but merely happened to have used it for conquest. This tells us nothing new. What matters most is nothing short of an interrogation into why the machine gun was invented in the first place; what made it possible, as an idea? What was the thought system that shaped the minds of the inventors? What was the relationship between this thought system and the purpose of invention? What was the relationship between the machine gun and the steamship, between the steamship and the misrepresenting text? If the misrepresenting text was "reinforced" by political and colonialist power, how did it turn itself around and reinforce, nay, make possible, that lethal power? To speak of such a text as being reinforced by power and as failing to engage the dispassionate scholarship that it claimed to embrace is in effect to say that the use of the machine gun merely tells of the violent disposition of its user, and that a machine gun's raison d'être is to maintain the peace, the very condition that would have made the very conception of the weapon impossible. Once the full implications of the narrative this chapter has offered regarding colonialism and its Orientalism are appreciated, it will be clear that Said insisted on drawing a picture in which the tail wags the dog.

As if the reversal of analytic priorities were not enough of a problem, Said went on to condemn Orientalism in toto. A charitable reader might indulge the attack as a rhetorical strategy or as hyperbole, but the price of this charitable act would be too high to pay, for nothing short of theoretical coherence and a clear analytical vision are at stake. The totalization also blurs vision as to how power works, and contradicts the very Foucauldian theory that Said claimed to have influenced him. In the next chapter, I attempt to sort out the problem of totalization through a theory of the author by giving, among other things, an account of an Orientalist who subverts Said's narrative in almost every way, going beyond the furthest reaches attained by Said.

CHAPTER III

The Subversive Author

I

If Europe had its resident manufacturers of Orientalist knowledge in the colonies, the likes of the French Morand, the Dutch Von Vollenhoven, and the British Jones, it also had large contingents of supporting Orientalists at home, those who, with their more active colonialist peers, made for a potent discursive tradition that fed into the local European culture of conquest and sovereign domination, all of which amounted to a complete set of conditions of felicity that made Orientalism merely another weapon in the war of Europe against everyone else, but a war that did not always aim to destroy out of existence. Wars, like genocides, often aim to rearrange existence, and not merely to create it ex nihilo. Yet, this cannot be the full account of Orientalism; such an account would merely commit the relatively minor sin of reductionism. The grave sin of this account is the elimination of the possibility of an inverse dynamic of power, of a complexity in the central domains that generates, as it has proven to do over millennia, a multiplicity of opposing forces within even the most hegemonic central domains.[1] Domains of power, in their very nature, must encompass force fields that often coordinate both their operations and their thrust in favor of the central paradigms governing a particular order, but they are not born, nor can they be nourished, without opposing force fields. This is no more conceivable or possible than a body in which all the organisms work in unison and toward an undivided balance of health. For if this were to be the case, no organism will ever die.

If variety, diversity, contrariety, and subversiveness are *inherent* in every structure of power and in every central domain, a fact we must take for granted, then we might well ask how these manifest themselves in Orientalism. Said singled out mainly two Orientalists—Gibb and Massignon—whose work was often sensitive to the objects of their scholarship, in this case Muslim Orientals, but the final verdict of *both* was negative. When all is said and done, neither scholar passed the test of adequate, accurate, truthful, and complete representation of the Orient. In other words, if either of the two had a "determining imprint," it was an imprint that, in the final analysis, conduced to the discursive formation in which Orientalism ultimately implicated itself, in colonialist power overseas, in political power at home, and in misrepresentation itself in the first place.

This categorical judgment ipso facto precluded a discriminating approach, and it is my strong suspicion that this error was precipitated by the lack of a complete theory of power. Foucault, as we have seen, was not himself attentive, by virtue of his preoccupations with the modern scene, to teasing out the full implications of his theory of "epochal" changes and transformations in either *épistémè*s or the discursive formations to which they give rise, although his last lectures at the Collège du France (1979–84) began to exhibit such an interest. When he speaks of "rules of formation," which are the "conditions of existence" for discursive formations, he is almost wholly interested in their modes of operation, and only incidentally in their rise or "disappearance," which he tends to note incidentally.[2] In *Orientalism*,[3] Said distilled his theory of power and knowledge, and appears to have taken from it only its schematic features. This explains his categorical and all-too-sweeping approach, which has exonerated no one who ever wrote anything about the Orient. Foucault's subversive "critique" makes no appearance in Said. This specifically Saidian legacy has spread among the current generation of scholars like fire in dry wood. Of course the reasons for the all-too-easy inflammability of this particular aspect of Said's writings are distinctively political, but like all political phenomena in modernity, they are rendered intelligible only when taken to deeper levels of analysis than conventional politics itself or political theory can afford.

If every writer on the Orient is potentially susceptible to the charge of Orientalism, then it is small wonder that any attempt by any writer to find any "civilizational glory" in the Orient turns out to be nothing more than wondrous awe that reduced the Orient to an exotic object. For Said, this constituted misrepresentation all the same. But for the legatees of this sweeping approach who still thrive today, misrepresentation and consequently "Orientalism" are what they disapprove in other scholars' work. The politicization in all of this stems from the fact that neither Said nor his followers set the necessary criteria that allow for grounded judgment, valuation, discriminating distinction, and assessment of what makes one Orientalist different from another, and what makes an Orientalist stand within a paradigmatic domain and another outside it. Turning thus to this structural feature of Said's understanding of Orientalism, I shall attempt to show, by proffering an account of the work of a versatile and accomplished Orientalist, that it is possible to demonstrate that (1) certain Orientalists can possess a "determining imprint"; (2) the imprint was inflicted in *specific* ways that distinguish it from the generic imprints described in *Orientalism*; and (3) crucial for our inquiry, Orientalism can provide, from within its own domain, a subversive discourse *structurally* critical of both colonialist and mainstream Orientalism, a critique that is more profound and meaningful than Said offers and one that derives its power from the fact that it goes, unlike Said's, to the heart of the central domain.

The account of this chapter therefore functions in a double-pronged manner: on the one hand, it complicates the phenomenon of Orientalism and at once defines it in sharper terms than Said has done; and, on the other, the account goes on to show that the subversive strategies within Orientalism can provide a critique of mainstream Orientalism that is more penetrating and certainly more *coherent* than Said has offered.[4] In a later section, I will attend to the fuller implications of setting up Orientalism as an exception to the standard of modern Western knowledge of the world, but for now I (re)turn to the concept of difference.

Said's argument that in the European imagination the Orient was *different* is not, on its own, informative, simply because the adjective is, by its very nature, both ambiguous and relative. To bear meaningful sense, it requires not only clarification but also differentiation and specificity. A potential witness's testimony that the bank thief looked different than he himself does, or even different from the police detective questioning him, would be for the policeman an utterly useless identification of the thief. It so happens that Said does articulate some aspects of the difference, an articulation that spans much of his book. The Orient is inferior, primitive, effeminate, superstitious, and the like, all of which are, for the Orientalist, negative attributes, or at least intended to be negative. But then Said expands his definition of "different" and includes positive qualities, such as the spirituality of the Orient, this time clearly intended by a few Orientalists to be a positive attribute with which they are stating their preference for the Orient over their Europe. As noted, Said saw in this an attitude that partakes in exoticizing the Orient, making it in the final analysis a negative quality. Yet, it is a given that the Orient is not Europe and cannot be Europe, nor vice versa, however either of them may look. Difference as a sum total of divergences in constitutive qualities, numerous if not countless, must, by necessity, be taken for granted, which leaves us in a quandary as to what would be the conditions of comparison that might satisfy this critic and the many who share this stance. Of course an obvious and easy answer is that the Orient should not be different from the West; it should not be more or less spiritual, more or less advanced, more or less domineering, more or less humane, more or less rational, more or less materialistic, more or less liberal, more or less superstitious, more or less effeminate, and so on. But then it is doubtful that the consequences of this answer would be satisfactory either, for such equations would produce an Orient in the image of Europe, precisely one of the major Orientalist creeds to which Said vehemently objected. For, after all, it was against Macaulay's doctrinal epitome—that, in effect, colonialist Europe endeavored to produce subjects black, brown, and yellow in color of skin but European in tastes, morals, and intellect—that he and many others have justly fought their intellectual and other battles.

It is difficult not to reach the conclusion that Said's objection to difference is precipitated by his foundational assumption of the West as a standard. This is evidenced in his position that even when the Orient is depicted as superior, the depiction amounts to nothing but fantasy, or, if not, an act of exoticizing. The exotic, every dictionary tells us, is that which is "out of the ordinary," that which is "not used for ordinary purposes." The ordinary in Said's mind is of course the normative, the standard, the paradigmatic. Or else, why should every positive depiction of the Orient be invariably exotic? Secular humanist, democratic values as well as the general cultural standards of the West, not secretly admired by Said, were so present and powerful in his mind that any claim to the Orient's superiority could in no way imply that the West should not, and cannot, be regarded as *the* standard—with the consequence that if there might be any attempt at bridging the much-abhorred *difference*, the act of bridging, with all the concessions that it might entail, self-evidently cannot come from the West. For Said is on record lauding these Western values and many others all the while deprecating tradition, religion, and much else of the like.[5]

That Said set up Western modernity as the standard is the most plausible conclusion to draw from his writings, because while Said, on the one hand, condemned Orientalism, he ennobled Western modernity and its achievements as *the exclusive standard*, on the other. His most-valued literature was Conrad and Kipling, not his compatriot Ghassan Kanafani or the other "Oriental" 'Abd al-Rahman Munif;[6] the music that thoroughly impassioned him, and that he himself performed, was Bach's and Beethoven's, not 'Abd al-Wahhab's, Riyad al-Sunbati's, or Sayyid Darwish's; and as a literary critic and intellectual, his entire academic apparatus and its Weltanschauung were profoundly Western, having never bothered, even in his senior years, to inquire into the dialogical potential of the exquisitely rich and fertile Oriental and Islamic intellectual traditions. It never occurred to him, for instance, to undertake research projects in literary criticism in which the highly refined Islamic contributions to this intellectual domain could be brought to dialogue with its Western counterpart, much less to critique it.[7] These were furthest from his mind, because Said was a secularist liberal, whereas these Oriental "traditions" were products of "religion," which, needless to say, he was not far from detesting. Massignon's condemnation rested precisely on this: he was "traditional." Difference, therefore, not only put Said in a bind, but created in his *Orientalism* an aporia of the first order.

To be understood properly, difference is situational, namely, it has both directionality and perspectivism inscribed into it. As a relative and perspectival phenomenon, difference also has an imaginary geography. Its sources may appear to perception to originate from one side of the difference's spectrum rather than another, in which case any diagnosis of difference's implications must account for these sources, their composition, inclination, value, implications, and historical situational presence, for the sources constitute the problem in the first place. It may be the case that in allocating responsibility for these sources, one may opt to resolve the difference from one side rather than another, depending on the results of the diagnosis. But in all cases, it is essential to understand the sources and their role in a potential bridging of the difference. I think Said did not get to the stage of sources, leaving his conception of difference unidimensional, one-sided, and, most importantly, one with a single directionality. A question must *also* be asked. What are the consequences that may ensue from a counterassumption: that the Orientalist ascription of difference to the Orient was a self-projection, that it is Orientalism itself as a mainstream academic discipline and its larger cultural props that were themselves the raison d'être of the difference, that they are the difference itself? Such a question opens up a different line of inquiry, one that forces new assumptions to make an entry into the debate, and one that may change the rules of the game, including those set by establishment Orientalism.

II

Enter our Orientalist. Raised as a Roman Catholic, and educated by the Jesuits, and later at the Sorbonne, René Guénon was a Frenchman whose formative years were spent in a country that promoted one of the most virile forms of European nationalism (this fact is relevant in light of Said's conception of an absolutely hegemonic national "ambience"). Belonging to the last generation of European Orientalists who mastered various Asian languages and knew more than one tradition (unlike their successors after World War II), Guénon produced some two dozen books on Hinduism, Taoism, and Islam, and his works were translated into some twenty tongues. He was a metaphysician of considerable weight, and his scholarship and intellectual activism worked hand in hand, straddling an interest in introducing Hinduism and Taoism to European audiences, and critiquing the modern West through much of his writings. His ideas about metaphysics and tradition guided a number of scholars and thinkers in what became the traditionalist school Philosophia Perennis. As a subversive author (an analytical category to which I shall attend later in this chapter), with a less-than-popular esoteric approach and profound contempt for academics, his place in mainstream Orientalism was uncertain, to say the least; but his work made for such a profound impact that a group of thinkers and writers continued to advocate ideas that he would spend his life articulating. What makes him an interesting case for my inquiry is not that he was an Orientalist who went against his own discipline—as significant as that may be for my overall argument—but that with all the esotericism and unusually unconventional thrust of his critique, he went against

Orientalism and all that which produced it, and *still* managed to leave a legacy. This phenomenon has profound implications for a theory of the author.

It is worth noting that Guénon does not make a showing in Said's *Orientalism*, not even a passing mention, although as a classical Orientalist, he and his work complicate the concept of Orientalism in the way they have given rise to a form of subversivity that survived the author himself. Obviously, Guénon does not meet Foucault's criteria for the discursive author, but his influence on major scholars within and without Orientalism, as well as the renewed relevance of his work during the last decade or so, attests to the durability of at least the thrust of his ideas to the crises of modernity[8] as well as to mainstream Orientalism as its subset. Guénon's relevance, in short, issues from the urgency of the questions he sketched close to a century ago, questions that are preoccupying, with renewed vigor, modern academia and its new subfields, ranging from postcolonial studies to environmental ethics and much else. This is another way of saying that just as Orientalism's performative power resided in conditions of felicity within the Enlightenment worldview and the formation of the nation-state, Guénon's critique finds its commensurate conditions in the oppositional force fields of power that were produced, per force, by none other than the Enlightenment-state formations themselves. No power can exist without creating within itself, within its own processes and dynamics, the potential for its own transformation, if not destruction. Guénon's legacy may not constitute such a potential, but his critique of modernity and its products is gaining enough appeal that it has become recently relevant for many intellectual concerns, including, as is the case here, a reassessment of what Orientalism is. That his ideas are esoteric in the extreme and at times outright objectionable is of no relevance here; after all, the discursive tradition of Orientalism itself—as a subset of liberalism—does not fare better, although for different reasons altogether.

The first extraordinary effect of bringing Guénon into conversation with the late-modern critique of Orientalism is the difference in the points of departure from which he and Said initiated their inquiries. Although writing a good half-century before Said, Guénon begins where Said ends, taking for granted much of what the latter endeavored to show in detail. His critique during his formative years was certainly shaped by ideas and reflections emanating from the European intellectual environment, but it increasingly, and later heavily, drew on an engagement with the Taoist, the Islamic, and, most prominently, the Hindu traditions, especially the Vedanta school. This is a matter not just of scope and quantity, but primarily of methodology, assumptions, a critical apparatus, and a determining worldview. When Guénon was writing his postformative work, postcolonial and so-called postmodern critique had obviously not yet existed, the Frankfurt School was being formed, Foucault and *his* Nietzsche had not yet emerged; and Heidegger's *Being and Time* would sweep European philosophy only toward the end of his life. His critique, summed up in his *Orient et Occident* (1924), was instead framed by an implacably negative reaction to European philosophy from Leibniz and Kant to Schopenhauer, and, in politics, to the configuration that was the legacy of World War I and the Bolshevik Revolution. Yet, translated into the idiom of the twenty-first century, and transcending its eccentric and unconventional style of expression, Guénon's critique synoptically captures much of the best in recent social theory, Critical Theory, and cultural criticism, but without admitting the legitimacy of the system on which these critical theories insist.

And here, I think, is where the reasons for Guénon's rejection by the "system" lie. Guénon had the intellectual courage to delve deep into modernity and reach the most negative conclusion possible about it: that it needs to go. Much of his work attempted to outline the "reform" through which modernity must be phased out, but this is not our concern. What is of relevance here instead is that Orientalism, like much else that is interconnected in modernity, cannot be properly evaluated without reference to the whole, and that the massive body of relationships that enveloped it and in turn produced it was affected by its operation and production, all this, in contrast to Said's microanalysis, entailing—in the strongest sense of logical and ontological entailment—the fundamental questions as to how and where Western modernity must be placed within the long history of world civilizations.

Unlike Marx and his predetermined stages of historical evolution, Guénon regarded history, under the influence of Hinduism, as a cyclical movement of generation and corruption, and did not see it as possessing any *Geist* that will inevitably lead to some goal or final purpose. An implacable enemy of the doctrine of progress, and of any conception of historical determination, he saw Western modernity as "a veritable anomaly," pointing to the rise of materialism as major cause for the West to go "astray," to take a "divergent course."[9] Among all the civilizations "known to us more or less completely, this civilization is the only one that has developed along purely material lines, and this monstrous development, whose beginning coincides with the so-called Renaissance, has been accompanied . . . by a corresponding intellectual regress."[10]

"Materialist" and "materialism" for Guénon are complex concepts intended to describe and analyze a system of relations that govern Western modernity, capitalism being just one of its major components. It is a political and sociological system of value that permeates the social order and gives it its meaning and worldview, and it is in this order that modern academia, scholarship, mass culture, and, specifically, Orientalism (as straddling all these) receive their shape and definition. The moral order—what he calls "moralism"—of the "contemporary" West "is really nothing but the necessary complement of practical materialism," for "both develop simultaneously along the same lines."[11] Pervasive and a wholly defining force, "materialization" is a dynamic force that affects all phenomena, giving them not only a particular physical structure and constitution, but remolding them as a particular idea or a structure of ideas, with unique symbols and significations, and a distinct way of seeing the world. Materialism is a general attitude that "underpins what is thought of as 'ordinary life.'"[12] The performativity of materialism's psychological and corporeal power amounts to the full weight of transformative processes that culminate in depriving the human faculties of the ability to see beyond the immediate senses. Trapped in the sensible world of the here and now, modern Western "man" has become self-enclosed in a locked system beyond which no other form of reality can be comprehensible.

Accordingly, with its capitalism and attendant cultural value system, materialism ab initio precludes the possibility of understanding, much less appreciating, the manner in which other civilizations and cultures articulate, and live in, the world. This is why Guénon never questions the "sincerity" of the intellectuals he collectively subjects to vehement criticism, because in effect he sees them as thinking and operating within a regime of truth dictated by what he would probably have called a discursive formation beyond their comprehension and control.[13] Yet, this tolerant judgment of the individual should not amount to the exoneration of the aggregate group that subscribes and contributes to materialism as a collective moral agent. The modern Western individual, though an unwitting contributor, is both object and subject of this performativity, for "he himself is one of the factors intervening actively in the changes affecting his world." The dialectic involved here is then progressive, between the individual and his human grouping, on the one hand, and mass culture and systemic structures, on the other. Once formed, the materialistic mind-set is disseminated and "cannot help but contribute to reinforcing" the same materialism that "made it possible in the first place."[14]

Echoing a Ghazalian perspective but on the level of the modern concept of "society," and not just of the individual as an autonomous agent, Guénon ascribes disjuncture between materialism and intellectuality, by which he means knowledge of the world that transcends the limits of rationality, reason, and the world of senses apprehended by these. "Material development and pure intellectuality go in opposite directions: he who sinks himself in the one becomes necessarily removed from the other."[15] For Guénon, this is ultimately a question of metaphysics, however much apprehension and understanding play a role. But for *our* own understanding of Guénon's attitude toward modern knowledge, modern academia, and its Orientalism, this is an issue of epistemological bifurcation of the first order. We will see later that Guénon complicates this picture by introducing the contributions of science, the doctrine of progress, instrumentalism, and much else into the overall phenomenon of "Western civilization." But taking these aggregate phenomena as being subsumed by the commanding category of materialism and its effects, we begin to understand how "establishment" Orientalism becomes an *epistemology* par excellence, one that misrepresents not because it is merely associated, as Said tells us, with political power and colonialism but because it is embedded in a system that understands and lives in the world in a particular way, one that represents for Guénon, as it did for Marx, Scheler, Heidegger, and many others, a distortion of reality and existence.

Yet materialism is not a performative and constitutive epistemological power that exists in solitude. It always stands in a dialectical relationship with other major spheres, what we have called central domains, and what Guénon describes in nontechnical, layman's language. Science is certainly one of them, and Guénon accords it much importance, since it also constitutes an epistemology that for him bars knowledge from transcending its closed world of the senses, a Western phenomenon that, precisely because of its epistemic limitations, derailed any proper comprehension of "Eastern civilizations." The status accorded to science in the West and the "unbounded admiration and superstitious respect" for it stand in "perfect harmony with the needs of a purely material civilization."[16] But Guénon should not be mistaken for a Luddite:[17] every society needs science, he argued, and all civilizations had their own systems of science. Yet, the modern West (which is always for Guénon a culture and epistemology, not a geographical place) is the only civilization that created a form of science exclusively geared for the promotion of material benefit, accumulation of wealth, instrumentalism, and "bodily comfort," all the while limiting its sphere to "industrial purposes" and "mechanical inventions." Because "it is limited to the sensible world, which it takes for its sole object," Western science is myopic, and represents, in the words of an anonymous Hindu scholar that Guénon approvingly quotes, "ignorant knowledge."[18]

Being a system of "very relative knowledge," and nourished in a specifically materialist environment, Western science tends to exclude more than include, having been "purchased at the expense of forgetting all that [is] truly worthy of interest."[19] What is worthy of interest is the enveloping structure that must frame and control science, giving it its meaning within a larger order of things. There is then a determined continuity between science and the higher forms of knowledge, the former issuing from and directed by the latter. Western science has not just lost this continuity, but also exacerbated the discontinuity to a degree of exclusion; it has, in effect, taken the place of metaphysics and God himself, thereby dethroning religion and sitting in its place. It may be for Guénon that Western science "lacks a principle" or that it is not "attached to any principle of a higher order,"[20] but this in effect amounts to what I earlier called epistemic sovereignty.

Guénon's diagnosis of science as a field of knowledge, ideology, propaganda, and mass worship[21] amounts to a discursive formation that includes, excludes, reorganizes, and makes intelligible a certain reality that creates what he calls a gap between cultures and civilizations. As in the case of materialism, this culture of science is of course an overarching reality, but it is undeniable that the epistemological component in it and its consequences and effects are grave in terms of viewing and dealing with the other. Science comes to dialectically augment materialism in setting in stone a vision of the Other (Guénon's "Eastern civilizations") that is intent on judging it by Western standards, not only because of a sense of "superiority" and "prejudice"—two attitudes that Guénon fully recognizes—but because there are genuine barriers in the very constitution of Western knowledge. And since these barriers are not intentional on the personal level, and are beyond the control and determination of authors and scholars, Western knowledge is largely unconscious of its own "ignorance." It is in this sense as well that the Hindu's description of Western knowledge as ignorant is to be understood; and this is also why Guénon repeatedly uses the metaphor of a child who, upon learning a few things that he fancies to be exceptionally important, purports to teach the adults whom he thinks to be ignorant. This child is the West preaching at the Orient.[22]

I earlier discussed the Is/Ought distinction and the separation between Fact and Value (to which I gave the label "Distinction") as integral to the conditions of felicity that gave Orientalism its performative power. Guénon does not use these terms of description, but his diagnosis is largely the same. Modernity cannot conceive of reality except in empirical terms: things, to be comprehensible, must be measurable, countable, or weighable, since

> It is to these alone that the quantitative point of view is applicable; and the claim to reduce quality to quantity is most characteristic of modern science . . . a fact which in itself shows very clearly how incapable modern Westerners have become of raising themselves above the realm of the senses; there are many who do not know how to distinguish between "conceiving" and "imagining," and some philosophers, such as Kant, go so far as to declare "inconceivable" and "unthinkable" everything that is not capable of representation. . . . The fact is that spiritualism and materialism, in the philosophical sense of these expressions, have no significance apart from one another: they are simply two halves of the Cartesian dualism, whose radical separation has been turned into a kind of antagonism; and since then, the whole of philosophy has oscillated between these two terms without being able to pass beyond them.[23]

Echoing Charles Taylor's and Alasdair MacIntyre's critiques of the Is/Ought distinction,[24] and within a largely similar context, Guénon, with a sting, charges modern Western philosophy with "arbitrary demarcations" and "useless subtleties" that reflect "ceaseless confusions" and "aimless discussions." The arbitrary demarcations are nothing but the free will to fix the "rules of discourse" according to a particular perception of reality, positing, rather than demonstrating, its status as value-free, all against long-standing traditions and worldviews that were eventually subverted into near extinction. The Distinction imposed on moral philosophy was, in one important sense, inevitable because this "philosophy cannot admit the existence of true metaphysics without destroying itself."[25] Of course the denial of metaphysics in the name of science, or of any such entity as can determine the truth of matter, is itself a type of metaphysics, but Guénon choses for it the less-charitable term "superstition." He rejects the very possibility of studying the sensible world as a self-sufficient endeavor. Science and philosophy cannot be judged as justifiable and worthy of respect unless the means have been found of anchoring them, to one degree or another, in "something stable and permanent."[26] Whether the Distinction and the severance of the study of reality from its cosmological anchor are a matter of arbitrariness or sheer free will to decide what is or is not value-free, the fact remains that only a sovereign mind can undertake, with decisive success, such a determination. If Western science, like its twin sister philosophy, can establish, "under the pretext of 'freedom of thought,' the most chimerical beliefs that have been seen at any time,"[27] it is because this freedom of thought is sovereign. That Guénon did not articulate the issue in terms of sovereign will should not mask the fact that he in effect fully understood and appreciated its force.

Propelled by materialism and justified by philosophy, science led Europe to material progress, a doctrine invented during "the second half of the eighteenth century." Having an illusory structure, "progress" is identified not only with "material development that absorbs the entire activity of the West," but also with its twin term "civilization."[28] In the name of civilization, progress is articulated as "moral progress," when in fact it is nothing more than "material progress," the result of "experimenting upon matter for solely practical purposes"; whatever the choice of name or description, this constructed reality cannot "in the least make us modify the judgment . . . that the Western civilization is altogether material."[29]

As there is nearly nothing to this development other than material ambition, the West in all its phenomena has come to exist without principles, progress being likewise characterized as having no purpose or terminus. And a drifting system produces drifting individuals, which explains why the Western individual is fragmented, "inconstant," "directionless," and "unable to find his balance." This precarious state of affairs has been habituated within the illusion of progress, "as if it were enough simply to walk, quite regardless of direction, to be sure of advancing. As for the goal of his advance, he [the individual] does not even dream of asking himself what it is."[30] Guénon explains the thorough conditioning of the individual into seeing this state of affairs as normal in terms of Aristotle's concept of second nature as habit, a social technology of creating a subject within what Bourdieu came to call much later a habitus.

III

Since sacred progress has no terminus, the individual has also been thoroughly conditioned into constant striving, being never content with the present. Progress is an endless, perpetual yearning for the ultimately *unknowable*. For Guénon, as we just saw, this mode of existence is planted in acquired habits that shape individual and social action, what Scheler more trenchantly described as an "innate drive," although for Scheler it is specifically a drive that culminates in an unceasing struggle for knowledge geared toward the penchant for domination.[31] For Guénon, however, the ceaseless "effort" of the Western individual has become a habitus that is to be problematized in relation to what Isaiah Berlin at a later stage termed "positive liberty," a concept in which freedom is attained by liberating the self—through what one might call a Maussian training, an inner cultivation of one ethical form or another—from need, especially for the materiality of the world. Instructive for our purposes, and an understanding that goes to diagnosing Western and Orientalist attitudes to the Orient, Guénon instructively contrasts the "Easterners" with the "Westerners" on this crucial phenomenon, saying that the former do not need the results of the always materialistic Western progress, because "he who has reached a state of equilibrium no longer feels this need, just as he who has found no longer seeks."[32] I say "instructively," because Guénon, in an effectively casual manner, goes to the heart of two important points.

First, Berlin's passing over the concept of positive liberty—in his famous essay[33]—with near silence is indicative of the general dismissal of it in Western thought, a concept that otherwise bears much significance for other forms of the individual's psychosocial development, and for social and political organization. Of course Berlin's virtual dismissal of positive liberty was directly linked to deeply seated fears of Soviet Communism, which he did not attempt to hide. By contrast, Guénon's frame of reference was the ancient and long-standing "traditional civilizations," those systems of acculturation that cultivate ethics and moral technologies of the self precisely for the attainment of this "positive" freedom. The quality and type of ethical formation may be different in the case of Soviet Communism from its "Eastern" counterpart, but the idea of cultivating the self as freedom is one and the same, however much Communist thinking remained constrained by concepts of materialism. This is not a negative freedom that curbs external interference and control while conditioning the subject into a materialist view of the world, one that is intended to enhance the subject's freedom not only to need, but, more importantly, to convert wants and material cravings into needs.

Berlin's setting aside of positive liberty in favor of its negative counterpart reflects not only a clear bias in favor of capitalism and a particular mode of political rule and governance, but, more importantly for us, an avoidance of, repugnance toward, and virtual hostility for positive liberty. This is so because capitalism, integral to Guénon's critique of materialism, cannot survive positive liberty, yet it cannot live without its negative counterpart. Setting up the latter as the benchmark, desideratum, and ideal is not just a political or economic way of seeing the world; rather, it is constitutive of a worldview, a general attitude, a culture—all of which went into making the mainstream Orientalist, whether he knew it or not. Guénon was in effect saying this in detail, though in a different idiom, and not without a measure of hyperbole. Yet, his critique remains both daring and cuttingly penetrating. Being a central domain, capitalism and its enveloping matrix, materialism, create a particular subject, with a particular value system, and a definite way of seeing the world and valuating, but not necessarily valuing, all its perceptible components.

Second, Guénon diagnosed what amounts to the effects of habitus to explain the "unintentional" prejudices of Westerners in general and Orientalists in particular toward the subjects they have come, directly or indirectly, to rule. Here progress, as a justificatory and legitimizing materialistic doctrine, is tied directly to the lazy, passive, and even supine "Oriental" whose invention by Orientalism Said rightly condemned. Yet, importantly, Said does not recognize, much less hint at, any element of this inner/outer formation of the subject, a formation without which no sociology of knowledge can ever be possible, or any credible evaluation of what *constitutes* the Orientalists as socioepistemically conditioned beings. Said's secular humanism and liberalism, two qualities that presuppose in every important way an Enlightenment conception of materialism, could not allow for any variety of positive liberty or for any form of ethical formation of the self.

A Berlinian by any indication, Said would have militated against himself, against his own education, and thus against the very ideas and values he cherished and on which he based his critique of Orientalism, had he ventured into critiquing even the outer edge of negative liberty. The difference between Said and Guénon, as "authors," is therefore not merely formal, nor is it a matter of preference or approach. It is one that determined their location within the central domain and its discursive formation. In due course, we will see that the difference is pregnant with further profound implications for a proper understanding of Orientalism, and *why* the Saidian narrative was both inadequate and politicized, all at once.

Just as the theology of progress was, on the one hand, developed within a system governed by materialism, driven by science, and legitimized by philosophy and more generally the academic profession in its entirety, on the other hand, materialism, science, and philosophy were structured within a narrative of progress. A penetrating understanding of the dialectic within the system and among its central paradigms is unmistakable in Guénon, however cloudy his manner of expression may be. Yet, much else was also captured, including the role that modern forms of history and historiography played in this systemic picture. Being essential to, if not a defining practice of, Orientalism, modern historical writing reflects, both accurately and poignantly, the inner dynamics of the systemic dialectic I have been expounding in Guénon. History is not so much an account of how people in the past lived; it is the mirror in which the image of the historian herself appears. Guénon, I think, generally and intuitively, understood this much, and as such he condemned modern history not only for its conclusions about the "Easterners," but because it issued from the inner dynamics of this dialectic. Having lived during the last part of Europe's nineteenth century, Guénon might well have said that modern history has the same genetic makeup as the tradition of science-philosophy-materialism-progress-technicalism from whose mentality it was inevitably bound to hail. As a "singular object," and "standing for all others of the same class," history, like all paradigmatic instances, "defines the intelligibility of the group of which it is a part, and which, at the same time, it constitutes."[34]

This history exhibited its doctrinal substrate in Comte's Law of Three Stages, where, like Bacon and Pascal, Comte "compared the ancients to children, and others, more recently, have thought to improve on this by likening them to savages, whom they call 'primitives.' "[35] The assignment of the ancients to the childhood stage of development is obviously the function of the illusion generated by the doctrine of progress and of the elision of materialist advance into intellectual progress.[36] Of course it did not escape Guénon that modern forms of history are not only a matter of scholarship subjected to the ideological influence of science, materialism, and the doctrine of progress. History, a product of institutions sponsored by the nation-state, was thus required to fulfill certain functions, chief among them the propping of nationalism and nationalistic paraphernalia. This is why, Guénon insists, "certain methods" in the study of history "are officially imposed to the exclusion of all others," just as, we have seen, *modern* philosophical narratives perform the same operations in ousting other, contending points of view. History is specifically designed in a manner that makes it impossible "to see certain things clearly, and that is how 'public opinion' is formed." The possibility of opening up the gates of historical investigation to what Guénon calls "ordinary history" is out of the question, because this "might endanger certain political interests."[37]

History thus rides on the back of the Comtean concepts of civilization and progress, yet it is through it—in what we might call now performative discourse—that these concepts acquire their "illusory" meaning. History, in other words, gives force to the imaginaries of "civilization" and "progress" and makes them "suitable for imposing on a mob," at least in moments of "collective hallucination,"[38] what the historian Dirk Moses aptly described as a "genocidal moment." Needless to say, this understanding anticipates Hannah Arendt's critical philosophical and political elaborations on Nazi atrocities, as well as her more sophisticated analysis of the political concepts of "masses" and "mob";[39] but for Guénon history is already seen as informing politics as much as it is informed by it. And politics played a crucial part, through Orientalism and colonialism, in determining the fate of his "Eastern Civilizations." The implications of this line of critique will become clearer in the next chapter.

It might not be trite here to dwell on a striking instance in which European history justified colonialism through Orientalism, an instance in which Guénon offers perhaps the most penetrating analysis, which was not to be matched until six decades after he wrote. Summing up a doctrine that dominated Orientalist discourse since the third quarter of the nineteenth century, and placing it not only within the Islamic tradition but also within the larger context of attitudes toward the entirety of the major cultures of Asia, Guénon observes that among "the many things that Westerners often blame the Eastern civilizations for [is] their fixity," what the Orientalists of the first half of the twentieth century have described, among other things, as "ossification," "rigidity," "encylose," lack of adaptability, and the like. As we saw earlier, the Shari'a (governing much of the Muslim world from North Africa to the Malayas) was a particular target of attack, and all these adjectives were applied to it with prejudice, since "reforming" it, through the method of "demolish-and-replace," would have first needed the justification. But this strategy was also equally applied to Hindu and other Islamic institutions. Fixity, Guénon continued, amounted for the Westerners "to a denial of progress," but to see in this denial a fault "one must believe in progress." For Guénon fixity is no indication of the rigidity ascribed to the Orient's institutions or systems of thought; what is "immutable" in these civilizations are the "principles upon which [these civilizations] are based," since the constancy of such first-order principles "is one of the essential aspects of the idea of tradition."[40]

Since the debate over rigidity and ossification within Orientalism was crucial in rewriting the history of Islam and its "law," not to mention that of Hinduism and others, and since this discursive act of rewriting charted the course of hegemony over, and colonialization of, most regions of the world, it is worth quoting Guénon's definition of tradition, a concept that was to become foundational for many writers and thinkers who followed in his steps:

> What we call a traditional civilization is one that is based on principles in the true sense of the word, that is, one where the intellectual realm dominates all the others, and where all these, science and social institutions alike, proceed from it directly or indirectly, being no more than contingent, secondary, and subordinate applications of purely intellectual truths. *Thus a return to tradition and return to principles are in reality one and the same thing.* . . . When we speak absolutely of principles, without any specification, or of purely intellectual truths, it is always the universal order, and no other, that is in question.[41]

The conception of "intellectuality" is not to be confused, Guénon cautions, with reason and rationality, for these are merely the means through which, if harnessed correctly, one arrives at intellectual truths. These truths represent our understanding of the cosmos and its order, an idea reminiscent of Scheler's philosophical position on the matter. Scheler argued that it is in the essence of the cosmos to exhibit an underlying ethical order, one that is the work of a transcendental deity; and it is because of the very existence of this moral character that humanity is bound by it as a doting code, an *ordo amoris*.[42] It is precisely because this Schelerian code, or the Guénonian "principle," is lacking in Western civilization that it is "eminently unstable," eminently without fixity. Note the directionality of difference we have spoken of earlier in the context of Said's concept of the same. The standard here is never Western civilization, for, after all, it is the one civilization that forms the exception, the one that "strayed" from the pattern that was constituted by all other civilizations, through what the world historian Marshall Hodgson has aptly called the "Great Western Transmutation."[43] Fixity, so Guénon argues, is an *essential*, not contingent, requirement for living in the world as an ethical order, as one that does not separate the material from the moral, or matter from value. This ethical order is then an intellectual realm at one and the same time, dictating the rules of play all the way down to the most mundane of matters. Yet

> one should not imagine that the stability we speak of goes to the length of excluding all change; what it does is to reduce the change to being never more than an adaptation to circumstances, by which the principles are not in the least affected, and which may on the contrary be strictly deduced from them, if they are resorted to, not for themselves, but in view of a definite application; and that is the point of all the "traditional sciences." . . . These sciences cover the range of all that may happen to proceed from the principles, including social institutions. It would be wrong to confuse immutability with immobility; such understandings are common among Westerners because . . . their minds are inextricably bound up with representations dictated by the senses. . . . The immutable is not what is contrary to change, but what is above it.[44]

Guénon's understanding of Islam and its Shariʻa (as integral to his "East") in terms of fixity, immutability, and change is governing, and has an unmatched potency. Legal Orientalism dismissed even the very grounds on which such an understanding could be reached, and it took until the end of the twentieth century for scholars critical of this tradition to rehabilitate, against the Orientalist narrative, the concept of change in the Shari'a.[45] As it turned out, this revisionist scholarship, mindful of Orientalism as a colonialist discourse aiming at justifying, if not charting, the reengineering of Islam through its Shari'a, reached the same understanding that Guénon had offered, an understanding that came without the complex details that writing legal history demands.

Yet Guénon shrewdly ties the concept of change in "social institutions"— by which he means all institutions that pertain to society, whether legal, economic, or strictly social—to first-order principles, making the metaphysical stand in dialogue with the mundane, temporal, and worldly. (A concrete example of how first-order ethical and moral precepts maintain a continuum with worldly affairs, especially—in light of the phenomena of Western materialism and capitalism being discussed here—matters of finance and economics, is that of the cap that was placed on the rise of the corporation, an example we discussed in chapter 2, section 3). The inability of Westerners to see the unity of the world as a moral order (bringing us back to the Distinction as being a condition of felicity) and hence seeing Eastern civilizations as fixed and rigid are the source of a "very real opposition . . . between the East and the West, at least as things are at present." This "divergence is one sided," it "being like that of a branch which grows away from the trunk," a divergence that made "Western civilization" go "astray" from the rest of the world, but not without devastating consequences.[46]

IV

We are now in a position to streamline Guénon's proffered causes for the divergence of Western civilization and how Orientalism fits in this picture. It is obvious that a central role is played by materialism, a concept that is intended to encompass particular attitudes to the world as matter (that is, the Distinction), capitalism as a system of exchange and material greed (whether personal or collective), and love for material things and wealth, all of which form the subject of what he might have called "negative liberty." Being inherent in this materialist system, science and philosophy contribute to a discursive stripping of value from matter, and then they are turned around to study the world as such. Progress comes to clothe all these practices with a doctrine that converts vice into virtue;

and history is the application of this doctrine to the study of how people lived in the past, especially the different "Easterners." Materialism is thus at the root of the European transformation that made it into an anomaly. Yet, it seems that for Guénon even materialism is itself an effect of a higher cause, rather than a final cause. Materialism seems thus intelligible only within a framework in which the loss of principles is fully appreciated. But the loss of principles is in turn a function of yet another act. "The modern world has precisely reversed the natural relations between the different order of things," a reversal that resulted in the "depreciation of the intellectual order" and "exaggeration of the materialist and sentimentalist order,"[47] this latter meaning all the dogma, doctrine, "moralism," and ideological paraphernalia that came to justify and legitimize this reversal, elevating "depreciation" into appreciation. The West, in other words, has lost "a principle of a higher order," which stands as the ultimate cause for its "divergence," for its arrogance (expressed in "racism," "prejudice," and a sense of "superiority" over others), and, most importantly, for its "barbarity."[48]

It cannot be overemphasized that Guénon sees all this as a systemic phenomenon, one in which a colossal dialectic is at work, producing—out of the massive interactions of economy, science, philosophy, progress, nationalism, and much else—a civilization that is not aware of itself. Hence the distinctions he often makes between the individual author's intentions and the use into which his work is put within this system, although he is fully aware that certain authors' intentions are consistent with their malevolent teachings.[49] In the majority of individual cases, and as a collectivity, the problem is one of "utter failure to understand," or perhaps of "blindness," pure and simple. Yet, blindness for Guénon is a purely epistemological matter, not a rhetorical condemnation. "Westerners" are "like blind men who deny, if not the light itself, at least the existence of sight, for the sole reason that they are without it. To declare that there is not only an unknown but also an 'unknowable' (to use Spenser's word), and to turn an intellectual infirmity into a barrier which no one may pass—that is something whose like was never seen or heard before."[50] This "blindness" to the self first, and consequently to the Other, is not Guénon's diagnosis alone, for the same metaphor or its exact equivalent was to play an important part in the analysis of Horkheimer and Adorno (in their *Dialectic*), as well as of the Argentinian philosopher Enrique Dussel, all of whom wrote after Guénon. It is instructive that Dussel characterized the blindness of Europe (and, later, of modernity in general) to its mythic quality as one that continues to carry on irrational processes concealed even to itself.[51]

This epistemological blindness, being the result of "reversing the order of things" and then believing it to the exclusion of every other possibility of knowing the world, is what makes the West a barbarity. And barbarity is just another name for colonialism and the wars that Europe wrought upon itself within its own borders. However, typical of Guénon's attitude that what the West does to itself is its own business, he is never concerned with what goes on within Europe (= the "West"). The bulk of his critique is geared toward how the West sees and deals with the East, the "dealing" being only the practical result of the more important "seeing." Seeing, or rather not seeing, is the issue. Hence his repeated reference to ignorance, whether as a direct charge, or as a charge placed in the mouth of a Hindu or some other Eastern pundit. It is sheer ignorance then that makes Westerners hostile to Eastern civilizations and its principles, because they are all the more afraid of them the less they understand them, "being themselves without [these principles]." "Lack of principles," then, characterizes Western civilization "in every domain," and this lack, being unique to the West, makes it an abnormality, an anomaly of an unusual type.[52]

Western epistemological blindness produced the "most terrible offence," "proselytizing fury," a unique feature among all civilizations.[53] The "spirit of conquest," embedded within the inner existence of Westerners, "goes under the guise of 'moralist' pretexts, and it is in the name of 'liberty' that they would force the whole world to imitate them!"[54] They "force everyone to interest themselves exclusively in what interests them, to put economic concerns above all, or to adopt the political regime which they happen to prefer. . . . And the most extraordinary thing is that they have similar pretensions not only with regard to the peoples that they have conquered, but also with regard to those among them,"[55] referring perhaps to the Irish, the Basques, or other oppressed groups within Europe. "Proselytizing fury" thus stands at the heart of the matter. Conquest of other peoples is recognized by Guénon as unpreventable,[56] and so, in and by itself, this is not the real problem. Rather, it is the imposition of Western knowledge and Western views of the world on others, under the pretense of acting in the interest of "civilization," that makes the difference between ordinary historical conquests and their Western counterparts. The difference amounts to "abuse," one whose "chief object . . . is to exploit the country, and . . . its inhabitants."[57] This in effect is compounding the economic abuse of the colonized by an attitudinal sense of superiority that invariably involves treating even "civilized peoples" like "savages." Not just the colonists and state officials but also "Europeans almost without exception"[58] "went out to seek the Easterners, not to learn from them, as behooves youth in the presence of old men, but to strive, by brutal or insidious means, to convert them to their own way of thinking"[59] through exporting schools and a Western system of education and through "assimilation."[60]

The civilizational configuration that produced this "abnormality" is systemic and colossal, yet Orientalism does play a part in it, although the overall thrust of his writings—and this is crucial for our own argument—gives the distinct impression that Orientalism occupies a position secondary to materialism, science, philosophy, and the doctrine of progress. This position contrasts sharply with Said's, where Orientalism, aside from its collusion with power and colonialism, is treated as a discrete category, largely unrelated to the wider intellectual and materialist environment that produced Orientalism in the first place. Said's references to "culture" as a participant in this collusion remain empty of meaning and substance. There is nothing in *Orientalism* in the way of critiquing modern science, technology, capitalism, materialism, liberalism, the doctrine of progress, philosophy, and the like.[61] Nor is there any reference whatsoever to the embeddedness of all of these in a particular structure of thought, one that can be grounded in the Enlightenment. "Culture" remains a vacuous concept, and if not vacuous, then a political category at best. For Guénon, it was a systemic phenomenon of the first order. And it was within this phenomenon that the Orientalists were *positioned*.

Yet, despite the deeply structural understanding that Guénon attained (with the implication that a powerful discursive formation is at play), he was not so categorical or totalizing about the Orientalists. He acknowledged the existence of "certain individual exceptions" among Orientalists, but on the whole, these exceptions do not avert, much less subvert, the dominant and dominating tendencies. His position thus allows for exceptions that nonetheless do not amount to an effect that can alter or modify in any remarkable way what we now call a discursive formation or a central domain. In "most cases," he argues in line with this understanding, it is even better not to read the Orientalists' works, because "their chief effect" has been to "mislead the Westerners."[62] What makes this matter of grave concern is that the Orientalists are the only source of knowledge about "Eastern civilizations," leaving the Westerners with no other means to inform themselves correctly about these civilizations. As Guénon has in mind a proposed outline aimed at reforming Western civilization, the misrepresentations of "official" Orientalism pose to him a serious problem since this expert knowledge of the Orient would have otherwise mediated common grounds for understanding. But instead of attempting to create a kind of knowledge that leads to rapprochement between East and West, "Orientalism is widening the gulf" between them, for Orientalist discourse produces one of two effects, and neither is reassuring in the least. The reader of Orientalist works either develops a distaste for the East that "strengthen[s] his Western prejudice" or finds them "so absurd or so devoid of sense" that he will lose all interest.[63]

A strong theme in Guénon, misrepresentation has its sources in more than one place. The very methods of the Orientalists, which are general to academia, are problematic, pointing the finger specifically at historical criticism. The choice of material suffers as well, since the general approach is to confine research "to historical or philological works," and to call the amassing of detail scholarship. It is writing a lot about very little. Worse of all, however, is the Orientalists' pretension to understand Eastern traditions better than the Easterners themselves, having made "the most incredible travesty of them." Of course there is no question in the Orientalist's mind of "accepting the opinion" of learned Easterners as sources for his writings; "instead they act as if called upon to reconstruct vanished civilizations" out of a trenchant and entrenched "belief in their superiority."[64] But not all Orientalist misrepresentations are negative. *Some* Orientalists, out of "sympathy for Eastern conceptions," endeavor "at all costs" to make these conceptions "fit into the frames of Western thought," with equally harmful results, "disfiguring them altogether" and demonstrating yet again how little they understand these civilizations and their repertoire of thought.[65] In this case, it is not just a matter of not being able to "see," a case of epistemic blindness generated by the overwhelming power of the cultural formations that the West has produced, and that have swept the "official" bulk of Orientalism, but rather one of "exactly seeing what is not there." Among the national groupings of Orientalists, the German received the critical wrath of Guénon, who charges that no one "has ever pushed these *assimilations* further than they," partly, it seems, because they have come to "monopolize almost entirely the interpretation of Eastern doctrine."[66] A striking case in point is Schopenhauer, who, with his student

Karl Robert Eduard von Hartmann, managed to misrepresent Asian doctrines, making pessimism the basis of Hindu thought.

There are two profound points raised by this category of Orientalists, qualified by the quantifier "some." First, the charge of "assimilation" in Guénon is pregnant with meaning, for he invariably employs the term in the context of the French Orientalists' writings on Algeria and its "native" inhabitants, as well as of the French colonialist and home-government policies in absorbing the country into France.[67] Although not involved in a formal colonialist setting, and no colony in particular is on their mind, the German Orientalists' "scholarly" act nonetheless possesses the same structural features, the same frame of mind, and the same epistemological underpinnings.[68] In other words, colonialism or not, ill intentioned or well wishing, the discursive power of the West, philosophical, political, or otherwise, cannot but produce the same effects of distortion and misrepresentation. The association of German scholarship with French colonialist scholarship and policies begins to bestow a dialectical dynamic on the idea of "fitting the West in the East" (as Guénon may have put it), and one that does not stop at the mere production of misrepresentation, a unidirectional trajectory. "Fitting" is not merely misrepresentation that discolors the Western mind; it is a project of assimilation that requires and presupposes the remaking of the "Eastern" subject. Guénon does not express the matter in quite these terms, but he inches very closely to this conception. That there is further depth to assimilation in European soil, which Guénon did not see, is a matter that will concern us in the next chapter. That he did not see this depth is a function of historical location, having (when he wrote on the subject) not yet seen the atrocities of Nazism, World War II, and the rest of what has been called the genocidal century.

Second, although Guénon subsumes the weighty German Orientalism under the quantifier "some," he still deems this type of "sympathetic" Orientalist as a minority that fails to match in size or importance "official Orientalism," which I take to be establishment Orientalism. This is all the more impressive, since this "sympathetic" tendency, having started in Europe in the nineteenth century, was to become much more than mere tendency, one that conscripted a wider range of Orientalism and a vast number of "Easterners" themselves. Guénon did not live long enough to see the Easterners at work,[69] but Said did. Nonetheless, this category of assimilationist Orientalists, Western or not, does not appear to constitute one of Said's concerns. What disturbed Said was negative depictions and stereotyping, on the one hand, and "exoticizing," on the other. The latter, as we have seen and will continue to see, is a highly problematic category, for no other reason than this: Had Said discussed Guénon, he would have, almost certainly, concluded that Guénon belonged to the second category, an "exoticizer." Be that as it may, the absence (or at best near-absence) of this category from Said is pregnant with significance, going beyond a mere understatement of a problem and speaking loudly of a clear case of misdiagnosis.

However terse, Guénon's diagnosis remains more penetrating than Said's. It is likely that even if Said had attended to German Orientalism, he would still not have transcended the limits he set in *Orientalism*. Guénon, on the other hand, exhibited a great deal of prescience, having detected the complicity of German Orientalism in the workings of political power that was to introduce the horrors of Nazism. He patently ties the "hypothesis of 'Indo-Germanism' " to politics, averring that it "scarcely exists but for political reasons: the German orientalism, like their philosophy, has become an instrument in the service of their national ambition." What is more striking is his intuitive understanding, anticipating Arendt's analysis of the Holocaust through Eichmann, that this complicity is neither aware of itself nor, therefore, malicious in intention, for "it does not mean that the [hypothesis's] representatives are necessarily dishonest."[70] What strengthens Guénon's intuitive but shrewd diagnosis is that the German case is not exceptional in the least. Even "official" Orientalists, who partake in both misrepresentation and colonialism, and whose work sits on "political undercurrents," have "in their favor . . . an honesty that is generally indisputable," although this does not change the fact of their "daydreams" and "gross errors, made still worse by methods of the lowest charlatanism."[71]

Guénon does not take the complexity of this *seeming* internal contradiction—what Arendt called the "banality of evil"—to its logical conclusion, stopping descriptively at the political level; nor does Said reach Guénon's limited understanding even of the complicity of "banal" Orientalism in mere "political undercurrents." Nor, still, does he come close to the pattern of thought set by Guénon, which makes it abundantly clear that the function of Orientalism in "Western civilization" is eminently dialectical, a dialectic that rests within the deep structures of the Enlightenment and of Europe as a modern project, in all that its materialism, science, philosophy of the world, and much else of the same implied. Orientalism, on the one hand, feeds on the "culture without *the* principles," in all of what we might call today discursive formations that are played out by the forces just enumerated, augmented by a pernicious theology of progress, and, on the other hand, feeds back into this civilization a bundle of errors and mis-representations, all done with a striking banality.[72]

This dialectic is missing in Said's analysis, even when Orientalism is correctly associated with power formations of the colonialist, political, and economic type. The narrative is unidirectional, mostly traveling from colonialism to the Orientalists who misrepresent. And if there is an element of reciprocity, it remains as vague as his diagnosis of the "cultural forces" in which Orientalism operated. We are given no account of the place of Orientalism in modernity at large, in academia, in liberalism, in capitalism, in the on-the-ground colonialist practices, in engineering the colonized subject, in the juridico-political concept and practices of sovereignty, in genocides, and in much else.[73] Nor is there an account of the wherefore of Orientalism. Like liberalism, capitalism, secular humanism, anthropology, science, economics, and law, Orientalism is a taken-for-granted phenomenon. It just went wrong, somewhere, somehow. That Said did not go into the conditions of felicity, the necessary conditions for expounding the dialectic that Guénon in effect undertook to expose sixty years before him, is not a mere oversight. It speaks of the limits that a critique imposes upon itself when it does not develop itself, from beginning to end, outside its object. Which is to say that when critiquing a domain, especially a central domain, the critic must consciously stand outside the paradigmatic structures defining that domain. To critique a phenomenon of which the critic is an integral and integrated part is nothing short of collusion; it is as if two branches of power cease to maintain their check on each other, producing a tyranny. The critic's collusion produces an epistemic tyranny.

V

Guénon's analytical project then not only exceeds that of Said in its diagnostic force of Orientalist and Western scholarship and its genealogy, but also offers possible solutions for the future that only match the depth of his diagnostics. If I am interested in briefly dwelling on these proposed reforms, it is not for their actual value for my overall argument as such, although, I think, we would do poorly to dismiss them out of hand. Their value instead lies in further explicating and pinning to the ground the deep structures of Orientalism and its intimate and dialectical ties to modernity as a new phenomenon in human history. Because Said navigated mainly at the conventional political level, and shirking—unknowingly to be sure—the engagement of the full weight of "undercurrents" in Europe that gave rise to the unique phenomenon called Orientalism, he had nothing to offer in the way of a solution other than comforting words aimed perhaps at engendering a glimmer of hope, but little else.

At the end of *Orientalism*'s introduction, and summing up what he saw as a possibility for the future, he writes: "Perhaps the *most important task of all* would be to undertake studies in contemporary alternatives to Orientalism, to ask how one can study other cultures and peoples from a libertarian, or nonrepressive and nonmanipulative, perspective. But then one would have to rethink the whole complex problem of knowledge and power" (24, emphasis mine).[74] Considering that such a task is "most important of all," it is striking that Said would, first, not say anything else about it throughout the book (nor, to my knowledge, in any other writing of his),[75] not even an allusion or intimation (although he does acknowledge that this task is "left embarrassingly incomplete in this study" [24]). Second, Said would see this all-important task as defined in terms of knowledge and power, however "complex" it may be. Said's complexity here is horizontal, not vertical, not because it was limited to the superstructures of political, colonialist, and economic discourse (which are indispensable to any analysis), but because these superstructures are not, as he himself said of Orientalist discourse, "merely decorative" (25). And third, Said would see Orientalism—and this is of central importance to my later argument—as a sort of an anomaly within European-Western academia, especially in the interwar period and thereafter (305).[76] The anomaly, it should be added, was for Said *within academia*, not within *modern* Euro-America and modernity at large.

Of course one wonders if Said understood the "complex problem of knowledge and power" as being limited to certain phenomena, Orientalism included, because for him to generalize the problem, as it should be systematically generalized, he would have been forced to eliminate the ascription of anomaly to Orientalism alone; the anomaly would then cease to be an anomaly, and would instead be a general characteristic of Western modernity, the (original) producer of Orientalism, liberalism, materialism, and secularism. Traveling this distance was not on Said's mind, however. In the very few times in which he spoke of "the crises of modernity," there is nothing beyond a mere intimation that the crises may be found in anything beyond the political sphere. The crises, perceived or real, are "caused in part by the diminishment of Western suzerainty over the rest of the world" (248, 257). First, it is not obvious that such a diminishment did occur, especially when the United States and its NATO allies renewed their hegemony with a new configuration after the Second World War, and when neocolonialism replaced the old with reinforced and indeed more hegemonic and vicious political and economic domination. In this respect, no serious scholar can argue that such a "diminishment" occurred.

Second, it is at least curious that the other "part" or "parts" of the crises should remain shrouded in utter silence when Said's topic of discussion is the perfect invitation to exploring the real crises in terms of modern state abuses, widespread social injustice, disintegration of the social structures, and a deplorable ecological degradation and environmental destruction, about which even Guénon, writing half a century before him, remarked.[77] If one part of the causes was in effect nonexistent and the other the locus of utter silence, then we must conclude that for Said the crisis was at best political in nature, having to do with the fall of empires (British, French, Dutch), who were probably alone in thinking of their decline as a crisis. This interpretation of Said is consistent with all his other views about problems in modernity, including that which mattered most to him—the question of Palestine. All of them for him were political, essentially related to empire and its malevolent power. That these were sourced in the deep epistemic structures of the modernity that gave him his own secular humanism and liberal values is a question that he seems to have never entertained. Guénon the Orientalist, on the other hand, having dug deep into the overall phenomenon of modernity, was able not only to offer a formidable critique of it but also to formulate solutions that are just as profound as the powers that made the "anomaly" of modernity possible.

Said's fleeting statement about alternatives to Orientalism I have just quoted finds a deeper and more far-reaching parallel in Guénon's declaration that "nothing would be more desirable, in our opinion, than the reconstitution of a truly Western civilization on normal foundations," which would still be as unique as any other civilization.[78] Taking the uniqueness and "diversity of civilizations" for granted, as Guénon does, in no way means that difference in forms excludes "agreement on the principles." Perhaps against liberal intellectuals and the Orientalist "sympathizers," he insists that "concord and harmony do not mean uniformity, and to think that they do would be to defer to those theories of utopian equality which are one of the things we denounce." Inasmuch as a civilization is expected to, and should, be unique, it should be "normal," which means that "it will always be able to develop itself without being a danger to other civilizations."[79]

Surely, Guénon does not use the word "danger" in its common sense, for most, if not all, civilizations in world history, at one point of time or another in their lifetime, did effectively constitute a danger that threatened other civilizations. The larger context of his writings bestows on "danger" another meaning, one that is intensive and that transcends occupation, sacking, and then ruling, even with an iron fist. "Danger" here encompasses what he terms "assimilation," an act of obliterating not the human element, but that element as a meaningful creature situated in what Scheler called an ethical order of the world. For he repeatedly explains that a "normal" civilization will always "abstain from proselytizing." And "proselytizing," as we have seen, is nothing but a secularized term bearing the same, though somewhat more general, meaning as "assimilation," however religious its lexical connotation may be. Proselytizing is "barbarity" because it *inescapably* leads to it. The *inescapability* is absolute, for the relationship is one of strict logical entailment.

"In short, the Western outlook must be completely reformed."[80] Note here that the target of attack is not Orientalism, colonialism, materialism, politics, philosophy, or science, or any "institution" that the "West" has produced. For Guénon, all these are expressions of a much deeper problem: an "outlook." With this single word, he is in effect insisting, as I have been trying to show throughout, that the problem lies in an "attitude," also Scheler's term to express what he saw as the fundamental problem of "Western man," this man being the prototype of the West as a cultural constellation. The outlook must be made to vanish, and nothing less; and to accomplish this goal, the central domains of Western modernity must be abolished, changed, or transformed. As I will argue momentarily, it is in this aspect that Guénon qualitatively differentiates his project from that of the exoticizers, the aesthetic worshipers of the Orient, as Karatani called them.

The implications of Guénon's insistence are clear: expressions of a problem are just that, expressions, and can be no more than predicates of a subject. If any meaningful or effective reform is to be undertaken, the first step is to begin with the root problem, the "outlook," the "attitude." In all cases, however, the subject, and with it the entire subset of predicates, must be "completely reformed." The ultimate responsibility thus rests with the West, with all the change that may be required, be it structural or substantially systemic. The East may adopt some aspects of Europe's "industrial development" as long as its traditions are not affected, as long as this material development remains subservient to the principles they have enshrined.

Guénon could have as well been speaking, and quite accurately, of such concrete matters of finance and economics as we have seen in the *waqf/* corporation conception and practice in premodern Islam,[81] as well as of numerous other institutions. But his point, I think, was that there is an inverse differential in reform between the East and the West, namely, that the more the West needs to reform, the less the East needs to match it. This understanding applies to the argument of an interlocutor, who seems naively to argue that in order for the East to avert the "danger" and belligerence of the West, the East must establish only a "purely economic relationship with the West." This Guénon finds objectionable, if not an illusion. There cannot be such an uneven relationship without first reaching an "agreement in the domain of the principles," for once such an agreement is achieved "all secondary difficulties will be smoothed away automatically, or else no real agreement of any sort will ever be reached." It is certainly not a coincidence that Guénon's proposition of "agreement on principles" as preemptive of conflict is identical to the liberal adage that democracies never go to war with one another, the assumption being that a true liberal existence, which presupposes the upholding of liberal principles, generates symbiosis, if not harmonious coexistence, between them. But Guénon insists on excluding from any "agreement" precisely the liberal "worldview" along with the entire set of principles that this worldview produced. Materialism, wealth, and economics are always a source of conflict and discord, unless regulated by "the principles."[82] Accordingly, since the "cause of the most dangerous understandings" lies in the West, Westerners must "rid themselves" of it through reforming their civilization and by taking "the first steps toward an effective renewal of intellectual relations." If carried out properly, or "deeply effected," this reform is the only guarantee "to prevent a return to barbarism."[83] This is not all: such a reform should not preclude the possibility of the West "taking advantage of [the East] for supplying itself with what it may still lack," for "lessons or inspirations may be taken from others without giving up one's independence."[84]

Guénon's proposed outline of reform is no doubt daring and ambitious, and its discursive extent spans a substantial part of his *East and West* as well as other writings of his. Its boldness, which rests on an equally bold diagnosis of modernity's "barbarism," earned him excommunication from certain academic quarters in the truest secular sense of the term. That he converted to a Sufi *tariqa* (the Hamidiyya Shadhiliyya order) did not help his case either, given French and European virulent racism and Islamophobia. Nor did his direct, unconventional, and heavily hyperbolic style mitigate any of these prejudices either. Reading Guénon is like dealing with a diamond in the rough. Yet, to knowingly dismiss the substance of his thought is to assign oneself to the status of Foucault's "dead author." The author's death, however, is not as innocuous as common death. If anything, authorial death is deadly. In one rather strong sense, the next chapter represents a sustained argument to demonstrate the truth of this proposition.

Thus, this very stance toward Guénon and his likes is inextricably linked to the act of self-positioning within a system of power, entailing the often unconscious epistemological placing of oneself in a particular position within a discursive formation. But reversed, this self-positioning is rendered the object rather than the subject. It becomes an act of self-death, as Foucault has judiciously argued. The implications of an assessment of Guénon thus invoke our earlier discussion of the meaning of the author, which now compels a question: Where do Guénon and Said himself fit in?

VI

Before I proceed to answer this question, I wish to dispose of the argument that Guénon may be no different than any other Orientalist sympathizer, that he was what Kojin Karatani called an "aesthetic worshiper" of the "inferior other." In a penetrating article, Karatani argued that the Orientalist treatment of the non-West as the inferior Other went "hand in hand with an aesthetic worship" of that very Other, producing "an uneradicable self-deceit: Those with an Orientalist attitude come to believe that they, unlike others, treat non-Westerners more than equally—they treat them with 'respect.'"[85] Looking down upon the Other as an object of scientific analysis and looking up to the same Other as an aesthetic idol are not a contradictory attitude but in fact an interdependent and mutually corroborating activity. Nor is the attitude necessarily traditional but rather "rooted in modern science and aesthetics, which together produce the ambivalent worship." Drawing on Kantian aesthetics, in which the human relationship to objects in the world is divided into the realms of cognition, ethics, and taste, Karatani argues, following Kant, that these three domains always operate all at once, despite the contradictions they engender, but in the process certain domains must be bracketed so that the remaining domain becomes the center of appreciation. A certain object can be pleasant even if it is evil, and true even if unpleasant. A urinal in an art gallery that is displayed along with the comment "This is an artwork in an exhibition" demands of the audience to bracket the object's daily use and instead see it as a work of art.

Thus essential to the aesthete is the constant exercise of bracketing, for without bracketing none of the three domains, making up all our experience of the world, can be accessed. "An aesthete kneels before something not because he has really submitted to it but because he derives pleasure out of bracketing the displeasure of obeying an object that *he can dominate if he wants to.*"[86] Which is to say that such admiration can have a long leash but one that is at the end predicated on the maintenance of the "ultimate security" of the aesthete. African art can be allowed to influence Cubism, but only insofar as it is absorbed within the comfortable zone of a distinctly European artistic mode. It is in this sense that Orientalism "exists within the aesthetic exceptionalization of the other," and it is this, Karatani argues, that "Said meant by the term of *Orientalism.*"[87]

Guénon's case fits none of the conditions set by either Kant or Karatani. Key here is the "ultimate security" of the aesthete in bracketing the cognitive and the ethical. Guénon neither entertained his cultural, intellectual, or political security nor bracketed it in favor of aesthetic pleasure. If anything, he demanded the dismantling of this security, insisting that nothing short of reform, and perhaps total removal, could satisfy his quest. He was much more than the "learned and intransigent critic" that Mircea Eliade thought him to be.[88] Nor did his project and proposal necessarily require the absorption of Eastern forms into Western culture, for he insisted on the uniqueness of all cultures, including that of Europe. If bracketing is a temporary state of mind, one that, as Kant tells us, always requires an act of unbracketing, then Guénon can be said to have bracketed nothing because his project had no room for unbracketing in the first place. That he "intransigently" rejected the West's materialistic, scientific, philosophical, and political structures in toto, that he left France for Cairo (where he raised a family with an Egyptian wife), and that he joined the ranks of a Sufi order leave nothing in his modes of being susceptible to the kind of analysis Karatani served the Orientalist aesthete and Said served, fairly or not, Massignon and his likes.

We are now in a better position to return to Foucault's theory of the author. As we saw, Foucault schematically typified the author into two categories, the author who has died, a type that we may call the "docile author" (again, after Foucault's own identification of the docile subject as an effect of subjection to power and to its discursive formations), and the discursive author, exemplified by Marx and Freud. As I have argued, Foucault's own theory of power bears further distinctions and further schematic typification. It is impossible for a discursive author (and Marx and Freud are nothing more than "schematic" examples, which is to say that they cannot provide an *exclusive* model) to arise within any formation without undergoing stages in between, however schematic they may be in turn. Said and Guénon happened to provide schematic examples of two more stages that we should recognize, and in fact have no way of avoiding, if we are to make full sense of the changing *épistémès* and of the power of critique that characterizes human history, and which Foucault himself acknowledged.[89] The docile authors, the type that characterizes the greatest majority of authors (whatever authorship might mean),[90] stand conscripted in the system of power, mostly not knowing that they are being conscripts. The discursive author, on the other hand, (unintentionally) defines the general contours of a discursive formation, without having control over the appropriation of his or her "work." This author, in other words, provides the ideological paraphernalia by which the central domains legitimize, sustain, and define themselves, although this very provision reflects the conditions of felicity that empower their discourses and give them their performative edge. This much is clear enough. But in between these two types, there are at least two others, my account being—no less than that of Foucault—also schematic.

Given all that has been said here thus far, I think it is quite plausible to recognize the categories of the dissenting and subversive authors, the latter having been alluded to earlier. Within our context, Said represents the former type while Guénon the latter. A dissenting author refuses the assumptions, the findings, and the received wisdom that characterize the docile author. The latter may engage in a critique of other docile authors, usually over details or relative details, but the critique never transgresses the boundaries of the commonly accepted assumptions of the discursive "tradition" or formation in which he or she operates. The *épistémè*, as Foucault would say, is never the issue. The docile author's critique pertains to detail, to a revision of or addition to a preexisting and accepted narrative. The general assumptions about the culture in which such interrogations are posed represent a received and established common denominator between the critic and her audience. This is a typical scenario in the discourse of mainstream Orientalism over the last century, as it is in all other academic fields. There is no doubt that Orientalism is and has been dynamic, internally, and debates in it over such issues of detail—what I call "paradigmatic instances"—have raged ever since Goldziher and his likes laid down the foundations of the field. But mainstream Orientalism, as Said aptly argued, remained a closed system, in the sense that all critique in it, whenever that happened, could never pass beyond an affirmation of the foundational assumptions that made the field what it has been for the last eighteen decades. A docile author, it must be also said, can distinguish herself over and above all her colleagues and peers, but will always remain within the rules and boundaries of the discursive "tradition" the field has set.

The dissenting author transcends the critique of individual projects of scholarship as such, which is to say that when she advances a critique, and when the work of individual scholars is subjected to criticism, it is not to critique these scholar's *specific* findings but rather to illustrate a major problem, an anomaly, *within* the system or *within* the discursive "tradition" in which they are writing. Clearly, key here is the word *within*. A dissenting author, however considerable the questions she poses are, does not question the mainstays of the system, or the epistemological structures or forms of knowledge that define the worldview through the prism in which problems in the field are solved. All these foundations and epistemic edifices are left in place, accepted and intact. What is interrogated, however, is the mode or modes in which the system is operated, analysis in it is conducted, methodological issues are defined, such interrogation aims to demolish and replace old approaches, the efficiency of its discourse or its modus operandi is managed, and so on. It amounts, in other words, to a correction *within* the system or to the system, but the system nonetheless, which remains in its foundational principles and structural modes of existence and operation more or less the same. If anything, the role played by the dissenting author is not just to keep the discursive tradition alive—for which purpose the dead author was specifically designed—but to *perform* a correction to the system, and to carry it to a *more* consolidated existence.

The dissenting author does not just fulfill the function of "loyal opposition," which no doubt she does; she also engages in changing the system from *within*, rendering it stronger and more robust. John Maynard Keynes is a typical example in point; his dissenting economic theories managed to displace earlier ones and to acquire wide influence and application, but there is nothing in Keynes's dissenting works that interrogates or attempts to challenge the theoretical foundations of capitalism, its validity, or the larger principles of its practice in the world. His theories were intended, and in fact were used, to improve the system, the perception—at least—being that the system would have suffered without his contributions. At least until Milton Freedman appeared on the scene as a strong challenger, Keynes's "authorial" output was thought to strengthen capitalism and enhance its efficiency. It is noteworthy that because the correction, whatever kind, happens inside the larger boundaries of the system, or what the system can tolerate, the dissenting author in turn is not only tolerated but usually welcomed and clothed with prestige, it being the case that his or her dissent, due to the perception of originality and innovation, is regarded as either improving on the system or cautioning against faults that may cause it to decline or suffer in one way or another. Yet, this "originality" almost invariably provokes resistance, but resistance that does not affect this author's status. In all cases, the critique produced by the dissenting author—and it is usually a critique that is involved—is received as integral to the discursive formation or set of formations within the larger system of power. The dissenting author does not experience death because he or she, far from being just another uniform or nameless voice within the discursive formation, *contributes* to the system and its flourishing and is likewise seen to do so. That the dissenting author cannot be given an epithet analogous to Foucault's biological metaphor of "dead author" ("dormant author"? "comatose author"?) is testimony to his or her theatrical language, which we surely cannot take too seriously.

Said's contribution to Orientalism, however strong the resistance to it may have been, is a case in point (in fact, resistance to Keynes was much more vehement, widespread, and robust than Said faced). It exposed the problems of the humanities in forceful ways, leading to the training of a new generation of scholars who have rearticulated the means by which the "Orient" is to be studied. The field of Near Eastern and Islamic studies (a new name for "Oriental Studies") is nothing but a more sophisticated version of its former self, largely due to Said's influence. Its intellectual composition today has no doubt grown in refinement, but all this has not changed its location and *function* on the scholarly grid. Nothing in the props of the system that produced such discourses was interrogated by Said, and nothing fundamental has in fact really changed. Like Keynes, Said believed in the soundness of the overall structure of the system, of its liberalism, secularity, and humanism, and even of its capitalism and bourgeois ethic. Said's culture, for all the reservations he expressed in *The Text, the World, and the Critic* and elsewhere, "resembles nothing so much as that of Arnold, Eliot or Leavis—there seems to be no irony intended at all when Said, the great campaigner against racism and ethnocentrism, laments in Leavisite tones the loss of culture's 'discrimination and evaluation.'"[91] His New York City, the highest manifestation of capitalism and liberalism in the world, was for him iconic; it was not only where Columbia University was found, but also where Bach's "rational music" and Gould's sonatas could be heard. Through his powerfully dissenting voice, Said reinforced modern academia and the foundations on which it stands.[92]

The subversive author, on the other hand, interrogates the foundational assumptions and epistemological mainstays of the discursive formations as well as of the larger system of power that sustains them. Marx was one such author, but after 1917, he rose to the rank of a discursive author. Freud, however, was almost "born," in one important sense, into a discursive authorship, having gathered discursive momentum some three decades before his death. (It is not the place here to interrogate in any detail Foucault's lumping together of Marx and Freud, since their discursivity is not of a type, and thus should be further distinguished, schematically and typologically. Since our authors do not belong to any of these categories, it is not essential to engage that issue.)[93] What differentiates the subversive author from his discursive counterpart is the absence in a central domain of a discursive momentum that is integral to a formation. A subversive author is thus synonymous with a latent, potential, or at best *embryonic* discursive momentum that never rises to the level of a formation, one that is oppositional to the dominating *épistémè*. For once that level is attained a subversive author obviously ceases to belong to that category. Yet, while the subversive author shares certain qualitative attributes with the discursive author (chief among them systemic or foundational critique, typified by Marx and Freud, respectively),[94] this type also shares quantitative attributes with the dissenting author. By virtue of dissenting on major—but not foundational or systemic—issues within the system, the dissenting author invariably and inevitably provokes opposition and countercritique. The subversive author likewise tends to generate a measure of critique, at times rather vehement and overwhelming, while at others less so—the latter by virtue of a tendency to marginalize and isolate, whether consciously or not. Yet, the quantitative analogy between the two authors does not only lie here. It is most remarkable in the parallel response in endorsement and following. The dissenting author attracts followers who, by virtue of their awareness of the need to critique the system, end up reinforcing and strengthening the system. The subversive author's followers stand on the opposite side, adopting the subversive author's critique with a view to changing the underpinnings of the system, creating another one, altogether different.

In this schema, Guénon occupies the category of the subversive author. His followers and disciples are relatively few but are many in absolute numbers. He generated a discursive momentum on a small scale, perhaps embryonic, but the relevance of his "work" to debates about modernity is increasing. It is unlikely that his "work" will evolve beyond the current stage of subversivity, but Foucault's discursive "analogies" may be at work, by which I mean that an "analogical" author—one who updates Guénon's "work" with reinvigorated relevance—may substitute for Guénon as Guénon.

I have already said that Foucault's theory of power and discursive formations allows for the category of the subversive author, and one reason for Foucault's insufficient theoretical attention to this category was likely to have been his preoccupation with the modalities and dynamics of modern power "at present" (a specification that abounds in his work). Foucault found Kant's "What Is Enlightenment?" striking because Kant essentially asked the question "What's going on just now? What is happening to us? What is this world, this period, this precise moment in which we are living?" More effectively put, Kant asked the fundamental question: "What are we, now?" Foucault undoubtedly appreciates the innovative nature of Kant's question, for what it meant for the end of the eighteenth century, but he seems to think that this is no longer a relevant question. It is worth quoting him at length. The "target nowadays" is not to discover what we are but to refuse what we are. We have to imagine and to build up what we could be to get rid of this kind of political "double bind," which is the simultaneous individualization and totalization of modern power structures. The conclusion would be that the political, ethical, social, philosophical problem of our days is not to try to liberate the individual from the state, and from the state's institutions, but to liberate us both from the state and from the type of individualization linked to the state. We have to promote new forms of subjectivity through the refusal of this kind of individuality that has been imposed on us for several centuries.[95]

If Foucault did not dwell, as a matter of elaborate theory, on such themes of resistance, it is because the focus of his analytic concerns lay elsewhere.[96] It is plausible to argue that emphasis has a decisive function in authorial exposition and production: an overstress on a side issue of an argument (or theory) at the expense of the main components of that argument can shift meaning, give undue importance to secondary issues, weaken the main argument, and possibly put it asunder. For Foucault to dwell at relative length on the subversive author would have meant that the performativity of the discursive formations would lose their force, and would open up possibilities that would potentially, even effectively, diminish the roles he assigned to them. It would have planted, in other words, a potent seed of doubt in the claim for the performative power of discursive formations. The claim need not be absolute (as some interpreters of Foucault, I think, mistakenly argue), but to make any claim or a sustained argument for a thesis is to stress it, elaborate it, expound it in detail, show evidence in support of it, and so on. To flesh out what are otherwise exceptions, side issues, or derivatives with the same force is to militate against the main thesis. This may also be the case with Judith Butler's theories of gender formation, as well as with several others.

Yet, Foucault could have still given an account of the discursive author without running such risks; for it is possible to argue, historically (and he certainly was a foremost historian), that épistémès and truth regimes have cyclical lives, that they rise and fall, and that, like the Khaldunian dynastic sequences, and even life cycles, they undergo formative periods, then periods of maturation and stability, before they decline and meet their end (without any of this entailing that cycles and cyclical time are identical). The thrust of Foucault's theories of power, knowledge, and the rest was explicitly and intensely concerned with the middle stage (mostly located in the nineteenth and twentieth centuries); and when he did dwell on the predecessors of the modern systems (for example, modes of punishment and surveillance, concepts of juridicality or pastoral power), it was not to show the workings of the earlier systems and their *épistémès* or modalities of the historical processes of change. Rather, it was to make explicit the *residues and effects* of a historical process so as to explicate in (his typically) forceful ways the modus vivendi and modus operandi of a modern, presently operating type of power. His account, implicitly grounded in a larger though unarticulated historical narrative, has a rather false synchronic appearance.

It is difficult therefore to draw the conclusion that Said appreciated the full implications of Foucault's theory of the author, and he seems to have in fact ascribed to him a theoretical narrowness of which Foucault cannot be accused. That Said overlooked Guénon altogether may be a chance or accident; yet, the introduction of this subversive author into a critique of Orientalism makes for an irony: Said himself could have been grist for Guénon's mill. As for the subversive author that Guénon was, Said's critique may be said to incur a double jeopardy. On the one hand, Guénon's narrative presence affirms the theoretical complexity of the concept of author in Orientalism, thus opening up further theoretical possibilities for diachronic critique and future action (the latter being the subject of chapter 5); and, on the other hand, Guénon's critique dwarfs that of Said, and for good reasons. Subversive authors always outmatch their dissenting counterparts.

Yet, for all the subversivity that Guénon mustered, his account lacks articulation insofar as the inner workings of Orientalism are concerned, insofar, that is, as the intimately structured organic connections between Orientalism and its epistemological, political, and cultural surrounds— those from which it emerged and with which it stood in a determined dialectic—are concerned. Guénon already made the first important step toward considering "official Orientalism" not only as integral to "Western civilization" but also as bound up with all corners of academia. For Guénon, there is no real distinction between the forms of knowledge that defined academic disciplines: they all issued from the same "civilizational" matrix, from the same worldview, one that possessed a single epistemological common denominator or a single foundational thought structure. For Said, the picture is not entirely coherent. Politically, he seemed to blame the West as a category for its destructive attitudes, but academically and epistemologically, he singles out Orientalism for indictment, letting the rest of the disciples pass unscathed (260). A strong man of the Enlightenment, Said could not see *where* the problem of Orientalism was, his view of knowledge being unsurprisingly provincial.

In the next chapter I shall argue that Said's placement of Orientalism as a sort of exception was problematic, not to mention arbitrary, and that Guénon's diagnosis did not go the full length that its potential allowed for. This is attributable, as I have intimated, to Said's ideological commitments, which, as a dissenting author, remained largely loyal to the system of power in which he operated, at times with passion, and mostly unconsciously. As for Guénon's lack of articulation, it seems that when he wrote about the subjects of our concern, he had not yet seen the full destructive forces of the twentieth century, some of which propelled major thinkers to *further* reevaluate much of what had by then been written and thought.

CHAPTER IV

Epistemic Sovereignty and Structural Genocide

I

There is nothing that should be clearer in this book than this: setting up Said's *Orientalism* for critique finds its reason, rationale, and conviction in the fact that the work's canonicity reflects not only its own power of argument but also its dominating effect on the whole range of discourse on the subject for almost four decades. This is not entirely a statement about the work, but rather about what and who make the work what it is. Canonical works ultimately undergo discursive accretions, including major revisions, interpretive "ameliorations," and qualifications that at once enunciate and suppress. Said's work, when not overlooked in its entirety (and there are those who deliberately disregard it), seems to continue to have a spell over the humanities and especially the field he particularly targeted and called "Islamic Orientalism." The work's canonicity, however molded, remains committed, in other words, to an iteration of central doctrines whose analytical force may be questionable. Cohesive within its own internal logic, Said's *Orientalism* displays microcosmic features that exhibit, each on its own, the structure of Said's thought. One such feature, a stubbornly troubling component of the work, is what I have been referring to as "difference."

There is no doubt that Massignon, whom Said studied in some detail, somewhat approaches the position of Guénon in his critique of the West and sympathies with the Orient, although Massignon established for himself a greater name in the field of Islamic studies, perhaps because he may have been a superior scholar but not because he "could refer so easily (and accurately) in an essay to a host of Islamic mystics, and to Jung, Heisenberg, Mallarmé, and Kierkegaard" (267).[1] Guénon had his own repertoire, ranging from the Greek, Taoist, Hindu, and Islamic intellectuals of the East, to Enlightenment one such as Kant, Comte, Schopenhauer, Hartman, Bergson, and numerous others. As I remarked earlier, this generation of European scholars as well as the one before them had garnered a kind of erudition in both language proficiency and area expertise that was to disappear, in large measure, from the field after World War II. This was the true philology that imperialist and colonialist Europe produced. Nor was Guénon the Islamicist that Massignon was, but he was the Hinduist. What matters to us in Said is that Massignon's fault was not his sympathies and endless advocacy of the Muslim and Palestinian causes, or the stereotypical distinctions he made between Arab and Persian Sufis, but his insistence that a fundamental "difference" existed between the modern West and Islam, the former being eo ipso modern, while the latter belonging to an ancient civilization. "Massignon's implication is that the essence of the difference between East and West is between modernity and ancient tradition" (269); "Massignon's vision . . . assigned the Islamic Orient to an essentially ancient time and the West to modernity" (270). It is almost certain, if I am allowed the conjecture, that had Said included Guénon for evaluation, he would have found him lacking on precisely the same grounds.

Said never bothers to excavate the reasons for the opposition that creates difference, nor does he seem curious about the meanings of the terms he himself assigns to the authors he critiques. We finish reading *Orientalism* without having an iota of information as to how Gibb understood nationalism or how Massignon himself articulated the concepts of modern and traditional, as well as those of "ancient civilization" and modernity. These pairs, by the fact of their appearance in any text, seem to cause Said an extreme case of anxiety. The categories of "religion," "tradition," "mysticism," and "ancient" are not amenable to analytical study, nor can they be even considered as serious objects of research. As critic W. J. T. Mitchell has poignantly remarked, Said characterizes religion "in terms of fairly reductive stereotypes," as "dogmatic, fanatical, irrational, intolerant, and obsessed with mystery, obfuscation, and human helplessness in the presence of the inscrutable divine (or demonic) design."[2] Said comes even uncomfortably close to mocking Massignon's own deep appreciation of mysticism, describing the mystical path as possessing a tendency toward the "nonrational and even inexplicable" (268).[3] Nor has Said cultivated any scholarly appreciation of the concept of "tradition" or an understanding of the implications of "ancient" in Massignon's work, which has a resounding similarity to that adopted by Guénon. For Said himself, the "ancient" was a strikingly oppositional category for the modern, that which is irrelevant, obsolete, defunct, not a continuous quality that has, through centuries and millennia, maintained a human and insentient ecology tested by time. The ancient for Guénon and Massignon is a long-standing tradition that undergoes piecemeal change, securely, steadily, and safely, but one that insists on maintaining itself within a principled order, ruled, as it were, by high-order governing ethical precepts. The "ancient" for Guénon, Massignon, and even some more recent anthropologists is the embodiment of tradition, one that operates by a principled logic, and one that extends its life into the modern, partaking in it and coping with its pressures.[4] The "ancient" for these two luminaries is a living and lived experience, however much this experience is threatened by colonialism and its modernity.

My point here is that Said's dismissal of these categories as they show up in Massignon's work (and, for us, in Guénon's as well) is a microcosmic and paradigmatic *instance* that illustrates his overall attitude to Orientalism. Hence his methodical insistence on treating this discipline as an exception to all other academic fields of inquiry. We might note the difference between Said and Guénon in how they locate Orientalism within the humanities in general. Guénon views the entire world of modern academia, including its humanities and natural sciences, as integral to Europe's discursive formations, all contributing, more or less, to the production of a particular view of the world, and all, at the same time, standing for him as the product of the "civilizational" soil in which they found themselves. Orientalism is just one of the many disciplines that reflected the "West's" attitudes, but one that happened to be geared toward the study of the "East." If Guénon paid attention to it, it was because he deemed it important as the bridge through which the West could learn something from the East, with a view to recovering "the principles" that Europe had lost. Said, on the other hand, isolates Orientalism in general and "Islamic Orientalism" in particular for a special treatment, assigning to them a second-rate intellectual competence and a problematic way of seeing the

Orient, having lagged behind in comparison with general academia and, especially, with the "human sciences" (260–61). Unlike Guénon, Said does not extend his critical acumen to anything beyond Orientalism, sheltering the "human sciences" from foundational critique, along with the surrounding environment, all the while constantly alluding to, but never showing the structure of, the ties between Orientalism and the "considerable dimension of modern political-intellectual culture" enveloping it (12). Nor did he even think that Orientalism may have the potential, in a better world, to come to the aid of the very culture that produced it, trying to reconstruct a concept of history that could at least shed light on modernity's sweeping crises. This is clearly because he himself did not think that the "Orient"—filled with religion, dogmatism, and sectarian conflict—has anything to offer. There is not a single word in *Orientalism* that even hints at the slightest potential in the Orient to instruct Said's liberal West.

Said's carefully buffered insulation of Orientalism as a target of massive critical conductivity was thus the function of his ideological commitment as a secular humanist and liberal, among much else that is *modernist*. He remained within the realm of "representation" as Orientalism's spectacular problem and could never go beyond it precisely because these commitments would have been destroyed to the core had he pursued his critique to its logical conclusion. This is a prime emblem of the dissenting author. As we have seen and as I will try to show shortly, representation is the least of Orientalism's problems, being in fact a superficial one. Indeed, the problem is not Orientalism at all, and if one insists that it is, then it is so only symptomatically and derivatively. Orientalism is not only just a microcosm of a much larger paradigmatic phenomenon, but it is little other than an instrument. To confuse an instrument with generative forces and creative structures that conceive, invent, and harness the instrument is nothing short of making the cart hide the horse, entirely, and out of view.

II

I shall have the occasion to dwell on the problem of setting up "instruments" as causes, but for now it is important to insist on Said's own advice, which he himself was per force clearly unable to follow. In the introduction to his work written in 2003, and in the context of defining the mission of "humanism" and "humanistic critique" (inspired by Vico, who was not, incidentally, an unqualifiedly secular humanist),[5] Said states "that every domain is linked to every other one, and that *nothing* that goes on in *our world* has ever been isolated and pure of any outside influence" (xxiii, emphasis mine). This, no doubt, is a remarkable statement, expressing a method, if not an entire (dialectical) methodology, that is sorely lacking—and for intelligible reasons—in the greatest bulk of modern scholarship. The use of the word "nothing" is equally remarkable, showing an admirable sense of systematicity that leaves us all the more bewildered. And one wonders how small Said's "our world" is. Obviously, it includes colonialism, which he clearly linked with Orientalism. But does this link have a thicker meaning? Does colonialism extend beyond a form of domination? Is it, like Orientalism, merely "a style of domination"? Does it differ from other, historically earlier forms? Does it have a structural connection with sovereignty over nature? What is the meaning of this sovereignty "in our world"? Does colonialism have structural connections with a genocidal structure of thought and with the very modern phenomenon of genocide? Does genocide itself even appear in Said's work beyond a passing mention? Does it have structural links with Orientalism? Does modernity have to do with genocide as a structure? Is genocidal modernity an analytical category, amenable to the much-cherished "humanistic critique"? Does modernity appear in *Orientalism* as a problem? Does humanist secularism have intimate structural ties with anthropocentrism? Does anthropocentrism appear at all in Said's critique? Does it have an organic connection with progress, racial theories, or genocides? Does progress appear in Said as an analytical category at all and does it have organic connections with secularism and genocide? Does liberalism itself have any connections with genocides? Do Orientalism and academia at large have an intimate connection with all of the above?

None of these questions was in the least entertained in *Orientalism*, much less articulated or answered, however partially or tentatively. It is to an outline of some[6] of these connections that we now turn, in an attempt to show that Orientalism is nothing more than the tip of the iceberg, the part that Said saw, but the part that, alone, could never sink a titanic.

I wish to begin by pointing out that Orientalism as a body of discourse is no different from any other field in modern academia, except that it happened to owe its formal existence to the fact of its specialization. Just as economics or business or engineering or English literature have their specialization in the cultivation of knowledge about their respective fields, Orientalism cultivates its knowledge with an exclusive regard to the "Orient." But the *inner structure of the intellectual attitudes* of an ordinary, typical, and mainstream economist is identical to that of his Orientalist, historian, anthropologist, scientist, or business-school counterpart. By "mainstream" I mean to isolate the subversive authors, who are a minority and who normally do not affirmatively partake in the plan of things I am about to describe.

I have already spoken at some length about Enlightenment philosophical discourse, beginning with its underlying moral thought, in terms of creating the arbitrary Distinction that was to become a determining force shaping arguments, modes of analysis, and an overall view of the world. The central domain of philosophy has been one that ennobled the quest for raw materialism and, one might even say, insatiable material greed by clothing it with a formation of legitimizing high-flying discourse that in turn acquired its own performative power. The concept of negative liberty that I discussed in the previous chapter is just one example in point. The sheer thickness and massiveness of this discursive tradition were such that it finally ousted from the central domain all rivaling views, until, that is, very recently, when this form of overwhelming domination was put into question. The rise of environmental ethics in the 1980s and 1990s, in particular, has been conducive to beginning the initial stages of shaking off not the discursive tradition itself, but its monopolistic grip over alternative narratives, although this critique, as I will argue in the next chapter, itself remains conflicted and uncertain of its method due to its inability to free itself from Enlightenment forms of rationality. But it is a fact that the discursive formations have had tremendous powers of performativity, and hence generative and reproductive capabilities shaping academia since the modern university came into existence. And science, acting largely on its own, has been replicating in technical, positivist, and highly practical terms this philosophical worldview, although, as I have been trying to show through a discussion of Guénon's critique, science stood in a dialectical relationship with philosophy, reinforcing its positivism and materialism, while imbibing the legitimacy that the lofty philosophical discourse provided.

My point is that these two fields have in fact laid the grounds for a vision of nature that denudes it of its ethical constitution, the kind that Scheler and Guénon spoke of. The psychoepistemic pervasiveness of this denuding act, which now itself becomes "natural" (which is to say, normative, habitual, and nothing short of a habitus), has exercised a hegemony that has constituted, I think, the most formidable obstacle facing the environmental ethicists in assigning intrinsic value to insentient creatures.[7] This psychoepistemic performativity has generated a form of rationality and reason that is, to use Guénon's and Dussel's expression, *blind* to any cognitive possibility beyond its own province, one whose scope and "binocularity" have been ultimately determined by the primacy of the Distinction. No wonder then that science, accompanied by the prestige of philosophical legitimation, the financial backing of the modern state and industry, and the all-powerful doctrine of progress, has managed in the span of less than two centuries to bring the natural world into severe crises. What I wish to emphasize here is not just the arbitrariness of the Distinction (for it could have hypothetically been conceived, and yet remain nothing more than ink on paper) but the very forces themselves that made of an arbitrary mode of thought an exclusive norm and an inviolable decree. The inviolability is such that with all the shelves in all the libraries in Western academia, there is not yet anything like a coherent, extensive, or even reasonably adequate narrative of the genealogy of the Distinction, or of the conditions of felicity that made it so powerful and performative. This absence, as well as the inverse *presence* that this absence designed and produced, speaks not just of the very heart of philosophical-scientific sovereignty but of its mind and one-sidedness as well.

There is nothing in the world in which humans live that can escape the sovereign decision of science. Whatever science, as a paradigm, says is the truth and nothing but the truth (however much certain individual scientists may disagree with this pervasive dictum). Yet, the indispensable and crucial addendum "nothing but the truth" is clearly intended to eliminate the possibility of including with the truth a nontruth, a lie, a deception, a malicious design, which creates for any rational being an insurmountable paradox made patently obvious by the destructiveness of science. It is after all science that created the means to effect ecological and environmentalist destruction, just as much as it created colonialism[8] and weapons of mass annihilation. Peace activists and decent spirits inexhaustibly condemn such weapons with tiring though justifiable repetition, but the question that is rarely asked is what made such destructive instruments possible in the first place, assuming the first answer included science as a culprit. The sovereignty of science and its genealogy are rarely in question.

Yet, science and philosophy are not alone. Departments of economics and business schools, to use two further examples, are single-mindedly geared toward the training of students to learn the methods and principles of economics and business, to teach them planning, organization, and techniques intended to cultivate and sharpen their efficiency. The ultimate purpose is to create the *homo economicus*, a subject whose machine-like faculties are harnessed to work the economy, improve it, make necessary corrections when needed, and, in the case of business, cultivate subliminal psychological and social techniques to promote consumerism and the circulatory flow of the market's power.[9] These desiderata of course come with the encouragement and blessing of the state that provides the necessary conditions to make the Berlinian negative liberty a fully functioning and boundlessly efficient technique. For the elaborate and intricately woven system that this worldview has created, the ultimate and single-minded purpose is not just profit and accumulation of wealth but the cultivation of a radical form of indifference toward the world and its Others. Negative liberty breeds the private, self-enclosed subject who is no more able to see and hear others than they can see and hear him. This subject formation and its single-mindedness are *essential* and central to such academic units, in which the very possibility of introducing any idea that threatens this teleology is eliminated ab initio. It is out of the question, for instance, that the quest for profit should be restrained by any other consideration, with the exception, however, of an idea that promises to yield more profit in the future. Corporate "charity" and "social responsibility" are major and classic examples on this point.

The corporate and institutional collectives' disregard for a genuinely motivated and ethically grounded social responsibility has long been observed as a symptom of disengagement with empathy that is in turn anchored in sociopathology. I will briefly attend to sociopathology momentarily, but it is important at this point to stress the links between institutional normative beliefs and "ideology," on the one hand, and deficit in moral and ethical education and upbringing, on the other. I do not assume that such an education fulfills its purpose only by means of engagement in internal psychological operations on the self and the body, what Foucault and Ghazali called, respectively, "taking care of the self" and "ethical training of the self by means of habituation."[10] This sort of training (*riyada*) requires an internal and introspective set of operations not only on the soul but also, and perhaps as much, on the body. As Foucault has aptly argued, in modernity "this notion is obscure and faded."[11] The psychological implications of the conflict that inevitably arises when such operations are conducted within a capitalist and consumerist system wholly located in an ideological conception of negative liberty are grave. Instead, moral and ethical education in an open-ended academic system of thought can be satisfied by a standard programmatic approach to course offerings. It is both striking and suggestive therefore that mainstream departments of economics and business schools—which is to say, their constitution as paradigmatic domains—generally have no course offerings on moral philosophy and ethics worth mentioning.[12] It would be, for example, a rare exception, if it exists at all, to find a business school in the United States that requires as an essential part of the student's education the completion of a course of study on such subjects as Aristotelian ethics or Kant's moral philosophy or even a general introduction to the history of ethics or of moral thought. It is less conceivable that such a course offering includes subject matter on "Oriental" philosophers, such as Hindu, Buddhist, or Islamic moral philosophers. My point is that the modern academic domains of economics and business (and, as in the case of Orientalism, there never was any equivalent in premodernity) exclusively and *intensively* operate within the single-minded frame of reference in which a large degree of moral neutrality is a *prerequisite*,[13] and in which the exploitation of matter and people for the single but highest goal of profit is a discrete yet mandatory category.

Business schools and departments of economics, sitting in academia alongside many others, and each with a province of expertise of its own, exhibit, by virtue of the unmasked nature of their interests, direct links with the nonacademic world that spans the length and depth of the market, the corporations, and their modus vivendi and highly destructive modus operandi in the social and natural orders. Both of them train and staff all forms of business, from small to large, although in our story business schools are always dependent on the latter, being not only structurally a derivative of but also determined by the economic and market behavior of the departments of economics. In other words, there are both structural and dialectical *modes of existence* between these academic outfits and the corporation, whose ethic and ethos are identical to those on which these outfits thrive. The fiscal dependence of these outfits on the corporation and "business" goes without saying; and I need not engage in the superfluous debate over academic freedom and the intellectual autonomy of academic discourse on business and economics, for the mere fact of their very position in the central domains, which they dialectically define and by which they are defined, is a matter not just of financial dependence but also, and equally importantly, of the performative power of the central domains that I have been trying to define.

The organic structural ties between the corporation and economic discourse (both philosophical—as in Adam Smith, J. S. Mill, and John Maynard Keynes—and purely academic), including that which has much later arisen in the form of business schools, are not attested only in late-modern capitalist systems but go back—and this is of immediate relevance to my account—to the very first decades of the corporation's life, and in no other place than in Britain's East India Company (and, to a somewhat lesser extent, in the United Dutch East India Company). It is not without great significance that the very first "theorists" of what has emerged as a new field of study, "economics," were mainly British, Thomas Mun (d. 1641) and Sir William Petty (d. 1687)[14] being two of the earliest, if not the earliest. The former also typically doubled as the director of the East India Company itself, and his writings were the direct result of his experience in that function and of the EIC's work as a colonialist entity.[15] It is instructive, and goes to the heart of our argument, that the Jesuit School of Salamanca, under the influence of the earlier and comparatively underdeveloped Spanish colonialist ventures, also put forth a nascent but a relatively sophisticated economic theory, as Marjorie Grice-Hutchinson has argued. But its teachings became soon defunct, because, there is every reason to believe, it insisted on certain ethical principles that were to become irrelevant to thinking about money, wealth, economy, and the corporation. The currents of emerging power that revived the legality of the company in the British Parliament—after outlawing it as an immoral entity[16]—appear to be the very same structures of power that made the School of Salamanca no more than a faint memory. It is not a coincidence, as Grice-Hutchinson notes, that the last advocacy of the school's ethical doctrines did not survive beyond the seventeenth century.[17]

The point I am trying to make is that there exists a direct *structural* link between these academic disciplines and the corporation, a largely colonialist entity that has been well known to engage in the exploitation of foreign (= "Oriental") labor, modern economic forms of human enslavement nearly everywhere, the virtual control of the host country's laws and public policies, and, no less important, the destruction of natural habitats. All of these forms of abuse as well as many others belong to the same structure of thought and the same general ethos and worldview that produced science with its destructive effects. As the Africanist scholar O. E. Udofia has argued, the multinational corporations lead the African economy and thus "constitute today's imperialism in Africa." The general characteristics of the multinational corporation are "ownership and control," both being manifestations of capitalism, whose quiddity is imperialism.[18] Udofia speaks about corporate discrimination against the African managerial class, the abuse of labor, and interference in the national economy, national elections, public policy, and so on, but does not tease out the full meaning of "ownership and control." Partly acting on behalf of the general interests of the mother country and partly on behalf of its own sovereign ambition, the corporation serves its private ambitions with virtual impunity. The natural manner of both neocolonialism and the corporation is one of "owning" the fields of their interest, disposing of them as they see fit. The host country's laws and regulations, and at times nationalist animosity, are mere annoyances to be "managed" and, as with everything else, disposed of. The long history of assassinations or removal of democratically elected leaders who oppose the exploitative American corporations in their countries is too well known and needs no rehearsal here.

The late-modern multinational corporation may not possess sovereignty in the full political sense of the term, but it often acts under the auspices of the home country that does. Still, in the manner they conduct themselves, and in their devastations of the natural environments and depleting of the "Orient's" natural assets (and the Orient for my purposes may as well be Africa or Latin America), these corporations have the right over life and death, not necessarily as a military and formal legal matter, but effectively. When Chevron dumps billions of gallons of toxic materials in the consumable waters of Ecuador, and when it hires mercenaries to shoot at and often kill peaceful protesters against its abusive activities in Nigeria, it is behaving effectively, though not "formally" or "legally," in the same way colonial governments conducted themselves in the colonies before the so-called national independence movement.[19] When Coca-Cola kills with impunity Colombians protesting the company's labor abuses,[20] it is acting within the same structure of thought: sovereignty over the instrumentalized human labor and the lives that make it possible. Chevron, like General Electric, ExxonMobil, Wal-Mart, General Motors, Nike, and a long list of others, has been behaving in much the same way, engaging in serious violations of human rights[21] and often causing continuous pain and suffering that many would argue is unimaginable.[22] In other words, sovereign domination over life and death has been the common denominator of both state colonialism and its subordinated associate,[23] the corporation, the latter having complicated the phenomenon of this sovereignty by resorting to sophisticated economic and political techniques that can command the right over life and death almost imperceptibly. But when these techniques fail, the corporation, like a miniature state, invokes the state of exception with the right to kill. It is only within this logic that the acts of Chevron, Coca-Cola, and many like them can be intelligible.

My point here is that the discursive formation lumping modern departments of economics and business schools (and associated fields, including law, politics, and diplomacy)[24] finds its conditions of felicity in the colonialist and corporate practices on the ground, these operating respectively—directly and indirectly—within a domination framework in which the state of exception inheres and which in turn reflects their sovereign structure of thought. As I intimated earlier, modern forms are not conscious of themselves, for they are invariably embedded in a thick cloud of ideology and a normative system of belief that masks their true nature. Psychologically, this self-unconscious collective and institutional psyche fulfills one of the essential requirements of the condition of sociopathology. Between the doctrine of progress and the redefining of human value in materialist terms, the typical student or professor in these academic units does not think of herself in any way as involved in such unethical ventures of human rights abuses, assassination, atrocious extraction of the natural wealth of other human populations, and destruction of the environment. And this is precisely what the typical student or professor in "Oriental" studies thinks and *feels* as well. Yet there is little difference between the two types of expertise, economic and Orientalist, and both culminate, on the structural level, in the absolute right to domination, one through the venue of economy, the other through cultural and, more important, juridical domination.

A word of caution is in order here. I have been trying to show the complexity of the structures of power within the Orientalist tradition through elaborating on Foucault's useful theory of the author. This theory, especially in the modified form I attempted to articulate, is consistent with Foucault's concept of power and knowledge, and is applicable to various fields of discourse. We might wish to extend the meaning of author slightly more than Foucault did. I take seriously his intimation that the informal jotting on the margins of a book constitutes "authorship," an intimation that opens up capacious theoretical space for including such concepts of author as a sophomore-taking-down-lecture-notes, which necessarily reflects the subjectivity of the student in the process of digesting the lecture. That the *typical* sophomore and her *typical* professor are authors of the dead type and that they constitute the subjects of the discursive formation in which they operate and live as "educated" beings are two matters to be taken for granted. That such students and professors should find it shocking that they are implicated, however remotely, in abuses, killings, and other kinds of atrocities is precisely where this theoretical space becomes productive. The question then is, Why this shocked reaction, and, more specifically, why does the dead author affirm her very status as dead author at the very moment she denies it? It is my contention that at the root of the problem of knowledge and power, and of all that which emanates from their dialectical relationship, lies a larger ethical problem, which is to say that Foucault's entire project, and almost everything he wrote, would remain unintelligible and lacking a truly unifying framework if it did not begin and end with this ethical problem. The indignation of the student at the very thought of being involved in such unethical behavior stems from the differential in the "intelligible rationality" between collective agents and the individuals inhabiting the collective entity, be it a university or, especially, a corporation. Yet, this rationality is not an autonomous source in itself, but reflects the difference in the normative anchors of these agents.[25]

This difference, however, does not appear to account for the full range of indignation, or, for that matter, for the student's affirmation of her very status as dead author at the very moment she denies it. Yet, the student hails from a society that defines, and is defined by, all the important institutions responsible for the charge, the state with all its departments, and the corporation with all its manifestations, including the scientific, technological, and industrial. At the same time, the student's "normative anchor" derives from a larger social world with diffused forms of morality, norms hardly consolidated or unified in the way government and corporate commercial institutions are.

It is here where the problem lies. Living in the space between the corporate and noncorporate social worlds is key. Psychoanalysis has shown the ways in which the collective psyche, unlike the individuals that make it up, can never develop self-awareness, which explains the common phenomenon of CEOs and high-ranking corporate managers who shun, mostly privately, the abusive practices of the very corporations they run. Because the student is not integral to the personnel of a business corporation, she feels justified in her indignation, whereas the CEO and the manager do not: they are, in the final analysis, morally, though not necessarily legally, implicated. But the moral anchor of the two is one and the same. In chapter 2, I have shown, through the Islamic case study, that the stubborn insistence on individual moral responsibility and liability was the *sufficient* cause for barring the rise of the corporation in the Islamic world, given that culture's colossal commercial and financial enterprise, which reached nearly all corners of the Old World.[26] This is not to say, however, that the student's normative anchor is driven by anything like the Islamic ethic, for the anchor is lodged deep in the waters that have already separated its elements of value from those of fact. The indignation lasts no longer than the moment when she has been made a generous offer by a corporation.[27] The typical student in business, management, or economics will decline such an offer at the peril of insanity. Once "in office" the indignation either vanishes or goes underground,[28] this latter replicating the familiar pattern of the CEO or manager who comprehends the immorality of her own corporation but continues nonetheless to serve it, often with enthusiasm and hard work.

In psychological terms, these managers may experience neurosis, even psychopathy,[29] but those who are not susceptible to fragmented consciousness are frequently identified as sociopaths, said to pervade the corporate world, and with increasing numbers, to boot. More generally, corporate personnel, including the sociopaths among them, are typically able to segregate their experiences in the corporation, thus leading, in effect, a dual existence. The world of the corporation, business, and money is one of fact; the world of children, of sisters and brothers and mothers, is one of value. But the distance between them is never great, and it could be bridged with systemic balance in favor of the former. The increasing power of the corporation, which stands commensurate with an increase in sociopathology[30] in the larger population, including academia,[31] has so far been a guarantee for an easy act of bridging. The overall result has been the further entrenchment of sociopathological behavior in the centers of power. As one psychologist concluded, corporate bodies, private and public, as well as "democratic" governments and their institutions—not to mention the nondemocratic—are typical cases of sociopathology.[32] The average or typical student's indignation—however genuine and sincere—is thus built into the discourse that enables the very attribute of dualistic, fragmented existence, which in turn becomes a necessary condition for forming humans into subjects of the discursive formation, a quality that functions as an unconscious coping mechanism. The indignation is thus indispensably built into the very system whose atrocities and destruction the indignation itself is intended to obviate, or at least disavow. This is what it means to be a subject of a discursive formation.

Yet, it would be wrong to confine corporate training (including in a university setting), mentality, and practice to sociopathological deviancy,[33] a diagnostic that subconsciously allocates responsibility for moral defect to a form of abnormality. While "sociopathology is a genuine phenomenon,"[34] the ethicist Joseph Heath argues, it is often simply the corporate constitution and corporate environment as such that create unethical and even criminal behavior. It is "the way people *think* about their actions and the situation [they are faced with in their corporate life that] has an enormous amount to do with their propensity to commit various crimes."[35] The common explanation of unethical and criminal activity in terms of deviant psychology has been persistent because such discourse provides "a source of assurance" to society that it is not itself, as a "normal" phenomenon, infected with deviancy. Nonetheless, it is society's ability to allow for "techniques of neutralization"[36] that remains the issue, for it is within these societies, which produce and are produced by corporate values, that unethical and criminal conduct takes a particular form and meaning.

The corporations and the markets generally

> are institutional contexts that generate a very steady stream of rather plausible (or plausible sounding) excuses for misconduct. This is the result of confluence of factors: first, corporations are typically large, impersonal bureaucracies; second, the market allows individuals to act only on the basis of local information, leaving them in many cases unaware of the full consequences of their actions; third, widespread ideological hostility . . . to regulation of the market; and finally, the fact that firms are engaged in adversarial (or competitive) interactions gives them broader license to adopt what would otherwise be regarded as anti-social strategies. The other major feature of the corporation, and of the business world more generally, is that it constitutes a subculture that in many cases isolates individuals from the broader community, and thus may serve to insulate deviant ideas and arguments from critical scrutiny.[37]

It seems that Heath's four explanations beg the question, unless we seriously take his argument, which he draws from Hannah Arendt, that bureaucracy is "rule by nobody."[38] In unethical and criminal corporate behavior, "it is seldom the case that one individual is clearly responsible for a particular action. Thus, when a crime is committed, everyone can, with some degree of plausibility, point the finger at someone else." Whether it is precipitated by sociopathological propensity or by what Heath calls a "cognitive" response to the "situation," it is clear that the very constitution of corporateness lies at the core of unethical and criminal misconduct. And it is within this very notion of nonpersonal liability that the Distinction finds one of its most powerful manifestations. The corporate subject, be it a student or professor, inasmuch as she is constituted by corporate culture, is herself the product of a society not only that is permeated by a general acceptance of corporate ethics but that does not question the legitimacy of such an ethic, much less of the corporation itself as a concept. Criminality and breach of ethical boundaries thus in no structural way represent exceptions to an otherwise moral conception and practice but are, respectively, two levels of maneuvering within one and the same system. Criminality begins not where ethics runs its course, but rather where the unethical has been entirely exhausted.

Now, cataloguing the entire range of university departments as a dialectic of power is beyond our bounds here. Nonetheless, it can briefly be said that the theory of central and peripheral domains allows a typification of these departments along these lines. I have noted that the sciences, in which I include biology, medicine, physics, and chemistry (in all their subdivisions), belong to the central domain, just as do philosophy (including its moral variant), law, psychiatry, education, journalism, history, archaeology, and even mathematics.[39] To the peripheral domains belong such departments as religion/divinity, literature, art, and music.

The less-than-obvious classification of, say, history in the central domain and literature and music in the peripheral domain understandably precipitates an interrogation as to the rationale of the choice. As I have intimated, the central domains require the support of discursive formations that legitimize, rationalize, and define their force fields and structures of power, all of which supports the effect of a dialectical production of performative power. In its modern reincarnation, professional history, unlike literature in general, is a nationalist discourse, based almost entirely on a doctrine of progress, without which it would suffer immediate collapse. This claim rests on the foundational argument that history, unlike literature, underwent structural change in the eighteenth and nineteenth centuries, a change that severed its organic ties to forms of historical writing characteristic of pre-modernity but one that simultaneously reenacted, through secularizing processes, what the philosopher Karl Löwith called "prophetic and messianic" Christian dogma.[40] Literature, on the other hand, being inherently aesthetic in nature, is less involved in proactive economic or political projects, especially of the colonialist type. That it exhibits coloniality in such forms as Said exposed in *Culture and Imperialism* is doubtless, but it is precisely its location in the peripheral domain that constitutes my point of contention with Said's diagnostics. For literature's collusion with power is subsidiary. Literature qua literature can survive power and remain literature. By contrast, modern historical writing, economics, and politics—as departments of modern academia—will vanish *as professional disciplines* once modern forms of power collapse, because they are constitutive of this power. Literature, music, and the like (all peripheral domains *partly* enlisted in nationalist and colonialist projects) are not, as such, constitutive of this power.

It was history as a methodology, including its associate Orientalism, that was at the core of redefining the "Orient's" temporal location, giving it a new identity and forming its colonial subjects who no longer can imagine their own past outside the purview of modern historical narrative. Furthermore, literature, like art and music, however much it is a participant in the same *épistémè*, is substantively and largely irrelevant to the business of domination and sovereign decision. It may be argued that an analysis of an Achebe or a Mahfouz is no less defining of the Oriental subject than an Orientalist analyzing an Urabi Revolt or an Averroes's commentary on Aristotle, and this is true.[41] Yet, literature, art, and music, because of their aesthetical constitution, are somewhat less effective than history and other discourses of the same category within the central paradigm. After all, the entire history of the colonial project in Asia and Africa has not been known to involve specialists in literature or music (however much these were supportive of the project), and if such figures did happen to be involved, it was not by virtue of their knowledge of these fields that colonialism thrived. We cannot forget that William Jones himself was an expert in literature and a poet of some status. He also was a linguist, but none of these scholarly accomplishments—which seem to have distracted Said—is directly relevant to his role as a colonialist functionary. What made Jones a potent colonialist was his knowledge of Hindu and Islamic "law," aided in forceful ways by his deep interest in history.

Literature, music, and art, however much they are partly constituted by modern categories, including the colonialist doctrine of progress, are not directly relevant to the force fields and power structure of central domains. Because of their aesthetic and artistically abstract constitution, they will, by definition, retain structures that inherently contradict the single-mindedness of the central domains, be it capitalism, science, or the realm of the political. This is precisely why they remain lodged in the peripheral domains, for when states, governments, and corporations jettison their armies, capital, corporate modes of domination, and sovereign structure of thought in favor of a dominating and overwhelming appreciation of a Quranic calligraphy, a Matisse, or a Pattachitra, making such objects the subjects of value and of performativity, art as a discourse, authorship, and discipline will ipso facto move to the central domain, defining it, and ousting departments of science and economics. Put bluntly, you cannot colonize a country, much less a whole civilization, through music, visual art, and literature, however useful it is for colonialism to force one "foot"[42] of these disciplines into the domain of colonial power (a foot that is undoubtedly planted therein). By contrast, capitalism and science, and their offshoots, have alone proven sufficient for colonizing the great majority of the world by the end of the nineteenth century.

When the visual arts—and for that matter music, literature, and the like—conduct and win their revolution that will demolish the theology of progress and a sovereign structure of thought, it is only then that science, philosophy, and economics will have to move to the peripheral domain or vanish in whole or in part; and being always subordinate and subservient to the imperatives of the central domain, these latter discourses will consequently shed their former structures of thought. Only then will some of them disappear forever (such as the business school) and others will be transformed into fields of discourse that place a premium on an aesthetic or epistemology that is determined by an ethical order of things. It cannot be then overstressed that inasmuch as colonialism and its various arms—including the trade company and the multinational corporation—are an extension of the state,[43] they are structurally interconnected with the discursive formations of their home cultures, especially the academic institutions and their central-domain specializations. That these academic-corporate structures are engulfed by a wide range of sociopathologies is taken here as a foregone conclusion.

III

Consistent with this narrative, I argue that colonialism, of the settler and nonsettler type, is inherently genocidal, in every shade this term implies, an implication that will require us to expand the meaning of genocide beyond its conventional physical forms. And if this argument is accepted, then one is compelled to conclude that central domain's academia—not only Orientalism—is also inherently disposed to laying down the discursive and material foundations of colonialist genocidal practice. There is then both a logical and an ontological concomitance between the academia of the central domain and colonialism, on the one hand, and the same concomitance between colonialism and genocide, on the other. I will argue that only the surface level of genocide possesses, like Orientalism itself, general political significance, and that, also like Orientalism, its genealogical roots go back to a philosophical worldview in which the concept of value suffered a significant reduction in scope and depth, and in which the shame of nature and thus self-hatred became the necessary conditions for the hatred of the Other.[44]

I should like to begin by engaging the historian Patrick Wolfe's formulation of the problem, as expounded in his outstanding article "Settler Colonialism and the Elimination of the Native."[45] I will contend, however, that, like Said, Wolfe remains committed to a "superstructural" analysis of the problem, one that has a "touch-and-go" relationship with the underlying structures of thought that characterize colonialism and genocide. Said confined the complicity of Orientalism to the political and economic, conventionally so defined, thus bestowing on Orientalism a cognitive structure of thought that, on the one hand, was integral to Europe's own discursive formations (the Foucauldian component) and, on the other, was an effect of its association with colonialism and Western hegemony over the Orient. When he came somewhat close to what I am calling here the sovereignty of knowledge, Said would not only passingly assign it to the internal dimension of the Orientalist text, but rather quickly retreat into the political domain. Wolfe does the same, except that his ranking of factors begins with property, represented in land and natural resources, among other such elements. The political factor ranks as a close second, but, as in Said, when he detects the odor of the sovereign *structure* of thought, he also retreats to the economic and materialistic, although his empirical data profitably allows for the type of analysis I am proposing here. This leaves his account tantalizing, for it is he who, after all, coined and insisted on the boundlessly insightful dictum that "genocide is a structure not an event." Wolfe gives due regard to the processual component of genocide's structure, but the structure of thought *within his* concept of "structure," that which drives action, remains unarticulated.

Nor are we entirely clear, in Wolfe's narrative, why genocides are not concomitant with colonialism ("though the two have converged") or why settler colonialism "is inherently eliminatory but not invariably eliminatory."[46] The explanation that genocide can occur without colonialism and colonialism without genocide is one of concurrence that explains difference but not commonality. It is, in other words, an external explanation that does not engage causal explication in any of its variants. Nor still are we clear as to why settler colonialism, at least in the American model, opted for implementing "cultural projects" with a view to remolding the "Red savage" in the image of the White man *after* a genocidal series had been undertaken, and not before. In British India, for example, genocide in its conventional meaning did not take place, and in the formally sovereign Ottoman Empire, genocide committed by the West was far from conceivable. How can all these phenomena be schematized under one encompassing explicans?

I would like to suggest that a satisfactory explanation resides in the structures of power that Foucault diagnosed and that was the "mother" structure that governed both colonialism and its concomitant genocide. If we see power not as a logic or as a logically structured domain, but rather as a system of tactics and strategies that operate under specific conditions in a specific manner, changing course and tactics as the situation requires, we begin to understand its instrumentalist nature, one that reflected and was reflected by the larger structure of instrumentalism and instrumentalist reason that is the hallmark of the Enlightenment. In this sense modern power is instrumentalism *meshed with, backed by, and fronted by* force. It is precisely here where modern power differs from its premodern counterparts, and not only in the order of its composition, but mainly in its very constitution. Premodern power was sheer force, backed and fronted by instrumentalism, but it was not meshed with it. Indeed, as I have noted earlier in the context of the benchmark principle, worldly force, violent as it may have been, operated under the benchmark constraints of higher principles, whether they were legal-moral precepts or the equally strong dictates of custom and its precepts.

Recognizing modern power as lacking an organizing logic—one of its most distinctive features—does not on its own explain Wolfe's purported distinction between genocide and colonialism. We need another explicans, which, once introduced, will remove the explanatory difficulties occasioned by the distinction and, I will argue, the distinction itself. The sophisticated Actor Network Theory has many parts, most of them are eminently useful, while some others are not without ideological biases, including a narrowly defined theory of agency that amounted, in certain writings, to reducing the culpabilities of nothing less than colonialism itself (through arrogating an indefensible form of agency to the "natives"). I am here interested in only one part of it, which I shall metaphorically call, not without a pun, "Latour's Stone."

Latour's Stone in my usage is a concept that ascribes *presence*, not agency, to the physical realities of the complex of land and people that was to become the colonies. Presence precludes a human structure of intent, a necessary condition for agency. Intent presupposes a rational action of choice, for when choice does not ontologically exist, there cannot be intent. I cannot intend to lift this chair if I operate without a concept of choice. As I suggested earlier, I do not have agency as a life-loving person if the only choice I have is to be killed by a bullet or by hanging. The locus of agency here is life itself, not the method of execution. In the colonial context, *presence* was the issue, not agency, according to the evidence of the existential, cultural, epistemological, political, legal, educational, psychological, and similarly profound transformations that were inflicted on the indigenous populations,[47] some of which I have explained in the second chapter.[48] Latour's Stone captures this presence within the overall structure of European power. As the ecological humanities scholar Deborah Bird Rose perceptively remarked, the native "got in the way" of the colonialists "just by staying home."[49] For the colonial settler, as Chaim Weizmann attests in his profoundly prophetic statement, the natives—in this case Palestinian—are nothing but "*rocks*" that present "obstacles that had to be cleared on a difficult path."[50]

Perhaps there is no better way of illustrating what I mean by Latour's Stone than by briefly dwelling on an ominous essay by Vladimir Jabotinsky, published in 1923 and titled "The Iron Wall." In this essay, Jabotinsky captured with equal measure both his own political present and the entire future of the Israel–Palestine problem, making prophesy a derivative of sovereignty. The power of his essay lies certainly not in any intellectual finesse or literary quality, but rather in the realpolitik of modernity that equipped the author with an assured grip over the concept of sovereign domination. Jabotinsky's text is of course a specimen of Orientalism, but it is also primarily a modern text in every meaning of the term. Like the project of Israel itself, "The Iron Wall" captures the entire range of Western knowledge as *structurally woven* into colonization, sovereign domination, and the decimation of the natives and their cultures. And just as the modern project presupposed such structures of domination, without which it could have never arisen, so did the conception and doctrine of our liberal revisionist Zionist. Whereas the distance between Said's academic Orientalist text and the colonial-genocidal activity on the ground was vitiated by a multiplicity of intermediaries, Jabotinsky's "Iron Wall" captures this activity as a textual representation in the most chillingly realistic form. "The Iron Wall" does not, as it would historiographically seem, just forecast the future; it in fact prescribes it, writes it, and creates it ex nihilo out of a sovereign impulse.

The range of Orientalist attitudes pervades "The Iron Wall" as a textual realpolitik. Jabotinsky's construction of the "enemy," the Oriental object, is highly calculated, for depicting the Palestinians as supine would of course preempt the very idea of an Iron Wall, since the Wall's necessity is predicated on the native rejection of, and resistance to, colonialism. It was therefore necessary, in order to justify military and violent ventures, to bestow a degree of rhetorical agency on the Palestinians as people who will resist any colonial power in its bid to dispossess them. But having decided for the Palestinians that they will resist the colonization of Palestine, he continues to decide for them the makeup of their national characteristics. "Culturally they are five hundred years behind us, spiritually they have neither our endurance nor our determination." Yet, they are "as good psychologists as we [Jews] are," because psychology is constructed here as having the function or power to unmask "our" plotting and cunning. In other words, their basic psychological instincts and "instinctive jealous love for Palestine" are sufficient to make them realize what "our" intentions are. For "they know what we want, as well as we know what they do not want."[51]

But what "they want" and what "we want" are not, and can never be, an equation, the latter *always* deciding on the fate of the former. Jabotinsky fully recognizes that colonization operates by its own sovereign logic: there is not a "solitary instance of any colonisation being carried on with the consent of the native population." Even when "the colonists behaved decently . . . the native population fought with the same ferocity against the good colonists as against the bad." Thus, no matter "which phraseology we employ in explaining our colonising aims," the Palestinians will resist. Yet, the Palestinians do not seem to apprehend what they are facing, and have little understanding of "us" as colonists. In horrific Schmittian language, Jabotinsky reminds the natives and his own readers alike that "*Colonisation carried its own explanation, the only possible explanation, unalterable and as clear as daylight to every ordinary Jew and every ordinary Arab.*"[52] It is "unalterable" because it is the highest truth, from which there is no escape. Colonization lies "in the very nature of things, and in this particular regard nature cannot be changed." Note here that for Jabotinsky nature is not only manipulable but also subject to change, control, and domination. But the only primordial aspect of it is colonization: it is the Law that governs all other laws. Domination is god, and it is in the name of this sovereign god that Jabotinsky seals the fate of the Palestinians. "*Zionist colonisation must either stop, or else proceed regardless of the native population.* Which means that it can proceed and develop only under the protection of a power that is independent of the native population—behind an iron wall, which the native population cannot breach."[53] The only difference between "our 'militarists' and our 'vegetarians'" is that "the first prefer that the iron wall should consist of Jewish soldiers," while the second "are content that they should be British."

Sovereignty does not only decide the fate of the natives; it also constitutes morality itself. If I say I am a moral agent, then I am a moral agent, even if I am a diabolical monster. Jabotinsky powerfully instructs us in the art of argument that disproves the impossibility of deriving the Ought from the Is: "Either Zionism is moral and just, or it is immoral and unjust. But that is a question that we should have settled before we became Zionists." And since "we have settled that question," the answer to the question is "in the affirmative. *We hold that Zionism is moral and just. And since it is moral and just, justice must be done.*"[54] This is the morality of colonialism, our morality, and it is so not only because "there is no other morality" but also because we said so.

What is it that should be done? The iron wall, needless to say, is no more than a means to an end. *The idea of this wall is to deprive the Palestinians of any possibility of resistance or action against the inescapable colonization of Palestine.* It is, in other words, any form of massive, impenetrable, and irresistible force. "Every native population in the world resists colonists as long as it has the *slightest hope* of being able to rid itself of the danger of being colonised."[55] If the Palestinians now resist, Jabotinsky declared, it is because there "remains a solitary spark of hope that they will be able to prevent the transformation of 'Palestine' into the 'Land of Israel.'" It is precisely this, the hope, that "we" should take away from them. For when "a living people yields in matters of such vital character it is only when there is no longer any hope of getting rid of us, because they can make no breach in the iron wall. Not till then will they drop their extremist leaders whose watchword is 'Never.'"

Had Jabotinsky's linguistic repertoire been accustomed to the notions of agency, he probably would have substituted the term "agency" for "hope." The idea was to take away agency from the hands and lives of the natives, to deprive them of any course of action, of any choice of their own. It is to throw them, like "stones," outside the system of power, the sufficient condition for eviscerating agency. And it is only when native agency is categorically eviscerated that "we" will be able to have an "agreement." The "only way to obtain an agreement is the iron wall, which is to say a strong power in Palestine that is not amenable to any Arab pressure. In other words, the only way to reach an agreement in the future is to abandon all idea of seeking an agreement at present."

The power of Jabotinsky's essay lies in the fact of its forecasting accuracy, an index of the power of sovereignty, not only over the present, but over the future as well. His was a brilliant diagnostic that, in a few pages, summed up and captured the entire structure of colonization in Palestine and elsewhere. The reduction of the Palestinians and many others to inertia was the point of the iron wall, whether Zionist, British, or French. Latour's Stone, exemplified and starkly manifested in the success of Jabotinsky's diagnostics, is a story of presence, not agency—that is, as long as the Stone remains in existence.

IV

The lack of power's organizing logic (in the way I have already described) together with Latour's Stone prepares the ground for an explanation of the variations on the single theme of genocidal colonialism, one that obviates and renders unwarranted Wolfe's distinction. Being itself bereft of an organizing logical principle (it being the defining feature of modern power), instrumentalism cannot, in and of itself, be an explicans, for it is made of what the term indicates, a conception or a composite conception of an instrument or instruments as applied to all value in the world. This conception is not just a way of thought or a mode of behavior that signals an attitude to things in the world, such as being cautious, cowardly, or judicious. The trio, among many others like them, does not involve an external component that defines what they are. If I am cautious, it is by virtue of an inner quality in my character that is not subject to a mechanism. If I am cautious, then I cannot be uncautious, no matter who and what I am dealing with, for this is my nature, irrespective of the particular circumstances. Instrumentalism, however, consists of the same element of a habituated disposition but it differs from such a trio in that it presupposes an object, one that, in order to manifest itself, is essential for the habituated quality in the process of projecting itself onto the object. If I am predisposed to being cautious, then I am just as cautious with my closest and most trusted friends as I am with strangers. The object of my caution is irrelevant. But instrumentalism is a structure of thought that always requires an object on whom instrumentalism is exercised. Instrumentalism, unlike prudence, caution, cowardliness, and much else of the like, is transitive and inherently transgressive, thereby presupposing an object of transgression. And because it is a structure of thought, instrumentalism not only uses people and things as instruments, but also devises the necessary instruments to exercise its transgression on the object.

An instrument in the very basic and primitive sense of a tool is therefore not a merely fortuitous physical object but, because of its architectural and epistemological composition, it becomes *itself* a structure of thought and action. To coin an adage, tell me what you invented and I will tell you *what* you are. The creation of a tool, instrument, or method therefore is never neutral, and never just a matter of need (as in the old adage "need is the mother of invention") but "a revealing"[56] of a structure of thought that establishes an epistemological continuum between subject and predicate, between the instrument and its maker. A gas chamber, a machine gun, an excavation machine, a drilling rig, a fighter plane, or a nuclear head embody within them structures of thought that establish an epistemological continuum with the minds of their makers. To explain genocides and holocausts as a result of the availability of modern technology, modern science, or bureaucratic efficiency is to misunderstand the very nature of instrumentalism as a structure of thought. The invention of nuclear weapons or of sophisticated military technology that wiped off the face of the Earth millions of innocent victims in the colonies, in Japan, and in Europe itself is not a neutral act of science or the result of neutral technological competence. Nor is there any neutrality in the use of otherwise "innocent" instruments to destructive effects. A carpenter's hammer used to smash the head of another human or a pet loses this epistemological continuum, rendering it anything but a carpenter's hammer as originally and conventionally conceived. The hammer is epistemologically reinvented at the very moment it is used for murder. It is therefore not the instrument and its availability that make for a rationally justifiable analytical explicans, but it is rather the mind behind its invention *and use* that must phenomenologically constitute the explicans.

A familiar and pervasive argument in this connection goes to the effect that had other "nations," "states," or "empires" possessed such a technology at earlier points in human history, they would have committed the same or similar acts as did the Nazis or the European colonists. But this does not account for the very raison d'être and genealogy of this kind of technology. Nor are the acts of violence committed by means of these weapons incidental to their invention. The architecture and epistemology of this very invention, on the one hand, and use of these weapons, on the other, are *both* integral to a structure of thought that made such weapons possible in the first place. What is more, this very explanation of them as incidental, if not an exception, to modern technical "evolution" is wholly integral to the theology of progress that in part constituted nothing less than a condition of possibility for these atrocities.

The nature of modern power (as described here) and its subset of the instrumentalist structure of thought go a long way, I think, in explaining how they bore on Latour's Stone. Yet, this structure requires further explanation, since its genealogical origins extend back to the Distinction I have been discussing. If we consider that the eminent effect of this Distinction was to remove value from nature, it is easy to see that humans, being an essential part of nature, especially the naked Adamic nature, have been deprived of value as well. They are no longer the creation of a higher deity, endowed in their essence with value precisely because they hail from a divine architecture and design. And the more naked they are, the lower their value is in the chain of being.[57]

In many cultures, including what Guénon called "Eastern civilizations," life is valued intrinsically, because of the unity of the universe as architecture; and architecture presupposes an architect, a rational/ intelligent plan, and an intent to design. The modern distinction obliterated this worldview, using racial theories and social Darwinism in order to classify creatures. Without the background of this structure, Locke's theories of freedom, government, and "democracy" and the very American Constitution will be rendered unintelligible, considering that Locke precluded non-Europeans from consideration as equally entitled to his notions of freedom and rule of law, evidenced in part in the fact that he himself invested heavily in the slave trade.[58] And when the American Constitution declared all men to be equal, the "Black man" was more or less in the rank of animals. Locke's philosophy and the theory and practice of the American Constitution—two remarkably influential sources of political thought and political practice—are on their own ample evidence of liberalism's organic embeddedness in the structure of thought I have been discussing. Of course the materialist and economic factors in the rise of such racist theories are undeniable, but materialism is not a sufficient condition or even the original culprit. (Had Marx been intimately familiar with Islamic economic, intellectual, and social histories—not to mention other Asian civilizational constellations—he probably would not have, I think, insisted on historical materialism as a monopolizing explicans for the rise of Western capitalism.) What led to the Distinction are a host of augmenting factors, eminent among them the political and social revolutions in Europe against the abuses of monarchies and church, secularized Christian concepts, and, quite likely, prior barbarian influences on Christianity itself. Irrespective of causes—which are in dire need of study on their own—what matters to us here is that once the structure of thought was shaped into the Distinction, the Distinction itself as a structure of thought became the engine driving the vehicle of the modern state in conducting the major forces.

Nor, I must stress, can racial theories be informative in the explanation of genocide or the general manner in which colonialism conducted its exploitative projects. First, racial and racialized discourse was no different from Orientalism's cultural depictions and stereotyping, a discursive method of high performativity, normatively installed as a "natural" means to legitimize and render intelligible and palatable the subjugation, and inhumane treatment, of the now human subhuman. Second, racial discourse was as instrumental as the instruments we have already discussed, namely, it was the consequence rather than the effect of a particular structure of thought. In fact, it was itself a *product* of that thought; and derivatives cannot logically or epistemologically supersede or obviate that of which they are derivatives.

Third, as Wolfe persuasively argued, using an empirical comparison between the treatment of "Black blood" and "Red blood" by American settler colonialism, racial theories operate differently in different contexts, often producing opposite results. They operate on their victims by the principle that it is not who you are but where you are. The "primary motive for elimination is not race . . . but access to territory. Territoriality is settler colonialism's specific, irreducible element."[59] While this is no doubt true, this greed for territory has no more explanatory value than race or a gas chamber, for the deep desire for all such material things can constitute neither a genealogical terminus nor a final cause.[60] The greed in accumulating territory is no different, in principle, than the greed in commanding a massive army and arsenal. These, in fact, stood more or less equal on Hitler's menu, and as indispensable supplements to each other, especially as evidenced in his Russian campaign's *Lebensraum* and *Unternehmen Barbarossa*. The White Americans and Spaniards were by no means unique.

Furthermore, if territoriality were *the terminus ad quem*, then one might ask why the Chinese, the Indians, the Muslims, and many others did not approach territory with the same mental attitude and methods of conquest; they did not systematically inflict physical or cultural or mental destruction on their subjugated populations, as the White settlers did on the Amerindians.[61] Furthermore, had territory constituted such a terminus or a final cause, why would this same territory be subjected to ecological and environmental degradation, and why was it eventually remade into a new nature, as William Cronon has argued?[62] In this larger story, territory is an instrument of a larger instrument, and this larger instrument is in turn an instrument of yet a larger one. Such instrumentalities therefore beg for a regressive series that can inhere in an intelligibly constituted, primary structure of thought.[63] It has been my argument that this structure is the Distinction from which all major modern phenomena, including instruments, instrumentalism, genocide and colonialism, and much else of the same vein, ensued, issued, resulted, and flowed. It is also within the inner core and kernel of the Distinction that the concept of sovereignty resided and continues to reside. It will not be an exaggeration to say that sovereignty constituted this innermost core and kernel.

V

Reality therefore was what the White man said it should be, and this man was not, as I noted earlier, a categorical term for all white men or all white women or all white children. This quasi-aristo-plutocracy therefore abducted the concept of sovereignty, laying the foundations for a worldwide concept of rule that relied primarily on a juridicality that is as instrumentalist as Europe could muster. This juridicality must be taken to rank along with all of the major instruments we have enumerated, and may rank second only to brute force, the most efficient of all. Juridicality—by its very nature as an apparatus of legality, as a socially pervasive system, one run by publicly manifest lawyers, judges, and ruling institutions—may possess, precisely by virtue of this nature, a more easily detectable structure of thought than that of a gas chamber, a nuclear missile, or even a race theory, but juridicality has nonetheless a similar power of decimation, in the sense I shall outline momentarily.

In the sense I use it, juridicality is any law, legal system, regulation, or decree used for coercing into obedience, governing, or regulating a human collectivity. It creates institutions through coercion, regulates their operation henceforth, and thereby regularizes and normalizes their modes of existence, all of these processes amounting to, and culminating in, an efficient performativity of the subject. Another distinguishing feature of juridicality is its arbitrariness, since it issues from sovereign power. We are accustomed to thinking of martial law as a deviation from the normative legal order, and the Schmittian "state of exception" is conceived and received as an exception precisely because it is founded on the assumption that a normative order is prior to it, constituting the normal state of affairs against which the "exception" stands as a kind of anomaly.

Giorgio Agamben disagreed with Schmitt on this point, arguing in effect that the state of exception lay neither in nor above the normative legal order, thus in effect constituting no exception in any qualitative sense.[64] It remains a primal form of modern juridico-political systems; rising out of its dormancy at any time, the perception of existential threat is awakened. It is constituted not as an essential difference but rather as a continuation of law by extrajustificatory methods. This elision from ordinary to extraordinary normativity becomes all the more intelligible if one does not take for granted the standardized and normative narrative of the history of the Euro-American political arrangement—one that has become, juridically speaking, globalized, and one that has also erased from memory all other premodern forms of governing; here, it is eminently arguable that the state of exception is not an exception at all, that it is not just a cherished, though residual, legacy of monarchical Europe. Instead, my argument goes, it is lodged amid the normative order, defining the *potentialities* of its force and *implicitly* determining its operations, even when the rules of the so-called normative order are in effect.

As I have argued elsewhere, what we call the rule of law in the Madisonian paradigmatic model is not, when contrasted with certain extra-European legal systems, as much a rule of law as it is a rule of the state itself.[65] That such a more robust extra-European model of the rule of law may not be readily comprehensible, or even conceivable, to, say, an American constitutional scholar is precisely testimonial to the same power of normativity that rendered the "state of exception" an exception. It is also this same power, driven by a progress theology, that renders the phenomenon of genocide, especially the Holocaust, an exception to modernity, when in fact genocide is inherent in it. This is not to say that the purported "state of exception" merely stands in an analogical relationship to genocide, in that they are both whitewashed by the doctrine of progress. My argument instead is that the two phenomena are structurally interconnected, genocide being one of the necessary conditions and manifestations of this "state," manifestations that do not always take on the form of genocide as an "event," but they remain—in structural terms—genocidal nonetheless.

Under the myth and fiction of popular sovereignty and popular will (a myth as true and believable today as racial theories were in eighteenth- and nineteenth-century Europe), we generally believe in *this* rule of law as an expression of that will. But serious political and sociological analysis, started by Marx but diversified later, speaks otherwise. Such analysis tells a story of interest and pressure groups, AIPACs, neodynastic families, class interest, and much else of the same that determine not only policies but the very form of government. In the case study discussed in chapter 2, Islam's rule of law was shown to have stood above executive, judicial, and legislating will, and no one could change the law at will or through an amendment. The change, as I showed earlier and in detail elsewhere, was piecemeal in substance and gradual in temporality, and was not subject to the will of any individual agent, institution, jurist, or power branch whatever. The overall dictates of the law ruled over sultans as much as over any common person or anyone in between.[66] The law of the land could not be suspended, and no exceptions were possible. And since that system, as I have shown through a discussion of the corporation, did not allow capitalism to break loose from a preset ethical benchmark, money and its derivative power could not affect the rule of law in any systemic or structural way. Nor could any other form of power. The enduring stability of first-order moral-legal principles guaranteed imperceptible mutations within an organically structured continuum of both polity and society. In that system, there was no need whatever for an ideological doctrine of progress whose function is in part to justify what in the long run of human history are radical changes and continuous but highly disruptive reengineering projects of the social and economic orders.

The fast-paced legal changes in the globalized Euro-American model are indicative not merely of the responsiveness and "rationally progressive" malleability of the law to social change and exigency, but rather of the sovereignty that deploys change and "exigency" in the service of power and domination in the first place, and for which "progress" becomes a legitimizing veneer. That the concept of change has become as normative as second nature in *homo modernus* does not, and cannot, oblige us to take it for granted. A question remains, provided we genuinely shed the doctrine of progress: How could humanity throughout at least six thousand years of recorded history undergo change, as it did, without having to experience the dimension of change as exists in modernity?

My argument is that integral to the modern variety of change is arbitrariness and self-arrogated freedom from restraint that can be defined only in terms of sovereign will. Which brings us back to the so-called state of exception, which is no exception at all. It is rather an integral part of a dominantly political and partially legal will that, because of its uncertain and necessarily inconsistent *substantive* constitution (for arbitrariness is, like power, by definition inconsistent), it is impractical to apply in a perpetually normative and consistently predictable manner. Normative law requires a degree of internal consistency and predictability that the so-called state of exception lacks. That this latter is inherent in law and political management is evident not only in the actual experience of the Euro-American juridico-political systems, but more so in the colonies, which exhibit the potentiality of extreme and exceptionally violent measures more than any other location; colonialism always encompasses the inherent potential of genocidal acts, even when it is seen to take place in the home country. As Dirk Moses has aptly argued, in a tactful response to Wolfe, even the Holocaust was articulated by Hitler and the leadership of the Third Reich as a defense against a perceived Jewish colonialist project.[67]

The political theorist Achille Mbembe argues that colonized territories are the location where sovereignty essentially consists in the exercise of a power outside the law, where "peace" is in effect a continuous and unending war, and where European rulers could decide upon matters of life and death absolutely: "the sovereign right to kill is not subject to any rule in the colonies." Colonialism's destructive forces were not, Mbembe argues, limited to pacification and forced cultural assimilation; they consisted in the sovereign right to kill the subject populations at will. Mbembe's account is eminently insightful, but he assumes too much when he speaks of such colonial practices as standing outside the law.[68] Being inherently instrumentalist, modern law is capable of adjusting to any situation at will, making exceptional measures integral not only to it but also to its normative mode.

In light of Agamben's and my insistence that the "state of exception" is not indeed exceptional and that it is more normative than is generally thought, the language of exception ceases to be adequate and, furthermore, becomes potentially self-contradictory. An exception that is integral to and that asserts itself as an exclusive and omnipotent quantum against the rule of law is no exception at all. The fact of its persistent presence in the actual practices of liberal democracies and the sheer volume of scholarly ink poured for its discussion—no doubt caused in good part by liberal anxiety about the implications of Schmitt's, and more so Agamben's, nightmarish reminders—make that "state" a near-ordinary practice and more than just a potentiality. It is anything, therefore, but an exception. It is not a differentiated quality but one of degree, and language tends to encounter distinctive problems when clear opposites or patent differences disappear, losing its crispness and sharp distinctions. For lack of a better term, it may be closer to a precise expression to call that Schmittian-Agambian moment a "state of extraordinarity," a somewhat awkward neologism,[69] but one that does not stray far from its adjectival equivalent. The state of extraordinarity, treading on the heels of the lexical "extraordinary," is integral to the *ordinary* legal and political order of the modern state; yet, the prefix "extra-"

carries the connotation not of the "supra-," but rather of occasional addition, partial displacement, and intensification of the state of the ordinary. The extraordinary is the moment of truth in the ordinary. It is the extra pressure and extreme stress that bring out the true character of what is masked, under usual circumstances, as a self-composed persona.

Because this state of extraordinarity *is*, among others, the governing state in the colonies, it acquires a measure of normativity that makes it ordinary. This is to say that the gradation from the ordinary to the extraordinary is just that, gradation, a changing quantity, an increasing or decreasing intensity willed by the colonist, but certainly not a qualitative difference. The colonies, I am in effect arguing, in line with Foucault's work on Europe, are the structural extension of the modern state's structure, rather than a mere attachment to it, an appendage that is accidental or contingent to it, but indeed one that is of its essence.[70] When Great Britain dropped India in 1947, it was not doing anything different than when Russia relinquished its southern and western republics and oblasts upon the collapse of the Soviet Union. Nor would the secession of Quebec from Canada after the referendum in 1995 have violated this logic (had it occurred), however unilateral it might have been.

Sovereignty and the state of extraordinarity are mutually constitutive of each other, law being no more than a malleable instrument in their cerebral and political operations. Here, the normal and abnormal as discrete categories do not exist, for they are constantly reconstituted, meshing with each other at every turn. Frantz Fanon assumed too much when he argued that colonialism is a "world turned upside down," that in this world the normal turns abnormal, where "the pathological came to occupy the space of the normal."[71] This, I have suggested, is only a matter of gradation, where the pathological constitutes metropolitan sovereignty as much as sovereignty constitutes colonial extraordinarity.[72] And if sovereignty and its law are constitutive of the pathological, then the modern state and its genealogy of thought structure mask a criminality sanctioned by that law.

Sovereignty runs the entire gamut of the modern sociopolitical order, and can be said to have manifested itself with increasing robustness since the sixteenth century. It is therefore a mistake to see it as belonging to, or definable by, an exclusive political framework. Consider the four major units defining the structure of the colonialist project, all infused with various forms of sovereign knowledge and action. Of course the first and commonly recognized unit is the obvious metropolis whose colonialist conduct is organized and driven by the sovereign state as a fairly well-defined political body. Then comes the unit of the officially appointed colonists themselves, who appear in the form of organized armies and trade companies, the British in India and the Dutch in Indonesia being prime examples. What are often missed in this larger picture of European colonialism are two additional elements—the third and fourth units—of no less significance to the entire project. These are the so-called lawless rabble[73] and the colonist as a private individual.

There is certainly nothing lawless about the rabble, for lawlessness presupposes a fixed, stable, normative, and steady rule of law. As both a phenomenon and a category of analysis, sovereignty was intrinsic to the four units of the colonialist project. It ran through the entire project and defined its evolutionary form and substance in every way. Rather than being a separate force operating in any way contrary to the colonialist vision of the metropolis, the "murderous activities of the frontier rabble constitute its principal means of expansion."[74] As the political historian Lorenzo Veracini persuasively argues, settlers, individual, collective, or official, systematically saw themselves as independent agents and thus as founders of political orders: they "interpret their collective efforts in terms of an inherent sovereign claim that travels with them and is ultimately, if not immediately, autonomous from the colonising metropole."[75] But it is significant that the quest for sovereignty was driven by the mother country's sovereign domination of its own deployed colonizers. The constitutional historian Aziz Rana effectively argues that at least in the North American case, the settlers enjoyed legal and political rights not much different from the conquered populations and African slaves. The Crown arrogated to itself as much right to exercise against them discretionary and coercive power as it had against the conquered and slave populations.[76] If violence breeds violence in the world of Europe, then sovereign domination breeds its own offspring.

My main argument here is that sovereignty saturated the colonial participants at all levels, and if the individual did not, on the surface, exhibit a pronounced sense of sovereignty, it is because all colonialist projects possessed a corporate nature, and the individual was forced to corral himself within the boundaries of any collective body that permitted the closest expression of his sense of sovereignty. It is no coincidence that the first rise of the company as a corporatized body was squarely situated within a colonialist venture: the British East India Company was well known for its claims to sovereignty or quasi-sovereignty, as well as for its corrupt actions that exhibited the length and width of sovereign behavior. The self-constituting capacity of the colonists traveled from the highest to the lowest echelons of the project, and had no necessary or exclusive connection with mere greed for wealth or territory. The project, individual and collective, was about sovereign domination of a new land, in which the natives were incidental and little more than a disposable attachment, and where will to power was restrained, if at all, by none other than the will itself.

The capacity for self-constitution was possible only through a conception of autonomy that subordinated all conceptions of "normative" law, including the law of the metropolis, which was often seen by the colonists themselves as oppressive. American settler colonialism, from its beginnings until the Civil War, and Israel's West Bank settlers are representations of the two extreme ends of a single spectrum in which colonial sovereignty exhibits itself. The former was a story of a successful sovereign action, the latter, thus far, considerably, though partially, successful. The "lawless rabble" are no less lawless just because they declare themselves sovereign. Sovereignty is productive not of a normative law or a rule of law, but rather of the will to law. To confuse the two is to confuse cause with effect. Sovereign will in the colonial project militated against the native's presence as natural "rocks" to be removed from its path, and the law came to execute this will.[77] It changed as the circumstance required, for if self-constitution meant entitlement, political and otherwise, then the Schmittian existential threat is always integral to colonial consciousness and presence. Upon any perception of such a threat the "exception" ceases to be an exception, even in the metropolis. The colonies, more susceptible to incurring such a perception, exhibited an intense degree of "exception," one that was routinized as a norm.

VI

All of the preceding now permits a schematic overview of the relationship between colonialism and genocide. Developing Raphael Lemkin's concept of genocide, Wolfe aptly argues that there are positive and negative dimensions to the phenomenon.

> Negatively, it strives for the dissolution of native societies. Positively, it erects a new colonial society on the expropriated land base. . . . In

its positive aspect, elimination is an organizing principal of settler-colonial society rather than a one-off (and superseded) occurrence. The positive outcomes of the logic of elimination can include officially encouraged miscegenation, the breaking-down of native title into alienable individual freeholds, native citizenship, child abduction, religious conversion, resocialization in total institutions such as missions or boarding schools, and a whole range of cognate biocultural assimilations. All these strategies, including frontier homicide, are characteristic of settler colonialism.[78]

Insisting that the concept of genocide includes what I call total reengineering of the colonized culture and its subject (in the performative sense of subjectivity, subjecthood, and identity), Wolfe wishes to avoid the problematics that such designations as "ethnocide" and "cultural genocide" engender because, being "not the real thing, they threaten to undo themselves." But Wolfe also points to a central problem in all discourse on genocide, academic or popular, namely, that the modern frame of mind has been stuck in the Holocaust as the "paradigm,"[79] one that has diminished the importance of the more complex forms of what he calls structural genocides.

Wolfe may have added that the persistence of the meaning of genocide as a singular occurrence of mass and summary killing (that is, as an event) is also due to the modern discursive practices of normalizing structural genocide. In fact, it is the standard received academic and popular wisdom in the modern world, especially among the current descendants of the peoples of former colonies and their modern institutions, that their history over the last two or three centuries was an inevitable process, a "natural" course on the path of progress. This was possible not only because they have not seen or experienced anything else (and are thereby left bereft of a comparative perspective) but also because these have been nurtured as true believers, like their Western counterparts, in the theology of progress, which was in turn one of the most essential and potent tools of imperialism. My point here is that the very strategy of the theological discourse of progress that made the Holocaust an exception worked concurrently to make structural genocide integral to the normativity of modern history, whereby the totalizing act of decimating "traditional" cultures comes to be regarded as a "natural" development.

Wolfe also argues that the Holocaust "exonerates anti-Semitic Western nations who were on the side opposing the Nazis," and that "those same nations have nothing to gain from their liability for colonial genocides." This is true, but it would make better sense not to limit the explanation to political strategizing but rather to view this particular phenomenon as integral to the overall narrative of progress that made of the Holocaust an exception, not only because of the well-known sensitivity of the issue, but because to argue, as the sociologist Sigmund Bauman, Hannah Arendt, and others have, that the Holocaust is a manifestation and an inherent feature of modernity is to invite further investigations into the deeper levels of modernity's destructiveness, including a meaningful look at structural genocide, *the historical basis of the modern project itself.* Here as well, the core issue lies not in politics but in thought structures. The Holocaust as a "paradigmatic" event, structure, and narrative was *as such* made as the immediate result not of Nazi evil but rather of the modern theology of progress. Nazi evil indeed brought out the modern potentiality into actuality, but the exceptionalizing was the handmaiden of this theology.

Wolfe's notion of structural genocide opens up capacious venues of investigation that potentially have the capabilities to rewrite the history of colonialism and thus of modernity. An essential requirement for such revisions in writing history is to recognize political phenomena and then go beyond their political implications and political significance. Toward that effort, we might see colonialism as a modern project of total transformation, one that *perpetually* aims at reengineering the subject as nature. This, not territory, is the ultimate desideratum and *terminus ad quem* of colonialism, in its settler form or not, in its Orientalism, secularism, or economics. Settler colonialism only intensifies the phenomenon of colonialism, but does not create a different underlying structure of thought, a structure that governs categorically. The levels of intensification determine the quantity and volume, but not the quality, of the state of extraordinarity.

The sources of European colonialism, eo ipso located in the European homeland,[80] were more or less the product of the same systems of power, be they British, French, Italian, Swedish, or Dutch. What made them exhibit certain difference in the way they conducted their colonialist projects was Latour's Stone, a Stone that in turn assumed different forms, sizes, and qualities in various colonized spaces. There was no issue of agency here, but one of how to carve the Stone. Some stones were too hard for carving, and were accordingly smashed or, if small enough, pulverized into dust. Others were too big, and thus were split, carved, and redesigned. Obviously, Latour's Stone in India was too large to be removed, leaving carving as the only option. In Amerindia, the Stone, having been split asunder by biological forces (influenza, typhus, cholera, and the like), became small enough for pulverization, keeping in mind that in the view of the Europeans, the Stone was simply not amenable to carving. In other words, it was not the thought structure that undergirded and governed colonialism that was the variable, but the feasibility of implementing its logic and values. The "natural" givens in the colonies thus determined the course and form of colonization.

The manner of conducting the project was one of *style*, but not a differentiated quality of a structure of thought. The French colonialists are generally seen as more bloodletting and more vicious than their British counterparts, but this is a mode of instrumentalism, *not a different quality of it*. The oft-made argument that the British went the "smarter" way than the French about running and managing their respective colonies means little other than this: the British were more efficient in translating that structure of thought into reality. Given the right conditions—that is, optimal colonialist efficiency plus total seizure and control of Latour's Stone—that reality would come into existence through the shortest route and in as full a manifestation as possible.

That settler colonialism is a graded quantity of the same colonialist quality also implies that colonialism has as many subtle forms of presence in the colonies as not so subtle ones. The most classic example is the Ottoman Empire, the Sick Man of Europe. Formally speaking, the Ottoman Empire was, by common parlance, a sovereign entity, and was not subjected to what is otherwise commonly regarded as colonialism; yet, as I have shown in detail earlier and elsewhere, it was subjected to various pressures that forced it to undertake a *structural* transformation (to invoke Wolfe's structural genocide) that was as aggressive and expedited as that which India underwent under direct British rule.[81] The Ottoman structural genocide was no less successful than any other. By the time Europe was finished with the Ottoman Empire, and after several decades of relentless domination and manipulation, there was virtually nothing left of it except a distant and distorted memory. Not only was it demolished institutionally, socially, economically, culturally, intellectually, and, concomitantly, politically, but even its memory was tarnished to the core.

If Ottoman society, like many "Oriental" others, meant anything, it was not for its political forms, but rather for its distinctive institutions, its social practices, a unique educational "system," its moral-mystical modes of expressing the self, its particular ways of existing in the natural and cosmo-logical world, and an overall system of value that was as robust and as sustainable as any other, for the sustainability had been a gradually adjust-ing continuation of earlier forms of existence that stretched back to ancient Babylonia and the world that surrounded it. Never has there been a single instance in the entire history of that region of the world—and I suspect elsewhere as well—where a society, small or large, was structurally trans-formed from within the subject outward, leading to the totalistic erasure of a mode of existence out of the world. It is particularly because Euro-pean colonialism never carried on a genocidal "event" against the Otto-mans that the Ottoman genocide represents perhaps the most classic case of a structural genocide, even more so, within my meaning, than the geno-cide committed by Euro-Americans against the Amerindians.

VII

Insofar as structural genocide is concerned, the Ottoman case may accord-ingly be located at the far end of a spectrum whose other end is occupied by such cases as the American, Australian, and Israeli cases, however dif-ferent the results of these three may be. Most other colonial situations fall in between. It is worthwhile, however, to briefly stay with the Israeli case because it manifests one of the widest ranges and greatest depths of settler colonialism, one that brings to the fore the role of academic knowledge, including Orientalism, in the project of direct colonization.[82] To the extent that the various modes of colonialism constitute a phenomenon analogical to the normative modes of politico-legal existence, Israel is a normative case of extraordinarity. Wolfe's account is remarkably helpful here, but it needs supplementation. As is well known, the Zionist project was integral to European colonialism,[83] having originated on European soil and repli-cated much of the European colonialist patterns, especially the American one. Although formally Israel does not have, like the British in India or the French in Algeria, a mother country or a colonial metropole, it does substitute for this particular tie strong and powerful connections with, if not dependency on, politically and financially influential diasporic Zionist communities in the West,[84] who lend it ideological and material support to the extent of subverting the national foreign policies of their home coun-tries, notably the United States.[85] These ties, coupled with the unqualified support it receives from the government of the United States and in large part the European Union, largely compensate for the formal absence of a mother nation.

Israel was largely founded on the myth of a Jewish people without a land finding a land without people. In the common Zionist register, the Palestinians were not people, just as the "Blacks" never counted as such in the American Constitution. The Zionist case, however, is particularly acute, since the Palestinians inhabited the land for millennia, and were not brought to it as subjugated slaves. And when Palestinians were occasionally noticed in the form of Latour's Stone, as happened with the Zionist ideologue Jabotinsky, they were given a choice: accept Zionism and its lordship and sovereignty or leave the country.[86] The option that they be the masters of their own home, the Jewish emigrants being guests who sought asylum in Palestine under the governance of its inhabitants, was not only out of the question, but not a question at all. It was not a question precisely because they did not exist, however much they materially existed. They were nothing more than an extension of nature, to be domesticated and dominated, just as the land itself was.[87] This conception stretched from the first moments of the rise of the Zionist movement to the present, having been reaffirmed by Israel's leaders in often dramatic but real terms.[88]

But Latour's Stone was too large for the Zionist project to carve or pulverize. The Palestinians far outnumbered the Jewish immigrants into Palestine, and they constituted part of a larger Arab nation that surrounded Israel from every direction but the sea. And because of this demographic, cultural, and geopolitical fact, the Palestinians were not readily amenable to a project of cultural and epistemic reengineering, a situation that finds an almost perfect analogy with the attitudes of Europeans to the Amerindians. It is not that their identity and subjectivity were more firmly entrenched in ancient traditions than the Hindus and Muslims of India; it is because the Zionist project was exclusivist by nature and too weak institutionally to embark on such a massive "cultural conquest" of the indigenous Palestinian population. When the British embarked in earnest on converting India, especially after the Great Mutiny of 1857, they had already set up and made stable their cultural and state institutions, having been politically and militarily a superpower and a leading player in the creation of modernity long before. The Zionist movement, even as late as 1948, had not established a mature identity as a state, or even as a culture, which rendered the undertaking of such a cultural reengineering project impossible.

This, together with the exclusivist nature of the movement, left Israel with another of colonialism's notorious methods: expulsion. Hence, the Palestinian exodus of about three-quarters of a million people in 1948, a method that was pursued again in the War of 1967, and that has never stopped ever since, although more recently the scale of the project has tentatively abated, so it appears.

The diminishment obviously has its reasons, all to do with a careful calculation of the best and most efficient means to complete the colonialist project. As the distinguished historian Ilan Pappe insightfully argued in the conclusion to *Ethnic Cleansing of Palestine*, there are "many Palestinians who are not under occupation, but none of them . . . are free from the potential danger of future ethnic cleansing. It seems a matter of Israeli priority rather than a hierarchy of 'fortunate' and 'less fortunate' Palestinians."[89] The increasingly depopulated West Bank is under effective control, having been largely taken over by the Jewish settlements. The colonization there is near complete. In the highly populated Gaza Strip, a narrow stretch of land that is home to nearly two million Palestinians, Israel created an open-air killing field, with massive bombardment campaigns pursued with some regularity. Together with the siege laid to the Strip since 2007, Gaza is the site of a process of gradual elimination, yet another distinguished colonialist method. Elimination may be the function of the impracticality of a one-off genocide (that is, genocide as an event) because of the attention of the world community and because of a fear of consequences similar to the case of "terminating apartheid" in South Africa. Yet these political and psychological constraints on Israel do not in the least preclude the plotting and implementation of an unconventional form of mass elimination, as Pape has suggested.

Given the global discourse of progressive modernity, in which the Holocaust appears as an exception (one that, among other things, is designed to enhance the acuteness of anti-Semitism and thus render its singularity serviceable in garnering support for Israel), and given the role of Israeli propaganda in nurturing this discourse, the Holocaust, as Wolfe aptly notes, emerged as the "non-paradigmatic paradigm."[90] Thus, like structural genocide, other forms of mass elimination would not, so Israel's leaders in effect appear to think, be detectable, precisely because of a piecemeal approach. In this approach no artificially constructed concentration camps, or an explicit bureaucratic machinery, or gas chambers are involved. What is involved instead is a semblance of traditional warfare, cast in the form of reprisals against militant groups who are perceived to threaten the security of the Jewish state. However, the construction of such an existential threat is by no means unprecedented, for as Schmitt taught us, this threat is integral to the concept of the political, to the distinction between enemy and friend, and thus to the modus vivendi of *all* modern states. Yet the enemy need not present itself as a state at all. Even groups within states can be *perceived* to create or represent such a threat, however imaginary the perception may be. Given the subjugated status of the Palestinians and their overall incapabilities, cleansing campaigns iterate the fundamental structure of a security-based existential threat, and are furthermore grounded in a *founding* ideology that assigns to the Palestinians a subhuman form of existence, all the while constructing the colonizers as "God's chosen people."

Existential threat is one of the foundations of the modern state's conditions of possibility, a cornerstone of the political and the offspring of total sovereignty, epistemic as much as political. It is a latent potential quickly awakened by everyday international relations. In the case of the United States, the threat experienced transference from Communist danger during the Cold War to Islamic danger, especially after 2001. The imaginary threat, subjective and arbitrary to the core (especially in the case of the latter), cannot be better illustrated than in the false conviction of Saddam's Iraq as possessing weapons of mass destruction. Yet, a more complex and relevant example may be Germany's Third Reich. In his infamous *Mein Kampf*, Hitler constructed the Jews not just as a menace but as an existential threat to the security of the Reich and the integrity of the Aryan nation. The Jews in Hitler's book, as they were commonly regarded by the general leadership of the Reich, were *effectively* constituted as a colonial threat, a power that was intent on subjugating the German nation through money, banking, and much else.[91] But such subjugation was not to be even entertained, especially considering the "superiority" of the Aryan race and the "inferiority" of the Jews (a construct that was in part brought into existence, we shall not forget, by German philological Orientalism). It was therefore a short step that Hitler had to take in *Mein Kampf* to convert the "racially inferior" Jews into a colonizable species. And it was on precisely this ideological basis that Jews were incinerated by the millions in central Europe and hunted down in the Eastern Soviet territories by equal numbers during the Russian campaign. Gradual genocides, settler colonialism, genocide as an event, nonsettler colonialism, structural genocide—different forms and different methods issuing from the same frame of mind, however much the active agents change, or appear to be different from one another.

In addition, the Israeli Arabs (those who were allowed to stay during the so-called war in 1948) are not immune from expulsion. Israeli discourse is replete with ongoing discussions about the Transfer Plan,[92] a plan that has been proposed as a possible strategy to create a decisive Jewish majority in Israel.[93] As Wolfe persuasively argues:

> For comparative purposes, it is significant that the full radicalization of assimilation policies in both the US and Australia coincided with the closure of the frontier, which forestalled spatial stop-gaps such as removal. In infra-continental societies like those of mainland Europe, the frontier designates a national boundary as opposed to a mobile index of expansion. Israel's borders partake of both qualities. Despite Zionism's chronic addiction to territorial expansion, Israel's borders do not preclude the option of removal (in this connection, it is hardly surprising that a nation that has driven so many of its original inhabitants into the sand should express an abiding fear of itself being driven into the sea). As the logic of elimination has taken on a variety of forms in other settler-colonial situations, so, in Israel, the continuing tendency to Palestinian expulsion has not been limited to the unelaborated exercise of force. As Baruch Kimmerling and Joel Migdal have observed, for instance, Israeli officials have only permitted family unions "in one direction—out of Israel." The Law of Return commits the Jewish state to numerically unlimited but ethnically exclusive immigration, a factor that, formalities of citizenship notwithstanding, militates against the assimilation of gentile natives. Thus assimilation should not be seen as an invariable concomitant of settler colonialism. Rather, assimilation is one of a range of strategies of elimination that become favoured in particular historical circumstances.[94]

The Israeli case thus captures the entire range of options usually pursued by colonialism and the modern colonial state: Massive demographic cleansing of the Palestinian land within the Green Line (1948); an equivalent cleansing of the West Bank in and after 1967; total decimation of Palestinian infrastructure, institutions, cultural traditions, and more than four hundred villages,[95] and their replacement with exclusively Zionist entities (namely, through the method of "demolish-and-replace");[96] killing en masse, coupled with an effective method of assassination of individuals;[97] dozens of discriminatory laws against the state's own Arab citizens, including the no-right of return;[98] highly destructive military campaigns against the Gaza Strip; and a structural genocide, in progress, against its Arab citizens of 1948. Zionism's inherent predilection for colonization—which is to say, its internal constitution as a thought and mental structure that defines its quiddity—means that such considerations as may bar it from undertaking genocide as an event or the implementation of the Transfer Plan are contingent realities, not essential attributes whose potential comes to the fore with fully tangible force once they are removed. Israel, in other words, is not only a nonexception to the modus vivendi of the modern state as constituted by the Distinction, but it represents in effect a paradigmatic exemplar of this state.

In the very argument that Israel is a paradigmatic modern state, there is the clear premise that because of the fact of being a state it is able to accomplish its virulent project, a premise that brings us back not only to the two necessary conditions making up the structure of thought I have been articulating but also to the state of extraordinarity, a state of sovereignty integral to these two conditions. Israel does not merely violate international law at will, but it does so partly in the process of creating new international norms. In other words, so-called violations of the norm are re-created as norms. What is significant in this productive process is that the law and its sociological agents—the lawyers and jurists—instate themselves (no less than the medical profession or technological sciences) as the handmaidens of the state. Engaging in what the law scholar George Bisharat has aptly called "legal entrepreneurialism," Israel pursues a policy of taking illegal actions under prevailing norms of international law "with the hope that they will, ultimately, gain approval." That this is made possible is due to the very nature of the structure of this law. Constituted as much by customary state practice as by treaty and contract, this law in its elaboration rests heavily, as it has since its rise, on the understanding that what states do as routinized practice acquires acceptance by other states—expressly or tacitly—thereby gaining the status of a lawful practice. "In other words, the determination of an act's legal status turns on the responses of other states, which are not always immediate, explicit, or uniform. Hence, it is sometimes unclear whether a particular state action that deviates from settled international law is, indeed, simply illegal, or whether it is, instead, the leading edge of a new international legal norm."[99] While it is true that "Israel's effective capacity to write law through violence is a function of power,"[100] it is equally true that this power is ultimately the function of a sovereign sense of domination. When compared with military might in the context of our Islamic case study, it becomes all too obvious that not all such might translates into self-authorizing force in the service of genocidal behavior.

All this brings us back to the central point I have been pursuing in this book: that colonialism, in all of its variants, is inherently genocidal, and that this genocidal quality is ultimately connected, in the most structural and structured ways, with a thought structure that has defined modern academia and the discursive formations that academia has largely shaped and continues to reproduce. In this picture, Orientalism plays a considerable part, but by no means the most important one. And all this, again, cannot be any clearer than in the Israeli case. First, Israeli academic institutions as well as public discourse and national narratives are densely derivative of their Euro-American parent, a fact that explains the strikingly near-identical similarities between the Zionist and American colonizations. From their inception, Israeli academic institutions (foremost among which is the Hebrew University in Jerusalem) were replicas of their Euro-American counterparts, and did not evolve, for instance, as did universities in most Asian countries, namely, through having to suppress their long-standing traditions of learning and the institutional structures by which they were sustained in favor of the imposed institutions of a foreign and colonizing intruder. In other words, Israel's academia is effectively a transplantation from European soil. Academically and intellectually, Israel is largely a replica of the average Western European country, "average" because those who established, staffed, and operated its academia were predominantly emigrants into Israel from those very countries. The more recently established institutions, now populated mostly by Jews born in Israel, simply followed the already-established tradition.

Second, Israel has one of the most intense exchange programs that any educational system in the world can have with Euro-American universities and other academic and quasi-academic institutions, including military academies, with a stunning flow of visiting scholars, especially from Israel outward. Which is to say that Israeli academia not only originated in the Western tradition of knowledge but also continues to maintain and update the thought structure of sovereign domination and genocidal colonialism on an ongoing basis.

Third, Israeli academic institutions of science and technology have been put to the service, among other things of course, of "developing" the country's infrastructures, including the military one. Israeli technology has touched nearly every inch of the natural habitat of what was Palestine, and its products have gone to the building and strengthening of the state's institutions and its military apparatuses that play a crucial part in colonizing the country. It is clearly significant for my account of the Distinction that the subjugation and destruction are not limited to the Palestinian population, but to the very natural habitat of the country. Just as the Western industrialized countries (and now China and Asian others) have contributed to the greater part of environmental degradation, Israel, in its domains, has too—notwithstanding its remarkable record in green technology. For instance, the Dead Sea, a unique natural habitat in the world, is experiencing, by any account, an "environmental calamity," largely due to Israel's exploitative industries.[101] Furthermore, the effects of Israel's technology and science have left an indelible mark on the promotion of violence around the world. Israel is one of the biggest arms exporters in the world, ranking as high as sixth from the top.[102] "Israel invests more money in [military] research than most other countries—and in no other place are research institutes, the defense industry, the army and politics as interwoven. . . . The enormous role played by the military in society also plays a role. 'The links between scientists, engineers and technology developers and the security situation in Israel is even more intertwined.'"[103] This connection between science and violence can nowhere pass as a normal state of affairs, particularly in a colonial space whose ideological foundations rest on a salvation project in which the Jews are rescued from genocidal Germany and European racism. The choice of excelling in weapon exportation—especially to politically unstable regions and to dictatorial regimes[104]—as a means of promoting the interests of a "Jewish homeland," rather than excelling, say, in environmentally friendly technology, connects back to the "genetic" constitution of colonialism as integral to a particular structure of thought. That modernity's victims are exact replicas of their victimizers and that they are blind imitators of their actions are perhaps the most powerful testimony to the entrenchment of this structure.

Fourth, Israeli academia represents the equivalent of the state of extraordinarity in the otherwise general (or ordinary?) rule that is the typical academic world. In other words, it brings the hidden but real potency of academia into plain view, just as sovereign colonial rule makes the state of extraordinarity the apparent norm of domination. As I intimated, Israeli science is instrumental in the maintenance of the state's grip over the Palestinians, including the medical profession, whose expertise is likewise essential for the torture of Palestinian political prisoners.[105] It is a solid a fortiori argument that if humanitarian medical ethics are routinely violated in the interest of domination, then the involvement of science in the project of elimination is to be taken for granted. As the Israeli intellectual Eyal Weizman incisively shows, the best of Israeli science and technology, especially as exemplified in the fighter plane, has systematically defined the architecture of Israeli occupation of Palestine.[106]

Yet no less important for our central argument is that the field of Israeli Orientalism (*Mizrahanut*) has been structurally and outwardly connected with the state intelligence and the military apparatus, the Israel Defense Forces.[107] Here as elsewhere in academia, *Mizrahanut* is an extension of, and in small part also a contributing participant in, Western Orientalism. The same ethos and mentality of inquiry and research in Euro-American academia dominate here as well, except that the nineteenth-century formulations and racial overtones of Western Orientalism have now been shed in the West but oftentimes not so in Israel. This is partly because the Israeli colonialist model still labors in good part under nineteenth-century forms, employing, among other things, a virulent racial discourse that many Orientalists had harnessed in their colonialist representations of the "Orientals." The most prominent category among the latter are the "Arabs," depicted primarily as submissive, supine, lazy, and irrational—antimodern and anti-Enlightenment qualities that render them inherently colonizable. Like the Jew of Europe, the Palestinian Arab is mostly a "dirty Arab," expressed in the nauseatingly common "'*Aravim milokhlakhim*."[108] A major study of Israeli school textbooks in 1999 found that these textbooks "portrayed Palestinians as 'murderers,' 'rioters,' 'robbers,' 'bloodthirsty,' and generally backward and unproductive."[109] While this street language is the daily staple of the average Israeli Jew, the Orientalist's dated language of description, discordant with its contemporaneous counterpart in the West, is often sequestered from international public view through investment in the mainstream (and national) Hebrew-language periodical of Israeli Mizrahanut, *Ha-Mizrah Ha-Hadash* (*The New East*, a title not without suggestive gesturing toward the ambition of creating a new East, one perhaps devoid of Palestinians, if not of many others as well).

Furthermore, while the ties in Euro-American countries between an education in "Orientalism" (now mostly known as Middle Eastern or Islamic studies) and service in government or military institutions remain somewhat covert, in Israel it is a supremely normal and open state of affairs. "Oriental" research institutes publicly announce their political agenda, declaring the fruits of their academic work to be in the service of political ends.[110] An education in *Mizrahanut* is a powerful ticket for rapid promotion in the army and an essential requirement for joining the Israel Intelligence Agency, the Mossad, the rough equivalent of the CIA. The flow between *Mizrahanut* and the IDF and intelligence is not unidirectional, to be sure, but largely dialectical. It is not uncommon for an army officer, a general, or a commander to serve, *concurrently*, as a professor. The militaristic overtness of the enterprise of Israeli academia is such that at times an army general appears in full military attire in the classroom.[111] This otherwise minor detail cannot, nonetheless, be taken as an "event," as a singular occurrence, or as a collection of singular incidents; rather, it should be read as a semiotic sign of an underlying relationship and of a structure of power in which knowledge is *publicly seen* as indispensable for the political, and in which the distinction between a military general and a university professor, even formally and overtly, ceases to exist. Indeed, the event is a paradigmatic instance exhibiting a structure of thought whose geography and genealogy extend far and wide and deep into the condition of modernity. It is the continuing dynamic of the state of extraordinarity that brings to the surface the true nature of the inner layers of the system and the thought structure that defines it.

Had Said begun with such a sign, located in the university, embedded in entrenched discursive formations, and rooted in systems of power that stem from an understanding of the world as a dispensable matter readily amenable to arbitrary will, he would have begun his project elsewhere, and ended it in an investigation of the modern project as one of genocidal sovereignty, a sovereignty of knowledge in the first place. Misrepresentation, one instrument among many that genocidal modernity employs, would have been one of the last villains to worry him. This kind of critique remains sorely unsatisfactory, failing to change the benchmark that allows authors, such as the academic and diplomat Samantha Power, to offer a "critical" account of US foreign policy on the grounds that it never acted in all of its history to stop a genocide or even to condemn one while it was proceeding.[112] Again, as with Said, and as with nearly all explanations offered for the Western European and North American countries' egregious failure to stop the Nazi Holocaust, the critique always navigates at the surface, going no deeper than common political analysis can afford. It is little recognized that the stunning failure of such critique and analysis, as Power exemplifies in her book, never gets to the real point, that the leading countries in what later became the Alliance that stood and watched the Nazi genocide against the Jews were *themselves constituted, formed, and shaped* by a genocidal process in the colonies, a process whose origins lie in a thought structure that fashions worldviews that have become the bases for action.

Finding satisfactory explanations in the processes of politics, itself a modern invention, can yield nothing better than a *petitio principii*, a hopelessly circular argument. Political discourse, to follow on George Orwell's brilliant formulations, is the chemical formula that dissolves real complexity into myth; it is, itself, constituted as a barrier that suppresses causality, connections, modalities, dialectics, and much else, even intelligence. Samantha Power's interrogation, like Said's own political aspersion, is not only superfluous because a genealogy of genocide was not undertaken before critiquing US foreign policy on genocides; it also reinforces the very system that the critic purports to scrutinize. By keeping the critique within the chemical formula, the critic not only places herself within its transformative power, an act of self-subjectification; she also enhances its reproductive capabilities for perpetual myth creation.

The critique of policies on genocides, just like the critique of Orientalism ever since Said wrote, is meshed with myth, which is to say that it is engulfed in a deep state of denial. No one can forget that myth's function is to make tolerable that which is otherwise intolerable. To dig that deep, to the intolerable, is to discover that evil—the metaphysical hatred of the human for the human and for all nature—was an art perfected and consummated in, and by, modernity. Yet, for a human to hate another with such intensity as to be able to incinerate her—and with an indescribable "banality" to boot—the victimizing human must be able to hate himself *first* before hating his victim who is nothing but a reflection of himself. He must be able to despise his own humanity and, *more importantly, his very nature*, before committing his acts, for that nature is the first thing he sees.[113] To ask, as Said does, how "one can study other cultures and peoples from a libertarian" perspective and then to say that this "task" requires "rethink-ing" the "whole problem of knowledge and power" (24) is not only to severely misunderstand the depth of meaning residing in "libertarian"; it is to affirm the very thing he denies. For "libertarianism," expressively cap-tured by Locke, J. S. Mill, and their likes, has always been constituted by *this* self-hate. That Said could do it with blithe impunity is a testimonial to the power of liberal myth, where contradictions are made, in a deceptively casual but characteristic manner, into common sense, often with eloquence and style.

CHAPTER V

Refashioning Orientalism, Refashioning the Subject

I

The study of any culture, as of any phenomenon, is ineluctably framed by the value-system and cultural imperatives of the scholar, irrespective of any claim to objectivity. This is what it means not to have—or the impossibility of having—a neutral point of view from which to study anything in the world. This I have taken for granted, as evidenced in my critique of Said's notions of prejudice and exoticizing. When Muslim scholars "studied" their Shariʻa system,[1] or any aspect of their world, they took it as a given that they were teaching and writing as expositors of the values in which the system itself was grounded and enshrined. The entire range of the discursive traditions they have constructed—be they literary, theological, Sufist, philosophical, linguistic, logical, or "legal"[2]—not only responded to the moral *grundnorm* (a foundational act *strictu sensu*) but continued to react and adjust themselves to the evolving challenges that the system and its practitioners continued to pose. Thus the jurists, for instance, wrote for their fellow Muslims about the norms and principles of their own society, whether for theoretical or practical ends.

The theorized foundational ethics that shaped their intellectual systems within the central domains stood in an intricate dialectic with their practical concerns, which in turn were elaborated as an intellectual formation of "applied ethics." They assumed or took for granted a considerable amount of knowledge about the system (precisely that which historians take most pains in the twenty-first century to unravel, often without success), but they also had much to say that was not taken for granted. Within the internal logic of the system in which they found themselves, and within the constraints and conditions that made their system possible in the first place, they rationally responded to the arising stimuli as any community of scholars and "legal" practitioners would. And as in any legal or intellectual community, there was nothing "objective" about their project except for the resultant social reality produced by the rationality that the internal logic of their world imposed.

As of the early nineteenth century, Orientalists too made it their business to study what they perceived as "Islam"; but the manuscripts, archives, and artifacts of that world were patently not deciphered within an Islamic cultural context, or within a profoundly ethicized framework or habitus, a crucial absence in their enterprise. For the first time in the history of Islam, its cultural production, especially its text-based traditions (now narrowly conceived and stripped of their cultural and psychological surrounds), was to be subjected to an entirely foreign, but also hegemonic and *transformative*, hermeneutic. This was not only an enterprise intent on organizing Europe's "scholarly curiosity," but one that effectively appropriated, refracted, and redefined the ways Muslims themselves thought of, and about, the world. Thus, by the end of the nineteenth century, when imperialism in all of its forms had completed its main mission, no Muslim historian could even attempt—much less be capable of producing—a Tabarian, Masʿudian, or Kathirian history, these standing at one time as indubitable exemplars of Islamic historiographical narratives. Nor was it conceivable in the least that a Juwayni, a Razi, or a Nasafi could be replicated in the central *sharʿi* domain—or any other for that matter. These paragons of paradigmatic Islamic learning effectively and fairly quickly became expressions of a dead past.[3] This Oriental epistemic transformation, which was not possible without *performative* colonialist institutions on the ground, did not represent the culmination of a European Orientalist discourse inside the Orientalist text that was geared to the Western reader, as Said had thought, but it was rather the product of the actual operations of an Orientalism on the ground, one in which forces larger than Orientalism as a scholarly and philological discipline were at play. This is in good part the meaning of what I have referred to in the previous chapter as structural genocide.

The context of interpretation and the assumptions of Orientalist herme-neutics were entirely and solidly grounded in a distinct and unprecedented intellectual and material European formation, one dominated by a newly forged Enlightenment whose values reflected a particular—though nar-rowly corralled—conception of reason and specific, if not unique, notions of secularism, religion, humanness, materialism, capitalism, instrumental-ity, emotion, pain, violence, and much else. All these categories were no doubt found in the Islamic East and elsewhere (however their boundaries and substantive thickness or thinness may have been defined) but were manifested there in often dramatically different ways, expressed in differ-ent forms, and, most importantly, *marshaled and utilized for different ends.*

The Muslim project may be said to have largely been geared toward self-construction—the psychological, moral, mildly mystical, and "legal" being paramount and overriding in importance and scope the materialist (a category emerging as *paradigmatic*[4] only with modernity). These aspects were exemplified in the emergence and maintenance of particular theo-retical and practical technologies of the self/subject, narratives of collective moral engagement, discursive codes of juridical and mystical conduct, and a socioeconomic system that ranged in its interests from social organiza-tion to economic activity and civil society, to a limited conception and practice of politics,[5] and to much else. The project was chiefly one carried out by the civic order on behalf of and for the sake of that order.[6] In this project, "Islam," as a collectivity of cultural, intellectual, spiritual, indi-vidualistic, communal, and material ways of living, was the subject, the predicate, and the object, all at once.[7] It is also in this project, as I have been arguing, that education, learning, and cultivation of the ethical self—all standing in mutually enhancing dialectic and integral to a habitus—were products of "civic" societies, articulated by ordinary individuals, governed by communal "self-rule," and largely without the dictates of "totalization and individuation"[8] by an all-dominating biopolitical power.

The Orientalist project, on the other hand, though similar in some ways, was yet profoundly different in others. The subject matter of Ori-entalism, always the object,[9] was by definition not European, although the enterprise itself was conducted by Europeans for Europeans, and mostly for the exercise of their sovereign domination over the Orient. An instru-mental building block of colonialism, the enterprise was an essential part of constructing modernity that initially—but undoubtedly—reconstituted the life values and worldview of Europeans. They came to inhabit that modernity, the only world they recognized as having full and autonomous ontological, epistemological, and cultural status, and thus legitimacy. The essential difference between the two projects thus pertained not to the processes of constructing the cultural or psychological self (however different these were in each case), but rather *to the teleology of humanity and of the subject, and their place in the world.*

II

As I have been arguing, Said's narrative, reflecting a particular and narrowly defined conception of power and knowledge claimed to hail from Foucault, remained faithful to the Enlightenment notions of secular humanism[10] and anthropocentrism. Blind to the profound effects of the Enlightenment Distinction (which he does not seem to problematize in the least), he consequently overlooked the *necessary* effects of the modern project in general and the liberal project in particular. Said's work, liberal in every important way, saw light at the end of an era, one that seemed, ever so deceptively, to hold some promise for a better future. But since the 1980s and the 1990s, Said's cherished values of secular humanism, especially its implied but ontologically and epistemologically *entailed* anthropocentricism, have been at the center of critique that recalls the disenchantment with the modern condition of a number of major intellectuals starting in the the eighteenth century (ranging from Herder and Nietzsche, to Max Scheler, the Frankfurt School and beyond).

But the critique has become both more urgent and more trenchant since Said wrote. The crucial matter of the survival of the human species and other forms of life was not atop that philosophical agenda, and certainly not on Said's when he wrote his *Orientalism*;[11] but it has recently been increasing in force and velocity. One can now speak even of a scientific consensus on climate and ecological crisis.[12] Colossal environmental destruction; massive colonialist and imperialist atrocities and dehumanization; unprecedented forms of political and social violence; the construction of lethal political identities; the poisoning of food and water; the extermination of alarming numbers of species; increasingly worrying health threats; indecent disparity between rich and poor; social and communal disintegration; the rise of narcissistic sovereign individualism and sociopathology; a dramatic increase in individual and corporate psychopathologies;

an alarming spread of mental health disorders; a "growing epidemic" of suicide, and much more (the list is long enough to require, literally, an entire ledger)—all of which aggregately constituting a phenomenon that calls attention to a revaluation of modernist, industrial, capitalist,[13] and chiefly (though not exclusively) liberal values. The increasingly proliferating and widespread understanding that the modern project, together with its knowledge system, is unsustainable[14] (even in the relatively short run) is in the process of taking over center stage, and not only in Western industrialized countries. Influential activist groups and prominent intellectuals in India, China, and several other countries in Asia, Latin America, and elsewhere have come to realize that a major restructuring, if not overhauling, of the paradigmatic systems of modernity is now in order. The crisis affects the global village, and is not the concern of only particular groups or countries, although the genealogy of the sources of destruction is widely recognized as European and more recently Euro-American.[15]

In the argument I am setting forth here, a series of premises should be made explicit: (1) the ecological and environmental crisis is endemic to the very modern system producing it, which is to say that the crisis itself is systemic, not contingent; (2) the modern system that cohesively marshals capitalism, technology, industrialism, and a legal system that regulates their conduct is based on forms of knowledge that are claimed to be rational and thus are far from haphazard or accidental; (3) this rationality, in its fully fledged practical manifestations, in effect amounts to nothing short of an epistemology, a conscious, deliberate, and fairly consistent way of understanding, interpreting, and living in the world; and (4) this epistemology lacks sufficient moral and ethical restraints so as to (a) allow living in the world without—to put it minimally[16]—a noticeable penchant for destructiveness, and (b) successfully remedy (if not preempt) ecological and socioeconomic problems as may happen to arise.

The upshot of these premises is that the present crises are not only indicative but in fact *an integral effect* of the forms of knowledge and of what Guénon called the "moralism" commanding modernity as a way of living in the world. They are to be lined up alongside the entire set of problems I have been assembling throughout the last four chapters. It is then wholly plausible to argue that there is "no area of ethical thinking that pushes us to examine the foundations of ethical thought more than environmental ethics."[17] Here, the "foundations of ethical thought" must be understood as entailing virtually the entire range of modern forms of knowledge, especially those lodged in the central domains, involved as they are in violent and destructive ventures. Nor should "environmental" in the quotation be understood to mean anything less than the entirety of being, including the human and dehumanized Other. In my conception, "environment" is all that exists in the world. It is not therefore a liberal conception that segregates the environmental from the political, seeking to solve the "green" crisis while overlooking the systemic and systematic dehumanization effected by imperialist and colonialist sovereignty.

The critical global situation during the last three decades calls for a more profound critique of the Orientalist project—as it does of most others in the sciences, the social sciences, and the humanities—even as Orientalism stands now in its modified form. Or is it because it stands in this modified form? As I have attempted to show, Said's own foundational premises and methods were not adequate for a penetrating critique of Orientalism, and they are even less useful, if not utterly useless, for any serious attempt at redirecting, much less refashioning, this discipline or any other. Secular humanism, anthropocentricism, Enlightenment rationalism, and liberalism (all of which rest on a mechanistic impulse and sovereign domination of the world) are increasingly viewed as too costly to maintain and as an excessive and unjustifiable—if not immoral—overreach, all this notwithstanding their benefits (undoubted benefits with equally undoubted disastrous side effects). In fact, it is precisely these benefits—supposed and real—that are directly tied to the pervasive destruction of nearly every aspect of modern human, animal, and insentient life (all of which, one can safely say, are experiencing, and *living*, the modern condition). As I have attempted to show, these benefits are furthermore grounded in, and derive from, less obvious but nonetheless very real projects of imperialism, colonialism, structural genocide, and much else without which these benefits would not have been possible in the first place.

It is therefore the benefits that we claim to derive from the modern project that do the work of vindicating the moral basis on which the project itself becomes both rationalized and justified. This has been the cornerstone and thrust of Jeremy Bentham's and J. S. Mill's philosophies, among others, which continue to flourish in various, yet pervasive, forms in the twenty-first century, whether intellectually, institutionally, or materially. Their effects have not been merely practical, in the sense that they afford a guide to an actionable way of life premised on certain foundational conceptions of utility, pleasure, and pain. Rather, the effects have gone deep into the formation of the modern subject, determining not only the manner in which that subject understands and interrogates the world, but also, and consequently, how it cognitively situates itself *in the world.*

In order to reckon with the unbearable heaviness of the ensuing contradictions within its fabric, modern understanding of the world had to be framed as a theory of morality (Guénon's "moralism"), a necessary myth that, as I have been trying to show, makes irreconcilable contradictions not only bearable but eminently justifiable. Hence, we often encounter the distinctly theological argument that modernity has developed its own concept—if not system—of morality, including the morality (even virtue ethics) of its liberalism, its capitalism, its Marxism, its scientism, and of course the interminably but deliberately vague dogma of progress. The structure of justification of this morality has behind it a venerable philosophical tradition that begins with Machiavelli and Hobbes and goes down to H. L. A. Hart, John Rawls, and Joseph Raz. The venerability is of course partly associated with intellectual integrity, but not wholly. Venerability and particularly the much-acclaimed validity and relevance of universalism rest on foundations that also have little to do with the honorable weight of intellectual attirement, and much to do with the politics of knowledge and its function in the production of regimes of truth. Upon entry into any debate about the nature of this morality as compared to, say, premodern cultural or religious systems, the contention that inevitably arises is one to do with the superiority of the modern system of value and thus of its moral basis (an honest position openly admitting its structural associations with power-based forms of knowledge) or, at best, of the relativism (and thus subjectivity) involved in weighing one moral system against another (a relativism that does not acknowledge the absolutism of the very system of knowledge that gives rise to it in the first place).[18] The balance between superiority and subjectivity has paradigmatically worked in favor of modern forms of morality, and largely of epistemology, for the coliseum of debate, including its presiding Caesar, remains undeniably modern. In a system that a priori sets limits to what can and cannot be acceptable standards of legitimate discourse, subjectivity and relativism work hand in hand and complement the stance of superiority—that which we know by the other names of racism and progress.

The modern constitution of moral value rests on a posited metaphysic[19] of individual freedom and rationality that in turn inheres in an enveloping political and capitalist system of value that shapes the qualities, and therefore

specific types, of freedom and rationality—all this being a process formative of the self but one that was kept distinct from *that* (unacknowledged)
metaphysic. Which is to say that it was necessary, in order to maintain
the idealized conception of freedom and rationality, to set this ideal apart
from the otherwise determining and dominating effects of economy and
materialism and therefore of its metaphysic (and to some extent even from
state policy of inventing and managing citizenship).

Thus the subjectivity of moral value is not to be confused with unintelligible abstractness. When all else fails, a moral system can be judged and
adjudicated on less abstract grounds than metaphysics, whether in its coherent or blurred (unacknowledged?) versions. If the structures of technology/
technique,[20] industrialism, science, rationality, instrumentalism, capitalism, and, no less, the nation-state are admitted to be paradigmatic, defining in the most decisive of ways the contours and substantive content of
modern life, then it may not be implausible to regard them as having
failed the consumers of the good life who live *in* and *with* the world rather
than *above* and *against* it, be these consumers human, animal, or insentient
(this last being determined as such, like much else, by the constrained forms
of modern knowledge).

Our concern in all this is of course rationality—presumably that discrete and autonomous process that remains, despite all claims to autonomy,
necessarily conditioned by the paradigmatic structures of modernity (not
least of which are capitalism, nationalism, industrialism, technology, science, and in part the entire range of peripheral domains that give it sever-
ally and aggregately their perspectival props). This rationality, *of a specific
type and structure*, may not be disentangled from modern forms of life, the
very forms that have led to the state of current crises. The crises have clearly
been precipitated by a human agency (and no other), one that is self-
professedly rational,[21] but also one whose quest for knowledge is garnered,
as Scheler put it aptly, for *systematic* control and domination.[22] And it is this
sovereign rationality that has dictated the way we construe ourselves as well
as the Other in the world, including Islam and its history and cultures.

III

What are the implications of this crisis in the modern project for the study of
the Other? Or, should we say, cutting straight to the point, for the study

of the self? To begin with, the implications are foundational, profound, and entirely psychoepistemic, which is to say that much of the way of understanding and doing things in the world now requires rethinking, but rethinking that transcends Said's proposal for a "libertarian" approach, itself a large part of the problem. This is also to say, in the first instance, that the very questions we ask must reflect the new critical reality of the last three decades, the culmination of abuses inflicted on the environment and the Other over the two preceding centuries. This claim, however, demands a clearer vision than I have thus far offered of the context in which such questions might be formulated.

When Europe developed Orientalism, it was a project integral to the rise of new modes of thought, economics, and forms of politics directed and commanded by the nation-state. But the project, as a subset of the larger European experiment that created modernity through subjugation of the Other, was profoundly anchored in the paradigmatic concepts of the Enlightenment. It is in this sense that Orientalism was a project of power and culture, anchored deep in the sovereign thought structure I have been outlining, and not merely an academic enterprise. As such, it was most natural for the agents of this enterprise to operate, like all others, within the cultural boundaries that modernity had come to require or, more precisely, determine and impose. Orientalism, like any other field of modern knowledge, contributed to the formation of that culture, which we have seen to be deeply rooted in a massive colonialist project that involved a structured and pervasive market of slavery,[23] economic exploitation, structural genocides, and the control and subjection of the lives of countless tens of millions of non-Europeans (and disenfranchised Europeans as well).[24] This is the world that made Orientalism possible, and it was in this world that it lived and served.

By the middle of the twentieth century, and with the majority of "third world" countries gaining so-called independence, Orientalism entered a new, postcolonialist stage, one that left it with residues of the colonialist heritage, but with altered forms of power. This stage, beginning sometime after World War II and partly ending in the 1980s, shifted the focus of the field from direct forms of colonialism and its justification as *mission civilisatrice* to a reelaboration and adjustment of the ways in which the "Orient" was now to be seen. It was owing to a shift from a conception of the modalities of reconstituting and governing it in effective terms to a strategy of how to deal with it that it now gained "independence" and presumably the ability to represent itself in the way it has now become reconstituted. Whether under the colonialist forms of the nineteenth century or the still-hegemonic influences of most of the twentieth (now cast in terms of globalization), the prevailing attitude was always one of strength and sovereign power: what Euro-America has said and done was the norm, the standard and decisive way according to which the world must be seen and run. This remained the case despite, if not because of, Said's critique, although the attitude toward the Muslim world after the rise of Islamist movements was one heavily colored by a renewed fear of Islam and its "political" (and often cultural and "religious") threat. Nonetheless, Orientalism in this latter phase acquired a diversity that is patently unprecedented. Its narratives and subnarratives have been highly contentious, this time integrating two varieties of "native" scholarship: dissenting and subversive voices who, by the nature of things, remain largely in the minority; and an unprecedented *quantity* of voices who have, through their ardent liberalism, mostly enhanced Orientalism, thereby continuing a long line of indigenous scholars who were trained by, and served, the first colonial Orientalists. The discipline has come to include a vast array of critical scholarly voices who are otherwise ethnically and culturally embedded within the West and its dominant academic institutions. This last contingent has emerged entirely out of the traditional colonialist mode, and tends to shun such a mode in the profession, yet it has not transcended Said's critique. In this sense, it remains situated squarely within the same liberal (and political) boundaries in which Said operated and that he took for granted.

The paradigmatic narratives of this varied tradition thus remain highly politicized, preoccupied, as it is, with what might be called the relationship of Islam to the West and the world (the directionality of this relationship being precisely that). Whether sympathetic or hostile to "Islam" as a "religion" or culture, the concern is with representing it to the West with a view to equipping the latter with a "better" and "more accurate" way of "understanding" it. Clearly, a great many Orientalists are no longer sympathetic to their governments' policies as carried out in Muslim countries (a stark contrast with nineteenth- and early-twentieth-century scholars, notwithstanding the rare, even at times powerful, exceptions),[25] but the general preoccupation remains representation "so that we know how to deal with Muslims," although this "dealing" often aspires to a set of attitudes that show, in good liberal fashion, relatively more respect and tolerance than any preceding period. But the common denominator of Orientalist academia undoubtedly remains one of epistemic superiority, which is to say that respect and tolerance come with a dose of epistemic self-confidence (and often arrogance) that still assumes—consciously or not—the validity of the Euro-American modern project, especially as it has been guided by the paradigmatic principles of the Enlightenment.

Integral to "Orientalism Now" (Said's last chapter in *Orientalism*) is also a phenomenon that Said does not address, namely, the rise of a contingent of scholars, mostly of non-Western ethnic backgrounds, whose task is seen as representing Islam to the West in favorable terms, with a view to rendering it acceptable to liberal sensibilities. These have surely been around before Said wrote, but their weight in the field has increased steadily and significantly during the last three decades, although members of this contingent are the quickest to level charges of "Orientalism" against others, most particularly against those who detect in Islam not just an "inferior" quality but especially a "superior" attribute that has, in their mind, the potential to give rise to a conception of "clash of civilizations."

It is my argument here that such epistemic self-confidence, as well as the concomitant corrective measures and apologetic, is neither justified nor sufficient, and that the earlier they are abandoned the better. The radical crisis of the modern project in Euro-America, as elsewhere, demands a radical solution, a fact that bears directly on how we should henceforth study Islam, its "law," and nearly everything else. At the center of this argument stand two essential facts: (1) the crises of the modern project are global, in both causes and effects,[26] which is to say that the modern structures productive of the ill effects have spread, through imperialism and colonialism, to all continents and are currently found in nearly every country, to one degree or another; and (2) every sector of ill effect has impacted material and sociopolitical reality in virtually all aspects of existence. The disappearance of one species, the decimation of a human group, the reengineering of long-standing cultures, or the pollution or deforestation of one region— each of these has created chain reactions negatively impacting ecological, psychoepistemic, and social balance in other spheres. And if the crisis is undeniably common to all, in effect representing a serious threat to the natural and social commons, then the commensurate moral responsibility (assumed here to be more binding than any legal or political responsibility) must be borne by all those who have a say about it. Put succinctly, if the Other, human and nonhuman, has been the means to, and instrument of, the formation of imperialist and colonialist modernity, then it is this Other that must be retrieved as the critical center in the project of transcending modernity. In *The Impossible State*, I have suggested some means through which a segment of the human Other may embark on a restructuring critique of modernity. Here, I offer a complementary critique toward a reconstitution of the self.

IV

Since states and governments are integral to modernity's problems, and have generally contributed to them, it falls to the intellectual traditions of the world to take up the challenge, and Orientalism is undoubtedly one such tradition that must reckon with the new realities. Choosing Orientalism is not a privileging act, however; rather, it is an act that takes it for granted that what is good for the goose is good for the gander. What applies to Orientalism must apply to all central domains of intellectual inquiry, including their founding principles, which are identical with the principles on which the central domains of modernity are founded. What Agamben argued with regard to the panopticon applies in equal measure to Orientalism: it "is a singular object that, standing equally for all others of the same class, defines the intelligibility of the group of which it is a part and which, at the same time, it constitutes."[27] Yet, there is something quite obvious about Orientalism that makes it a good candidate for representing the other domains, the other members of the group: its explicitly declared professional preoccupation with the Other. Thus, what applies to it applies to the others in both the *a minore ad maius* and *a maiore ad minus*.

It is through undertaking the challenge of reconstituting the self in meaningful and profound ways that Orientalism can transform its inner thought structures with a view to contributing, however modestly, to pioneering and building a sustainable path for all humanity, *beginning with a due consideration of the Other*. If the equivalent traditions in China, Latin America, and India can chart innovative ways in this direction, as they are beginning to do, there is no reason why Orientalism cannot find its own way toward such a goal. This, for Orientalism, is a particularly urgent requirement, keeping in mind two things: that it has been a contributor, among others, to the dehumanization of the Other and that environmental "crisis is the product of a culture, originating in Western Europe, which now dominates the world."[28]

Representing, if not encapsulating, what I have called the paradigms of modernity and the Enlightenment, Orientalism has been defined by a potent doctrine of progress, with an omnipotent and metaphysically latent concept of linear history. Yet, as a largely liberal tradition it also lends itself to the characterization of being, in the coinage of Alasdair MacIntyre, a rational tradition of inquiry, one that embodies the imperatives of the Euro-American modern paradigm. In its entirety, and with all its internal disagreements and divergences across two centuries of its existence, it continues to lend itself to the definition (again by MacIntyre) that it is an extended argument through time in which fundamental agreements are defined and constantly redefined in the context of debates within it and (tacitly) outside it.[29] If it does not exhibit on the surface all the features of a tradition (such as a conception of justice or a particular view of practical rationality), it is not because these features do not exist in it: they do, albeit in a tacit and unarticulated manner, for such paradigmatic features as a particular conception of rationality, a doctrine of progress, a linear notion of history, and a liberal conception of reality (including a latent theory of justice and ethics) all discretely govern its narratives *and internal logic* in structured ways.

As a tradition of rational inquiry, Orientalism directly confronts other traditions of an equally rational nature but that differ in their conception of rationality (the assumption being that every tradition has its own version of rational method derived from its own experience and view of the world, including traditions based on what—as outsiders—we might characterize as mythological, metaphysical, cosmological, or otherwise).[30] These have been called rival traditions, not necessarily in the sense of incompatibility that bars dialogue, but rather in the sense of difference that in fact compels these rival traditions to engage in dialogue with a view to (re)evaluating their own narratives, defending, justifying, or modifying them as a response to the challenge from another tradition or traditions. In some cases, a rational tradition becomes associated with political and military power that overwhelms and eventually destroys a rivaling tradition. An example in point is Orientalism itself, as it existed and operated in the nineteenth and early twentieth centuries in the lands of Islam. Since Napoleon's conquest of Egypt, it has come to be conjoined with military force that ensured its victory during the process, and in the aftermath, of the institutional destruction of indigenous forms of education and intellectual life (among much else). But there are other examples of traditions that have been forced to modify their internal narratives under the intellectual pressure and stress of other rival traditions, of the sort that MacIntyre studied in *Three Rival Versions of Moral Inquiry*. It is this kind of pressure that is at the center of my present narrative.

Before suggesting ways to cope with this challenge, I must note certain difficulties in MacIntyre's position with a view to making it useful for my purposes here. It is quite clear that MacIntyre has ignored the relationship between traditions and power,[31] limiting the conflict between traditions to the challenge of rational inquiry. More a case of deontological aspiration than an actual description of reality, his account fails to consider the success of a tradition as a result of sheer raw power, and not necessarily rational power. MacIntyre's work on tradition has, for instance, virtually nothing descriptive or analytical in it that accounts for the demise of the premodern Islamic tradition in its encounter with Orientalism as the handmaiden of colonialism and imperialism. That encounter did not involve any rational debate, but was one that took place, as I have just intimated, only *after* the fact of initial domination through hegemonic, military, economic, and political colonial ventures.[32] Yet, his account, as I will propose, might be the most promising prescription for future action if we agree that (1) what all traditions currently share is a *rationally* recognized global threat of disaster, and thus a set of globally shared concerns, (2) this threat ensues from a conception of the world that *demands* dehumanization of the Other (as I have defined it globally here), and (3) this situation is specifically a modern phenomenon (as I have argued throughout the book).

But to modify MacIntyre's theory of tradition does not necessarily mean that it must be reinterpreted in light of the Saidian theory of power as adapted from Foucault. As I have shown, Said's work on Orientalism remained anchored and defined by a series of premises and assumptions that reinforce the very modernist and liberal positions that gave rise to Orientalism in the first place. I have been showing throughout the last four chapters that Said misunderstands Foucault, failing to take the power/knowledge structure seriously, and that his concept of the author, including Foucault's theory of the same, is deficient, if not virtually nonexistent, and that because of these inadequacies his understanding of what a discursive formation is continued to labor at the surface. By contrast, as I have argued, Foucault's work, however much it remained underdeveloped concerning the author, continues to be most constructive and extraordinarily fruitful. Seen within the theory of central and peripheral domains, which have the added advantage of providing a historical dimension to his mostly synchronic analysis, Foucault's dynamic notion of power, knowledge, and author affords exits that replace the foreclosures that Said created.

Going along with MacIntyre then, I shall assume that rationality itself (as expansively redefined by him) is one component of power, which would partly bridge the divergence between his position and that of Foucault. This is so because a rearticulated rationality would then operate as an integral "tactical" element in the "field of force relations," providing ammunition for the subversive discursivity I have been speaking of. In other words, this rationality would be located within, and as part of, the mechanics of power. And it is precisely here, in the most unlikely of places, that Orientalism, once refashioned, can provide an oppositional discourse that facilitates the change needed to deal with the crises generated by the modern project. In a formal sense, Orientalism occupies an epistemic position that can allow it to accomplish this task, precisely due to its specific location in the current systems of knowledge. First, it is, along with anthropology, the most obvious academic discipline whose declared purpose is nothing other than the study of the Other, the "Oriental" Other who can now instruct in the art of forming the new self. Second, it is uniquely equipped with proficient philological tools and direct access to texts and archives of that Other. In this respect, Orientalism dwarfs anthropology, which on the whole continues to suffer from a serious deficit in philological talent, although anthropology has developed a cutting-edge theoretic still lacking in several quarters of the Orientalist discipline. Third, and related to the foregoing consideration, Orientalism is the single academic discipline in the Western hemisphere that has access to the "esoteric" and highly complex philosophical, moral, "legal," and mystical expressions of the Orient. This, as I will argue, is both the privilege and the burden of the discipline, the latter ensuing from the liabilities of Orientalism's location in a history of colonialism and genocide and within a larger project that led to the global crises of which I have been speaking.

In the face of the environmental crises, symptomatic of deep structural problems in the modern project, the need for a reassessment of the central domains is no longer in doubt. For Orientalism to survive as a tradition of rational inquiry, it must reckon with the emerging need for an internal critique, *one that rationality demands.* In addition to the "Green philosophers" of Euro-America, India, and China, the academic fields of history, philosophy, environmental science, and even engineering, among others, are currently undergoing self-evaluation, however meager these efforts have been in relation to the colossal magnitude of the crises. Entire programs, departments, institutes, scholarly journals, and much else are being established with a speed that only underlines the sense of urgency. Surely, the fundamental questions have not yet been asked, and thus real answers continue to be far from sight, but the severe anxiety that underlined academia for the past three or four decades is the beginning of a promising development. Orientalism has not so far picked up on these trends in any remarkable way, which is to say that it has not yet attained the necessary stage of anxiety. But, as I have intimated, its privileged epistemic site and vast erudition give it great potential to catch up and perhaps even provide leadership, precisely because of its proximity and access to the traditions and experiences of the Other.

During the last three decades or so,[33] there have emerged important voices in China and India that bank on a heuristic retrieval of premodern tradition and religion in an effort to combat the modern structures of epistemic power that have contributed to the deterioration and destruction of the natural habitat. They have rejected the modern Western attitude toward nature and the environment, especially its nonorganicist and mechanical view that has denuded nature of value as well as of any brand of metaphysics. Science of the kind that is harnessed with a single-minded ambition to serve the ends of capitalist ventures and to exploit the natural commons is now regarded as violent in the extreme, destroying the lives of people, cultures, and sustainable habitats and traditions.[34] They have also rejected the exclusivity of a linear concept of history, having stressed the need to expand the concept to include what has been called circulatory history, a rich and fertile notion that converts the modernistic view of history from a nationalist and thus ideological project into an ethical conception that treats the Other, now and in history, with appropriate epistemic respect. Most significantly, they have come to spurn the worldview of fragmented reality, a worldview that has proven its utter failure to see the interconnectedness of the various aspects of life in the world—human, animal, and insentient.

The common denominator of Asian environmental movements is their general refusal to separate ecology, environment, and the physical world, on the one hand, from an enveloping frame of metaphysical unity, on the other, where the intrinsic value of physical objects is rationally posited rather than "rationally" proven (just as we presume people innocent until proven guilty, without having to develop an entire philosophical field to prove the rationality of this proposition). This is precisely where Euro-American environmentalism faces a crucial difficulty, for its essentially Enlightenment concept of rationality has been incapable—as I explain below—of providing the logical and epistemological link necessary to assign intrinsic value to insentient life.

The failures of Western anthropocentricism and rationality therefore invite further reflection on the heuristic sources needed to supplement, if not displace, the unproductive Western search for an exit from the current ecological (and thus epistemological and hugely political) predicament. Such an exit, however, cannot consist of yet another "modern" solution to a modern problem. A solution to the crises of modernity cannot be modern—as I have argued earlier[35]—in the sense of applying the paradigmatic methods of the central domains to problems caused by these domains themselves.[36] The solution furthermore cannot be limited to an in situ, localized diagnosis—again a perception that is the result of a notoriously fragmented modern view of reality. Rather, the diagnosis must go to the deep structures of modernity, and thus of existence, for it is quite obvious that an economic problem is never just *in* or about economics, and a political problem is never just *in* or about politics. The core values of the system—political, economic, psychological, social, and otherwise—must be subjected to scrutiny *as an aggregate group* of problems, as a holistic phenomenon. The foundational thought structure needs to be rethought in its entirety.

The segregation of the political from the environmental, the ecological from the dehumanizing colonial, remains at the core of proposed modernist solutions, a segregation patently evident in nearly all Western environmental movements. These continue to speak of "saving the planet" but they consistently overlook the forces that were responsible, in equal measure and dialectically, for *both* environmental destruction *and* dehumanization. In speaking of one dimension, all the others must be included, either directly or by necessary implication. As the African diaspora scholar Zaki-yyah Iman Jackson incisively remarks, the "appeals to move 'beyond the human' may actually reintroduce the Eurocentric transcendentalism this [very] movement purports to disrupt."[37] In foregrounding the nonhuman as the proper site of analysis, environmental studies tend to relegate the human, especially the global poor, to the status of moral depravity. Linking the human and the nonhuman on a structural continuum permits a narrative that actively interrupts "the creation of deficient and inferior surplus populations that are distinguished by their monocultural, criminal, patriarchal, homophobic, and anti-environmental dispositions."[38] The categories of human and nonhuman must therefore indiscriminately collapse into each other.

V

Thus Orientalists, particularly equipped in the ways I have been describing, may now be forced to shift direction and develop a new theory—philological or otherwise—for their study of the subject, a theory that simultaneously presupposes a subject at variance with that which produced this and other fields of academic inquiry over the last two centuries. The needed change, it cannot be overemphasized, will have to involve a move *from an extroverted concern to an introverted one*. The study of Islam (as of any Other), insofar as it has been conducted up to this point, has in effect resulted in domination and violence, notwithstanding the various contributions of individual scholars. In harnessing the Islamic and other "Oriental"[39] heritages for self-constructive techniques and projects, the new approach will simultaneously convert failed intentions into effective, if not performative, discourse. This would be introspective Orientalism, a scholarly approach whose goal is reconstructing the self *first*, thereby changing its relationship to itself and then to the Other. This approach involves understanding the ways in which Oriental cultures of premodernity—in their organicist view of the world and their reflective ways of living in it—can provide heuristic sources for articulating new ways of thinking the world and of living in it.

The first task in the study of Islam (and for that matter all other major traditions of inquiry) is to treat it as a rational project, however much (or precisely because) its rationality differs from the thinking to which the modern mind has grown accustomed. Once the *internal logic* of this tradition is unraveled, the project would make as much *heuristic sense* as any other (despite the nonconformity of certain of its derivative features to modern taste, features we may set aside without prejudice to the general and higher precepts from which they derive). In light of a certain critical assessment of modernity, this logic may be deemed normative and readily accessible to Orientalists and others alike. Max Scheler's critique of modern life, for instance, can hardly be dismissed as anything less than modern in its general sensibilities, despite its radical disenchantment with modernity. Scheler very much echoes the worldview of Muslim jurists or theologians when he argues that the cosmos contains an underlying ethical order, and that it is integral to its essence to be connected to a transcendental deity. The cosmos, for him, *is* a divine order, a Quranic and cherished Islamic concept par excellence. Because the *ordo amoris* exhibits the moral character of the cosmos, humankind is intimately connected to the world in every way they are able to love. Much like Muslim intellectuals, including jurists and mystics and a combination thereof, Scheler argues that the heart (Ar. *qalb*) "deserves to be called the core of man as a spiritual being much more than knowing and willing do."[40] The Muslim intellectual may add the proviso that "knowing" (*'ilm*, as both an activity and habitus) is effectively constituted by the heart.[41]

Timothy McCune has perceptively argued that one need not be inclined toward theistic views or accept any traditional concept of divinity to appreciate, or even accept, Scheler's argument.[42] If belief is an intellectual argument, as Guénon has averred, then an intellectual argument can construct belief, as it has always done. For example, the entire range of Islamic traditions—Quranic, *shar'i*, *sufi*, theological, metaphysical, historical—rests on this kind of attitude, an attitude that dictates much of what these traditions, in general and in particular, consider essential on the cosmological, ontological, and epistemological levels. Likewise, these traditions—the Shari'a and Sufism no doubt foremost among them—cannot conceive of the world as anything other than interconnected, the unity of the cosmos reigning as a supreme doctrine. Stemming from the idea of ontological design—that everything in the world has an unconvertible and permanent reason to exist, irrespective of whether its role is subordinate to a higher order of being or not—emerges the concept of the sacredness of life, human or otherwise. This is an overwhelmingly foundational concept in the Islamic and other Asian traditions, and it stands at the core of many principles and norms across the entire span of their doctrines. Equally pervasive and countermodern is the primacy of human value over material worth in human relationships. In this worldview, capitalism and instrumentalism are relegated to a secondary and *subordinate* status, answering to the diagnosis that in modernity humans have lost a sense of who they are and what their purpose in life is. In this system of thought and action, the value of humanity paradigmatically resides in communal love, the community being the ultimate measure of existence. This is not just a

Fanonian concept of communal restoration; it is a worldview that fore-grounds community and communal love in a cosmological psychology.

For such a view to realize its full potential, it must escape the trappings of what MacIntyre has called the liberal interminable disagreement, a vast body of discourse that hovers around the liberal subject but never chal-lenges the *very constitution* of that subject. To make my argument in more specific terms, it may be instructive to dwell at some length on a funda-mental issue that illustrates the challenges with which the new Orientalist in particular and new scholar in general must contend, challenges that go to the heart of the Distinction and provide a manner of rethinking what it means to engage in scholarship. More importantly, it is an issue that engages the fundamental question of what kind of human being a scholar ought to be. In other words, it is with this question that scholars, in whatever field, must begin, for any other beginning, or no beginning at all, is the surest way to seal one's fate as a dead author, one who, in effect, partakes in the very knowledge and in the discursive formations that not only effaced him as an autonomously moral and thinking human being but also have caused unprecedented destruction.

To ask such a question is to inquire about the place of the human in the world, an inquiry that begins with an awareness of the location of the ques-tion within distinctly modern surrounds. As I have been arguing, a funda-mental category of modern thought shaping and reshaping our modernist existence is the mechanical view of the world, a view that not only dis-tanced human life from the life surrounding the human and nonhuman environment but also created a sovereign reason that took away value from life. To ask such a question is to begin with the very concept of "environment" that was converted by the mechanical worldview from an otherwise complex form of existence—which encompassed as much cos-mology *and epistemology* as the stones, the trees, and the air making up that environment—into a merely material object. Environment is all that sur-rounds the human agent, *and makes that agent in the process*, but the crisis within and challenge to the modern world consist precisely in the recog-nition of that which has been excluded from the very processes of think-ing, that which is value-laden but has ceased to have value.

This challenge—summed up in the language of the impossibility of missing what is unknown—stands at the core of the Schelerian problem, that *homo modernus* has lost sight of who and what he is. This problem is not merely physical, material, or even, when all has been said and done, just environmental. It is conceptual and epistemological in the first degree, and it is one that dictates the very terms of thinking about the predicament. The death of traditional metaphysics and cosmology, for instance, has determined the language of modernism in ways that the death foreclosed on any extramodern or contramodern critique of the issues raised by the problem. Which is to say that one of the major difficulties of the modern condition is the inability of its dominant discourses *to transcend their own categories of thought*, which is precisely where the challenge for the scholar lies. It is my argument that an ethical undertaking of redefining the place of the human in this environment and *internalizing this positioning as a moral technological operation on the self* is the starting point for, and end of, any engagement with scholarship and learning. The following discussion proposes a point of entry that intends to open up critical space for reassessing the Distinction and the sovereignty to which it gave rise.

VI

In an important article on what she called "the rationality of feeling gratitude toward nature," the environmental ethicist Karen Bardsley contends with the Enlightenment paradigmatic conception of a denuded, mechanical, and disenchanted nature. In this conception, the feeling of gratitude as a key concept is seen as inappropriate in response to someone's unintentional decisions, so that if nature is viewed, as is in fact the case, as mere inanimate subject matter, even "stupid,"[43] then the requirement that we ought to feel gratitude to it falls apart. Gratitude, in this conception, is called upon when the benefit accruing to us is motivated by intentionality, and being inanimate, nature cannot choose to help or harm us. Thus the question that arises for Bardsley is, "Is it rational . . . to feel gratitude toward something that has no intention?"[44]

The core dilemma here, as Bardsley acknowledges, is that the problem of ingratitude is the preserve of the secularists. People who believe in God or gods do not seem perturbed by such issues, as premodernity across time and space abundantly attests. Secular modernity's failure to organically integrate gratitude into nature and into fellow humans as integral to its view of the world seems not only unique to it; it also "deprives living without God of much of its coherence and meaning."[45] While gratitude seems for the theist a matter of course, for the secularist and atheist[46] it is nothing less than a "hopeless conundrum." But this conundrum and lack of coherence and meaning may not be a source of our worry about the atheists, if that is what the atheists have chosen for their own fate. The worry, rather, stems from the fact that these atheists and secularists often happen to occupy the centers of political, industrial, and technological power, and that what they felt and continue to feel about the world has led to actions that proved disastrous for the rest of humanity.[47]

Marshaling an impressive array of writings on the concepts of gratitude and gift, Bardsley frames her analysis in terms of what she calls two foci, one related to the gift itself and the other to the source of the gift, the supposed "benefactor." These are two different elements of consideration, each needing its own analytical attention, although they are interrelated in ways that make them both necessary for each other in order to fulfill the sufficient condition of gratitude. Ultimately, on Bardsley's own analysis, appreciation for the gift hinges on the gift-giver, the benefactor. The challenge raised with regard to the latter is that the "benefactor, i.e., nature, cannot have—in the atheist view of the world—any intentions, and intentions to benefit someone are deemed essential for feeling gratitude." To address this challenge, many writers have attributed "something akin to agency to non-sentient elements of the natural world," in order to bestow on nature qualities "similar enough to intentions."[48] One such argument draws on the way we are said to appreciate institutions, which have no intentions as such but possess "purposes and functions" as an integral part of their character. Thus, it is argued, one could feel gratitude to character "rather than [to] conscious intentions." In the final analysis, however, Bardsley recognizes the weakness of such arguments, on the grounds that many people cannot accept that the natural systems "possess anything like good intentions," which are prerequisites for a "rational" justification for feeling gratitude.[49] The weakness is such that Bardsley's philosophical bar drops significantly, leading her at the end to be satisfied with the absence of "bad intentions" instead of conscious, deliberate, and proactive ones. Thus, gratitude would be an "appropriate response to undeserved benefits from sources that (a) do not have bad intentions toward us and that (b) are not benefiting us as a result of accidental or regrettable aspects of their character."

All this, however, brings us back to square one, to the initial problem against which Bardsley has argued. If the natural systems have no bad intentions, then they cannot have good ones either, simply because they cannot have intentions at all; and the absence of any intention is detrimental to the argument in favor of feeling gratitude. We are also back to a dumb nature to which we paradoxically ought to be grateful just on the grounds that it is sustaining us, accidentally. There is no place in Bardsley's argument, or in any secularist argument that I know of, for a philosophical demonstration that the natural is nonaccidental, that it is a world created, by someone or something, by design. But even if we were to acquire a sense of gratitude despite this impediment (gratitude whose force has undoubtedly been significantly diminished by Bardsley's argument itself), we would still be showing gratitude to a dumb and stupid entity nonetheless, a stance that in turn considerably diminishes the rationality of our behavior. Whatever changes the concepts of human and rationality have undergone in late modernity, they continue to have the same structure that governed their nineteenth-century predecessors.

It is remarkable that with all her own arguments and the arsenal of arguments derived from countless other philosophical positions, Bardsley in conclusion frankly admits that "much more work needs to be done before we can argue that a failure to feel gratitude toward nature is a moral failing of any kind. Nor has it been proven that gratitude to nature provides any legitimate grounds for moral obligations to protect natural ecosystems . . . [or] to create obligations to act in certain ways."[50] It would seem that the uniquely *correlative and temporal concomitance* between Enlightenment reason and modernity, on the one hand, and systematic and global-scale destruction of natural ecosystems, on the other, is not sufficient rational reason for Bardsley to conclude that premodern world systems provided "legitimate grounds" for moral obligations to protect natural ecosystems or to create obligations on their part to act in ways that did not lead to their degradation and virtual destruction. We are therefore forced to conclude, on behalf of Bardsley, that the survival of ecosystems fairly intact until modernity was consummated had no causal relationship with the ways these systems viewed and lived in the world, and that the modern concomitance is a matter of sheer accident. Her argument, then, not only begs the question, leaving us wondering why she would interrogate atheism and its inability to engender gratitude in the first place, but also betrays the very liberal attitude that universalizes and distributes moral and ethical liability for the crises that it was largely responsible for creating.

In Bardsley's narrative, then, moral obligations have been shown to be unnecessary and, as a direct result, no modes of conduct can be prescribed for any action of protecting ecosystems that these moral obligations would have engendered. Put differently, and unlike, say, the nearly unquestioned technology of the self that demands the sacrifice of the citizen for the sake of the nation-state,[51] the duty to protect nature falls far from a corresponding course of action or defense of nature—to such a degree that it fails to engender in the soul or psyche even the conviction that such an action is a necessary, conscionable duty, whose violation creates in the subject a sense of violation and remorse. The absurdity arises from a value system that does not think twice about the utter willingness to have your son or daughter die for the cause of the country in a Schmittian, violent world of the political, but that remains at best uncommitted to a psychology of gratitude toward the very world that is sustaining human and nonhuman life.

But Bardsley and other environmental ethicists must contend with a more significant difficulty than just showing philosophically that gratitude to nature is a rational attitude, an argument that nonetheless encounters, as we have seen, major difficulties, if not a dead end. Even if we suppose that these difficulties can be overcome, there remains a colossal gap between philosophical discourse and actual practice. Gratitude to nature is not just a matter of philosophy, nor is philosophy, at the end of the day, the only or even major vehicle for the construction of an attitude that is integral to pervasive social conduct. Gratitude cannot be and is not limited to philosophical abstraction, as many philosophical issues are. Nor should it be so, since the issues involved within the scope of gratitude affect the ways in which humans live on a daily basis, ways that have themselves contributed to the ecological and environmental crisis and most dangerously to an increasing thrust of the sovereign structure of thought. In other words, since philosophy, especially in modernity, can never amount to popular, grassroots social norms and values, there remains a significant gap between ideas and intellectual discourse, on the one hand, and practical ethics, on the other. As the Muslim moral philosopher Taha Abdurrahman has argued, such gaps are endemic to liberal modernity, giving it the characteristic of a "civilization of speech,"[52] a notion dubbed more diplomatically by Alasdair MacIntyre liberalism's interminable disagreement.

Bardsley's critique and philosophical position, however thoughtful they may be, remain positioned within liberal discourse, attempting to refine and expand conceptions of rationality from a posited (and by necessity nonconvertible) liberal position. The scope of the two foci she identifies is constrained by considerations of gift and benefactor, and how these may be reinterpreted to engender gratitude to nature. But the constraints ab initio precluded a reinterpretation, and much less a critique, of the very subject who analytically stands before the two foci, a subject taken by Bardsley for granted and without adequate interrogation. Bardsley's overall argument does not reckon with the quality of the modern subject and the temporal, "progressive" changes that this subject has been undergoing through modern time. The evolution of this subject has been characterized by a marked increase in the subjectivity of the sovereign individual, where freedom to act in self-interest abnegates a sense of debt, and therefore gratitude, to others, nature included. The presumption that I do what I do for myself negates the intention to deliberately help or bestow benefit upon others. This comports with the assumption that individual interest, which I am entitled to assert and pursue, does not include the component of either debt or obligation toward others, who themselves, under the same rules, "owe me nothing either." And since I do not intend to make my act stand in your service, or result in your benefit, then I will feel no more gratitude toward you than I expect you to feel gratitude toward me if one of us, or both, happened to benefit from the deeds of the other. The modern subject's capacity to feel gratitude to others is diminishing (rather than increasing) because the feeling of debt chips away at self-entitlement, a major component in the constitution of modern subjectivity. In other words, gratitude threatens the notion of the autonomy of the individual's rights, if not sovereignty, and takes away the sacred feeling of self-entitlement. This is to say that Bardsley is entirely silent about the quality of the subject who stands before the "two foci" she has identified, and without whom these foci would have no meaning. In the study of gratitude, the subject is clearly more central as an analytical category than the elements of gift and benefactor, the source of the gift, since the problem lies therein, if it is not indeed the most central.

The issue for Bardsley, as it has been for liberal thinkers since J. S. Mill, is how to bring the world to liberalism, but never how to bring liberalism to the world. Which is to say that the secular-atheist subject in Bardsley's narrative is not himself the locus of the problem, for he is the agent for whom the world must be made sense of in accordance with her rational requirements. This, simply put, is where Bardsley's position suffers a fatal blow,[53] since it in effect entails the violation of the Law of Excluded Middle. It is either that an atheist agent denudes nature of intrinsic value or that a value-laden nature presupposes a believing subject; it cannot be both.

By contrast, for instance, the philosophical anthropologist Max Scheler focused his attention on the subject who needs to change who he is. His argument (not unlike that of Foucault himself)[54] goes to the core of subjectivity, questioning not only who the modern subject is but also his very knowledge of his own place in the world. For Scheler, modern man lacks a unified and coherent idea of who and what he is, and even more so lacks a unified and coherent idea of what he is capable of becoming. That modern man is lost to himself and in the world represents a function of the disconnection between *homo modernus* and the cosmos, which, for him, is an order of existence structured according to an ethical plan. The problem with modern man is that he lost touch with his inner self, including the faculty of love and sympathy. Instead, modern man, by which Scheler meant the "modern Westerner," has become a *homo capitalisticus*, a locution that transcends the meaning of an economic sphere and signifies a state of mind, a way of seeing and existing in the world. Utilitarian and instrumentalist to the core, the ethos and value structure of this man has been "marked by an insatiable drive for acquisition and a prioritization of the two lowest value-ranks: the useful and the agreeable."[55] The structure of the modern subject, designed by selfish interest, love for material things, and a self-centered view of the world, has resulted, according to Scheler, in ever-increasing levels of suffering and estrangement from nature, which has been dominated in systematic ways. Equally important, trenchant anthropocentrism has created a species that possesses a partial and limited view of life, reality, the world and nature at large.

What is needed, Scheler argues, is a profound transformation of the subject who must, in order to accomplish this transformation, alter his interior subjectivity so that the "inner power" wins over "inferior, non-spiritual, psychological 'life.'"[56] The fight within the self is squarely about inverting, if not subverting, the entire value structures of modernity, amounting to a revolution not only against how we think but, more importantly, against who we, as humans, ultimately are. Integral to this revolution is a major adjustment in our attitudes that have objectified and commodified nature, an adjustment geared toward compelling us—initially and until it becomes ingrained in us as a second nature—to see the world as a unity. And this cannot be successfully undertaken without realizing the full potential of our capacities of love, sympathy, and solidarity, capacities that may reestablish the desideratum of harmony within life and the world (and capacities whose absence, as I have discussed in the previous chapter, constituted the sources for self-hatred responsible, inter alia, for genocide).

Yet this harmonizing is not merely a slogan or a discursive claim; rather, it involves reengineering the self by means of certain technologies of self-cultivation, the restructuring of interpersonal relations and our relations to the nonhuman world. Harmony is also intimately tied to this notion of sacrifice: "Suffering is an ontological actuality—reality, recall, is resistance. Like the Buddha, Scheler offered an insight into essential existence, namely that 'one cannot want the one without the other; not love and the unison (community) without death and pain; not the higher development and the growth of life without pain and death; not the sweetness of love without sacrifice and its pains.' . . . It is the surrender of the part for the whole, and a lesser value for a higher one, though without diminishing the importance and uniqueness of each part and value."[57] In short, Scheler's phenomenology appears to require a particular technology of the self akin to that of Buddhism and Islam, but it certainly runs counter to the core of the liberal attitude toward pleasure and pain. It is a mental technology of the spiritual comportment of the self that depends on curbing drives and relating the inner being to the larger world and life.

Bardsley's and Scheler's positions capture two distinctively different Western ways to approach the crises that the modern subject is undergoing. However "green" and sensitive it may be, Bardsley's is a conventional liberal account of the subject. It assumes a status quo of subjectivity that merely needs, in a typical liberal fashion, to maneuver *hermeneutically* around the problems posed. The subject's constitution itself is never interrogated, and no demands are made of it to change its conception of itself, its value structures and ontological priorities, or its place in, and relationship to, the world. The result is yet another verbal contribution: a problem is talked about from the side or from above, but never confronted head-on with root solutions and with a causative diagnosis. To put it in popular jargon, Bardsley offers a "bandage solution," typical of how liberalism has dealt with all other major problems, be they related to poverty, health care, crime, education, military spending, or political intervention; and ecology, environment, and dehumanizing colonialism have been and continue to be no different.

Scheler, on the other hand, offers a profound conception of change—and a structural change at that: the inner layers of the self *demand* a complete revaluation. Undertaking such drastic methods is clearly not in liberalism's order, for any such attempt as Scheler has offered will per force change both the face and the substance of liberal subjectivity, and with it the very project of liberalism, which is precisely why the likes of Scheler and those calling for inverting and subverting values—from Herder to MacIntyre—have remained relatively on the margins of discourse, having been swept away by Enlightenment and post-Enlightenment doctrines amenable to liberal predilections (hence the dominance of neo-Kantianism, the concept of negative liberty, and the consequent validation of Said's liberal critique).

However, the reemergence of voices like Scheler's within the ecological and environmental movement (as well as within anticolonialist discourses) signals the insufficiency, if not inadequacy, of the liberal tradition in dealing with the crises in the natural habitat, and hence with the self as being itself the seat of the problem.[58] That is to say, the required changes are wide and deep, going into the very values of the modern subject and no less into the very technologies of the self that can reconstitute not only a new conception of rationality but also, and equally importantly, certain types of ethical formation.

Scheler's call for a restructured view of the world's unity amounts, with hindsight, to a devastating critique of the fragmented liberal subject who is formed within a narrow conception of particular competing interests and values of the good life that revolve mostly around material considerations. It is, in effect, an implicit but powerful attack on the concept of negative liberty, the political basis of the liberal subject formation. The absence in this subject of spiritual, metaphysical, and coherent psychological formation[59] has distanced it from its surrounding natural habitat, which, on a different conception of reality, remains tied to the cosmological background that gives rise to the subject in the first place.[60] This is precisely where the value of traditional world cultures and "religions" might reside. Since the present and the future offer no guides, these cultures and "religions" can provide, at least heuristically, a starting point for a revaluation of the place of humans in the world. In the case of the Islamic—as well as the Chinese and Indian—there is much to gain by reflecting on the coherent unity of the subject as situated in the cosmic and metaphysical world.

As a rational stance, gratitude in these traditions is enshrined as an integral part of living life—hence its indexical importance to my argument. It is not a *post eventum* justification or a desperate solution to eminent crisis, but rather a way of conceiving and making sense of the world and of life as it is lived. A measure of myth is of course always involved in the process of thought we call metaphysics or cosmology, just as the modern doctrine of progress, universal reason, and much else modern possess similar myths, despite all vigorous denials. Gratitude, in other words, is integral to the fabric of thought and practice, needing no philosophers to instruct people in the art of feeling and living. The epistemology of its practical ethics is woven through the weft of living life, which is to say that it is embedded within the substantive benchmark[61] of the technologies of the self.

Like Guénon's, Scheler's philosophical narrative essentially captures much of what the Oriental traditions, including the Islamic, have to offer. The overall structure and values of these traditions represent the substrate of a world of discourse that may be utilized heuristically for a study of the Orient within the context of the critique of modernity's current crises. Such a study—of Islam, Hinduism, and Buddhism, among many others—holds limited promise and viability as long as it is not informed by the most pertinent and overarching theoretical concerns of our day, concerns having almost exclusively to do with self-critique. Orientalism will thus be required to shift the focus of its interests by inverting the subject for the object, amounting in effect to a new philology centered on what may be called *heuristic historicism*; the Oriental traditions will cease to be the locus of revaluation and reengineering, and will instead stand as the repertoire of thought that will instruct in refashioning a new Orientalist self. This is another way of saying that Orientalism's philological work will constitute the constructive medium through which the sovereign subject, the *homo modernus*, can embark on a project of retraining the soul and spirit, in the process cultivating a new ethical technology of the self that will provide a model, an exemplarity, for the rest of the Orientalist's society to emulate. Amounting to a reversal of function, this operation would no longer be about the Orient, about understanding it so "that we can deal with it"; it would rather represent an ethically self-centered process of what Foucault called "taking care of the self," recovering what has "faded." There is no reason for Orientalism and the Orientalist to exist other than to fulfill this purpose. And once this goal is achieved, the rest, including a truly humane historiography, an empathetic philological method, and much else that the scholarly apparatus requires, will follow on their own.

If Orientalism has always been about Europe, as the bulk of Said's project claims, then the methods and lessons to be drawn require rethinking, being, after Said, a self-conscious project.[62] Yet, this is not to suggest that the Orientalist alone is to bear the burden of correcting the ills of her society—admittedly an unbearable burden—but the Orientalist happens, by virtue of her location within the formation of modern knowledge, to stand at the intersection in which knowledge of the Other is her expertise, par excellence. As I intimated earlier, if Orientalism was the most obvious bridge through which the Other was so badly constructed, then it is this bridge that can begin refashioning the self through a heuristic accessing of an instructive Other. Alien to modernity, epistemic humility, an antidote to sovereignty, is a much-needed remedy.

VII

Preoccupation with what we call microhistory cannot be validated without reference to, and an understanding of, the structural and paradigmatic features not only of macrohistory and *longue durée*[63] but also of an emerging critique whose starting point is the thought structure that gave rise, among other things, to environmental crisis—crisis, we have insisted, that is symptomatic of a larger epistemological and therefore ethical deficit (one that stems from a structure that is designed to operate *exclusively within* materialist and political considerations). It might seem to us a perfectly legitimate project of research to study, say, a ruler's intervention in market activity during a particular dynastic period, the economic life of a city, or marriage relations within a particular community. Yet, the legitimacy of the project rests on a host of broader questions inevitably informed by even larger philosophical and theoretical considerations. Reducing methodological concerns to the common modernist assumptions about, say, the role of "state" in the management or control of the Shariʿa in fourteenth-century Cairo is not only a narrow and highly biased way of studying history; it also represents a distorted view of reality, both of Islam's and of ours. While they seem on the surface acceptable and valid, research projects of this kind clearly lack theoretical and even conceptual clarity, not to mention intellectual maturity, in the sense I have been trying to elucidate. They only presume to tell us how things happened in an Islamic instance (what we call "a particular context") from a modernist perspective, the same perspective that is now being critiqued and rejected as the source of the very crises that humanity is experiencing.

The links between such scholarly assumptions and their deep foundations in the sovereign Enlightenment structure of thought may be subtle, but they cannot be too subtle for a scholar with a deep sense of ethical responsibility. Such conventional historiographical ventures, it must be recognized, are nearly always situated within a latent context of (oppositional) comparison with a modern (or rather modernist) situation, one that has driven the question of research in the first place.[64] This has been the general approach of the overwhelming bulk of recent scholarship, as evidenced, among other things, in the proliferation of studies on women and gender issues "in Islam," on social and economic practices within the parameters of "Shariʿa and state," and on what might be called a "hero history" that reentrenches (after early forms of Orientalism) the "civilizational influence" that a master-jurist exercised over an entire legal-moral tradition, thereby disregarding the dialectical traditions without which no jurist could have been constructed as such an authority in the first place.[65] These topics of research, like countless others, have no future promise without reckoning with the immediate and critical questions of the day, those that are increasingly compelling us *to interrogate the very ethical foundations of the premises underlying these fields.*

An inquiry of the sort I am proposing will have to contend with a revaluation of the very questions asked of other traditions, a situation that presupposes the interrogation of their ethical groundings. An illustrative instance may provide some clarification. Take, for example, a fairly large body of Orientalist discourse that has been geared, for nearly three-quarters of a century, to the study of the Quran, the Islamic foundationalist text par excellence, in the formative period of so-called Islamic law. This early historical phase has been dominated by a narrative of "borrowings" and "debts" to the preceding cultures of the Near East, most notably the Greco-Roman, Byzantine, and Jewish. "Islamic law," also misnamed "Mohammadan law," is said to have accumulated such a debt by a wholesale incorporation, under an Islamic "veneer," of the former cultures' institutions and legal concepts, since the overriding but often undeclared racial assumption is that the impoverished tribes of the desert-filled Arabia who conquered the entire belt stretching from Morocco to Transoxiana could not have built an empire with such sophistication on their own. Through forging an Islamic narrative in the name of Islam's Prophet, the early Muslims legitimized and thus domesticated these "foreign influences." Issues of originality and authenticity are clearly at stake here, but equally clear is that their implications are to be located squarely in the project of legitimizing structural genocide.

Yet, this is not the entire story. It remains a focus of intense curiosity that the Quran, with all its importance to Muslims from the beginning, did not make it to the rank of a "legal" source, but was instead kept on the side for nearly a century before it was brought in, as "an afterthought," to endorse, with a final stamp of approval, the naturalization of the process of "borrowings." Seen as a veneer, the Quran then had no real formative dimension as a creator of normativity, and its performativity in the production of a new moral subject of the "law" remained unrecognized by Orientalism. Hence the persistent difficulties that engulfed this scholarship in explaining why the caliphs of Islam, and later its sultans, never as much as attempted to seize the law, particularly its "legislative branch." What is even more striking is that this narrative never reached the stage of asking the fundamental question: If these rulers never entertained such an ambition, then would the emerging picture be one of an entrenched concept of rule of law? This stage of scholarly inquiry was precluded ab initio because the very possibility of asking the question would have necessarily opened up a whole range of other questions that would ultimately demolish the entire Orientalist narrative of an arcane and despotic Shariʿa. A Shariʿa offering a concept of the rule of law that is as robust as, if not more robust than, the modern Euro-American model not only would diametrically run against the doctrine of progress and the Western sense of superiority over the "Orient," but also would contradict the very cultural and legal discourse that was put in the service of justifying colonialism and, later, "legal reform" in the Islamic world, one whose effects I have discussed in detail in chapter 2.[66] If the Shariʿa possessed such robust features—the rule of law being, no doubt, a premiere feature—then why demolish it through an aggressive series of "reforms"?

The factors that went into making this scholarly myth about the Quran as a veneer and an afterthought are surely many and complex, but there is no doubt that a general attitude to religion as primitive and a thing of the past is one of them. This attitude, however, is not separate from the Distinction, especially in its Is/Ought component, of which a central proposition is that value cannot be derived from fact. The Distinction stands thus at the root of modern legal positivism, which cannot articulate the world in any terms other than through state coercion and interference. Law without a state's coercive power of enforceability is no law at all. Hence the impasses suffered by Orientalism in interpreting the role of the Quran in both constitutional organization and "law's" formation—as a substantive body of juridico-moral norms—during the first century of Islam's history. The idea that a divine-command ethics can provide the basis for, and drive, a legal system was *posited* as both obsolete and irrelevant to any modern construction of legal normativity. As I have shown with regard to the ab initio ousting of any competing view from the process of positing the Is/ Ought distinction as an exclusive point of view from which to see the world, here too there was no room for alternatives. There was even less room for the possibility that a divine-command ethics has a certain heuristic value, with this having to entail the adoption of, or indebtedness to, another legal culture. For this exercise, normal as it was for many cultures (including the Islamic in its encounter with Greek and Indian intellectual systems), would have been seen as chipping away at Western superiority and its unqualified theology of progress.

Yet it is my argument that the Islamic intellectual debates over the nature of law continue to have heuristic relevance to modern thinking about modern law's performativity as a coercive mechanism producing an externalized subject, rather than one that presupposes an individual who is operating with internal moral restraints constituted by the systematic workings of ethical technologies of the self. Depriving the individual of this eminent potential (brought to the fore by other cultures and their human populations for millennia) was clearly the work of a domineering and an all-powerful state, one that could not depend on the moral agency of its subjects to do its bidding in nationalist wars, conquests, and various forms of oppression. But this deprivation also stems from self-imposed limits within the Western intellectual traditions of modernity, limits having to do with unquestioned assumptions about such categories as "religion," divine-command ethics, and nearly any nonsecularist conception of reality. These categories are seen not only as unworthy of serious consideration, but also as standing beneath the dignity of serious scholarship. This is of course epistemic arrogance pure and simple, but it exhibits all the features of Scheler's man-lost-in-the-world, one who can no longer conceive of the possibility that the world is made of countless structures of thought that can provide at least serious heuristic value.

As one scholar has insightfully argued, the Islamic theological and legal debates culminate in the *fundamentally epistemological* view that reliance on divine-command ethics in norm construction finds its justification in the very limitations that secular modes of thought impose on reasoning in general and on moral-legal reasoning in particular. Which is to say that Muslim intellectuals have long before modernity reflected on the epistemological implications of a secular system of thought, and have judged it as unsatisfactory, if not harmful (akin to Hinduism's critique of the Buddhist *nastika*). The dominant Ash'ari School, for instance, has found it necessary to resort to revelation-based ethics precisely because of the inadequacy and limits of individual human experience in providing any guidelines for the construction of general principles. To avoid the epistemic implications of this experience, and of all the skepticism that necessarily ensues from it, an interruption of these experiences was needed, namely, through miracle. In other words, the miracle is precisely the source of universalizable norms, one that takes away the arbitrariness and subjectivity of individual and relativist experience. Whereas mainstream Muslim intellectuals have moved from skepticism, as a distinctly epistemological impasse, to the absolute necessity of theism, the paradigmatic line of modern thinking moved from theism to the unavoidability of skepticism.[67] In yet other words, a divine-command ethics, whose theoretical and substantive principles are elaborated—as I have been arguing throughout—by spatially and temporally dispersed communities of scholars, was the surest way to install a system of rule of law that was not subject to any individual or state agency.[68] Here, the *very concept of miracle that genealogically formed the basis of the Schmittian state of exception was turned on its head to generate a rule of law without exception.*

This conception is not to be understood, as it has invariably been, to mean that divine-command ethics must entail theistic tyranny and the absence of individual moral autonomy. Such an understanding may accurately apply to the ways in which Christian Europe conducted itself, and against which the Reformation and the Enlightenment constituted reactions. But this was not what Islam stood for, at least not what the dominant and mainstream Ash'ari School and generally the paradigmatic duo of Shari'a and Sufism theorized and practiced. Aside from a miniscule body of rules directly stipulated in the body of revelation, God's justice *was* the-world-as-his-creation, which is to say that it was not a specific divine will but one that infused the order of being as goodness (something quite reminiscent of Scheler's world-as-ethical-order). The interpretation of this goodness was left to the moral subject whose rational-intellectual apparatus would dictate to her, from within her soul, the necessity of the inclination to see the world as goodness and to act in it as requiring such goodness. This doctrine of *kalam al-nafs* presupposes the moral subject, which is to say that *before the subject becomes an interpretive subject*, a hermeneutical agent, there exists a moral drive to render interpretation nothing but an ethical exercise. As I have argued elsewhere, the modern question as to why be moral did not arise in the same way for Muslim jurists and theologians.[69] Ethics was not a challenge, but a question of how best to put it into practice.

That legal ethics, the moral law, was indeed articulated and applied in practice by a temporal-cum-spatial community of scholars that could not itself change the law except through a case-by-case temporal-cum-spatial interpretive communal effort was indeed one of the landmarks and most distinguishing features of that civilization. *Both* the individual and the "state" would be under the law, and the latter cannot stand above it, as the modern state does. Note here—at the risk of repetition—that whereas miracle in the Schmittian-Agambian conception produces what I have called the state of extraordinarity[70] (Schmitt's "state of exception"), in Islam miracle produces a rule of law that cannot allow for any such exception—much less a state of extraordinarity—to exist.[71] There are no exceptions within the "law," either in theory or in practice. Yet, the implications of adopting a divine-command theory extend even beyond the political, for in the very act of making it a starting point for reflection on the world there lies the profound assumption that this world is saturated with goodness and that everything in it is made in accordance with an ethical plan. By contrast, an epistemology that leads to skepticism is bound to land the skeptic in what Bardsley has called (as we saw earlier) a "hopeless conundrum," without this guaranteeing a more robust moral agency than the theist would possess. If anything, a whole line of philosophical-historical analysis shows the opposite, a line that ranges from Foucault's discursive formations to the problem of moral neutrality and Arendt's banality of evil and moral agency's resignation to bureaucratic and other forms of domination.

VIII

There is here much food for thought, although the stupendous army of Orientalists has not picked up on the significance of these and similar topics of inquiry even after subjecting the Islamic Orient to study for almost two centuries. It is neither reductionism nor an overstatement to say that at the source of the failure lies a deep disconnection with the central importance of individual ethical formation, one that Foucault has famously declared to be an art that is now "obscure," having "faded" in the landscapes of modernity.[72] There is no route to understanding the Quran's role in constitutional organization and its centrality in the answer to skepticism outside this ethical formation, for it is this very formation that provides the foundation of critique for assailing the dominance and performativity of modernity's discursive formations. Which is also to say that this understanding is not to be conducted on behalf of the Orient or its Muslims, but rather for the sake of the Orientalist himself. If anything, she, like all her colleagues in other disciplines, needs it more than anyone else.

If we assume, as we should, that knowledge is never innocent of the social, conceptual, material, political, and power networks within which it is cultivated, then engaging in knowledge production—inter alia the mission and, indeed, raison d'être of the scholar—comes with a grave ethical and moral responsibility, but one that can no longer be formed through the liberal tradition or exclusively within the central domains' discursive formations. As an instrument of power and one that in modernity stands in dialectical relationship with it, knowledge is a weapon that can inflict cruel violence, including, as we have seen, genocide and much else.[73] To cultivate it within an ethical framework is to engage, first and foremost, in a series of self-interrogations about the justifiability of the very concept of scholarship in the first place: Why, that is, choose to enter into *this* domain of production? What forms of scholarship are ethically justifiable and what forms are not? How can a scholar, through a specific and precisely formulated research project, partake in ethical self-formation? Which comes first, the material comfort as a sole consideration or the ethical obligation toward the self and the Other, the "object" of one's research? But whatever supposes itself to be an explanation, justification, or rationalization of the choice of entering into this field does in no way circumscribe or circumvent the ethical quality of the derivative questions that the scholar asks of the field, and of what it is that the answers to these questions aim to accomplish.

The prevalent attitude within professional historiography is of course that history is a field of knowledge, and as such, any question posed within its boundaries is as legitimate as the next. In other words, who is to say what is a legitimate or valid historical question and what is not? The entire range of historical space and time is equally open to investigation, without prejudging the legitimacy of membership qua membership. Only the results or answers given to the formally posed question are subjected to evaluation as good, bad, solid, persuasive, flimsy, or otherwise. But as a rule the very questions or choices of historical topics are never themselves interrogated. No one, to my knowledge, has ever cast doubt on a historian's work insofar as the topics chosen for study are concerned, be they minting practices under the Qing dynasty, the uses and economy of salt in the New Kingdom of Pharaonic Egypt, the structure of Mamluk armies, filth in nineteenth-century Paris, the history of mosquitos in the Malayas, or, for that matter, the conditions of felicity in the speech of a Pennsylvania village idiot. The extent to which this state of affairs is integral to the modern sovereignty of knowledge has never been a topic of investigation, much less a serious one.

The nonrestrictive, freely open attitude is largely the function of the foundational assumption that history is there for us to discover, that its truths are ultimately objective, and that it is—in a mimesis with the natural sciences (a model that history always subconsciously aspires, however unsuccessfully, to replicate)—knowable. History, in other words, is ours, and our knowledge of it is sovereign. If we are the subject, the active knower, then history is the object, the terrain that *our* minds chart. Undeniably, the widespread belief among professional historians is that history and historiography are cumulative in nature and revisionist along the way, but ultimately destined toward a teleology, namely, discovering a particular truth about a period, a field or subfield, an event, a dynasty, an emperor, an economy, or an "issue" in an endless series of "issues." Thus while history is commanded by our sovereign knowledge, and we therefore epistemically own it, it is not really "about us." Furthermore, this race for the "truth" of history is also claimed to be self-evident, as an endeavor that is intrinsically valuable and in need of no prior justification. Knowledge, including historical knowledge, is self-justifying, since it stems from a sovereign structure of thought, one that has been at the center of this book's critical gaze. In an intellectual world in which the Distinction prevails, sovereign knowledge, the source of so-called intellectual freedom, translates into precisely the kind of questions whose answers yield the destructive effects of oppression, colonialism, and genocide. None of these, it must be remembered, would have been possible without history, and if these are distinctly modern phenomena, as we have seen, then it is the modern form of history that *manifests* the problem. Sovereign knowledge is not freedom, but one that is by definition reckless, violent, and devoid of ethical content, as the history of modern history amply attests.

The inquisitive freedom afforded by the discipline of historiography, including philology, furthermore replicates those freedoms propounded in liberal democracies, freedoms unquestioned as long as they operate, more or less, within both the acceptable norms within the profession and the forms of knowledge that regulate a particular view of history (the liberal parallel to these is the sociopolitical order and the knowledge forms governing capitalist modes of production, forms that in turn determine the perpetually uncertain teleology of that order). It is, for instance, a canonical truth of professional historiography to reject any understanding oppositional to its concept of Enlightenment reason that, for instance, separates between fact and value, a sacred distinction in the very natural sciences that it strives hard to imitate. It would be an incurable sacrilege therefore to even gesture toward the possibility that history has, in the main, no other function than to provide ethical instruction, or that myth and magic are scrutable through *their own* structure of rationality.

Such a heresy is inextricably entailed by another pervasive creed that dominates the very course and content of historiographical practice. Walter Mignolo argues that modernity's concept of history is singular, recognizing, that is, a single line of narrative. When a new development occurs, what existed before it is pushed back into the past, precisely into "history" and the "historical."[74] This process, pervasively epistemological, carries with it profound implications, since the very conception of linear, singular history, coupled with a trenchant theology of progress, always locates the past within the marginal and less privileged. History is history, less "developed" and thus wholly or partially primitive, medieval, antimodern, and most importantly irrelevant to the new and modern, to the "true" expression of "progress."[75] Beginning with Vico and early Nietzsche and ending more recently with Hayden White and de Certeau, this conception has been critically interrogated, creating anxiety but little change among professional historians. Deeply implicated in nationalism and modern state domination, modern historiography and historical imagination remain implicated in imperialism and colonialism, that is, in the mechanics of destructive power.[76] My analysis of historical and other forms of academic knowledge throughout this book has in effect shown the same results, with the caveat that history and Orientalism are extensions of each other, just as philosophy, science, and economics divide among themselves the labor of conquering the world. History, to play on one of White's famous terms, *plots* violence, and as such it has the selfsame epistemic structures of Orientalism. By contrast, in its circulatory model—the form that prevailed in premodern Islam, China, and India—history possessed, as Nietzsche vehemently argued in another context, a moral and ethical backbone.[77] Instead of being an instrument of building destructive political and national identities, it contained narratives of ethical instruction (precisely the central themes of classical Islamic history, which stood at no remove from *shaṛi* and mystical discourses). Once we recognize that our modern historiography is plotted in no less mythical and imaginary ways than any other (a thesis argued forcibly and convincingly by de Certeau, White, and a number of others),[78] we will be on our way to articulating a healthier conception of the value of human and nonhuman life as embedded in a complex environment not only that sustains this life but also that instructs us in our "study" of the Other. The study of history, Orientalism, philosophy, science, and any other field of intellectual inquiry is essentially an exercise in an ethical self-construction, a technology for ethicizing the self. It is the only teleology that can be justified on ethical grounds.

Notes

Introduction

1. The confusion is readily apparent in a piece written by the historian Bernard Lewis, one of the foremost Orientalists of the twentieth century. In an attack on Edward Said's *Orientalism* and on all critics of the discipline, he says that the "term 'Orientalist' was not ('in the past') as vague and imprecise as it appears now." It is "by now . . . polluted beyond salvation . . . and had been in fact abandoned by those who previously bore it. This abandonment was given formal expression at the Twenty-ninth International Congress of Orientalists, which met in Paris in the Summer of 1973." After a long debate in that congress over the designation and what it meant to the participants, the "institution was strong enough to prevent the dissolution of the congress." The "movement to abolish the term 'Orientalist' was, however, successful." In the last sentence of his diatribe, as indeed throughout the body of his text, Lewis nonetheless continues to use the term (arguing, interestingly, that the "most rigorous and penetrating critique of Orientalist, as of any other, scholarship has always been and will remain that of their fellow scholars, especially, though not exhaustively, those working in the same field"). Bernard Lewis, "The Question of Orientalism," in *Islam and the West* (New York: Oxford University Press, 1993), 99–118, at 101, 103, 118. See also Ivan Kalmar, *Early Orientalism: Imagined Islam and the Notion of Sublime Power* (London: Routledge, 2012), 18–21. As I will show in due course, Said's work, in isolating Orientalism for special analysis, had the effect of reifying

a category of modern discourse that masked deeper structures of what might be called non-Orientalist Orientalism.

2. Harry Oldmeadow, *Journeys East: Twentieth-Century Western Encounters with Eastern Religious Traditions* (Bloomington: World Wisdom, 2004), 7. See Anouar Abdel-Malek, "Orientalism in Crisis," *Diogenes* 11, no. 44 (1963): 103–40; A. L. Tibawi, "English-Speaking Orientalists," *Islamic Quarterly*, pt. 1, vol. 8, no. 1 (1964): 25–45; pt. 2, vol. 8, no. 3 (1964): 73–88.

3. Oldmeadow, *Journeys East*, 14.

4. Sociology of Islam List, June 4–8, 2016.

5. For a powerful argument that challenges the rehabilitation of company Orientalists against Said's charge (thereby confirming Said's narrative and in effect going beyond it), see Siraj Ahmed, *The Stillbirth of Capital: Enlightenment Writing and Colonial India* (Stanford: Stanford University Press, 2012), esp. 161–88. For a more general overview, see Betty Joseph, "Dredging Orientalism," *Eighteenth-Century Life* 38, no. 2 (Spring 2014): 120–26.

6. Michel Foucault, "The Subject and Power," in *Power: Essential Works of Foucault, 1954–1984*, ed. James D. Faubion, trans. Robert Hurley et al., vol. 3 (New York: New Press, 1994), 326–48, at 330.

7. A critique of these liberal positions is the concern of the last chapter.

8. On the problematics of Said's secular humanism, see note 33 of this chapter; chapter 2, notes 62 and 137; and chapter 5, note 10. On anthropocentrism, secularism, and atheism, see chapter 5, especially section 6. For an ethical critique of secular humanism, see Basil Mitchell, *Morality: Religious and Secular* (Oxford: Clarendon, 1980). A more insightful critique of the same may be found in the various important contributions of Talal Asad.

9. See, in particular, Alasdair MacIntyre, *After Virtue: A Study in Moral Theory*, 3rd ed. (Notre Dame: University of Notre Dame Press, 2007), chap. 2.

10. I think Sudipta Kaviraj puts the matter well when he says that "what Said described and analysed was not what is called colonial discourse in the narrow sense. His work was concerned primarily with European, and subsequently, Western representations of the Orient. He rarely concerns himself with the question of what happened in the reception of these ideas in the very different context of colonial societies. . . . But there is no doubt that his side of the picture exerted great influence on the debates about colonial discourse and knowledge. Strictly, these two things are different." Sudipta Kaviraj, "Said and the History of Ideas," in *Cosmopolitan Thought Zones: South Asia and the Global Circulation of Ideas*, ed. Sugata Bose and Kris Manjapra (New York: Palgrave Macmillan, 2010), 58–81, at 75–76.

11. James Clifford, *The Predicament of Culture: Twentieth-Century Ethnography, Literature, and Art* (Cambridge, MA: Harvard University Press, 1988), 266.

12. Clifford, 268.

13. Perhaps the most succinct account Foucault gives of discursive formations is to be found in Foucault, *The Archaeology of Knowledge and Discourse on Language*, trans. A. M. Sheridan Smith (New York: Pantheon, 1972), 31–39.

14. See note 2 of this chapter.

15. As I will attempt to show in chapter 4, German Orientalism, operating from a landlocked country, developed its own internal Other, and did not necessarily require distant colonies to exhibit colonialism or genocide. That Germany "did not have colonies" (partially incorrect) is an argument that bolsters my thesis to the effect that, irrespective of varied forms of colonialism, modern structures of thought operated in principle in the same way wherever they were to be found. That German Orientalism behaved differently before the Third Reich—arguing for Asian rather than Judeo-Christians origins of Germania and Europa—is no less damning, in the sense that certain components of it exhibited anti-Semitism while others were "enrolled in a highly significant revision of German rhetoric about identity formation, both individual and cultural." Suzanne Marchand, "German Orientalism and the Decline of the West," *Proceedings of the American Philosophical Society* 145, no. 4 (December 2001): 465–73, at 473. The "explosion of specialized knowledge about the East," Marchand continues, "had destroyed the biblical foundations of European identity, and exploded the Graeco-centric world of the nineteenth century. Of course, it was the Arian strain that flourished under the Third Reich; but what we might call the Keyserling version was reborn again in the 1960s as a means to complete the critique of classical antiquity's normativity, European imperialism, and the desiccation of the academy. We may well be, as Said argues, the heirs of the imperialist 'gaze'; but we are perhaps equally the descendants of German orientalism, a much more ambiguous and irreversible strain of thought." With the benefit of hindsight, it is difficult to see how German Orientalism's engagement with the "East" and its attendant critique of European imperialism and the academy contributed anything to the betterment of the East and its fortunes, or to changing the central paradigmatic discourses of Western academia, that is, if we grant that the entire project was about anything other than self-redemption. (I am indebted to my colleague Avinoam Shalem for fruitful discussions about Marchand's work.)

16. Said adopted the same method in *Culture and Imperialism* (New York: Vintage, 1993), xxii: "My method is to focus as much as possible on individual works, to read them first as great products of the creative or interpretative imagination, and then to show them as part of the relationship between culture and empire."

17. Said, xxii: "As I discovered in writing *Orientalism*, you cannot grasp historical experience by lists or catalogues, and no matter how much you provide

by way of coverage, some books, articles, authors, and ideas are going to be left out. Instead, I have tried to look at what I consider to be important and essential things, conceding in advance that selectivity and conscious choice have had to rule what I have done. My hope is that readers and critics of this book will use it to further the lines of inquiry and arguments about the historical experience of imperialism put forward in it. In discussing and analyzing what in fact is a global process, I have had to be occasionally both general and summary."

18. Page citations in the body of the text are always to Said, *Orientalism* (New York: Vintage, 2003).

19. As my conception of central and peripheral domains contends (throughout chapters 1 and 2), the Enlightenment is neither a monolithic nor a consistent project, having encompassed multitudes of voices and representations, not to mention various internal "breaks" or "turns." However, for all these varieties and permutations, it constituted, in its central paradigms of rationality, materialism, and a single-minded vision of politics, a rupture from what had preceded it, even by Europe's own historical standards. To confuse the breaks and turns within its history with being continuous with paradigms from before the sixteenth century is to misunderstand modernity's uniqueness as an epistemic, teleological, and colossally destructive project.

20. See, for instance, Aijaz Ahmad, "Orientalism and After: Ambivalence and Cosmopolitan Location in the Work of Edward Said," *Economic and Political Weekly* 27, no. 30 (July 25, 1992): 98–116.

21. In her remarkable book, *Colonialism/Postcolonialism* (London: Routledge, 1998), Ania Loomba speaks of the "historical sweep" of modern European colonialism that "makes summaries impossible. It also makes it very difficult to 'theorize' colonialism," since "some particular instance is bound to negate any generalization we may make about the nature of colonialism or of resistances to it." Yet, Loomba has to concede, just "because colonial studies encompass such a vast area, it does not mean that we should only confine ourselves to study of particular cases, without any attempt to think about the *larger structures of colonial rule and thought*" (xiii–xiv, my emphasis). It is these larger structures, I argue, that the theory of paradigms can bring into sharp relief and make intelligible, and that should be the focus of our analytical and critical thrust.

22. Nowhere in *Orientalism* does Said question modernity as a problem (nor does the index identify "modernity" as a topical entry). It is curious that despite his fairly intimate knowledge of the works produced, among others, by the early Frankfurt School, especially by Adorno and Horkheimer, Said lags behind on this score, leaving the project qua project immune to critique. The "antihumanity" of Orientalism never transcends into the modern, but is

rather the prerogative of the Orientalist and his discipline. "My argument takes it that the Orientalist reality is both antihuman and persistent" (44).

23. Joseph Massad effectively sums up the Saidian project: When *Orientalism* came out, "few books unraveled the archaeology of Western identity the way *Orientalism* did. Said's book ingeniously exposed the connections, relationships, modulations, and displacements in Orientalism's production of an Orient that was a ruse for the production of the Occident. If Franz Fanon argued 'Europe is literally the creation of the Third World,' Said elaborated on that brilliant summation. Thus, for him, Orientalism was never about the Orient and its identity and culture but about the production of the West and *its* identity and culture—in short, a kind of Western projection; the West could not exist if the East were not invented as its antithesis, its opposite, its other." Massad, "Affiliating with Edward Said," in *Edward Said: A Legacy of Emancipation and Representation*, ed. Adel Iskandar and Hakem Rustom (Berkeley: University of California Press, 210), 23–49, at 25.

24. Foucault, "The Subject and Power," 337.

25. Even Foucault scholars and commentators continue to labor under modern moralities in interpreting Foucault on the relationship of knowledge and power. Colin Gordon, for instance, in his introduction to Foucault's volume *Power: Essential Works of Foucault, 1954–1984*, ed. James D. Faubion, trans. Robert Hurley et al. (New York: New Press, 1994), xix, argues: "The reason the combining of power and knowledge in society is a redoubtable thing is not that power is apt to promote and exploit spurious knowledge (as the Marxist theory of ideology has argued) but, rather, that the rational exercise of power tends to make the fullest use of knowledges capable of the maximum instrumental efficacy. What is wrong or alarming about the use of power is not, for Foucault, primarily or especially the fact that a wrong or false knowledge is being used. . . . [Rather, it is that] the knowledge that guides or instrumentalizes the exercise of power is valid and scientific. Nothing, including the exercise of power, is evil in itself—but everything is dangerous." Note how knowledge, despite its instrumentalist potentialities, remains beyond doubt or suspicion, and how both power and knowledge are mythologized as transcendental entities. The "valid and scientific knowledge" that modern power depends on is, as such, never questioned. Why it is that *this* knowledge, and not "spurious knowledge," is the desideratum of power neither Foucault nor Colin questions.

26. Michel Foucault, *Discipline and Punish: The Birth of the Prison*, trans. Alan Sheridan (New York: Vintage, 1995), 3ff.; for telling the truth about ourselves as subjection, see Foucault, *On the Government of the Living: Lectures at the Collège de France, 1979–80*, trans. Graham Burchell (New York: Picador, 2012).

27. See chapter 2, note 133.

28. Critics of my *The Impossible State: Islam, Politics, and Modernity's Moral Predicament* (New York: Columbia University Press, 2013) may also make here the claim that I ignore modern Islamic discourse; see, for instance, Nathan J. Brown, "A Discussion of Wael Hallaq's *Islam, Politics, and Modernity's Moral Predicament*," *Perspectives on Politics* 12, no. 2 (June 2014): 464–65. But since I agree with these critics that contemporary forms of Islam are modern, they must also agree with me that the constitution of modern Islam replicates the central and peripheral domains existing elsewhere in the world, not least in Euro-America. To take these domains as having the analytical power of comparativity is to indulge in redundancy. It is impossible to speak, for instance, of an economic system in (or of) modern Islam that is in any structural way different from the central domain of modern capitalism. The same can be said of all major political concepts and institutions governing the Muslim world today. By contrast, Islam's (central) domains before the nineteenth century—decimated at the hands of colonialism *precisely* because they contradicted the desiderata of Europe's central domains—provide powerful models for such juxtapositions. Furthermore, while it is true that modern Islam has developed creative dialectical relationships with Western modernity, it remains the case nonetheless that, as Humeira Iqtidar persuasively argued, Islamism was predicated upon colonial secularism: "Islamism is closely related to the secularism that helped define its limits, its contentions and its focus; the relationship between Islamism and secularism is not one of straightforward antagonism but a dialectical and creative one. Critically . . . the type of secularism that the British sought to impose in colonial India created the possibility of this novelty in Muslim thought and practice that is called Islamism." Iqtidar, "Colonial Secularism and Islamism in North India: A Relationship of Creativity," in *Religion and the Political Imagination*, ed. Ira Katznelson and Gareth Stedman Jones (Cambridge: Cambridge University Press, 2010), 235–53, at 235. On the reproduction of Islam as a form of liberalism, see Joseph A. Massad, *Islam in Liberalism* (Chicago: University of Chicago Press, 2015).

29. In my account, therefore, the naturalization of massacre and war, as Maldonado-Torres argues, after Tzvetan Todorov, Emmanuel Levinas, and Enrique Dussel, is an inadequate *explinans* of the modern paradigm. A "philosophical and historical account of modernity as a paradigm of war" and as a "community of masters" over slaves does not offer sufficient explanatory power as to why war in premodernity did not yield structural effects similar to the modern paradigm, nor does it explain how "a community of masters" can sustain itself within the logic of "eliminating the slaves," the latter being a prerequisite to the maintenance of the "community of masters." Nelson

Maldonado-Torres, *Against War: Views from the Underside of Modernity* (Durham: Duke University Press, 2008), 3–4, 13, 15.

30. See, on this "Occidentalism," Walter Mignolo, *The Darker Side of Western Modernity* (Durham: Duke University Press, 2011); Panjak Mishra, "Bland Fanatics," *London Review of Books* 37, no. 23 (December 3, 2015): 37–40, 55–56. For another important meaning of Occidentalism as a concept subtending Orientalism, see Joseph Massad, "Orientalism as Occidentalism," *History of the Present* 5, no. 1 (Spring 2015): 83–94.

31. The unidimensionality of traveling from the text to "worldliness" has been Said's preoccupation throughout, manifested most clearly in his literary critique of Western canons in *The World, the Text, and the Critic* (Cambridge, MA: Harvard University Press, 1983). For an illustrative argument capturing this approach, see Moustafa Bayoumi and Andrew Rubin, eds., *The Edward Said Reader* (New York: Vintage, 2000), 218–42.

32. "Paradigmatically" is intended to invoke the theory of paradigms and central domains on which an understanding of this book depends. It is not used in the conventional or general sense of the term.

33. The sensitive reader of *Orientalism* is thus struck by Emily Apter's statement that "Said, in his own work, never lets the reader forget the human in the humanities": Apter, "Saidian Humanism," *Boundary 2* 31, no. 2 (2004): 35–53, at 53. Said's "human"—especially in his *Orientalism*, and even as Apter wants to portray this category in Said's thought—is a Western, textual human. In fact, *Orientalism*'s Orientals never emerge as real human beings, as mothers, friends, children, laborers, scholars, "organic" intellectuals, peasants, banished and dispossessed communities, or prisoners of various forms of colonial imprisonment. This humanization of the colonized was reserved by Said for his later writings, passingly in *Culture and Imperialism* (for example, page 59) and more robustly in his work on Palestine, a "question" that was for him, as it was for many others, a largely, if not entirely, political problem. Judging it from the stark reality of colonized space, *Orientalism* may easily come across as an elitist academic work whose concern for the oppressed is driven by the hem and haw of a bourgeois ethic.

34. The only other reference to "law" in *Orientalism* is introduced in the context of confirming "the disparity between East and West" (255–56). Otherwise, "law" does not make a showing in the index, and has no noteworthy role to play in the colonialist project.

35. Alexander Anievas and Kerem Nışancıoğlu, *How the West Came to Rule: The Geopolitical Origins of Capitalism* (London: Verso, 2015); Timothy Mitchell, "Stage of Modernity," in *Question of Modernity*, ed. Timothy Mitchell (Minneapolis: University of Minnesota Press, 2000), 1–34.

36. The political economists' argument makes the largest claims, which I am addressing here, but the argument extends to various fields of inquiry, particularly those with a focus on colonialist ventures. In his remarkable article on genocide, Patrick Wolfe speaks of genocide as a structure, which includes, among other important features, the complex process of assimilation "whereby the native repressed continues to structure settler-colonial society." Wolfe, "Settler Colonialism and the Elimination of the Native," *Journal of Genocide Research* 8, no. 4 (2006): 387–409, at 389. Said himself, both in his *Orientalism* and in its sequel, *Culture and Imperialism*, also argued that the very idea of Europe as a superior culture is "never far" from the Orient, and was constructed in ideological opposition to it. Said, *Orientalism*, 7. All this is true, but as I shall continue to argue throughout this book, the position that construes "colonial effects" as amounting or contributing to non-European participation in the formation of the modern project altogether misses the foundations of the problem, and this largely—though not exclusively—due to the liberal-thought limitations I shall be discussing throughout.

37. For a definition of benchmark, see chapter 2, section 3.

38. It is, I think, here, in the span of this process, that the work of such scholars as Mignolo and Dussel intersects with my arguments. Their somewhat earlier dating of the origins of modernity as an actual colonialist project should be seen as the stage that prepared for and immediately generated the better-crystalized phenomenon I identify as the beginning of modernity par excellence. See Dussel, "Eurocentrism and Modernity," *Boundary 2* 20, no. 3 (Autumn 1993); Mignolo, *The Darker Side of Western Modernity*.

39. Anievas and Nişancioğlu's argument in *How the West Came to Rule* is no more sustainable than similar others. The Ottoman threat to Atlantic Europe is said to have contributed to the rise of capitalism by virtue of forcing Western European countries to find markets and economic opportunities westward, through the Atlantic. At the same time, the capitulatory commercial privileges given to them by the Ottomans permitted access to raw materials and staple commodities of which they would have otherwise been deprived. The idea being conveyed here is that the emergence of capitalism cannot be explained through an exclusive focus on the English countryside. While the idea of the need for a more "global" and *longue durée* approach is irreproachable, it fails to account for the uniqueness of the capitalist structures arising in Western Europe (mainly in Britain and the Netherlands). The Ottoman threat itself cannot be linked to that particular structure, just as the alleged "breakthrough to capitalism" already made in medieval Buddhist China and pre-Tokugawa Japan can hardly be said to have developed, much less articulated, the structural features that became necessary for the rise of European capitalism. See Randall Collins, "An Asian Route to Capitalism: Religious

Economy and the Origins of Self-Transforming Growth in Japan," *American Sociological Review* 62, no. 6 (1997): 843–65. Collins realizes that these Asian forms could not sustain the development of an industrial revolution, a puzzle left for "further study." Any student of Islamic history can make similar arguments. The question to which the present work attempts to provide an answer is what made that differential possible, a differential that possessed exclusively European roots but one that undeniably harnessed the global world as its laboratory.

40. George Saliba, *Islamic Science and the Making of the European Renaissance* (Cambridge, MA: MIT Press, 2007); Jonathan Lyons, *The House of Wisdom: How the Arabs Transformed Western Civilization* (New York: Bloomsbury, 2009); John M. Hobson, *The Eastern Origins of Western Civilization* (Cambridge: Cambridge University Press, 2004); Jack Goody, *The Theft of History* (Cambridge: Cambridge University Press, 2006); Edward Grant, *The Foundations of Modern Science in the Middle Ages: Their Religious, Institutional, and Intellectual Contexts* (Cambridge: Cambridge University Press, 1996), 22–26.

41. See works cited in the previous note.

42. And however much Said's "secular criticism" is directed at "secular beliefs" themselves, as Mufti argues. See Aamir R. Mufti, "Critical Secularism: A Reintroduction for Perilous Times," *Boundary 2* 31, no. 2 (2004): 1–9, at 2–3. As I will argue throughout this book, the very concept of secularism, in its most positive, productive, and sensitive forms, is as problematic as the very structure of thought that gave rise to Orientalism in the first place. Further on Said's secular humanism, see note 33 of this chapter; chapter 2, notes 62 and 137; and chapter 5, note 10.

43. In *Culture and Imperialism*, 12–13, Said admittedly expands his circle of inquiry, including a wide variety of "cultural formations." Yet, his concerns with "education," "science," and "art" invariably, and in the nature of his interest, revert back and are reduced to literature, whose style and content bespeak its connections with, even dependency on, imperialism. Nowhere is there a hint at the roots of the problem that constitutes and explains the peculiarities of modern imperialism, always taken as the ultimate and readily posited frame of reference for "national culture." The narrative, dialectically and endlessly traveling between "culture" and imperialism, remains bereft of a causality that can break out of this circle. The problem with "culture," for Said, is that it is unconscious of its associations with imperialism, and so we must account for the forces within the latter that feed the former, and vice versa: "There is, I believe, a quite serious split in our critical consciousness today, which allows us to spend a great deal of time elaborating Carlyle's and Ruskin's aesthetic theories, for example, without giving attention to the authority that their ideas simultaneously bestowed on the subjugation of inferior peoples

and colonial territories. . . . Unless we can comprehend how the great European realistic novel accomplished one of its principal purposes—almost unnoticeably sustaining the society's consent in overseas expansion— . . . we will misread both the culture's importance and its resonances in the empire, then and now. Doing this by no means involves hurling critical epithets at European or, generally, Western art and culture by way of wholesale condemnation. Not at all. What I want to examine is how the processes of imperialism occurred beyond the level of economic laws and political decisions, and—by predisposition, by the authority of recognizable cultural formations, by continuing consolidation within education, literature, and the visual and musical arts—were manifested at another very significant level, that of the national culture, which we have tended to sanitize as a realm of unchanging intellectual monuments, free from worldly affiliations. William Blake is unrestrained on this point: 'The Foundation of Empire,' he says in his annotations to Reynolds's Discourses, 'is Art and Science. Remove them or Degrade them and the Empire is No more. Empire follows Art and not vice versa as Englishmen suppose.' What, then, is the connection between the pursuit of national imperial aims and the general national culture? Recent intellectual and academic discourse has tended to separate and divide these: most scholars are specialists; most of the attention that is endowed with the status of expertise is given to fairly autonomous subjects, e.g., the Victorian industrial novel, French colonial policy in North Africa, and so forth. The tendency for fields and specializations to subdivide and proliferate, I have for a long while argued, is contrary to an understanding of the whole, when the character, interpretation, and direction or tendency of cultural experience are at issue. To lose sight of or ignore the national and international context of, say, Dickens's representations of Victorian businessmen, and to focus only on the internal coherence of their roles in his novels is to miss an essential connection between his fiction and its historical world. And understanding that connection does not reduce or diminish the novels' value as works of art: on the contrary, because of their worldliness, because of their complex affiliations with their real setting, they are more interesting and more valuable as works of art." This passage, quoted in full measure, sums up, I believe, Said's project, both in *Orientalism* and in *Culture and Imperialism*. My point is that, while important, the project remains constrained by a horizontal concern, where "education" and "science," and much else in academia and "culture," are elided into an analytical mode of literary crisis that never acquires attention as discrete phenomena that arise from a profoundly problematic but foundational structure of thought.

44. For a critique of modern science that largely comports with the vision advanced in this book, see the incisive contributions of Claude Alvares, Shiv

Visvanathan, Manu L. Kothari and Lopa A. Mehta, and Vandana Shiva in Ashis Nandy, ed., *Science, Hegemony and Violence: A Requiem for Modernity* (Delhi: Oxford University Press, 1988); Jean-Pierre Dupuy, *The Mark of the Sacred*, trans. M. B. DeBevoise (Stanford: Stanford University Press, 2013), 54–89. See also Sandra Harding, ed., *The Postcolonial Science and Technology Studies Reader* (Durham: Duke University Press, 2011); Mark Harrison, "Science and the British Empire," *Isis* 96, no. 1 (2005): 56–63; Michael A. Osborne, "Science and the French Empire," *Isis* 96, no. 1 (2005): 80–87.

45. In his *Culture and Imperialism*, for instance, Said likewise argued, as did many others, that such openings and fissures are productive sites of critique, but his and many others' arguments rest on paradigmatic fissures that always lie within central domains, secularism and Enlightenment reason being prime examples. What the present book attempts to show, by contrast, is that regenerative critique demands extraparadigmatic fissures and openings, ones relegated to the peripheral domains—precisely because they are either irrelevant or antithetical to the central domains. Thus, nonparadigmatic "openings, cracks, fissures, and fractures" would give critique a wholly different meaning and quality.

1. Putting Orientalism in Its Place

1. Page citations in the body of the text are always to Said, *Orientalism* (New York: Vintage, 2003).

2. This feature in Said's work was critiqued by Aijaz Ahmad, though to a somewhat different effect. See Ahmad, "Orientalism and After: Ambivalence and Cosmopolitan Location in the Work of Edward Said," *Economic and Political Weekly* 27, no. 30 (July 25, 1992): 98–116, at 100.

3. Said, *Culture and Imperialism* (New York: Vintage, 1993), 15–16.

4. Émile Tyan wrote several books, the best-known of which are *Histoire de l'organisation Judiciaire en pays d'Islam*, 2 vols., 2nd ed. (Leiden: Brill, 1960); *Institutions du droit public musulman: Tome premier; Le califat* (Paris: Recueil Sirey, 1954); *Institutions du droit public musulman: Tome deuxième, Sultanat et califat* (Paris: Recueil Sirey, 1956). For a critique of his ideas about Islamic forms of political organization, see Wael Hallaq, *The Impossible State: Islam, Politics, and Modernity's Moral Predicament* (New York: Columbia University Press, 2013), 60–63. Said's critique of Lewis takes up pp. 315–21 of his *Orientalism*.

5. Joseph Massad provides discriminating nuances to this statement in "Orientalism as Occidentalism," *History of the Present* 5, vol. 1 (Spring 2015): 83–94, at 87–88, but since the issues Massad discusses remain concerned with Europe's

self-formation against the Oriental Other, they do not—as I have stated earlier—bear on my present discussion.

6. Foucault does on occasion identify the Reformation as a point of beginning, but does not attribute to it the confluence of power relations that were brought together during the seventeenth, eighteenth, and nineteenth centuries. See Foucault, "The Subject and Power," in *Power: Essential Works of Foucault, 1954–1984*, ed. James D. Faubion, trans. Robert Hurley et al., vol. 3 (New York: New Press, 1994), 326–48, at 332.

7. Daniel Martin Varisco, *Reading Orientalism: Said and the Unsaid* (Seattle: University of Washington Press, 2007), 43–44. It must be noted that Varisco's book is valuable not so much for its own critique of Said's work as for its compilation of the many critiques of the work.

8. One of the best analyses of Said's problematic ideational relationship with Foucault is to be found in James Clifford, *The Predicament of Culture: Twentieth-Century Ethnography, Literature, and Art* (Cambridge: Harvard University Press, 1988), 266–71. See also Sudipta Kaviraj, "Said and the History of Ideas," in *Cosmopolitan Thought Zones: South Asia and the Global Circulation of Ideas*, ed. Sugata Bose and Kris Manjapra (New York: Palgrave Macmillan, 2010), 58–81, at 71–75.

9. See chapter 3, section 6.

10. This statement was received by many at face value, without pitting it, as a theoretical matter, against Said's actual application, which was at variance with it. See, for instance, the otherwise insightful article of Nadia Abu El-Haj, "Edward Said and the Political Present," *American Ethnologist* 32, no. 4 (November 2005): 538–55.

11. It is therefore puzzling to read in the writing of one of Said's students and ardent followers that Said was "far from viewing Orientalism as totalizing and absolute system of representation," and that those who attribute to him this understanding are "careless readers." Aamir R. Mufti, "Orientalism and the Institution of World Literature," *Critical Inquiry* 36, no. 3 (2010): 458–93, at 462. I find it striking that through Mufti's writings Said is barely recognizable, as if Mufti has read a different Said. No less striking is the confidence with which so many "readers" have been dismissed as "careless."

12. One critic has argued that Said's starting point is "without foundation." Taking over "Foucault's archaeology and genealogy, [Said] is in the awkward position of condemning not only most, but all, Orientalists because he has virtually presupposed that there is no such thing as the understanding of other cultures, that statements or representations can be nothing but exercises of power as parts of discursive formations. And at the same time he has undermined any basis to justify his own critique." Arran E. Gare, "MacIntyre, Narratives, and Environmental Ethics," *Environmental Ethics* 20 (Spring 1998): 3–21, at 315. For

a different take on the same issue, see Gil Anidjar, "Secularism," *Critical Inquiry* (Autumn 2006): 52–77, at 56–58.

13. I have offered a version of this theory in Hallaq, *Impossible State*, 6–12. Here, I develop it further, partly with a view to engage the theory of author.

14. This is in explicit reference to the theory of relevance in analogy.

15. I am referring to the title of the English translation of *Les mots et les choses*, a title that seems to me more apt than the French original. It should be noted in this context that my take on paradigms is greatly indebted to Carl Schmitt, M. Foucault, and to a lesser extent Thomas Kuhn, although I harness their ideas for my own purposes, creating modifications and adjustments as necessary. The relevant work of Schmitt is "Age of Naturalizations and Depoliticizations"; of Kuhn, *Structure of Scientific Revolutions*; of Foucault, *History of Sexuality*, *Les mots et les choses*, and *Archaeology of Knowledge*. See also Giorgio Agamben, *The Signature of All Things* (New York: Zone, 2009), 9–32.

16. See Schmitt, "Age of Naturalization," 84–87; quotation at 86.

17. Schmitt, 85.

18. For a definition of benchmark, see sec. 3 of this chapter.

19. Schmitt, "Age of Naturalization," 86, emphasis mine.

20. Schmitt, 87.

21. A case in point is the otherwise conservative domain of classical music, where physical and sexual beauty (exemplified in performances by such artists as Yuja Wang and Khatia Buniatishvili) has emerged as implicit preconditions for a successful career.

22. The painting is "The Head of a Young Woman" and the billionaire is the Spanish Jaime Botín. Of course there are more notorious cases, particularly the acquisition of Bacon's work for a nine-figure sum by a Russian billionaire.

23. In Islamic cultures of premodernity, for instance, charity and philanthropy were integral to the concept of moral technologies of the self, constituting themselves within the very structures of the central domain. See Amy Singer, *Charity in Islamic Societies* (Cambridge: Cambridge University Press, 2008); Hallaq, *Impossible State*, 146–52. As I will discuss later in the context of benchmarks, the materialistically ulterior transformations of philanthropy in modernity and their ethically driven equivalents in other cultures should not be taken to render modernity bereft of ethically driven acts of charity, or to bestow any idealism on premodern cultures (a rash judgment that some of my critics have been all too ready to pass). The theory of paradigms and central domains accounts for such diverging components within power formations and in fact deems them necessary to such formations, as I continue to argue throughout. Yet, the theory, running against the doctrine of progress, makes possible a vision of premodern cultures that defines and articulates their existence

through differently structured rationalities, governed by different systems of value.

24. See previous note.

25. Kojin Karatani, "Uses of Aesthetics: After Orientalism," *Boundary 2* 25, no. 2 (Summer 1998): 145–60, at 150, emphasis mine.

26. John Gray, *Enlightenment's Wake: Politics and Culture at the Close of the Modern Age* (London: Routledge, 1995), 123.

27. Gray, 124. See also Carlton J. H. Hayes, *The Historical Evolution of Modern Nationalism* (New York: Russell and Russell, 1968), 13–14.

28. Such an all-too-common argument as expressed by Gordon T. Stewart, "The Scottish Enlightenment Meets the Tibetan Enlightenment," *Journal of World History* 22, no. 3 (2011): 455–92, is blind to the concept of paradigm (even structure) and prone to an atomistic vision of reality. In his otherwise remarkable *Enlightenment Against Empire* (Princeton: Princeton University Press, 2003), Sankar Muthu wishes to "pluralize" the Enlightenment by showing that Diderot, Kant, and Herder stood against empire and colonialism. While this is an eminently worthwhile project and an immense credit to Muthu, pluralizing the Enlightenment (driven by a humanistic impulse no less powerful than Said's) will not change the ultimate fact that as a central domain, it not only massively promoted colonialism on the intellectual level but was in fact instrumental in building the projects of empire and colonization. We need nothing more than Muthu's own testimony, on the first page of his book, to the effect that the anti-imperialists represented a "historically anomalous" and "unique" phenomenon. Strikingly, Muthu argues, "virtually every prominent and influential European thinker in the three hundred years before the eighteenth century and nearly the full century after it were either agnostic toward or enthusiastically in favor of imperialism" (1). Numbers and statistical majorities need not always count in paradigms, but in this case they distinctly constitute additional evidence. That the exceptions Muthu studied should render unwarranted our speaking of "an overriding Enlightenment project" is itself an unwarranted proposition, for the very fact that the anti-imperialists were buried under the dominant narrative of imperializing and that they remained "understudied" until Muthu discovered that they should not be so is further testimony that, insofar as empire was concerned, there was in effect one Enlightenment. This affirmation rests on certain conditions of felicity that gave teeth to the project, whereas the project of Muthu's heroes had no effective or paradigmatic intellectual force to speak of.

29. See, for instance, Michael N. Forster, *After Herder: Philosophy of Language in the German Tradition* (Oxford: Oxford University Press, 2010), esp. intro. and chap. 1.

30. See Hallaq, *Impossible State*, 89–97, and notes.

31. M. Foucault, *The History of Sexuality*, vol. 1, trans. Robert Hurley (New York: Pantheon, 1978), 101–2.

32. Examples of this arena in colonialist discourse may be seen in the important contributions of Susan Buck-Morss, especially her "Hegel and Haiti," *Critical Inquiry* 26, no. 4 (Summer 2000): 821–65. See also Muthu, *Enlightenment Against Empire*.

33. Foucault, "The Subject and Power," 329.

34. J. L. Austin, *How to Do Things with Words* (Oxford: Clarendon, 1962). Austin speaks of felicity as well as of conditions that make propositions felicitous, but he himself did not use the phrase "conditions of felicity." See Austin, "Performative Utterances," in *Philosophical Papers*, 3rd ed., ed. J. O. Urmson and G. J. Warnock (Oxford: Clarendon, 1979). For further on this and on Searle's position, see Benjamin Lee, *Talking Heads: Language, Metalanguage, and the Semiotics of Subjectivity* (Durham: Duke University Press, 1997).

35. In the same obfuscating vein, and in all likelihood under Said's influence, Ziauddin Sardar (*Orientalism* [Philadelphia: Open University Press, 1999], 18) not only assigns John of Damascus (d. 749) the role of an Orientalist but declares him to have laid the foundation of Orientalism.

36. On the complexity of these transformations and acts of superseding Christian forms, see chapter 2, section 4.

37. For an excellent account of one instance of such phenomena in the rise of modernity, see Margaret C. Jacob, *Radical Enlightenment: Pantheists, Freemasons and Republicans* (Lafayette: Cornerstone, 2006).

38. On some aspects of the distinction between Is and Ought in the legal and political spheres, see Hallaq, *Impossible State*, 75–82, 89–90, 160–61.

39. As, for example, in his distinction between discursivity in science, on the one hand, and discursivity in the social sciences and the humanities, on the other. In fact, he seems to argue that discursivity does not exist in science, because a "Re-examination of Galileo's text may well change our knowledge of the history of mechanics, but it will never be able to change mechanics itself." M. Foucault, "What Is an Author?," in *Textual Strategies: Perspectives in Post-Structuralist Criticism*, ed. Josué V. Harari (Ithaca: Cornell University Press, 1979), 141–60, at 156. If at a certain historical time we come to believe in the truth of a scientific theory about mechanics, then this theory constitutes our knowledge of mechanics itself, just as in a particular era it might be believed that the size of a skull is supposed to tell us something important about the cultural or intellectual capacities of certain ethnic groups. Edifying scientific knowledge as an extramental reality, knowable on its own and accurately representing an independently existing reality, runs against much of what Foucault himself has stood for. It should be noted that a few lines after what I think are unwarranted statements about science, Foucault does admit the

difficulties involved in his own account, saying that it is "not easy to distinguish between the two" and that, "moreover, nothing proves that they are mutually exclusive procedures" (157).

40. Foucault, 144.

41. Foucault, 154.

42. See next chapter, section 2.

43. Foucault, "What Is an Author?" 145.

44. Foucault, 154.

45. Foucault, 154–55.

46. Foucault, 157.

47. Colin Gordon, "Introduction," in Faubion, *Power: Essential Works of Foucault*, xxxix.

48. Cited in Gordon, "Introduction," emphasis mine; see also Alan Milchman and Alan Rosenberg, "Review Essay: Michel Foucault, *On the Government of the Living*," *Review of Politics* 77 (2015): 683–87, at 683–84.

49. Foucault, "The Subject and Power," 336.

50. Foucault, "What Is an Author?" 158.

51. Foucault, 158.

52. Foucault, 159.

53. See quotation in chapter 3, at note 95.

54. Foucault, "What Is an Author?" 158, emphasis mine.

55. It may be argued that had Said been adept at professional historiography, a discipline critiqued throughout this book, he would likely not have fared any better in his historical diagnosis. This argument would be valid only if we assume that his critique rests squarely on the narratives of modern historiography, which obviously is not the case. "Historical sense" only requires Said to detect the full meaning of modernity as an epistemic transformation in human history, to see that Orientalism is the creation of *a distinctly modern structure*.

56. By "proper historical outlook," I mean to say that the past is treated with the same epistemic respect extended to the present, allowing for its own forms of rationality and internal logic, and not as an inherently deficient form of life on a permanent quest for self-fulfillment, one that seeks to arrive at "progress." For more on this, see chapter 5.

57. For an insightfully critical genealogy of the doctrine of progress, see Nauman Naqvi, "The Nostalgic Subject: A Genealogy of the 'Critique of Nostalgia,'" in *Centro Interuniversitario per le ricerche sulla Sociologia del Diritto e delle Instituzioni Giuridiche*, Working Paper 23 (September 2007), 4–51. For a more general critique, see Hallaq, *Impossible State*, 14–18.

58. On chance as a factor in epistemic breaks in Foucault, see Thomas Flynn, "Foucault's Mapping of History," in *Cambridge Companion to Foucault* (Cambridge: Cambridge University Press, 1999), 28–46, 31.

59. It is curious, to say the least, that a good part of Said's critique had already been put forth, a decade and a half earlier, by the Egyptian Marxist Anouar Abdel-Malek ("Orientalism in Crisis," *Diogenes* 11, no. 44 [1963]: 103–40). A promising topic of research into the subject of authorship and canonization might be why Abdel-Malek's penetrating critique—though cast in a laborious style and at times terse to an enigmatic point—never managed to gain anything near the canonical status that Said's liberal work achieved.

60. Said expresses "difference" also as "remoteness." When speaking of the *Cambridge History of Islam*, "a regular summa of Orientalist orthodoxy," he says that "to *all* the authors Islam is a remote, tensionless thing." Said, *Orientalism*, 305, his emphasis.

61. Akeel Bilgrami, "Occidentalism, the Very Idea: An Essay on Enlightenment and Enchantment," *Critical Inquiry* 32 (Spring 2006), 381–411, at 389.

62. It should be noted that Bilgrami's first and second features collapse into the first "structural feature" in my account.

63. Bilgrami, "Occidentalism," 389.

64. Robert Young has perceptively argued that "Said's most significant argument about the discursive conditions of knowledge is that the texts of Orientalism 'can create not only knowledge but also the very reality they appear to describe' [*Orientalism*, 94]. At the same time his most important political claim is that as a system of learning about the Orient, Orientalism . . . can be seen to have justified colonialism in advance as well as subsequently facilitating its successful operation. Said's wish to make both these points poses, however, a major theoretical problem: on the one hand he suggests that Orientalism merely consists of a representation that has nothing to do with the 'real' Orient, denying any correspondence between Orientalism and the Orient . . . while on the other hand he argues that its knowledge was put in the service of colonial conquest, occupation, and administration. This means that . . . Orientalism as representation did have to encounter the 'actual' conditions of what was there, and that it showed itself effective at a material level as a form of power and control. How then can Said argue that the 'Orient' is just a representation, if he also wants to claim that 'Orientalism' provided the necessary knowledge for actual colonial conquest?" Robert J. C. Young, *White Mythologies: Writing History and the West* (London: Routledge, 1990), 168–69.

65. As evident on the first page of that book. Said, *Culture and Imperialism* (New York: Vintage, 1993), vi.

66. Said, xiv.

67. Emily Apter, "Saidian Humanism," *Boundary 2* 31, no. 2 (2004): 35–53, at 40–41.

68. Apter, 43.

69. Apter, 45, 46–47, partly quoting Riccardo Fubini.

70. Apter, 44.

71. Anidjar, "Secularism," 69. See also Jean-Pierre Dupuy, *The Mark of the Sacred*, trans. M. B. DeBevoise (Stanford: Stanford University Press, 2013), 90–124.

72. That such literary and linguistic projects were anything but harmless is brilliantly demonstrated by Siraj Ahmed, *The Stillbirth of Capital: Enlightenment Writing and Colonial India* (Stanford: Stanford University Press, 2012), 175–78, contra, for example, the less discerning Michael J. Franklin, *Orientalist Jones: Sir William Jones, Poet, Lawyer, and Linguist, 1746–1794* (Oxford: Oxford University Press, 2011).

73. Of the trio, genocide and company Orientalism, not to mention the corporation, never make an appearance in *Orientalism's* index. Of course this is the book Said chose to write, but the point of remarking on these omissions is that Said's narrative does not delve into the *performative structures* that underlie the phenomena he is critiquing. The corporate business and economics are not just material factors, as Said seems to think (*Culture and Imperialism*, 12). They are rather the manifestations of the deep structures of thought that explain and explore the full dimensions of what Said was complaining about but that he never articulated.

74. See Clifford, *Predicament of Culture*, 260.

75. On the vibrancy of modern Islamic tradition, see Humeira Iqtidar, "Redefining 'Tradition' in Political Thought," *European Journal of Political Theory* 15, no. 4 (2016): 424–44.

76. "Destructive and intolerant" in the sense I elaborate in chapter 4.

77. The Tang dynasty, representing one of the highpoints of China's history, roughly coincided with the first century of Abbasid rule in Baghdad, a century (ca. 760–860) that also represented a sort of "golden age."

78. Ahmad Ibn al-'Abbas Ibn Fadlan, *Ibn Fadlan's Journey to Russia: A Tenth-Century Traveler from Baghdad to the Volga River*, trans. Richard N. Frye (Princeton: Markus Wiener, 2005); Muhammad b. Ahmad Ibn Jubayr, *The Travels of Ibn Jubayr*, trans. William Wright (Leiden: Brill), 1907; Abu 'Abd Allah Muhammad Ibn Battuta, *Travels of Ibn Battuta*, trans. H. A. R. Gibb (New Delhi, 1929).

79. Muhammad b. Ahmad al-Biruni, *Alberuni's India*, trans. Edward C. Sachau (New York: Norton, 1971).

80. See, for instance, Abu 'Ubayd al-Bakri, *Jughrafiyyat al-Andalus wa-Urubba: Min Kitab al-Masalik wal-Mamalik*, ed. 'Abd al-Rahman 'Ali al-Hajji (Beirut: Dar al-Irshad, 1968), 74–82. In his remarkable study of ancient Mesopotamia, Egypt, and China, Mu-chou Poo (*Enemies of Civilization: Attitudes Toward Foreigners in Ancient Mesopotamia, Egypt, and China* [Albany: State University of New York Press, 2005]) offers a textured narrative of the stereotypical views that these civilizations held vis-à-vis the foreigner, views that seem to be based

in cultural difference, rather than in race or even ethnicity: "Even though Mesopotamia was a multiethnic society, there was still a sense of the unity of 'Mesopotamian/we' people, as opposed to 'foreign' or 'enemy/they' people. . . . When the Egyptian texts mentioned a foreign people or country outside Egypt, they often employed stereotypical and hostile expressions to characterize the foreigners. . . . In the theological line of representations, the foreigners were of necessity evil force from without" (147). "In fact, even the Greco-Roman rulers, or their representatives in Egypt, found no need to discontinue the traditional hostile or condescending attitude" (149). In China, the *Zhouli* genre depicted the world as a circle in which China is located at the center, whereas "the vassals and the barbarians [stood] in the outer circles. . . . This world system, although an ideal construction that never existed in reality, nevertheless became the basic political rhetoric of subsequent governments and ruling elites regarding the relationship between China and foreign cultures and peoples" (150). "In fact, a sense of cultural superiority existed in all the three civilizations studied here" (152).

81. Austin, *How to Do Things with Words*, 8; Austin, "Performative Utterances."

82. Judith Butler, *Gender Trouble: Feminism and the Subversion of Identity* (New York: Routledge, 1999), 4. For a complex and nuanced analysis of juridicality in a colonialist setting, see the important work of Samera Esmeir, *Juridical Humanity: A Colonial History* (Stanford: Stanford University Press, 2012).

83. I have here partially revised the position on language I adopted in "On Orientalism, Self-Consciousness and History," *Islamic Law and Society* 18, nos. 3–4 (2011): 387–439.

84. In the introduction from 2003 to *Orientalism*, 21, Said makes the following statements: "The things to look at are style, figures of speech, setting, narrative devices, historical and social circumstances, not the correctness of the representation nor its fidelity to some great original. The exteriority of the representation is always governed by some version of the truism that if the Orient could represent itself, it would; since it cannot, the representation does the job." A few lines later, he says: "Another reason for insisting upon exteriority is that I believe it needs to be made clear about cultural discourse and exchange within a culture that what is commonly circulated by it is not 'truth' but representations" (his emphasis). Said here appears to critique positivism through a positivism of his own. How can "historical and social circumstances" of the Western text and the supposed inability of the Orient to "represent itself" be extricated from "truth" or a version thereof? More generally, against what criteria can representation or misrepresentation be evaluated? Said's insistence on (mis)representation as enclosed and judged by "style, figures of speech," and "narrative devices" internal to the text belies a latent yet ever-present reference to something

outside these texts (otherwise, the entire project of *Orientalism* in fact becomes utterly unintelligible).

85. Karen Barad, "Posthumanist Performativity: Toward an Understanding of How Matter Comes to Matter," *Journal of Women in Culture and Society* 28, no. 3 (2003): 801–31, at 802, emphasis Barad's.

2. Knowledge, Power, and Colonial Sovereignty

1. As evidenced, for example, in Bernard Lewis's reply to Said. Lewis categorically denies any structural connection between scholarship and power, taking the role that many Orientalists played in the actual administration of colonialist projects to be no more than exceptions. See Lewis, "The Question of Orientalism," in *Islam and the West* (New York: Oxford University Press, 1993), 99–118.

2. As I argue in chapter 5.

3. Page citations in the body of the text are always to Said, *Orientalism* (New York: Vintage, 2003).

4. See the incisive analysis on this point by Sudipta Kaviraj, "Said and the History of Ideas," in *Cosmopolitan Thought Zones: South Asia and the Global Circulation of Ideas*, ed. Sugata Bose and Kris Manjapra (New York: Palgrave Macmillan, 2010), 58–81, especially at 58–60. I am not disputing Kaviraj's claim that "*Orientalism* can be seen and read therefore—legitimately—as a piece of political theory"; my argument is that reading the work through this prism masks deeper problems in *modern and modernist* forms of knowledge.

5. See Said, *Culture and Imperialism* (New York: Vintage, 1993), 225: Here Said is more explicit about colonialism's devastating effects, but ultimately underrates these effects through allocating a measure of "mythmaking" to the "nationalist" narrative of devastation: "Let me give three examples of how imperialism's complex yet firm geo-graphical *morte main* moves from the general to the specific. The most general is presented in Crosby's *Ecological Imperialism*. Crosby says that wherever they went Europeans immediately began to change the local habitat; their conscious aim was to transform territories into images of what they had left behind. This process was never-ending, as a huge number of plants, animals, and crops as well as building methods gradually turned the colony into a new place, complete with new diseases, environmental imbalances, and traumatic dislocations for the overpowered natives. A changed ecology also introduced a changed political system. *In the eyes of the later nationalist poet or visionary, this alienated the people from their authentic traditions, ways of life, and political organizations. A great deal of romantic*

mythmaking went into these nationalist versions of how imperialism alienated the land, but we must not doubt the extent of the actual changes wrought" (emphasis mine).

6. Islamic literature, for instance, did produce a number of travelogues and annals treating of the Other, but the so-called *adab al-rihla* (travel) literature did not exceed a few dozen books, only a small number of which are known to us in their entirety. Biruni's study of India—a scientific study that resembled Orientalist works in its interests and scope—was relatively rare, and one would be hard-pressed to identify even a few similar others throughout the entirety of Islamic history. This is to be compared with *shaŕi* (legal) works produced over the same historical span, works whose count requires at least a six-digits register. By contrast, Orientalism and anthropology combined produced in a mere century a totality of works that far exceeds in number those produced in any major discursive tradition in Islam, perhaps to the exclusion of Shari'a, Sufism, and their subdivisions, fields that defined two central domains of the Islamic tradition at large.

7. Louise Levathes, *When China Ruled the Seas: The Treasure Fleet of the Dragon Throne, 1405–1433* (New York: Simon and Schuster, 1994); Edward L. Dreyer, *Zheng He: China and the Oceans in the Early Ming Dynasty, 1405–1433* (New York: Library of World Biography, 2007).

8. This phenomenon provides a further contrast: whereas European scholars attached to colonialist ventures saw themselves as charged with "understanding" the colonized lands and their peoples and cultures for purposes—needless to say—of management and domination, the Islamic jurists accompanied sultans as learned men who could function as emissaries but mainly to opine on what is lawful and unlawful in the practice of conquest and war. In other words, knowledge in the first case was outward, directed toward and exclusively concerned with the Other and the means of controlling it, whereas in the Islamic case, it was chiefly geared toward the Self and the necessity of conforming to the juridico-moral principles of the Shari'a. On the participation of *ulama* in military campaigns, see Asya Sulayman Naqli, ed., *Dawr al-Fuqaha' wal-'Ulama' al-Muslimin fil-Sharq al-Adna fil-Jihad Didd al-Salibiyyin Khilal al-Haraka al-Salibiyya* (Riyad: Maktabat al-'Ubaykan, 1423/2002); 'Abd al-Rahman b. Muhammad b. Abi Hatim, *Kitab al-Jarh wal-Ta'dil*, vol. 7 (Haydarabad: Majlis Da'irat al-Ma'arif al-'Uthmaniyya, 1952), 227; Muhammad Ibn Hibban Abu Hatim al-Tamimi al-Busti, *Kitāb al-Majruhin min al-Muhaddithin wal-Du'afa' wal-Matrukin*, ed. Mahmud Ibrahim Zayid, vol. 2. (Aleppo: Dar al-Wa'y, 1975), 275; Isma'il b. 'Umar Ibn Kathir, *al-Bidaya wal-Nihaya*, ed. 'Ali Shiri, vol. 14. (Beirut: Dar Ihya' al-Turath al-'Arabi, 1988), 14.

9. Arguably, by 900 AD, Baghdad's Bayt al-Hikma had the largest library in the world, and housed astronomical observatories as well as other scientific

instruments. The institution dwindled after the tenth century and was sacked by the Mongols in 1258. See Jonathan Lyons, *The House of Wisdom: How the Arabs Transformed Western Civilization* (New York: Bloomsbury, 2009).

10. W. J. T. Mitchell, "Secular Divination: Edward Said's Humanism," *Critical Inquiry* 31 (Winter 2005): 462–71.

11. See, for instance, Marshall Hodgson, "The Great Western Transmutation," in *Rethinking World History: Essays on Europe, Islam, and World History*, ed. Edmund Burke, III (Cambridge: Cambridge University Press, 1993), 44–71.

12. The driving methodological vehicle of the dialectical traditions is suitably illustrated in the art of juridical *jadal* and *munazara*. See Walter Edward Young, *The Dialectical Forge: Juridical Disputation and the Evolution of Islamic Law* (Bonn: Springer, 2017) as well as Khaled El-Rouayheb, *Islamic Intellectual History in the Seventeenth Century: Scholarly Currents in the Ottoman Empire and the Maghreb* (Cambridge: Cambridge University Press, 2015).

13. Hallaq, *Shariʿa: Theory, Practice, Transformations* (Cambridge: Cambridge University Press, 2009), 172, 181–82, 125–26, 136.

14. George Makdisi, *The Rise of the Colleges: Institutions of Learning in Islam and the West* (Edinburgh: Edinburgh University Press, 1981); Jonathan Porter Berkey, *The Transmission of Knowledge in Medieval Cairo: A Social History of Islamic Education* (Princeton: Princeton University Press, 1992); Daphna Ephrat, *Learned Society in a Period of Transition: The Sunni Ulama of Eleventh-Century Baghdad* (Albany: State University of New York Press, 2000); Hallaq, *Shariʿa*; Michael Chamberlain, *Knowledge and Social Practice in Medieval Damascus, 1190–1350* (Cambridge: Cambridge University Press, 1994).

15. Kamal al-Din Ibn al-Humam, *al-Musayara fi ʿIlm al-Kalam* (Cairo: al-Matbaʿa al-Mahmudiyya, n.d.), 175–85. The centrality of action and practice to knowledge (*ʿilm*) in the premodern Islamic tradition has understandably drawn much ink from Taha Abdurrahman's pen. See Abdurrahman, *al-ʿAmal al-Dini wa-Tajdid al-ʿAql* (Casablanca: al-Markaz al-Thaqafi al-ʿArabi, 1989); *Ruh al-Hadatha* (Casablanca: al-Markaz al-Thaqafi al-ʿArabi, 2006); *Suʾal al-ʿAmal, Bahth ʿan al-Usul al-ʿAmaliyya fil-Fikr wal-ʿIlm* (Casablanca: al-Markaz al-Thaqafi al-ʿArabi, 2012), 13–37 and passim.

16. See Wael Hallaq, *The Impossible State: Islam, Politics, and Modernity's Moral Predicament* (New York: Columbia University Press, 2013), chap. 5.

17. This spectrum can be gleaned from a comparison of any *fiqh* work with Ghazali, *Ihyaʾ ʿUlum al-Din*, 5 vols. (Aleppo: Dar al-Waʾy, 1425/2004), and these in turn with Farid al-Din al-ʿAttar, *Mantiq al-Tayr* (*The Conference of the Birds*, trans. Afkham Darbandi and Dick Davis [London: Penguin, 1984]).

18. The main focus of Ghazali's *Ihyaʾ ʿUlum al-Din*. See my analysis of this theme in his work in *The Impossible State*, chap. 5.

19. "Searcher," as opposed to mere researcher, a word that conveys the *murid* and *talib*, those, among others, who seek *'ilm*, in the final analysis a moral quest.

20. Badr al-Din Ibn Jama'a al-Kinani, *Tadhkirat al-Sami' wal-Mutakallim fi Adab al-'Alim wal-Muta'allim*, ed. 'Abd al-Salam 'Ali (Cairo: Maktabat Ibn 'Abbas, 2005), 140; al-Khatib al-Baghdadi, *al-Faqih wal-Mutafaqqih*, 2 vols. (Beirut: n.p., 1975); 'Abd al-Qadir al-Jaza'iri, *Kitab al-Mawaqif al-Ruhiyya wal-Fuyudat al-Subuhiyya*, ed. 'Asim al-Kayyali, 3 vols. (Beirut: Dar al-Kutub al-'Ilmiyya, 2004), I, Mawqif 19.

21. See, for instance, Robert G. Morrison, *Islam and Science: The Intellectual Career of Nizam al-Din al-Nisaburi* (London: Routledge, 2007), 95–125.

22. The works of Makdisi and Berkey remain authoritative in validating this point. See note 14 of this chapter.

23. The early caliphs did contribute to the body of "legal" knowledge, among others, but they did so in their capacities as companions and successors, which is to say that, when they did so, they were wearing their scholarly "hats," rather than the caliphal ones. For a detailed discussion of this matter, see Wael Hallaq, "Qur'anic Constitutionalism and Moral Governmentality: Further Notes on the Founding Principles of Islamic Society and Polity," *Comparative Islamic Studies* 8, nos. 1–2 (2012): 1–51, at 29–34; Hallaq, *Shari'a*, 38–45. It must also be noted that even when the Ottoman sultans of the early sixteenth century established a syllabus for the imperial *madrasa*s, they did so through recourse to the works of private scholars whose habitus was neither political (in any specifically Ottoman sense) nor state-grounded (for the state, as we know it, had not yet come into being). That this move was "unprecedented" is further attestation to the marginal role that Muslim rulers played in the larger system of Muslim education. See Shahab Ahmed and Nenad Filipovic, "The Sultan's Syllabus: A Curriculum for the Ottoman Imperial Medreses Prescribed in a Ferman of Qanuni I Suleyman, Dated (1565)," *Studia Islamica*, 98/99 (2004): 183–218; reference to the "unprecedented" nature of this practice occurs on page 183.

24. Hassan Khalilieh, *Islamic Maritime Law: An Introduction* (Leiden: Brill, 1998), and sources cited therein; Khalilieh, "Legal Aspects from a Cairo Geniza Responsum on the Islamic Law of the Sea: Practice and Theory," *Jewish Quarterly Review* 96, no. 2 (Spring 2006), 180–202; Dionysius A. Agius, *Classical Ships of Islam: From Mesopotamia to the Indian Ocean* (Leiden: Brill, 2007). On trade in the Indian Ocean in general, see K. N. Chaudhuri, *Trade and Civilization in the Indian Ocean: An Economic History from the Rise of Islam to 1750* (Cambridge: Cambridge University Press, 1985).

25. See, for instance, the contributions in Frederick de Jong, ed., *Sufi Orders in Ottoman and Post-Ottoman Egypt and the Middle East: Collected Studies* (Istanbul: ISIS Press, 2000).

26. Due in good part to Abu Hamid al-Ghazali's efforts as exhibited in *Ihya' 'Ulum al-Din*, a work that became highly influential in both the Sunni and Shi'i traditions.

27. Hallaq, *Shari'a*, 1–353, 543–55; Hallaq, *An Introduction to Islamic Law* (Cambridge: Cambridge University Press, 2009).

28. The implication being that, while the general moral norms, or "moral universals," are fixed and thus cannot be changed, the legal norms, which must necessarily occupy a second and subservient rank, can be modified in accordance with the demands of place and time. Here, a constant dialectic exists between the demands of the moral universals and those of life and legally regulated acts. And it is here that Ought continuously regulates and restrains the Is. For an extended analysis of this and related issues, see Hallaq, *Impossible State*, 74–90, 160–61.

29. See, for instance, George Saliba, *Islamic Science and the Making of the European Renaissance* (Cambridge, MA: MIT Press, 2007); Lyons, *The House of Wisdom*; John M. Hobson, *The Eastern Origins of Western Civilization* (Cambridge: Cambridge University Press, 2004); Jack Goody, *The Theft of History* (Cambridge: Cambridge University Press, 2006); Edward Grant, *The Foundations of Modern Science in the Middle Ages: Their Religious, Institutional, and Intellectual Contexts* (Cambridge: Cambridge University Press, 1996), 22–26, and passim (relevant entries not listed in index). For the contributions of Indian science to modern science, see Gyan Prakash, *Another Reason: Science and the Imagination of Modern India* (Princeton: Princeton University Press, 1999).

30. The most obvious of these are hadith and *ahkam al-Qur'an* studies, including the interconnected subdisciplines of *asbab al-nuzul* and *tafsir*, all of which were the "basic" disciplines that *usul al-fiqh* and *fiqh* studies presupposed.

31. In fact, the principles governing many fields of scientific and "legal" interest, among others, were often captured in poetic form. Poetry was as much a scientific and "legal" mode of expression as it was aesthetic and literary. Examples of such works are Ibn al-Haytham's poem in astronomy, "Qasida fi Tarhil al-Shams" (uncertain attribution); 'Abd al-Rahman al-Akhdari's *al-Sullam al-Munawraq*, explaining the use of Aristotelian logic in law; and al-Hajj Mulla al-Sabzawari's *Ghurar al-Fara'id*, a "systematic and complete presentation of the philosophy of the (Ishraqi) School of Mulla Sadra." See John Cooper, "Al-Subzawari," in *Routledge Encyclopedia of Philosophy*, ed. Edward Craig (London: Routledge, 1998), 440.

32. The legal stratagems of *hiyal* are perhaps most noteworthy, but these remained, as is well known, a minor element in the "law," with increasingly diminishing relevance after the early centuries of Islam. On this theme, see Hallaq, *Impossible State*, 10–12 and 175n42.

33. I have dealt with these issues at some length in Hallaq, 48–70.

34. The occasional abuses of the system were almost always recorded in our sources because such conduct was seen to violate the norm. Historical works and especially so-called biographical registers, among other genres, made it their mission to record not the thousands of details of day-to-day routine practices of the judiciary or of legal life (which were taken for granted), but rather the exceptions. This interest, as I have been trying to show, is intimately connected with personal integrity and thus personal moral and legal liability and accountability. A violator of the system, especially a judge, a scholar, a ruler, a market inspector, or any person in a position of power, went down in history as the man he was, which is to say that he would be located on a grid that would determine how he is judged, literally, by history. An abusive judge, for instance, would be discredited in every way: his judicial record would be tarnished for all generations to come, and if he had, say, narrated hadith, his transmission would be dismissed as untrustworthy. The same would be the case with a transmitter who forged his materials or part thereof; not only would he be suspect and out of the pale of "reliable" transmitters, but he would also have his entire record as a judge, scholar, or otherwise tarnished as well. See Wael B. Hallaq, *The Origins and Evolution of Islamic Law* (Cambridge: Cambridge University Press, 2005), 190.

35. Henry Cattan, "The Law of Waqf," in *Law in the Middle East*, ed. Majid Khadduri and Herbert J. Liebesny (Washington, DC: Middle East Institute, 1955), 203–22; Murat Çizakça, *History of Philanthropic Foundations* (Istanbul: Bogaziçi University Press, 2000); Richard van Leeuwen, *Waqfs and Urban Structures: The Case of Ottoman Damascus* (Leiden: Brill, 1999); Makdisi, *Rise of the Colleges*; Hallaq, *Sharīʿa*, 53–54, 126, 141–46, 150, 191, 194, 195, and passim.

36. Hallaq, *Impossible State*, 119–20.

37. For a proper interpretation of my language here, two fundamental givens must be kept in mind: the first is the meaning I assign to the concept of "benchmark" as outlined in the preceding paragraphs; the second—answering to claims about the rulers' "arbitrary" and oppressive conduct—pertains to the premodern relationship between ruler and subject. In a system where political and executive power possessed no right over education at any of its levels and in its most expansive meaning, and lacked in addition the mechanism of raising the "state"-subject, the individual remained under the purview of "private education," which always was dissociated from such power, and often under the direction of Sharīʿa-Sufi associations as communal entities. Political organization and coercive power did not translate into the cultivation of the subject, as the modern state has made them to be.

38. Joel Bakan, *The Corporation: The Pathological Pursuit of Profit and Power* (New York: Free, 2004), 5–8, 12: In both Europe and America, the corporation was initially opposed on moral grounds because "it allowed investors to escape

unscathed from their companies' failures. . . . The critics believed it would undermine personal moral responsibility, a value that had governed the commercial world for centuries." See also David C. Korten, *When Corporations Rule the World* (West Hartford: Berrett-Koehler, 1995).

39. This of course assumes that profit and wealth are not, in themselves and on their own, justifiable in ethical and moral terms. For a different view that assumes the corporation as a sign of progress in the West and a cause of retardation in Islam (a view that does not seem to mind the unethical thrust and practices of modern, especially transnational, corporations), see Timur Kuran, "Why the Islamic Middle East Did Not Generate an Indigenous Corporate Law," University of Southern California Law School: Law and Economics Working Paper Series 16 (2004): 1–33.

40. Hallaq, "Qur'anic Constitutionalism and Moral Governmentality."

41. More on this, see chapter 5.

42. Q. 2:107; 2:255; 3:109, 189; 4:131–32.

43. Q. 51:19; 70:24.

44. Hallaq, " 'God Cannot Be Harmed': On Huquq Allah/Huquq al-'Ibad Continuum" (forthcoming).

45. Q. 56:78; 62:2; 85:22.

46. Abu Ishaq al-Shatibi, *al-Muwafaqat fi Usul al-Ahkam*, ed. Muhyi al-Din 'Abd al-Hamid, 4 vols. (Cairo: Matba'at 'Ali Subyah, 1970), II, 3.

47. On the popular origins of the Shari'a and its socially grounded system (a bottom-up, rather than top-down, system), see Hallaq, *Impossible State*, 48–73.

48. W. B. Hallaq, "Groundwork of the Moral Law: A New Look at the Qur'an and the Genesis of Shari'a," *Islamic Law and Society* 16 (2009): 239–79, at 261–64.

49. W. B. Hallaq, *A History of Islamic Legal Theories: An Introduction to Sunni Usul al-Fiqh* (Cambridge: Cambridge University Press, 1997), esp. chap. 5.

50. Max Weber, *Economy and Society: An Outline of Interpretive Sociology*, vol. 1 (Berkeley: University of California Press, 1978), 56.

51. Mathieu Tillier, "Judicial Authority and Qadis' Autonomy Under the Abbasids," *Al-Masaq* 26, no. 2 (2014): 119–31 (sound in its general conclusions, although interpretation of specific evidence at times replicates earlier Orientalist biases); Haim Gerber, *State, Society, and Law in Islam: Ottoman Law in Comparative Perspective* (Albany: State University of New York Press, 1994); Ronald C. Jennings, "Kadi, Court and Legal Procedure in 17th C. Ottoman Kayseri: The Kadi and the Legal System," *Studia Islamica* 48 (1978): 133–72; Jennings, "Limitations of the Judicial Powers of the Kadi in 17th C. Ottoman Kayseri," *Studia Islamica* 50 (1979): 151–84.

52. On law-finding in the Shari'a, see Wael B. Hallaq, *Authority, Continuity and Change in Islamic Law* (Cambridge: Cambridge University Press, 2001), 166–74.

53. Gary Lawson, "Rise and Rise of the Administrative State," *Harvard Law Review* 107 (April 1994): 1231–54; M. Elizabeth Magill, "Beyond Powers and Branches in Separation of Powers Law," *University of Pennsylvania Law Review* 150, no. 2 (December 2001), 603–60; Magill, "The Real Separation in Separation of Powers Law," *Virginia Law Review* 86 (September 2000): 1127–98; Harvey C. Mansfield, "Separation of Powers in the American Constitution," in *Separation of Powers and Good Government*, ed. Bradford P. Wilson and Peter Schramm (London: Rowman and Littlefield, 1994), 3–15; Richard A. Epstein, "Why the Modern Administrative State Is Inconsistent with the Rule of Law," *NYU Journal of Law and Liberty* 3 (2008): 491–515.

54. See sources cited in note 51 of this chapter.

55. I have discussed the Muslim rulers' search for legitimacy in relation to the "legal scholars" in *Shariʿa*, 197–221. The case with the Sufi scholars and their orders is very much the same.

56. It may simplistically be argued that the law of *jihad* is legal knowledge used by political and military power, but this argument encounters significant problems. First, understood properly, this law was in effect mostly defensive rather than offensive. *Jihad* is mandatory only when the lands of Islam are attacked by the enemy, and only those in relative proximity to the territory attacked are obligated to partake in the defense, not all Muslims within the kingdom or principality. Second, "power" insofar as the doctrine of *jihad* is concerned is restricted to military power, and lacks nearly all the features that Foucault expounded. In other words, the *jihad* doctrine did not precipitate, engage, or promote biopower, nor was it used to accomplish such ends; nor, still, did it allow for any environment in which the state subject, the citizen, or Foucault's docile subject could be as much as entertained as a preliminary idea. Third, unlike modern knowledge, which was engineered by the state through its educational institutions, *jihad* and law in general were, as we saw, the product of an autonomous juristic system, and as such were not always useful for military, executive, and political power. This explains why most wars to which the Islamic armies were a party were not *jihad* campaigns, but wars in the conventional sense, and mostly conducted against other Muslim armies. For more on these themes, see Hallaq, *Impossible State*, 93–95.

57. For lack of better terminology, I adopt the expressions "formal" and "substantive" to distinguish the relationship between executive power and what might be called "social knowledge" in Islam, the latter encompassing, among lesser others, Sharʿi-Sufi traditions of learning and social organization and discipline. Whereas in the modern state all these are intermeshed and woven into one largely sociopolitical fabric, in premodern Islam the executive will to power remained considerably disentangled from this fabric. For instance, political power in the biopolitical and Gramscian senses did not produce the

Muslim subject, which remained insulated from the sort of technologies of the self that are now managed by the Political (in the generally modern and specifically Schmittian senses). Regulation of markets and highways and appointment and dismissal of judges are two arenas where the formal relationship took a dynamic form. The latter, judicial example represents what I have been calling here a "genetic slice," which captures the relationship between the Sultanic/executive and the other "branches" of "power." The Sultan could appoint and dismiss judges, and even impose jurisdictional limits on their powers (thereby deciding, among other things, venue), but no sultan could decide what the law was and how to apply it. This consistently remained the legal, moral, and educational prerogative of the *ulama*. What the modern state possesses in terms of legal engineering powers of society and its individual citizens (so instrumental to the subject's formation) was entirely lacking in the premodern Islamic world; and it is to this notion that "substantive association" refers.

58. See introduction to P. Rabinow, ed., *Foucault's Ethics, Subjectivity, and Truth* (New York: New Press, 1994), xiii–xiv.

59. M. Foucault, "What Is an Author?" in *Textual Strategies: Perspectives in Post-Structuralist Criticism*, ed. Josué V. Harari (Ithaca: Cornell University Press, 1979), 141–60, at 158. Omid Safi, for instance, asks whether or not "one may legitimately question how successfully [Foucault's] theories can be applied to non-European and, perhaps more importantly, premodern civilizations. . . . One should seek to explore whether such systems of surveillance are uniquely a feature of modernity or possible only in a post-Enlightenment European context." He then proceeds to argue: "Our evidence suggests that already in fifth-/eleventh-century Islamdom, [the Saljuq vizier] Nizam al-Mulk had anticipated the importance of the system of surveillance and reconnaissance for imposing the Saljuq view of normative Islam and normative social order on the whole society." Thus, the vizier's "system of surveillance and reconnaissance was to keep a watchful eye on two groups: those who were likely to rebel against Saljuq authority and those within the Saljuq regime who were in position of power/knowledge," namely, "state's" employees, notably judges, for whom he "had a particular fascination" since they were "the deputies of the king" and as such reflected to society the ruler's sense of justice. Safi then tells us that the modalities of this system are "a postal service" as well as "undercover . . . mendicants and Sufis," whose function was "espionage." This "system of reconnaissance and surveillance" was "essentially a spy network." Safi, *The Politics of Knowledge in Premodern Islam: Negotiating Ideology and Religious Inquiry* (Chapel Hill: University of North Carolina Press, 2006), 83–85. None of this is integral to Foucault's theory of surveillance. This "system" had been in place for millennia, nearly in all Asian

domains, in Christendom, and certainly in West Asia before Islam appeared in the world. Safi's simplistic understanding of surveillance in the Foucauldian sense leaves out the more important components of biopower that were characteristic of Europe. European surveillance came not only with the rise of the modern state as a new political phenomenon but also with a system of incarceration, policing, bureaucracy, health, and education, none of which had an analogue in Islam. Furthermore, nothing in Safi's narrative speaks to biopower. What emerges is a top-down narrative of a "watchful eye." Here no regimes of truth or discursive formations are to be found. What is generally unprecedented about Foucault's ideas is that power wielded by people or groups by way of episodic or sovereign acts of domination or coercion is not a useful analytical category. Power is dispersed and pervasive; it is everywhere. In Foucault's conception, there is no king whose head may be cut off.

60. The philosophical literature on the Is/Ought distinction is vast and heavily, though expectedly, in favor of it. The basic writings, however, may be found in W. D. Hudson, ed., *The Is-Ought Question* (New York: St. Martin's, 1969).

61. I am aware that there are two registers to the Distinction: (1) that fact is a priori devoid of value, and (2) that factual and normative statements are two different logical propositions, where the latter cannot be derived from the former. In other words, the analytical position is to be both distinguished and dissociated from the ontological premise. While the rich discussions of analytical philosophers are not immediately relevant to my concerns here, it may be argued that their contributions are not only singularly predicated upon the ontological distinction, but also driven by its forceful role in Enlightenment thinking. Only a particular worldview of fact can allow for the rise of the logical problem as we have come to know it.

62. This allowance of a necessary condition, one among many, also accounts for Said's attribution of Orientalism to Christian Europe, and even for the charitable interpretation that Gil Anidjar (in "Secularism," *Critical Inquiry* [Autumn 2006]: 52–77) gives *Orientalism* on this point. But it must be clear that this allowance insists on a strict definition of necessary condition, namely, that the potentiality of that condition can, by definition, never be materialized without the presence of other, autonomous conditions that make a dormant potential active. Said, we have seen, insisted on the "formal" beginnings of Orientalism in the Council of Vienna, and in the same vein argued that Orientalism "is a structure inherited from the past, secularized, redisposed, and re-formed by such disciplines as philology, which in turn were naturalized, modernized, and laicized substitutes for (or versions of) Christian supernaturalism" (122). As I construe it, this is more an emphasis on the fantastic constructions that Orientalism carried over from Christian myths than it is a "Saidian" discovery akin to a Schmittian genealogy whereby political,

liberal, and other major concepts of modernity are said to be secularized Christian forms. See also Murray Bookchin, *Remaking Society: Pathways to a Green Future* (Boston: South End, 1990), 44–46.

63. Lynn White, Jr., "The Historical Roots of Our Ecological Crisis," in *Western Man and Environmental Ethics: Attitudes Toward Nature and Technology*, ed. Ian G. Barbour (Reading, MA: Addison-Wesley, 1973), 18–30. See also Peter Singer, *Practical Ethics* (Cambridge: Cambridge University Press, 1993), 265–69. For a critique of Christianity as a progenitor of secular modernity, see Gil Anidjar, *Blood: A Critique of Christianity* (New York: Columbia University Press, 2014).

64. This, I think, is the meaning of Talal Asad's argument when he states that "there is no simple move from a Christian idea . . . to the modern universal concept." The move's complexity, I argue, is unraveled through the imperatives imposed by the Distinction and the rise into central prominence of the modern state. Talal Asad, "Reflections on Violence, Law, and Humanitarianism," *Critical Inquiry* 41 (Winter 2015): 390–427, at 398.

65. Marjorie Grice-Hutchinson, *The School of Salamanca: Readings in Spanish Monetary Theory, 1544–1605* (Oxford: Clarendon, 1952).

66. These considerations somewhat problematize the arguments of several Latin American scholars and intellectuals, such as Enrique Dussel, Walter Mignolo, and Nelson Maldonado-Torres, who regard the "long sixteenth century" as the spatiotemporal site in which modernity and its peculiar forms of colonialism originated. Yet, insisting on Christianity as having fulfilled only a necessary, but not a sufficient, condition would simultaneously allow for their and my narratives to stand not only intact but also in complementary and mutually supportive ways. It is not essential for my account to deprive the "long sixteenth century" of the thrust of a protomodern colonialism, but it is clear that the later forms of colonial sovereignty transcended and qualitatively complicated those articulated in that century. It can hardly be argued, for instance, that the forced conversions of the Muslims and Jews in Andalusia possessed the same structures of domination as those embedded in juridicality and education of the nineteenth century, however particularly brutal these conversions were. Forced conversions surely existed for millennia and were practiced by several empires throughout Asia, but did not result in cultural, epistemic, or structural genocide.

67. See the analysis of Dussel in Ramón's Grosfoguel, "The Structure of Knowledge in Westernized Universities: Epistemic Racism/Sexism and the Four Genocides/Epistemicides of the Long Sixteenth Century," *Human Architecture: Journal of the Sociology of Self-Knowledge* 11, no. 1 (Fall 2013): 73–90, at 78–79.

68. Enrique Dussel, *The Invention of the Americas: Eclipse of "the Other" and the Myth of Modernity*, trans. Michel D. Barber (New York: Continuum, 1995); Dussel,

"Anti-Cartesian Meditations: On the Origin of the Philosophical Anti-Discourse of Modernity," *Journal for Culture and Religious Theory* 13, no. 1 (Winter 2014): 11–52.

69. I have in mind such landmarks as the rise of the British East India Company, the rise of Dutch East Indies, and the transformative Peace of Westphalia.

70. Lewis W. Moncrief, "The Cultural Basis of Our Environmental Crisis," in Barbour, *Western Man and Environmental Ethics*, 32–33.

71. Richard H. Grove, *Green Imperialism: Colonial Expansion, Tropical Island Edens and the Origins of Environmentalism, 1600–1860* (New York: Cambridge University Press, 1995), 4.

72. The discourse that generalizes European problems and overdistributes them unto "humanity" at large possesses such a grip over Western scholarship that even vehement critics of European Christianity and modernity all too easily slip into that universalizing mode. In his critical and important work, *The Domination of Nature* (New York: George Braziller, 1972), William Leiss endorses Lynn White's critique of European Christianity and acknowledges the "East Asian" modes as being distinctly different in their attitude toward nature. Yet, in his conclusion to chapter 2, he remarks: "One basic point emerges from an inquiry into the historical roots of the idea of mastery over nature: this idea has long been immersed in the darker side of the human psyche and has retained associations with evil, guilt, and fear even in its recent secularized form" (44). Note here the transference of the burden of guilt and evil from Christianity to the "human psyche," an argument that (unconsciously?) scores yet another point by making the "recent secularized form" a derivative.

73. For a representative debate, see various contributions in Barbour, *Western Man and Environmental Ethics*.

74. Paul W. Kahn, *Out of Eden: Adam and Eve and the Problem of Evil* (Princeton: Princeton University Press, 2007), 64.

75. Kahn, 115.

76. Kahn, 117. See also Achille Mbembe, "Necropolitics," trans. Libby Meintjes, *Public Culture* 15, no. 1 (2003): 11–40, at 14, arguing a similar point on the basis of Hegel.

77. Carl Schmitt, *The Concept of the Political*, trans. G. Schwab (Chicago: University of Chicago Press, 2007), 29.

78. Effectively summarizing the second part of William Leiss's *The Domination of Nature*, W. Warren Wagar observes: "As Bacon and his followers never understood, the struggle for mastery over nature in a world divided into rival classes and nations becomes, above all, a struggle for power over one's fellowmen. This brutal struggle for existence negates the gains made by technical progress. 'The more actively is the pursuit of the domination of nature

undertaken, the more passive is the individual rendered; the greater the attained power over nature, the weaker the individual vis-a-vis the overwhelming presence of society.' The central fact of our time is not wealth or freedom, but the persistence of social conflict at all levels, to which science and technology are insatiably subordinated. We are as far as ever from mastery of ourselves." Wagar, "The Domination of Nature," *Technology and Culture* 14, no. 3 (July 1973): 480–82, at 481.

79. Of course it is arguable that Schmitt's diagnosis is too bellicose and bleak, but the very fact of the political theorists' obsession with his thought despite his Nazi affiliation is testimonial to the gripping and staying power of his diagnosis. To invoke Schmitt on these and related issues is to come rather close to an undeniable reality. Hence the liberal nightmarish obsession with Schmittiana.

80. Max Scheler, *Problems of a Sociology of Knowledge*, trans. Manfred Frings (London: Routledge and Kegan Paul, 1980), 77.

81. It must be noted, as Frings (one of the most important Scheler scholars) does, that Scheler's theory of innate drive(s) "sets him apart from virtually all modern European philosophers." See Manfred S. Fringes, *The Mind of Max Scheler* (Milwaukee: Marquette University Press, 2001), 176, 244–47.

82. W. Stark, *The Sociology of Knowledge: An Essay in Aid of a Deeper Understanding of the History of Ideas* (London: Routledge and Kegan Paul, 1960), 114.

83. Scheler, *Problems*, 98; Scheler, *Philosophical Perspectives*, trans. Oscar A. Haac (Boston: Beacon, 1958), 1–5, 112–17. On the Judeo-Hellenic conceptual roots of the Western domination of nature, see Singer, *Practical Ethics*, 265–69.

84. Scheler, *Problems*, 118, emphasis mine.

85. J. R. Staude, *Max Scheler* (New York: Free Press, 1967), 191; Stark, *Sociology*, 19–21.

86. For a critique of the modern concept of "Man," see Sylvia Wynter, "Unsettling the Coloniality of Being/Power/Truth/Freedom: Towards the Human, After Man, Its Overrepresentation: An Argument," *CR: The New Centennial Review* 3, no. 3 (Fall 2003): 257–337.

87. By "ontological" here I do not mean a pregiven, independent order of existence, since such an order cannot exist without a particular form of knowledge that makes it what it is. The self, for instance (modern or premodern), is a particular formation that may lend itself to an analysis of quiddity, although it is a constructed entity. Which is also to say that the "ontological" is not a stable or fixed "natural" quality, incapable of mutation.

88. For an insightful account, see Margaret C. Jacob, *Radical Enlightenment: Pantheists, Freemasons and Republicans* (Lafayette: Cornerstone, 2006).

89. Charles Taylor, "Justice After Virtue," in *After MacIntyre: Critical Perspectives on the Work of Alasdair MacIntyre*, ed. John Horton and Susan Mendus (Cambridge: Polity, 1994), 16–43, at 18.

90. See Kant's manifesto, "An Answer to the Question: What Is Enlightenment?," in *Immanuel Kant: Practical Philosophy*, ed. Mary J. Gregor (Cambridge: Cambridge University Press, 1996), 17–22.

91. I. Kant, *The Moral Law: Groundwork of the Metaphysic of Morals*, trans. H. J. Paton (London: Routledge, 2005), 14–15 (translator's epitome), 63–78, and passim. For an overview of Kant's Categorical Imperative, see J. B. Schneewind, "Autonomy, Obligation, and Virtue: An Overview of Kant's Moral Philosophy," in *The Cambridge Companion to Kant*, ed. Paul Guyer (Cambridge: Cambridge University Press, 1992), 309–33.

92. Hannah Arendt, *The Origins of Totalitarianism* (San Diego: Harcourt, 1976), 290–91.

93. G. E. M. Anscombe, "Modern Moral Philosophy," *Philosophy* 33, no. 124 (1958): 1–19, at 1–2, 5; see also Alasdair MacIntyre, *After Virtue: A Study in Moral Theory*, 3rd ed. (Notre Dame: University of Notre Dame Press, 2007), 55.

94. Jacob, *Radical Enlightenment*; Guyer rightly argues that Kant's concept of freedom was most central, underlying his notions of reason and morality, and in effect overshadowing them. See Guyer, *Kant on Freedom, Law, and Happiness* (Cambridge: Cambridge University Press, 2000), 5, 8, 39–42, 51–59, 129–38.

95. Taylor, "Justice After Virtue," 20; MacIntyre, *After Virtue*, 56–61, 79–87; MacIntyre, *A Short History of Ethics* (London: Routledge, 1998), 130–31, 166–71, 189–91. See also Raymond Geuss, *Morality, Culture, and History* (Cambridge: Cambridge University Press, 1999), 170, for Nietzsche's similar attitude to the distinction between Is and Ought.

96. Taylor, "Justice After Virtue," 20.

97. Taylor, 20–21.

98. See, in particular, Max Horkheimer and Theodor W. Adorno, *Dialectic of Enlightenment: Philosophical Fragments*, ed. G. Schmid Noerr, trans. E. Jophcott (Stanford: Stanford University Press, 1987); Helmut Peukert, "The Philosophical Critique of Modernity," in *The Debate on Modernity*, ed. Claude Geffré and Pierre Jossua (London: SCM Press, 1992), 17–26.

99. Scheler, *Problems*, 119, his emphasis; 78.

100. Cited in Stark, *Sociology*, 118; see also Scheler, *Problems*, 129–30. For a critique of positivism, see Thomas A. Sprangens, Jr., *The Irony of Liberal Reason* (Chicago: University of Chicago Press, 1981), 196–310.

101. Of course, of all these names, Bacon was the advocate of this domination. See Leiss, *The Domination of Nature*, 45–71; Antonio Pérez-Ramos, "Bacon's Forms and the Maker's Knowledge," in *Cambridge Companion to Bacon*, ed. Markku Peltonen (Cambridge: Cambridge University Press, 1996), 99–120, at 110–13; and Jatinder K. Bajaj, "Francis Bacon, the First Philosopher of Modern Science: A Non-Western View," in *Science, Hegemony and Violence:*

A Requiem for Modernity, ed. Ashis Nandy (Delhi: Oxford University Press, 1988), 24–67.

102. Pérez-Ramos, "Bacon's Forms"; Paolo Rossi, "Bacon's Idea of Science," in *The Cambridge Companion to Bacon*, ed. Markku Peltonen (Cambridge: Cambridge University Press, 1996), 37–42.

103. Kahn, *Out of Eden*, 66. Contrast this with the scientific Islamic perspective on nature. A highly representative case is the scientist and astronomer Nisaburi, who argued that "an informed and accurate understanding of nature was bound to increase one's appreciation of God's role in creation and in nature." Morrison, *Islam and Science*, 115.

104. For an incisive analysis of these views, see Akeel Bilgrami, "Gandhi, Newton, and the Enlightenment," in *Values and Violence*, ed. I. A. Karawan, et al. (New York: Springer, 2008), 15–29.

105. Jacob, *Radical Enlightenment*, 6, as well as pp. xi, 3–4, 64–67, and passim.

106. Domenico Losurdo, *Liberalism: A Counter-History*, trans. Gregory Elliott (London: Verso, 2011), 3–4. See also Sven Beckert and Seth Rockman, eds., *Slavery's Capitalism: A New History of American Economic Development* (Philadelphia: University of Pennsylvania Press, 2016).

107. Bilgrami, "Gandhi, Newton, and the Enlightenment," 25 and passim.

108. One can no more dominate a nature that is infused with value than subordinate and transform the Other whose human and cultural worth and moral constitution create a similar demand. More importantly, however, and as some social scientists (neo-Marxists and nonmainstream sociologists) have argued, the separation that denudes intellectual/scientific inquiry of value "is ethically untenable," for it "disengages the observer from the social responsibility that should accompany his accounts, and it results in the status quo being presented as somehow natural and real, rather than as constructed and partisan." This ethical dimension, indeed moral accountability, can hardly be overemphasized. Charles Pressler and Fabio B. Dasilva, *Sociology and Interpretation: From Weber to Habermas* (Albany: State University of New York Press, 1996), 102–3, emphasis mine.

109. On concepts of domination and imperialism in late Antique empires, see Rolf Strootman, "Hellenistic Imperialism and the Ideal of World Unity," in *The City in the Classical and Post-Classical World: Changing Contexts of Power and Identity*, ed. Claudia Rapp and H. A. Drake (Cambridge: Cambridge University Press, 2014), 38–61.

110. On non-Muslims under Islamic governance, see Anver Emon, *Religious Pluralism and Islamic Law: Dhimmis and Others in the Empire of Law* (Oxford: Oxford University Press, 2012). While rich in its empirical presentation of legal literature on the subject, the book is heavily anachronistic and hopelessly ideological, succumbing to modern and distinctly liberal notions of equality and

state structures, thus overlooking—and thus misjudging—the internal social/communal logic of Islamic governance. In fact, treating the Islamic model of rule of law on its own terms may offer a rich source of critique or at least a productive heuristic exercise in the study of modern forms of "minority" governance, including the liberal. By contrast, an insightful and sensitive analysis of minority communities in Islamic domains is provided by Rachel Goshgarian, *The City in Late Medieval Anatolia: Cross-Cultural Interaction and Urbanism in the Middle East* (London: I. B. Tauris, 2018).

111. Ranajit Guha's concepts of both dominance and hegemony, notwithstanding their differentials, would thus be subordinate to the concept of sovereignty I am articulating here. See Guha, *Dominance Without Hegemony* (Cambridge, MA: Harvard University Press, 1998).

112. For the constitutive features of the state, see Hallaq, *Impossible State*, 19–36.

113. Foucault, "The Subject and Power," in *Power: Essential Works of Foucault, 1954–1984*, ed. James D. Faubion, trans. Robert Hurley et al., vol. 3 (New York: New Press, 1994), 326–48, at 333.

114. Foucault, 334.

115. Martin L. van Creveld, *The Rise and Decline of the State* (Cambridge: Cambridge University Press, 1999), 168–69, 417–18. On the further growth of prisons more recently, see Gary Teeple, *Globalization and the Decline of Social Reform* (Aurora, Ontario: Garamond, 2000), 122–26.

116. See van Creveld, *Rise and Decline*, 205–24. See also Christopher Lasch, *The Culture of Narcissism: American Life in an Age of Diminishing Expectations* (New York: Norton, 1978), 125–53.

117. This last reference is intended to evoke the analysis in Foucault, *The Order of Things: An Archeology of the Human Sciences*, trans. R. D. Lang (New York: Pantheon, 1970).

118. Foucault, *Discipline and Punish: The Birth of the Prison*, trans. Alan Sheridan, 2nd ed. (New York: Vintage, 1995), 138.

119. The mild qualification is occasioned by the recognition that the citizen must be, in certain restricted and narrow spheres, distinguished from the moral individual. But this is not a paradigmatic distinction, since the moral individual as an archetype—whose province neither enters the political nor counts in the legal—pales in significance when compared with his role as citizen. It is in this light that one should interpret Iris Murdoch on this point. See Murdoch, *Metaphysics as a Guide to Morals* (London: Random House, 2003), 357.

120. The frequency with which large sums of money are dispensed to support research related to "threats to national security" and "threats to democracy" is dizzying. An example is a recent e-mail announcement in my own institution calling for proposals to be submitted to the Andrew Carnegie Fellows Program. Awarding "thirty-five major fellowships of $200,000 each, lasting

one to two years," the program seeks to support "talented individuals whose vibrant, creative research addresses threats to our democracy, as well as to the international order." "Eligible topics for the 2017 competition" include "strengthening U.S. democracy." "All recipients must be U.S. citizens or have permanent U.S. residency status." Email: Sept. 28, 2016. See also David Nugent, "Knowledge and Empire: The Social Sciences and the United States Imperial Expansion," *Identities: Global Studies in Culture and Power* 17 (2010): 2–44. Nugent argues that the US government, the American corporations, and their educational foundations "considered the social sciences essential to the project of managing empire. At each major stage in the reorganization of that empire, state and capital have underwritten a massive reorganization in the production of social science knowledge" (2).

121. See Hallaq, *Impossible State*, 75–89.

122. On the social sciences in particular, see *Open the Social Sciences: Report of the Gulbenkian Commission on Restructuring the Social Sciences* (Stanford: Stanford University Press, 1996). For a critique, see Bruce C. Wearne, "Review Essay," *American Sociologist* 29, no. 3 (September 1998): 71–78.

123. For more on this matter in the context of Orientalism (a form of knowledge supported and sustained by the humanities and social sciences at large), see Wael Hallaq, "On Orientalism, Self-Consciousness, and History," *Islamic Law and Society* 18, nos. 3–4 (2011): 387–439. See also Nugent, "Knowledge and Empire."

124. N. Rose and P. Miller, "Political Power Beyond the State: Problematic of Government," *British Journal of Sociology* 43, no. 2 (1992): 173–205, at 182. It is surprising that Loïc Wacquant privileges "the so-called humanities, philosophy, literature, law, etc." over "the deeply regrettable exceptions of economics and political science," the former having risen up to the challenge of "critical thought." According to Wacquant, critical thought "weds epistemological and social critique by questioning, in a continuous, active, and radical manner, both established forms of thought and established forms of collective life—'common sense' or *doxa*." This critique puts "us in a position to project ourselves mentally outside of the world as it is given to us in order to invent, concretely, futures other than the one inscribed in the order of things. In short, critical thought is that which gives us the means to *think the world* as it is and as *it could be* ("Critical Thought as Solvent *Doxa*," *Constellations* 11, no. 1 (2004), 97–101, at 97–98, his emphasis). In light of the overall arguments of the present book, I fail to understand how a critique of the type Wacquant defines can privilege the "so-called humanities" (especially philosophy and law) over the "deeply regrettable exceptions," unless, that is, the critique is only rhetorically "radical" and "active."

125. Bill Readings, *The University in Ruins* (Cambridge, MA: Harvard University Press, 1996); David Harvey, "University, Inc.," *Atlantic Monthly* 282, no. 4

(October 1998): 112–16,www.theatlantic.com/magazine/archive/1998/10
/university-inc/377274/.

126. Henry A. Giroux, "Public Intellectuals Against the Neoliberal University,"
in *Truthout*, October 29, 2013, www.truth-out.org/news/item/19654-public
-intellectuals-against-the-neoliberal-university#XXXVI.

127. Giroux: "In the United States, college presidents are now called CEOs and
move without apology between interlocking corporate and academic boards.
With few exceptions, they are praised as fundraisers but rarely acknowledged
for the quality of their ideas. It gets worse. As Adam Bessie points out, 'the
discourse of higher education now resembles what you might hear at a board
meeting at a No. 2 pencil-factory, [with its emphasis on] productivity, efficiency, metrics, data-driven value, [all of] which places utter, near-religious
faith in this highly technical, market-based view of education.'" See also
Martha Nussbaum, *Not For Profit: Why Democracies Need the Humanities* (Princeton: Princeton University Press, 2010); Charles H. Ferguson, *Predator
Nation: Corporate Criminals, Political Corruption, and the Hijacking of America*
(New York: Crown, 2012). Note that Giroux, as much as Nussbaum, predicates too much criticism of corporatizing the university on the notion of liberal democracy (that "true" democracy contradicts this trend), when it is my
argument throughout the book that it is precisely liberalism, in both its classical and it late modern forms, that is inherently predisposed to various forms
of sovereign domination and exploitation. Apparently unaware of much
scholarship on the structural entanglements of liberalism in slavery, colonialism, and genocide, Nussbaum is able to declare, with astounding intellectual
innocence, that "Education based mainly on profitability in the global market magnifies these deficiencies [in liberal democracies], producing a greedy
obtuseness and a technically trained docility that threaten the very life of
democracy itself, and that certainly impede the creation of a decent world
culture" (142).

128. See introduction, sec. 3.

129. Kojin Karatani, "Uses of Aesthetics: After Orientalism," *Boundary 2* 25, no.
2 (Summer 1998): 145–60.

130. To say that Orientalism constituted a part of the machinery that remade and
re-created the Orient is not to contradict the claim that Orientalism exhibits
the entire range of features that became another name for modernity, a microcosm in which the entire range of paradigmatic features of the modern project is concentrated.

131. When Joseph Schacht, the "father" of Islamic legal studies in the West, sealed
the fate of the Shariʿa as stagnant and as having lost touch with "state and
society" since the ninth century, he was, in the 1950s and 1960s, describing
a fait accompli, a colonialist process that had already eviscerated Shariʿa's

system during the century before his writings became canonical. Schacht, *Introduction to Islamic Law* (Oxford: Oxford University Press, 1964), 69–85.

132. This is certainly one of the very few legitimate critiques that B. Lewis levels at Said's *Orientalism*. Bernard Lewis, "The Question of Orientalism," in *Islam and the West* (New York: Oxford University Press, 1993), 99–118.

133. Brett Bowden offers a succinct but excellent summary of the basic features of the doctrine of progress: "The idea of progress has two related components. The first is that the human species universally progresses, albeit at different rates and to different degrees, from an original primitive or child-like condition, referred to as savagery, through to barbarism, and culminates at the apex of progress in the status of civilization. The second component of the idea of progress holds that human experience, both individual and collective, is cumulative and future-directed, with the specific objective being the ongoing improvement of the individual, the society in which the individual lives, and the world in which the society must survive. For some thinkers it seems logical that what follows from the general idea of progress is the notion that progress is directed in a particular direction, or that history is moving forward along a particular path toward a specific end. History, in this conception, is not merely the cataloguing of events, but a universal history of all humankind, a cumulative and collective history of civilization, that is, History. The notion that different peoples or cultural groups are at different stages of development along the path of universal progress has led some to deem it necessary to try to ameliorate the condition of those thought to be less civilized. This enterprise has variously been known as the 'white man's burden,' the 'burden of civilization,' or the 'sacred trust of civilization.' The general aim of these often violent and overly-zealous 'civilizing missions' was to ameliorate the state of the 'uncivilized' through tutelage, training, and conversion to Christianity. With European expansion, wherever 'civilized' and 'uncivilized' peoples existed side by side, there soon developed an unequal treaty system of capitulations, also known extraterritorial rights. In much of the uncivilized world this system of capitulations incrementally escalated to the point that it became full-blown colonialism." See Bowden, "Colonialism, Anti-Colonialism, and the Idea of Progress," *History and Philosophy of Science and Technology, Encyclopedia of Life Support Systems,* ed. UNESCO-EOLS Joint Committee (Oxford: EOLSS, 2011), 1–2. For a critique of the residues of this doctrine in Critical Theory and in the early Frankfurt School thinkers, see Amy Allen, *The End of Progress: Decolonizing the Normative Foundations of Critical Theory* (New York: Columbia University Press, 2016). In the present book, I employ the expression "theology of progress," rather than "theory" or "idea" of progress for at least two reasons, the first having to do with the Christian origins of this trenchant belief, and the second its posited nature.

134. Bhabha, "Difference, Discrimination, and the Discourse of Colonialism," in *The Politics of Theory*, ed. F. Barker et al. (Colchester: University of Essex Press, 1983), 194–211, at 200.

135. Implicitly responding to such critics as Homi Bhabha, who argued that *Orientalism* does not allow for native agency, Said, in *Culture and Imperialism*, vii, states this: "What I left out of *Orientalism* was that response to Western dominance which culminated in the great movement of decolonization all across the Third World. Along with armed resistance in places as diverse as nineteenth-century Algeria, Ireland, and Indonesia, there also went considerable efforts in cultural resistance almost everywhere, the assertions of nationalist identities, and, in the political realm, the creation of associations and parties whose common goal was self-determination and national independence. Never was it the case that the imperial encounter pitted an active Western intruder against a supine or inert non-Western native; there was always some form of active resistance, and in the overwhelming majority of cases, the resistance finally won out" (emphasis his). Note that Said here accepts the narrative of decolonization and deems "cultural resistance" an important source (along with armed struggle) and a venue for "decolonization." Yet, Said's notion of decolonializing modalities squarely places these modalities within the dictates of the colonizer's terms: nationalism, "assertion of nationalist identities," political parties, "self-determination and national independence"—all of which are nationalist European legacies that were made, in the first place, to decimate the cultural traditions of the colonies and then create new realities in the image of Europe, only for these nation-based ontologies to return later in order to reassert hegemony and to further destroy many of these "nation-states" themselves, or at least wreak havoc with their lives. But this is not all. A little later in the introduction of the same book (xxiv), Said makes the stunning remark that "Western imperialism and Third World nationalism feed off each other." Are we then to conclude that Said accepts as a satisfactory explanation that the agency which permitted "winning" against the "Western intruder" was the very act that inscribed the colonized in the very paradigmatic structures of their colonizers? The point is that Bhabha's and Said's concepts of agency are not merely superficial; they could not transcend the very discourse that gives the theory of agency its raison d'être. See further on this point chapter 2, section 4, and chapter 4, section 3. In this context, Leonard Wood is to be commended for his insistence, supported by meticulous empirical research, that academia has inflated claims of agency. See Wood, *Islamic Legal Revival: Reception of European Law and Transformations in Islamic Legal Thought in Egypt, 1875–1952* (Oxford: Oxford University Press, 2016), esp. 262.

136. Daniel Martin Varisco, *Reading Orientalism: Said and the Unsaid* (Seattle: University of Washington Press, 2007), 55–56.

137. A poignant summary of Said's problems with religion is to be found in W. J. T. Mitchell, "Secular Divination," 466–67. "But it is the domain of religion that Said so often characterizes in terms of fairly reductive stereotypes: dogmatic, fanatical, irrational, intolerant, and obsessed with mystery, obfuscation, and human helplessness in the presence of the inscrutable divine (or demonic) design." Mitchell cited perhaps the most damning evidence from Said's own *Humanism and Democratic Criticism*: "Religious enthusiasm is perhaps the most dangerous of threats to the humanistic enterprise, since it is patently antisecular and antidemocratic in nature." Mitchell concludes: "Religion for Said is an expression of the alienated capacities of the human imagination, a system of ideological deception and coercive authority." Said, *Humanism and Democratic Criticism*, ed. Akeel Bilgrami (New York: Columbia University Press, 2004), 51.

138. Allen, *End of Progress*.

139. Walter Benjamin, "Theses on the Philosophy of History," in *Illuminations*, ed. Hannah Arendt (New York: Schocken, 1968), 253–64, at 260.

140. Theodor Adorno, *History and Freedom*, ed. R. Tiedemann (Malden, MA: Polity, 2006), 3–9, 138–41. See also Brian O'Connor, "Philosophy of History," in *Theodor Adorno: Key Concepts*, ed. Deborah Cook (Stocksfield: Acumen, 2008), 179–95, 181.

141. Christopher Dawson, *The Making of Europe* (New York: Meridian, 1956), 16.

142. Hallaq, *Impossible State*, 14.

143. Asifa Quraishi, "The Separation of Powers in the Tradition of Muslim Governments," in *Constitutionalism in Islamic Countries: Between Upheaval and Continuity*, ed. Rainer Grote and Tilmann J. Röder (Oxford: Oxford University Press, 2012), 63–73, at 65–68 (notwithstanding the anachronism of "mistake committed by an early Muslim state," p. 73).

144. This much is fully recognized by traditional Orientalism, although this scholarship consistently refused to draw the necessary implications of this constitutional arrangement. See H. A. R. Gibb, "Constitutional Organization," in *Law in the Middle East*, ed. M. Khadduri and H. J. Liebesny (Washington: Middle East Institute, 1955): 3–27, at 3.

145. Wael Hallaq, "From Regional to Personal Schools of Law? A Reevaluation," *Islamic Law and Society* 8, no. 1 (2001): 1–26.

146. Hallaq, *Authority, Continuity and Change*.

147. The title of chapter 3 in my *Impossible State*.

148. van Creveld, *Rise and Decline*, 209; Hallaq, *Impossible State*, 23–25.

149. For an outline of this conception of rationality, see Charles Larmore, *The Autonomy of Morality* (Cambridge: Cambridge University Press, 2008), 1–7.

150. van Creveld, *Rise and Decline*, 185. See also J. S. Mill, *On Liberty*, ed. David Bromwich and George Kateb (New Haven: Yale University Press, 2003), 81; Marc Ferro, *Colonization: A Global History* (London: Routledge, 1997), 22.

151. For an overview of "reforms" in the Ottoman Empire, see Hallaq, *Shariʿa*, 396–429.

152. Çizakça, *History of Philanthropic Foundations*; Cattan, "Law of Waqf"; van Leeuwen, *Waqfs and Urban Structures*; Makdisi, *Rise of the Colleges*; Hallaq, *Shariʿa*, 53–54, 126, 141–46, 150, 191, 194, 195, and passim.

153. Hallaq, *Shariʿa*, 433.

154. The remainder of this section draws on the empirical data I have utilized in *Shariʿa*, 371–83, 388–95, 401–10.

155. A more detailed account of this argument may be found in my *Impossible State*, 98–138.

156. See, generally, H. Driessen, ed., *The Politics of Ethnographic Reading and Writing: Confrontations of Western and Indigenous Views* (Saarbrücken: Breitenbach, 1993).

157. It is instructive in this context to note how individual and group Orientalist discourses operated within Orientalism's own discursive tradition. The French Orientalist production during this period was heavily geared toward France's specific colonialist project in Algeria, essentially serving its interests. This production then had a certain specificity, not only because it was about Maliki jurisprudence but mainly because it constituted a part of a clearly political project. Yet, when these discourses (now seen as "books" and "scholarly articles") were read in France and later in North America, the colonialist context was almost invariably subtracted from their constitution. They have now become just "scholarly contributions," to be read like any other book or article on Algeria, Islam, the Orient, the world. If the colonialist context was so routinely subtracted, it is because colonialism itself was an essential component of the Orient itself, the latter inconceivable without the former. Which is to say that colonization is not only routinized but also normalized. It then becomes a scholarly discovery when an American Orientalist notices, a century after the event, that there is something disingenuous about that discourse, namely, that it is more colonialist and less "scholarly." That this "bias" is brought to light a century after the event, when French settler colonialism and almost all such rudimentary forms of colonialism have lapsed, is remarkable in that in the very "critique" of such biased "scholarship" a new Orientalist scholarship sanctions the legitimacy of its own project, advancing its cause along the lines of a mutating discursive tradition of which this discourse is an essential part. For an instance of this American Orientalist "critique," see David Powers, "Orientalism, Colonialism and Legal History: The Attack on Muslim Family Endowments in Algeria and India," *Comparative Studies in Society and History* 31, no. 3 (July 1989): 535–71.

158. One can even add German Orientalism as a "mediated" political interest that "did not emerge due to any particular concern for the Orient"; see Ursula Wokoeck, *German Orientalism: The Study of the Middle East and Islam from 1800 to 1945* (London: Routledge, 2009), 211. The diminutive presence of the blatant colonial and political in German Orientalism is perhaps the best argument for my thesis, namely, that it is neither the political nor colonial-economic interests as such that primarily gave rise to the structure of thought of sovereign domination.

159. Powers, "Orientalism, Colonialism and Legal History," 536. However, see note 157 of this chapter.

160. Macaulay, "Minute on Indian Education," in *Selected Writings*, ed. John Clive and Thomas Pinney (Chicago: University of Chicago Press, 1972), 237–51, at 249.

161. An important and thickly constructed narrative is the entire Orientalist subfield that "investigates" the origins of Islam, essentially showing that the "heavy debt" Islam owed to previous legal cultures and "civilizations" (Greek, Roman, Byzantine, Jewish, even Persian) is commensurate with modern Islam's legal deficiency (namely, deficiency of the Shariʿa), which can be cured only by accepting and adopting the legal systems of the inheritors of these ancient civilizations, who happened to be represented by the modern Europeans. It is not readily detectible to the uncritical eye that a subfield which pretends to study legal history and so-called legal transplantation in the sixth and seventh centuries AD is driven by an ideology that is directly—though surreptitiously—connected with an ideological system constructed to justify the Westernization of Islam's legal system and consequently Islam itself. This involved narrative, it must be said, drew the arsenal of a number of Orientalists over several decades, and extended over a number of areas of expertise. On this particular theme, see Hallaq, "On Orientalism, Self-Consciousness, and History," 412–13; Hallaq, "In Quest for Origins or Doctrine? Islamic Legal Studies as Colonialist Discourse," *UCLA Journal of Islamic and Near Eastern Law* 2, no. 1 (Fall/Winter 2002–03): 1–31.

162. Hallaq, "On Orientalism, Self-Consciousness, and History," 409–15. Of course, this selective approach to *waqf* is not even the most important feature of Orientalist discourse. In all that Orientalism produced about Islamic forms of government and politics, there is a resounding silence over the relationship of these forms to the rule of law. As I have shown elsewhere, this silence, as silence, is the function of a discourse that was programmatically geared to justify the imposition of Western notions of democracy and political freedom on the Islamic world through the creation of a narrative of "Oriental despotism" that presumably dictated the conditions of political rule in Islam. See Wael Hallaq, "Quranic Magna Carta: On the Origins of the Rule of Law

in Islam," in *Magna Carta, Religion and the Rule of Law*, ed. R. Griffith-Jones and Mark Hill (Cambridge: Cambridge University Press, 2014), 157–76.

163. Allan Christelow, *Muslim Law Courts and the French Colonial State in Algeria* (Princeton: Princeton University Press, 1985), 20, 131.

164. Hallaq, *Shariʿa*, 435–38.

165. As I have witnessed throughout three decades of interaction with lawyers and judges from this region, as well as from South East Asia, particularly Indonesia. It must be said that the most striking of such discourse comes from Egypt, especially as articulated by a few who staff(ed) the Supreme Constitutional Court, as well as an increasing number of recent writers (both self-declared Islamists and liberals, without these being mutually exclusive).

166. Daniel Lev, "Colonial Law and the Genesis of the Indonesian State," *Indonesia* 40 (October 1985): 58.

167. Lev, 59.

168. M. B. Hooker, *A Concise Legal History of South-East Asia* (Oxford: Clarendon, 1978), 192–93. See also Hooker, *Adat Laws in Modern Malaya: Land Tenure, Traditional Government, and Religion* (Kuala Lumpur: Oxford University Press, 1972); Hooker, *Legal Pluralism: An Introduction to Colonial and Neo-Colonial Laws* (Oxford: Clarendon, 1975).

169. A critic, finding this statement impossible to refute for the premodern period, may nonetheless argue that there were jurists who may have encouraged rulers to embark on such projects in the early modern period, before the "legal order" of the Shariʿa suffered total collapse during the nineteenth century. Although I myself cannot document such juristic voices, their probable presence strengthens my argument rather than weakens it, for such voices had no hearing in the actual practice of Muslim "state" and empire during the sixteenth century and seventeenth.

170. In the manner I have distinguished this term from sovereignty. See section 4 of this chapter.

171. See, for example, Hallaq, *Origins and Evolution of Islamic Law*, 29–32.

172. A theme to be treated at some length in chapter 5.

173. J. F. Holleman, ed., *Van Vollenhoven on Indonesian Adat Law: Selections from Het Adatrecht van Nederlandsch-Indië* (The Hague: Martinus Nijhoff, 1981), 7–11 and passim. See also C. Fasseur, "Colonial Dilemma: Van Vollenhoven and the Struggle Between Adat Law and Western Law in Indonesia," in *European Expansion and Law: The Encounter of European and Indigenous Law in the 19th- and 20th-Century Africa and Asia*, ed. W. J. Mommsen and J. A. De Moor (Oxford: Berg, 1992), 240–62.

174. Lev, "Colonial Law," 66.

175. Takashi Shiraishi, *An Age in Motion: Popular Radicalism in Java, 1912–1926* (Ithaca: Cornell University Press, 1990), 28–29.

176. Macaulay, "Minute on Indian Education."

177. Werner Menski, *Hindu Law: Beyond Tradition and Modernity* (Oxford: Oxford University Press, 2003), 164–65, and passim.

178. Siraj Ahmed, *The Stillbirth of Capital: Enlightenment Writing and Colonial India* (Stanford: Stanford University Press, 2012); Garland Cannon and Kevin Brine, eds., *Objects of Enquiry: The Life, Contributions, and Influence of Sir William Jones, 1746–1794* (New York: New York University Press, 1995); Michael J. Franklin, *Orientalist Jones: Sir William Jones, Poet, Lawyer, and Linguist, 1746–1794* (Oxford: Oxford University Press, 2011); John Strawson, "Islamic Law and English Texts," *Law and Critique* 6, no. 1 (1995): 21–38.

179. Cited in Bernard Cohn, *Colonialism and Its Forms of Knowledge: The British in India* (Princeton: Princeton University Press, 1996), 69. See also Scott A. Kugle, "Framed, Blamed and Renamed: The Recasting of Islamic Jurisprudence in Colonial South India," *Modern Asian Studies* 35, no. 2 (2001): 257–313.

180. Ahmed, *Stillbirth of Capital*, 176–77: "The point of [Jones's] translation was . . . to provide the 1793 Permanent Settlement with its legal architecture. Jones considered the legal codes on which he labored . . . to be his most valuable contributions to history, not his many other Orientalist works nor the Indo-Aryan thesis, for which he is much more famous: he aspired to be 'the Justinian . . . of the East.' Jones wanted orientalism, in other words, to serve the demands of colonial property. . . . Jones's Orientalism gave the East India company's revolutionary rule of property the appearance of an ancient origin, folding it into the 'sakuntala Era,' at least as far as his European reading public was concerned. The Laws of Manu simultaneously authorized the Permanent Settlement and drew attention away from its material context and consequences. Its logic seemed to be dictated by immemorial traditions."

181. Cited in Cohn, *Colonialism and Its Forms of Knowledge*, 69. See also Michael Anderson, "Legal Scholarship and the Politics of Islam in British India," in *Perspectives on Islamic Law, Justice, and Society*, ed. R. S. Khare (Lanham, MD: Rowman and Littlefield, 1999), 74.

182. This is the main argument made by Ferdinand F. Stone ("A Primer on Codification," *Tulane Law Review* 29 [1954–55]: 303–310, at 303–4), although he also acknowledges that codification is the state's (and its reformers') tool for effecting a "new economic and social order."

183. S. A. Bayitch, "Codification in Modern Times," in *Civil Law in the Modern World*, ed. A. N. Yiannopoulos (Kingsport: Louisianan State University Press, 1965), 161–91, 164.

184. Obviously, the common law is an exception, but then the vast majority of Islamic states did not adopt this system, Egypt being a prime example of a British protectorate opting for French-inspired law.

185. This, according to Stone ("Primer," 303–4), being the raison d'être of the code.

186. Stone, 306.

187. See Bayitch, "Codification," 162–67. On the power of the law to create, constitute, and reconstitute subjects, see Clifford Geertz, "Local Knowledge: Fact and Law in Comparative Perspective," in *Local Knowledge: Further Essays in Interpretive Anthropology* (New York: Basic, 1983), 167–234; Teemu Ruskola, *Legal Orientalism: China, the United States, and Modern Law* (Cambridge, MA: Harvard University Press, 2013).

188. On this subject as the performative effect of the technologies of the self, see Hallaq, *Impossible State*, 110–38.

189. See Hallaq, *Shari'a*, 159–96, 200–8; Hallaq, "A Prelude to Ottoman Reform: Ibn 'Abidin on Custom and Legal Change," in *Histories of the Modern Middle East: New Directions*, ed. I. Gershoni et al. (Boulder: Lynne Rienner, 2002), 437–61.

190. On self-rule, see Hallaq, *Shari'a*, 200–8.

191. Hallaq, *Authority, Continuity, and Change*, 121–235.

192. Hallaq, *Impossible State*, 48–62.

193. Strawson, "Islamic Law and English Texts."

194. On this and related issues, see the work of M. B. Hooker, cited in note 168 of this chapter.

195. This is in reference to my discussion of central and peripheral academic domains. See chapter 4, section 2.

3. The Subversive Author

1. This argument is not to be confused with my argument in the next chapter with regard to what I have called Latour's Stone. Modern central domains are domains of power, the very domains that, in their constellation, made possible the colonialist venture in the first place. The indigenous central domains, while acting as such before the colonial encounter, were the object of evisceration and, often, decimation. In the case of evisceration, they also, ipso facto, lost their internal dynamics of power. Thus, the Latour's Stone thesis should not be seen as analytically amenable to the theory of central domains, for the central domains in the case of Latour's Stone are the very European domains that created the Stone.

2. Foucault, *The Archaeology of Knowledge and Discourse on Language*, trans. A. M. Sheridan Smith (New York: Pantheon, 1972), 38.

3. In his *Beginnings: Intention and Method* (New York: Columbia University Press, 1975), 295, Said gives a brief account of the historicity of *épistémès* in both

Foucault and his mentor, Georges Canguihelm. In *Orientalism*, however, he does not seem to consider the implications of this account upon his narrative.

4. This theme is taken up further in the next chapter.

5. See chapter 2, note 137; chapter 4, notes 2 and 48; and chapter 5, note 10.

6. To say, as Aamir R. Mufti does ("Global Comparativism," *Critical Inquiry* 31 [2005]: 472–89, at 472), that non-Western literature "animates" Said's work "even when its explicit preoccupation appears to be elsewhere" is certainly an overreach. One wonders why such a comparative interest needs to "be put into articulation" if it were indeed "present in relatively developed form in his [Said's] work." It is telling that Mufti views his own scholarship as an attempt to continue Said's work, "to pick up where he [Said] seemed to have left off, to pursue directions that were only hinted at in his work, or to explore possibilities that were implicit in them" (473). Here, as in Mufti's analysis of Said's understanding of secularism and "secular criticism"/"critical secularism," Said is made to bear larger claims than he in fact propounded. That Said *hinted* at the importance of non-Western literature and strove to provide for its integration the method of contrapuntal reading is undoubted, but this remained indeed implicit, and was never carried out, with any methodical thrust, *in correction* of the discourse he was critiquing. More crucially, such readings, had they been articulated and elaborated by Said, would not have mitigated the problems engulfing his liberalism, anthropocentrism, and secularism.

7. When Said expressed interest in the literature of the colonized, and when he vehemently critiqued the Eurocentric predilections for Euro-American literature, his final concern remained constrained by "understanding" Western literature as an expression of empire. Furthermore, this proposal never translated into even a preliminary methodological or theoretical attempt at bringing Euro-American literature into critical dialogue with literary and other cultural productions of the colonized, be it in their colonized present or in their largely autonomous histories. "I suggested that studying the relationship between the 'West' and its dominated 'others' is not just a way of understanding an unequal relationship between unequal interlocutors, but also a point of entry into studying the formation of meaning of Western cultural practices themselves." Said, *Culture and Imperialism* (New York: Vintage, 1993), 191. This attitude exhibits the same pattern of thought that governs *Orientalism*, as I have been arguing. It does not seem to have been on Said's mind that the *fundamentals* of Euro-American intellectual and cultural productions can be subjected to, and reevaluated by a critical engagement with and by means of, the intellectual-historical accumulation of the presently colonized cultures.

8. Which he himself articulately characterized as such in Guénon, *The Crisis of the Modern World* (London: Luzac, 1962).

9. R. Guénon, *East and West*, trans. Martin Lings (Ghent, NY: Sophia Perennis, 2001), 11, 85.

10. Guénon, 11.

11. Guénon, 22–23.

12. Cited in Graham Rooth, *Prophet for a Dark Age: A Companion to the Works of Rene Guénon* (Brighton: Sussex Academic Press, 2008), 201.

13. Guénon, *East and West*, 29–30: "We have no desire to question the sincerity of any scientist, historian, or philosopher; but they are often the apparent 'controllers,' and they may be themselves controlled or influenced without in the least realizing it. Besides, the use made of their ideas does not always correspond with their own intentions, and it would be wrong to make them directly responsible, or to blame them for not having foreseen certain more or less remote consequences."

14. Rooth, *Prophet for a Dark Age*, 201–2.

15. Guénon, *East and West*, 20.

16. Guénon, 38.

17. Guénon, 32–33.

18. Guénon, 30, 48, 88. See also Gyan Prakash, *Another Reason: Science and the Imagination of Modern India* (Princeton: Princeton University Press, 1999).

19. Guénon, *East and West*, 33.

20. Guénon, 30.

21. Guénon, 27–28, 36–37.

22. Guénon, 86.

23. R. Guénon, "A Material Civilization," in *The Betrayal of Tradition: Essays on the Spiritual Crisis of Modernity*, ed. Harry Oldmeadow (Bloomingdale: World Wisdom, 2005), 15–30, at 17–18. See also Guénon, *Reign of Quantity and the Sign of the Times*, trans. Lord Northbourne (Hillsdale, NY: Sophia Perennis, 1995).

24. Charles Taylor, "Justice After Virtue," in *After MacIntyre: Critical Perspectives on the Work of Alasdair MacIntyre*, ed. John Horton and Susan Mendus (Cambridge: Polity, 1994), 16–43, at 20; Alasdair MacIntyre, *After Virtue: A Study in Moral Theory*, 3rd ed. (Notre Dame: University of Notre Dame Press, 2007), 56–61, 79–87; MacIntyre, *A Short History of Ethics* (London: Routledge, 1998), 130–31, 166–71, 189–91.

25. Guénon, *East and West*, 91.

26. Guénon, 37.

27. Guénon, 28.

28. Guénon, 13, 15.

29. Guénon, 20, 21, 23.

30. Guénon, 26, 52.

31. W. Stark, *The Sociology of Knowledge: An Essay in Aid of a Deeper Understanding of the History of Ideas* (London: Routledge and Kegan Paul, 1960), 118; Max

Scheler, *Problems of a Sociology of Knowledge*, trans. Manfred Frings (London: Routledge and Kegan Paul, 1980), 129–30. See also discussion of Scheler in chapter 2, section 5.

32. Guénon, *East and West*, 26. Guénon's attitude toward the Easterners would change in his later *The Crisis of the Modern World*, 141: "It is true that the encroachments of the West are nothing new, but hitherto they have been confined to a more or less brutal domination over other peoples, whose effects went no deeper than the domain of politics and economics: despite all efforts at a propaganda that worked under many different guises, the Eastern attitudes of mind remained unaffected by all deviations, and the ancient traditional civilizations survived intact. Today, on the contrary, there are Orientals who are more or less completely 'Westernized,' who have forsaken their tradition and adopted all the aberrations of the modern outlook, and these denatured elements . . . have become a cause of trouble and agitation in their own countries."

33. Isaiah Berlin, "Two Concepts of Liberty," in *Liberty*, ed. Henry Hardy (Oxford: Oxford University Press, 2008), 166–217. See also John N. Gray, "On Negative and Positive Liberty," *Political Studies* 28, no. 4 (1980): 507–26; Charles Taylor, "What's Wrong with Negative Liberty," in *The Idea of Freedom: Essays in Honor of Isaiah Berlin*, ed. Alan Ryan (Oxford: Oxford University Press, 1979), 175–93.

34. Giorgio Agamben, *The Signature of All Things: On Method* (New York: Zone, 2009), 17, speaking of the panopticon, which exhibits what I have been calling paradigmatic instance or a "genetic slice."

35. Guénon, *East and West*, 19.

36. Guénon, 19.

37. Guénon, 15.

38. Guénon, 16.

39. Hannah Arendt, *The Origins of Totalitarianism* (San Diego: Harcourt, 1976), 107–8.

40. Guénon, *East and West*, 51.

41. Guénon, 107–8, emphasis mine.

42. Cited in Timothy J. McCune, "The Solidarity of Life: Max Scheler on Harmony of Life with Nature," *Ethics and the Environment* 19, no. 1 (Spring 2014): 49–71, at 57. Cf. Abu Hamid al-Ghazzali's discourse on *qalb*, in *Ihya' 'Ulum al-Din*, 5 vols. (Aleppo: Dar al-Waʿy, 1425/2004), I, 117–22, 209–24.

43. Marshall Hodgson, "The Great Western Transmutation," in *Rethinking World History: Essays on Europe, Islam, and World History*, ed. Edmund Burke, III (Cambridge: Cambridge University Press, 1993), 44–71.

44. Guénon, *East and West*, 119.

45. See, for example, Hallaq, "Was the Gate of Ijtihad Closed?," *International Journal of Middle East Studies* 16, no. 1 (1984): 3–41; Hallaq, *Authority, Continuity and Change in Islamic Law* (Cambridge: Cambridge University Press, 2001).

46. Guénon, *East and West*, 52. On page 37, he restates this opposition, saying that "the two mentalities appear to be decidedly incompatible, but since it is the West that has changed . . . perhaps a moment will come when its mentality will be modified for the better and become open to a wider understanding, and then this incompatibility will vanish of itself."

47. Guénon, 24.

48. Guénon, 24–25, 43, 69–70, 80; Rooth, *Prophet for a Dark Age*, 201.

49. Guénon, *East and West*, 70: "That is what we call 'moralist' hypocrisy: it is unconscious in the masses of the people, who never fail to accept with docility whatever ideas are inculcated, but it ought not to be equally so with everyone, and we cannot admit that statesmen, in particular, are dupes of the phraseology which they use."

50. Guénon, 31.

51. Dussel, "Europe, Modernity and Eurocentrism," *Nepantla* 1, no. 3 (2000): 465–78, at 472.

52. Guénon, *East and West*, 106.

53. It must be clear that in Guénon's usage "proselytizing" is anything but forced religious conversion, hence his unwavering insistence that it is a quality unique to the modern West. Easterners "let others think what they will, and are even indifferent as to what is thought of them. . . . They are not in the least given to proselytizing." Guénon, 26, 72. It is without doubt that the term is solely expressive of forcing others to agree to, adopt, and form themselves according to one's will—in other words, to remold them into different subjects that correspond to the proselytizer's conception of reality, whatever its form at any given point of time. Proselytizing, in sum, is an act of reengineering the Other. Guénon does not quite put it in these terms, but his thrust is unmistakable. See also Guénon, *Crisis of the Modern World*, 97–100.

54. Guénon, *East and West*, 25.

55. Guénon, 71.

56. Guénon, 70.

57. Guénon, 70.

58. Guénon, 71.

59. Guénon, 86.

60. Guénon, 26, 43.

61. The doctrine of progress never makes an appearance in *Orientalism* and is never problematized as a cornerstone of the mainstream Orientalist project. Science and philosophy as such are never implicated in anything to do with the "wider

culture" with which Orientalism stood complicit. And when Western liberal culture "was no more than a form of oppression and mentalistic prejudice," he does not recognize it by its name, liberal culture; it becomes "liberality" (Said, *Orientalism* [New York: Vintage, 2003], 254; page citations in the body of the text are always to this edition). Note the past tense as well. In the use of "liberality" in the past tense, liberalism as a structure of thought and action—as a *process* that extended from the late seventeenth century to the present—is exonerated. Nor does Said even use the words "anthropocentric" or "anthropocentrism." (The word appears three times in his text, all of which are in language he quotes from Anouar Abdel-Malek's "Orientalism in Crisis." Said, *Orientalism*, 97, 98, 108.)

62. Guénon, *East and West*, 95–96.
63. Guénon, 95–96.
64. Guénon, 97.
65. Guénon, 98, emphasis mine.
66. Guénon, 97–99, emphasis mine.
67. Guénon, 77.
68. See introduction, note 15, and chapter 2, note 158.
69. See, however, Guénon, *Crisis of the Modern World*, 141, and note 32 of this chapter.
70. Guénon, *East and West*, 100.
71. Guénon, 100.
72. Exhibited as well in the translation project that Orientalism conducted with overwhelming force, one in which the British excelled over other Europeans, but that was nonetheless devoid, mostly unintentionally, of "any concern for true understanding." Guénon, 96.
73. Herein lies the value of such contributions as that of Gil Eyal, who convincingly argues that in the case of *Mizrahanut* (see chapter 4) a shift in its conceptions of the Orient occurred only after the establishment of the state of Israel and the expulsion of the Palestinians, a shift—tellingly characterized as "disenchantment"—having to do with state formation. Although Eyal's narrative does not focus on Zionist prestate disenchantment (where the Palestinians and their Orient remained integral to the concept of domination of nature), it does complicate Orientalism's configuration through taking seriously state formation and facts on the colonialist ground as determining features of *Mizrahanut*. See Eyal, *The Disenchantment of the Orient: Expertise in Arab Affairs and the Israeli State* (Stanford: Stanford University Press, 2006).
74. Page citations in the body of the text are always to Said's *Orientalism* (New York: Vintage Books, 2003).
75. Said essentially repeats this desideratum in his article "Orientalism Reconsidered," *Cultural Critique* 1 (Autumn 1985): 89–107.

76. In critiquing *The Cambridge History of Islam*, "a regular summa of Orientalist orthodoxy," Said says: "The sections on economic and social institutions, on law and justice, mysticism, art and architecture, science, and the various Islamic literatures, are on an altogether higher level than most of the *History*. Yet nowhere is there evidence that their authors have much in common with modern humanists or social scientists in other disciplines: the techniques of the conventional history of ideas, of Marxist analysis, of the New History, are noticeably absent." Said, *Orientalism*, 305.

77. Rooth, *Prophet for a Dark Age*, 201.

78. Guénon, *East and West*, 81.

79. Guénon, 81.

80. Guénon, 80.

81. See chapter 2, section 3.

82. Guénon, *East and West*, 71.

83. Guénon, 80.

84. Guénon, 81.

85. Kojin Karatani, "Uses of Aesthetics: After Orientalism," *Boundary 2* 25, no. 2 (Summer 1998): 145–60, at 147.

86. Karatani, 151, emphasis mine.

87. Karatani, 153.

88. Harry Oldmeadow, *Journeys East: 20th Century Western Encounters with Eastern Religious Traditions* (Bloomington: World Wisdom, 2004), 189.

89. On the role of critique in subversivity according to Foucault, see chapter 1, section 3.

90. Again, this is to follow on Foucault's problematization of writing. Is the author someone who writes a book, a popular journal article, a memoir, private glosses on the margins of a book, or a letter to a friend?

91. Robert J. C. Young, *White Mythologies: Writing History and the West* (London: Routledge, 1990), 173.

92. Interestingly enough, "dissent" was the very term Said used (in his *Humanism and Democratic Criticism*, ed. Akeel Bilgrami [New York: Columbia University Press, 2004]) in describing the function of democratic and humanistic criticism, the ultimate desideratum of the true scholar and intellectual. See also W. J. T. Mitchell, "Secular Divination: Edward Said's Humanism," *Critical Inquiry* 31 (Winter 2005): 462–71, at 463. Furthermore, as Robert Young argues, "Said's difficulty is that his ethical and theoretical values are all so deeply involved in the history of the culture that he criticizes. . . . Said's culture always remains exclusively European high culture. . . . Nowhere does he feel it necessary to consider the role or significance of anything that does not correspond to the most traditional notions of culture and literature." Young, *White Mythologies*, 172–73.

93. Nonetheless, see next note.

94. I differentiate between systemic and foundational critique in the sense that the former radically transforms an *épistémè* and the system that it drives, including the entirety of its discursive formations, whereas the latter remains within the system but changes the epistemic foundations of a single discursive formation, with the possibility that this change may have ripple effects on other formations, but without effecting a foundational change in them. This distinction is illustrated by the nature of discursivity in Marx and Freud, the latter, as opposed to the former, having advanced a foundational critique. It is in this sense that I think Foucault undertook a categorical lumping of the two intellectual giants.

95. Foucault, "The Subject and Power," in *Power: Essential Works of Foucault, 1954–1984*, ed. James D. Faubion, trans. Robert Hurley et al., vol. 3 (New York: New Press, 1994), 326–48, at 336.

96. Interestingly enough, on the very same page quoted in the previous note (336), Foucault shows an ingenious sensitivity to the implications of asking certain questions that tend to occlude the answer to others. "If . . . I grant a certain privileged position to the question of 'how' [that is, 'how is power exercised?'], it is not because I would wish to eliminate the questions of 'what' and 'why.' . . . To put it bluntly, I would say that to begin the analysis with a 'how' is to introduce the suspicion that power as such does not exist."

4. Epistemic Sovereignty and Structural Genocide

1. Page citations in the body of the text are always to Said, *Orientalism* (New York: Vintage, 2003). In his *Post-Orientalism*, Hamid Dabashi eloquently critiques Said's sweeping brush by noting the attributes of I. Goldziher, one of the greatest Orientalists to have lived. Like Massignon, Goldziher was an "exemplary scholar of unsurpassed brilliance, . . . a humanist with a vast catholicity of learning rarely seen among his peers, a politically alert and intellectually diligent activist who opposed colonialism of all sorts as a matter of moral principle." Yet, Dabashi duly recognizes that "Goldziher's scholarship was integral to a mode of knowledge production at once exceedingly productive and insightful and yet at its very epistemic root predicated on European colonial interests in what they called the 'Orient.'" See Dabashi, *Post-Orientalism: Knowledge and Power in Time of Terror* (New Brunswick, NJ: Transaction, 2009), 107–8. We should remind ourselves that it was also Goldziher who single-handedly destroyed, via that epistemic root, the entire edifice of Islam's prophetic traditions (*hadith*), an act raised to perfection

by Said's Columbia colleague, Joseph Schacht. More importantly, it is the absence of this type of "root" from Guénon that marks this latter as, first, a different type of author and as, second, representing a genuine refutation of Said's categorical brush.

2. W. J. T. Mitchell, "Secular Divination: Edward Said's Humanism," *Critical Inquiry* 31 (Winter 2005): 462–71, at 466–67. Likewise, Ziauddin Sardar, *Orientalism* (Buckingham, PA: Open University Press, 1999), 74, rightly points out that "Said exhibits as much hatred for things non-Western as the Orientalists showed towards things oriental. In his books on Palestine, which even his strongest critics have praised, a distinct dislike for Islam and Islamic culture is more than evident. . . . That religion could have real meaning for people, that it can be just as rational as humanism, are totally alien notions for Said. Hence he retreats into the classical European depiction of the Oriental as a child-like entity driven purely by emotional needs. In Said's vision there is no place for alternatives and in his world there is no place for Islam or Muslims to exist by their own definition."

3. See chapter 1, section 2; chapter 4, section 1; and note 48 of this chapter.

4. See, for instance, the insightful article by Talal Asad, "Thinking About Tradition, Religion, and Politics in Egypt Today," *Critical Inquiry* 42 (Autumn 2015): 166–214.

5. See chapter 5, note 10.

6. I have attempted to address the remaining questions in the preceding chapters.

7. See chapter 4, sections 4 and 6.

8. Gyan Prakash, *Another Reason: Science and the Imagination of Modern India* (Princeton: Princeton University Press, 1999).

9. A leading business school describes its mission thus: "At Columbia Business School, we prepare our students for career success by connecting their classroom education to the trading floors, board rooms, and retail stores where theory is put into practice." www8.gsb.columbia.edu/about-us/theory-to -practice. As telling: "Columbia Business School enjoys many assets, including the valuable expertise and wide-ranging business ties that the Board of Overseers brings to the School community. These profiles of the Board of Overseers members attest to the School's reach across business, government, and the nonprofit sector. More than a distinguished calling card for the School, the Board of Overseers is an active body that supports and extends Columbia Business School's unique brand of education. Board members' expertise and leadership ensure that the School's centers and institutes are more connected to industry. And their involvement with students in the classroom and other settings demonstrates how academic theories influence and come to life in the real world. . . . The Board of Overseers works tirelessly to

promote an environment in which faculty members can advance the School's thought leadership and where students and alumni can continue to lead and shape the world of business in times good and bad. You are invited to get to know the Board of Overseers members, whose leadership and stewardship exemplify the talent of Columbia Business School's more than 40,000 alumni around the world." www8.gsb.columbia.edu/about-us/board.

10. Hallaq, *The Impossible State: Islam, Politics, and Modernity's Moral Predicament* (New York: Columbia University Press, 2013), 110–38.

11. Cited in Hallaq, 98.

12. In my own university, for instance, the department of economics offered, not including the summer session, around 160 courses in 2016. The courses covered everything from introductions to developmental economics and game theory to global economy and corporate finance, but only two or three courses were concerned with what I call ethical problems generated by economic development, and none with ethics or moral philosophy as integral to the training of students. While "dissenting" echoes can be heard in such offerings as "Inequality and Poverty Justice," "Environmental and Natural Resources Economics," and "Logical Limits of Economics," critical discourse stops right here.

13. On moral neutrality/disengagement, see Albert Bandura, "Moral Disengagement in the Perpetration of Inhumanities," *Personality and Social Psychology Review* 3, no. 3 (1999): 193–209.

14. On Petty, see Tony Aspromourgos, *On the Origins of Classical Economics: Distribution and Value from William Petty to Adam Smith* (London: Routledge, 1996). On Mun, see Lynn Muchmore, "A Note on Thomas Mun's 'England's Treasure by Foreign Trade,'" *Economic History Review* 23, no. 3 (1970): 498–503, especially at 503, where the connection between his new economic theories and EIC's colonial ventures is clearly made.

15. See previous note.

16. See chapter 2, section 3.

17. Marjorie Grice-Hutchinson, *The School of Salamanca: Readings in Spanish Monetary Theory, 1544–1605* (Oxford: Clarendon, 1952), 77.

18. O. E. Udofia, "Imperialism in Africa: A Case of Multinational Corporations," *Journal of Black Studies* 14, no. 3 (March 1994): 353–68, at 355–60; see also Bade Onimode, "Imperialism and Multinational Corporations: A Case Study of Nigeria," *Journal of Black Studies* 9, no. 2 (1978): 207–32, at 207: "In Nigeria as elsewhere, the giant multinational corporations are the basic units of imperialism in its contemporary neo-colonial stage."

19. See, for example, Francis O. Adeola, "Environmental Injustice and Human Rights Abuse: The States, MNCs, and Repression of Minority Groups in the World System," *Human Ecology Review* 8, no. 1 (2001): 39–59.

20. Coca-Cola's general conduct has generated much condemnation around the world. In 2006, the University of Michigan, New York University, and other colleges and universities in North American and Europe severed their ties with the corporation on the grounds that it refused an independent, third-party audit of its abuses in Colombia and India. Other groups have also condemned its practices in several other countries, including Peru, Chile, and Guatemala. See also *New York Times*, July 26, 2001.

21. For an excellent account of corporate abuse, see David C. Korten, *When Corporations Rule the World* (West Hartford: Berrett-Koehler, 1995). On the corporation and ethics, see Thomas Donaldson, *Corporations and Morality* (New Jersey: Prentice-Hall, 1982). For American clandestine interventions that were partly conducted on behalf of American corporate interests, see Jonathan Kwitny, *Endless Enemies: The Making of an Unfriendly World* (New York: Congdon and Weed, 1984).

22. Adeola, "Environmental Injustice and Human Rights Abuse," 40: "Among the recent cases of environmental injustice and human rights violations in the Third World are: the murder of Wilson Pinheiro and Francisco 'Chico' Mendes in the Amazon rain forest, the massacre of Father Nery Lito Satur and several others in the Philippines, and the public hanging of Ken Saro-Wiwa and eight other members of the Movement for the Survival of the Ogoni People (MOSOP) in November 1995 in Nigeria. The subsequent detention, torture, and repression of other members of MOSOP are among the most compelling cases of environmental and civil rights transgression in developing nations monitored by Human Rights Watch, Natural Resources Defense Council, Amnesty International, and other Non-Governmental Organizations (NGOs). There have been several other cases of government agents especially in the Third World, adopting a policy of systematic genocide against members of minority groups in order to appropriate their lands and natural resources." See also pages 41, 43–44: "The operations of MNCs [Multi-National Corporations] in underdeveloped nations involve the use of hazardous materials, extraction of natural resource base, environmental degradation, and the spread of toxic materials, emissions of noxious gases, which pose immediate and long-term health risks to the masses. Harper recently described the environmental impacts of MNCs as: 'At their outrageous worst, MNCs have promoted and sold pharmaceutical, pesticides, baby formulas, and contraceptives already banned or restricted as unsafe in their home country in the Third World. . . . They have brokered the international sale of solid and toxic wastes to poor nations. . . . Shipments of toxic industrial and medical wastes arrive in African nations from most European nations and in central America, the Caribbean, Latin America, and Africa from the U.S. MNCs have orchestrated the cutting of rainforests in Indonesia and Malaysia.

Similar to ecological degradation, ecocide, and genocide associated with Multinational Oil Companies in Nigeria, Texaco made a real mess in the Ecuadorian rainforests, where it dominated the nation's oil industry for over 20 years.'" Quotation within quotation from C. L. Harper, *Environment and Society: Human Perspectives on Environmental Issues* (Upper Saddle River, NJ: Prentice Hall, 1996), 373.

23. Philip J. Stern, *The Company-State: Corporate Sovereignty and the Early Modern Foundations of the British Empire in India* (Oxford: Oxford University Press, 2011).

24. A highly representative course offering in a school of international and public affairs is a module entitled "US Diplomacy in Africa." The "course is an introduction to the practice of U.S. diplomacy and statecraft in Africa. State-craft is the *art of applying the power of the state to other states and peoples*. It includes the construction of strategies for securing the national interest in the international arena, as well as the execution of these strategies by diplomats. Diplomacy applies this power by persuasive measures short of war, though it also serves to prepare as often as to avoid war. This course is taught from the point of view of the professional diplomat faced with developing strategies to advance the national interest in the context of a rapidly transforming, complex and multipolar global system. The current U.S. presidential election [2016] and candidate platforms will serve as case studies for students crafting Africa policy for the incoming Administration. Students will learn the tasks and skills of diplomats needed in integrating all elements of national power to successfully advance national interests and manage U.S.—Africa relations in a global context" (emphasis mine). www.columbia.edu/cu/bulletin/uwb/.

25. Maurice Yolles, "A Social Psychological Basis of Corruption and Sociopathology," *Journal of Organizational Change Management* 22, no. 6 (2009): 691–731, at 694.

26. Chapter 2, section 3.

27. Consider, for instance, the Panalba case, involving the pharmaceutical company Upjohn. Despite the fact that the antibiotic was decidedly shown to have serious side effects, including death, and that it "offered no medical benefits beyond those that could be obtained from other products on the market, the board of directors of the firm decided not only to continue marketing and selling the drug, but also arranged to have a judge issue an injunction to stop the FDA from taking regulatory action." When the FDA did finally succeed in having the drug banned in the United States, the firm continued to sell it in foreign countries, a practice that is not uncommon. In a study of this case as an ethical problem, respondents were nearly unanimous in deeming "executives who allow their firm to sell a drug with undisclosed harmful side-effects

as having committed a serious criminal offense, second only to murder and rape." However, "when management and executive training students *were put in a role-playing scenario (as members of a corporate board, faced with the same decision that confronted Upjohn)*, 79% chose the 'highly irresponsible' option, of not only continuing with the sales of the drug, but also taking action to prevent government regulation. The other 21% chose to continue selling the drug for as long as possible, only without trying to interfere with regulatory process. . . . *Not one group chose the 'socially responsible' action of voluntarily withdrawing the drug from the market.* These results were obtained from 91 different trials. . . . It is worth noting that Scott Armstrong, the investigator who conducted these studies, initiated them because he was puzzled by the Upjohn case, and believed that his own students at the Wharton School of Management could not possibly do such a thing. Unfortunately, it was his own students who became the first group to disprove his hypothesis." Joseph Heath, "Business Ethics and Moral Motivation: A Criminological Perspective," *Journal of Business Ethics* 83, no. 4 (December 2008): 595–614, at 598, emphasis mine.

28. See previous note.
29. Clive R. P. Boddy et al., "Leaders Without Ethics in Global Business: Corporate Psychopaths," *Journal of Public Affairs* 10 (2010): 121–38; Boddy et al., "The Influence of Corporate Psychopaths on Corporate Social Responsibility and Organizational Commitment to Employees," *Journal of Business Ethics* 97, no. 1 (November 2010): 1–19.
30. On the correlation between corporate success and psychopathy, see Paul Babiak et al., "Corporate Psychopathy: Talking the Walk," *Behavioral Sciences and the Law* 28 (2010): 174–93.
31. Stevens et al. argue that psychopaths are increasing in the general population and that the "successful psychopath" variety is adequately represented among university undergraduates. Gregory W. Stevens, Jacqueline K. Deuling, and Achilles A. Armenakis, "Successful Psychopaths: Are They Unethical Decision-Makers and Why?," *Journal of Business Ethics* 105, no. 2 (January 2012): 139–49, at 146.
32. Yolles, "A Social Psychological Basis of Corruption and Sociopathology." See also Fred Dallmayr, "The Underside of Modernity: Adorno, Heidegger, and Dussel," *Constellations* 11, no. 1 (2004): 102–20, esp. at 116–17.
33. Although this deviancy is often seen as a virtue, testimonial to the argument I am making here. It should come as no surprise then that in the business world narcissists are seen as good business people who are especially equipped to "bring added value to their organizations." See Alan Goldman, "Personality Disorders in Leaders: Implications of the DSM IV-TR in Assessing Dysfunctional Organizations," *Journal of Managerial Psychology* 21, no. 5 (2006): 392–414, at 410.

34. Heath, "Business Ethics," 598.

35. Heath, 596, 610, his emphasis.

36. Bandura, "Moral Disengagement in the Perpetration of Inhumanities."

37. Heath, "Business Ethics," 605.

38. Heath, 605.

39. "Even mathematics" because of the significant role it played and continues to play in industrial-scientific production geared toward military purposes. That it was the single academic discipline that contributed most to the development of military technology is attested and exemplified in the instructive instance of the rise of the computer, initially a military tool that was popularized much later. It was the German Enigma machine, the Polish Bombe, and especially the Turing machine that formed the genealogical basis of the modern computers, all these being instrumental in the project of domination and bellicosity. The inventers—Marian Rejewski, Gordon Welchman, and Alan Turing, among others—were all talented mathematicians, and heavily involved in the invention of military technology.

40. Karl Löwith, *Meaning in History: The Theological Implications of the Philosophy of History* (Chicago: University of Chicago Press, 1949), 19.

41. The culmination of Orientalist thought about Averroes is to be found most saliently in the work of the major Muslim thinker Muhammad 'Abid al-Jabiri. For a trenchant critique of his work, see Taha Abdurrahman, *Tajdid al-Manhaj fi Taqwin al-Turath* (Casabalnca: al-Markaz al-Thaqafi al-'Arabi, 2007), 29–71.

42. This is in reference to my earlier discussion of such artists as Picasso and Richter. See chapter 1, section 2.

43. Stern, *The Company-State*.

44. See chapter 2, section 4, for a discussion of this theme in the context of a theory of evil.

45. Patrick Wolfe, "Settler Colonialism and the Elimination of the Native," *Journal of Genocide Research* 8, no. 4 (2006): 387–409.

46. Wolfe, 387.

47. See chapter 2, note 108. For a useful summary of these transformations (though by no means exhaustive), see David B. Abernethy, *The Dynamics of Global Dominance: European Overseas Empires, 1415–1980* (New Haven: Yale University Press, 2000), 363–86.

48. In critiquing Said, Sudipta Kaviraj ("Said and the History of Ideas," in *Cosmopolitan Thought Zones: South Asia and the Global Circulation of Ideas*, ed. Sugata Bose and Kris Manjapra [New York: Palgrave Macmillan, 2010], 58–81) argues that Said flattened the power structures in the narrative and practice of colonialism, in effect depriving the colonized of a concept of agency. Referring to Bayly's work on the information order in precolonial India and

its transformation under British rule, Kaviraj commends this work for show-ing the "internal layering and diversity" in a "vast interconnected system. . . . The competencies involved, the skills, orientations, intellectual dispositions, personal and group purposes are all allowed their differentiated positions." Yet, it is "clear that the factual information that the earlier [Indian] order col-lected and classified was subsumed, after the colonial administration stabilised, into a larger cognitive system of radically different kind. But the Indian actors are not deprived of a minimal subjectivity; nor are European actors accorded an expanded sovereignty over the whole intellectual field." The earlier Indian "sophisticated network of collection and interpretation of politically relevant information," which was harnessed "for the use of Indian rulers and elites," was "subsumed" by the British and "supplemented" by "new techniques and requirements of new kinds of information demanded by their adminis-trative techniques. In time, Indians also learn the techniques of a modern cognitive apparatus" and produce "a new order of information about Indian Society." Kaviraj takes into account the rise of nationalism and how it turned the field of history "into one of intense contestation" and "a vast clamour of contending ideas." He concludes this long paragraph by saying that this is "quite unlike the implications often derived from Said's work of a sullen submission to an alien forms of knowledge." Kaviraj, "Said and the History of Ideas," 77–78. Despite the "internal layering and diversity" of such accounts, the fact remains that the entirety of the Indian cognitive structure and orientation "turned" into something else, something that was determined not by a long, historical, internal evolution but by the effective domination of an alien system. As I have argued, if we take away a theology of progress from any such historiography, what remains is nothing more than a rupture in which an intellectual formation was forced to adopt the cognitive struc-ture of an alien Other. That Indians had a space for some maneuver is unde-niable, but this is irrelevant. They chose to die by a proverbial bullet, not by hanging, as I discussed earlier. The real question about agency can be answered only under the assumption of an important hypothetical: Did the Indians want to be ruled by the British in the first place? And assuming they knew what they were getting into in terms of cognitive, structural, environmen-tal, materialistic, and spiritual transformations (all determined by the colo-nizer's systems of knowledge), would they have agreed to the proposition of living under such a system, with its effects on their lives? Indeed, Kaviraj, a little later in the essay, says that the "British information specialists had to depend on native literati for their basic information on Indian society; but the cognitive frame in which that knowledge was included was theirs, not of their native informants." Furthermore, the "implications" derived from Said's work on this point do not account for the larger intellectual landscape from which Said was speaking. I think Said did not work out a clear position on the matter. He condemned colonialist domination of Oriental knowledge but he himself seems to have shunned Oriental traditions and anything that is religious or traditional. We should recall that this was one of the grounds on which he censured Massignon, however highly he regarded him as a "brilliant" intellect. We still don't and will likely never know what Said really approved about the sort of knowledge systems, cultures, and psychologies the Orient itself embodied. For more on the issue of agency, see chapter 2, section 6 and note 135; chapter 3, section 3.

49. Deborah Bird Rose, *Hidden Histories: Black Stories from Victoria River Downs, Humbert River and Wave Hill Stations* (Canberra: Aboriginal Studies Press, 1991), 46.

50. Nur Masalha, *The Palestine Nakba: Decolonizing History, Narrating the Subaltern, Reclaiming Memory* (London: Zed, 2012), 54. See also note 87 of this chapter.

51. Vladimir Jabotinsky, "The Iron Wall: We and the Arabs," originally published in *Rassvyet* 4 (November 1923). I have used both the Lenni Brenner transcription and revision of the text (www.marxists.de/middleast/ironwall /ironwall.htm) as well as a PDF of an earlier translation, http://en.jabotinsky .org/media/9747/the-iron-wall.pdf.

52. Emphasis in original.

53. Emphasis in original.

54. Emphasis in original.

55. Emphasis mine.

56. Martin Heidegger, *The Question Concerning Technology, and Other Essays*, trans. William Lovitt (New York: Garland, 1977), 4, 12: "The possibility of all productive manufacturing lies in revealing. Technology is therefore no mere means. Technology is a way of revealing. If we give heed to this, then another whole realm for the essence of technology will open itself up to us. It is the realm of revealing, i.e., of truth."

57. See chapter 2, section 4, and, by way of contrast, the various contributions in Mohammad Hashim Kamali et al., eds., *Islamic Perspectives on Science and Technology* (Singapore: Springer, 2016).

58. Dominico Losurdo, *Liberalism: A Counter-History*, trans. Gregory Elliott (London: Verso, 2011), 3–4. In this context, see also the insightful analysis in Sankar Muthu, *Enlightenment Against Empire* (Princeton: Princeton University Press, 2003), 271–73.

59. Wolfe, "Settler Colonialism and the Elimination of the Native," 388.

60. This is precisely the limitation in Aijaz Ahmad's critique of Said's work. He was quite right to note that Said erred in seeing Orientalism and various forms of European prejudice as a "trans-historical process of ontological obsession

and falsity," but he too reduces the sources of domination to "colonial capitalism," which in turn "gave rise to other sorts of power." See Ahmad, "Orientalism and After: Ambivalence and Cosmopolitan Location in the Work of Edward Said," *Economic and Political Weekly* 27, no. 30 (July 25, 1992): 98–116, at 105. The question that needs to be asked is whence this "capitalism."

61. It may be argued that the Mongol invasions of the thirteenth century are both comparable and analogous to the European conquests of the Americas but this is a plainly erroneous argument. Despite their extraordinarily destructive effects, the Mongol conquests represented an "event" rather than a structure or a process. They represented a modus operandi of conquest, not a modus vivendi in the world, one that reflects a certain attitude and view of life, humanity, and nature writ large. Once the Mongols accomplished their initial military goals of conquest, they resumed the same modes of governance that had inhabited the world before them. Their three Western Khanates became Muslim and followed, more or less, the same patterns of governance as had existed in Muslim lands earlier, namely, a rule of law under the Shari'a. For a brief but authoritative survey, see Ira M. Lapidus, *A History of Islamic Societies* (Cambridge: Cambridge University Press, 1988), 276–79.

62. See William Cronon, *Introduction to Uncommon Ground: Rethinking the Human Place in Nature* (New York: Norton, 1996), 23–56.

63. This is why the analytical category of "spacio-cide," as suggested by Sari Hanafi, is no more helpful than territory, race, or genocide. See Hanafi, "Explaining Sapcio-cide in the Palestinian Territory: Colonization, Separation, and State of Exception," *Current Sociology* 61, no. 2 (2013): 190–205.

64. Giorgio Agamben, *State of Exception*, trans. Kevin Attell (Chicago: University of Chicago Press, 2005), 23: "In truth, the state of exception is neither external nor internal to the juridical order, and the problem of defining it concerns precisely a threshold, or a zone of indifference, where inside and outside do not exclude each other but rather blur with each other."

65. Hallaq, *Impossible State*, 37–73.

66. Hallaq, 37–73.

67. A. Dirk Moses, "Colonialism," in *The Oxford Handbook of Holocaust Studies*, ed. Peter Hayes and John K. Roth (Oxford: Oxford University Press, 2010), 68–80, at 73.

68. Achille Mbembe, "Necropolitics," trans. Libby Meintjes, *Public Culture* 15, no. 1 (2003): 11–40, at 23: "In modern philosophical thought and European political practice and imaginary, the colony represents the site where sovereignty consists fundamentally in the exercise of a power outside the law (*ab legibus solutus*) and where 'peace' is more likely to take on the face of a 'war' without end."

69. It is used in cognitive psychology in association with cognitive bias.

70. While this continuous quality comports with my general narrative of sovereign domination of man over nature/Other man, Arendt's distinction between genocidal colonialism and the Holocaust seems not only unwarranted but inconsistent with her general narrative about modernity's penchant to dominate "nature." "Far from trying to link European colonialism in Africa to Nazism and the Holocaust, then, the purpose of *The Origins of Totalitarianism* and [Arendt's] oeuvre in this respect was to disentangle them and distinguish the Holocaust from previous genocides." A. Dirk Moses, "Hannah Arendt, Imperialisms, and the Holocaust," in *German Orientalism: Race, the Holocaust, and Postwar Germany*, ed. Volker Langbehn and Mohammad Salama (New York: Columbia University Press, 2011), 72–92, at 78.

71. Fanon as characterized by Nelson Maldonado-Torres, *Against War: Views from the Underside of Modernity* (Durham: Duke University Press, 2008), 95, 100.

72. This is of course not to underrate Fanon's diagnosis but only to insist that the colonial is the clearest manifestation of a pathology that masks its own genealogy in the metropolis. Without this productive metropolitan pathology there can be no colonial pathology.

73. Wolfe, "Settler Colonialism and the Elimination of the Native," 391, a designation he borrows from James M. Mooney, *Historical Sketch of the Cherokee* (Chicago: Aldine Transaction, 1900), 124.

74. Wolfe, "Settler Colonialism and the Elimination of the Native," 392; see also Lorenzo Veracini, *Settler Colonialism: A Theoretical Overview* (London: Palgrave Macmillan, 2010), 56–58.

75. Veracini, *Settler Colonialism*, 53.

76. Aziz Rana, *The Two Faces of American Freedom* (Cambridge, MA: Harvard University Press, 2014), 37–40.

77. A poignant example is the juridicality of dispossessing the Amerindians in the United States. See Robert A. Williams, Jr., *Like a Loaded Weapon: The Rehnquist Court, Indian Rights, and the Legal History of Racism in America* (Minneapolis: University of Minnesota Press, 2005); Williams, *The American Indian in Western Legal Thought: The Discourses of Conquest* (Oxford: Oxford University Press, 1990); Linsday G. Robertson, *Conquest by Law: How the Discovery of America Dispossessed Indigenous Peoples of their Lands* (Oxford: Oxford University Press, 2005).

78. Wolfe, "Settler Colonialism and the Elimination of the Native," 388.

79. For the political uses of the Holocaust as "industry," see Norman G. Finkelstein, *The Holocaust Industry: Reflections on the Exploitation of Jewish Suffering* (London: Verso, 2003).

80. Another dimension of this argument is made in the introduction.

81. Chapter 2, part 2; see also Hallaq, *Shari'a: Theory, Practice, Transformations* (Cambridge: Cambridge University Press, 2009), 396–420.

82. For a particularly insightful political and ethical analysis on the complicity between Zionism and modern forms of knowledge, see Ilan Pappe, *The Idea of Israel: A History of Power and Knowledge* (London: Verso, 2014). See also Gershon Shafir, "Zionism and Colonialism: A Comparative Approach," in *Israel in Comparative Perspective*, ed. Michael N. Barnett (New York: State University of New York Press, 1996), 227–42, at 228. Shafir argues that despite the fact that "Zionist colonization" is a "particular cast," it has "not eliminated its fundamental similarity with other pure settlement colonies" (230). "Pure settlement colony established 'an economy based on white labor' which, together with forcible removal or the destruction of the native population, allowed settlers 'to regain the sense of cultural and ethnic homogeneity that is identified with a European concept of nationality'" (229, his emphasis). See also A. Dirk Moses, "Empire, Resistance, and Security: International Law and the Transformative Occupation of Palestine," *Humanity: An International Journal of Human Rights, Humanitarianism, and Development* 8, no. 2 (Summer 2017): 379–408.

83. See, for instance, Masalha, *Palestine Nakba*, 53–74.

84. Gershon Shafir's argument that Zionists did not have a "colonial metropole" is belied by the very empirical data he provides in his own article (Shafir, "Zionism and Colonialism," 230). While it is true that a mononational colonial metropole did not exist in the case of Zionism, the overall political and financial support the movement received and continues to receive, both directly and indirectly, from the influential diasporic communities more than compensates for that lack. By Shafir's own admission, the survival and relative success of the first Aliya (from 1882 to 1903) were due to the assistance of "a member of the Rothschild family" (232). Furthermore, and particularly since 1973, direct and indirect American financial assistance and near-unqualified political support lend themselves to analysis in terms of settler colony and metropole. On American financial aid to Israel, see Shirl McArthur, "A Conservative Estimate of Total U.S. Direct Aid to Israel: Almost $138 Billion," *Washington Report* (October 2015): 28–30, www.wrmea.org /congress-u.s.-aid-to-israel/u.s.-financial-aid-to-israel-figures-facts-and -impact.html. For an account by year, excluding loan guarantees, see "U.S. Foreign Aid to Israel: Total Aid (1949-Present [2017])," in *Jewish Virtual Library*, www.jewishvirtuallibrary.org/total-u-s-foreign-aid-to-israel-1949-present. Nor is it fortuitous that of the nearly two hundred countries that receive American aid, Israel is by far the largest recipient of military assistance. See "How Does the U.S. Spend Its Foreign Aid?," *Council of Foreign Relations* (April 11, 2017), www.cfr.org/backgrounder/how-does-us-spend-its-foreign-aid.

85. See, for instance, John J. Mearsheimer and Stephen M. Walt, "The Israel Lobby and U.S. Foreign Policy," *Middle East Policy* 13, no. 3 (Fall 2006): 29–87; Mearsheimer and Walt, *The Israel Lobby and U.S. Foreign Policy* (Toronto: Viking Canada, 2007).

86. See Benny Morris, "For the Record," *Guardian*, January 13, 2004: "The newly available material shows that the Israeli critics were wrong: the Zionist leadership in the 1920s, 1930s and 1940s, from David Ben-Gurion, Israel's founding prime minister, through Chaim Weizmann, the liberal president of the World Zionist Organisation, and Menahem Ussishkin and Zeev Jabotinsky, had supported the idea [of transfer]."

87. The leading Zionist Chaim Weizmann once declared that "Palestine shall be as Jewish as . . . America American" and that the native Palestinians were to be regarded as no different than "the rocks of Judea, as obstacles that had to be cleared on a difficult path." See Masalha, *Palestine Nakba*, 54.

88. Golda Meir, Israel's Prime Minister, 1969–74: "It was not as if there was a Palestinian people in Palestine and we came and threw them out and took their country away from them. They did not exist." *Haaretz*, May 3, 2015, www.haaretz.com/israel-news/.premium-1.654218; Raphael Eitan, Israel's Chief of Staff, 1978–83: "When we have settled the land, all the Arabs will be able to do about it will be to scurry around like drugged cockroaches in a bottle." *New York Times*, April 14, 1983, www.nytimes.com/1983/04/14 /world/most-west-bank-arabs-blaming-us-for-impasse.html.

89. Ilan Pappe, *The Ethnic Cleansing of Palestine* (London: Oneworld, 2006), 260.

90. Wolfe, "Settler Colonialism and the Elimination of the Native," 402. See also Amos Goldberg et al., "Israel Charny's Attack on the Journal of Genocide Research and Its Authors: A Response," *Genocide Studies and Prevention: An International Journal* 10, no. 2 (2016): 3–22.

91. Moses, "Colonialism."

92. On this plan in Zionist history, see Nur Masalha, *Expulsion of the Palestinians: The Concept of "Transfer" in Zionist Political Thought, 1882–1948* (Washington, DC: Institute for Palestine Studies, 1992).

93. The distinguished historian Ilan Pappe argues that those "who live under the greatest illusion of safety, the Palestinians of Israel, may also be targeted in the future. Sixty-eight per cent of the Israeli Jews expressed their wish, in a recent poll, to see them 'transferred.'" Pappe, *Ethnic Cleansing of Palestine*, 260.

94. Wolfe, "Settler Colonialism and the Elimination of the Native," 399–400.

95. Walid Khalidi, *All That Remains: The Palestinian Villages Occupied and Depopulated by Israel in 1948* (Washington, DC: Institute for Palestine Studies, 1992).

96. This method, common to all forms of colonialism, constitutes a conscious and deliberate component of Zionist ideology, and has since the end of the nineteenth century. Wolfe, "Settler Colonialism and the Elimination of the

Native," 388, notes: "As Theodor Herzl, founding father of Zionism, observed in his allegorical manifesto/novel, 'If I wish to substitute a new building for an old one, I must demolish before I construct.' In a kind of realization that took place half a century later, one-time deputy-mayor of West Jerusalem Meron Benvenisti recalled, 'As a member of a pioneering youth movement, I myself "made the desert bloom" by uprooting the ancient olive trees of al-Bassa to clear the ground for a banana grove, as required by the "planned farming" principles of my kibbutz, Rosh Haniqra.' Renaming is central to the cadastral effacement/replacement of the Palestinian Arab presence that Benvenisti poignantly recounts." See also Masalha, *Palestine Nakba*, 75–87.

97. Eyal Weizman, *Hollow Land: Israel's Architecture of Occupation* (London: Verso, 2007), 237–58.

98. A list of about fifty discriminatory laws may be found on the site of the advocacy group Adalah, www.adalah.org/en/law/index.

99. George Bisharat, "Violence's Law: Israel's Campaign to Transform International Norms," *Journal of Palestine Studies* 42, no. 3 (Spring 2013): 68–84, at 70.

100. Bisharat, 80.

101. Hagai Amit, "The Dead Sea Is Dying Fast: Is It Too Late to Save It, or Was It Always a Lost Cause?," *Haaretz*, October 7, 2016, www.haaretz.com/ israel-news/business/1.746258. See also "World Bank Overview," http://web .worldbank.org/WBSITE/EXTERNAL/COUNTRIES/MENAEXT /EXTREDSEADEADSEA/0,,contentMDK:21841536~menuPK:5174651 ~pagePK:64168445~piPK:64168309~theSitePK:5174617,00.html.

102. In 2013, Israel ranked as the sixth largest arms exporter in the world. Its sales for that year were 74 percent higher than they were in 2008. "Overtaking China and Italy: Israel Ranks as the World's Sixth Largest Arms Exporter in 2012," *Haaretz*, June 25, 2013, www.haaretz.com/israel-news/.premium-1 .531956.

103. "Israel's War Business," *Der Spiegel*, August 27, 2014, www.spiegel.de/international/world/defense-industry-the-business-of-war-in-israel-a-988245 .html.

104. "'Israel Would Be Embarrassed If It Were Known It's Selling Arms to These Countries,'" *Haaretz*, August 7, 2015: "All countries engage in military exports. The problem is that Israel is involved in places that the United States and Europe decided to avoid exporting weapons to. We know Israel is selling arms to Azerbaijan, South Sudan and Rwanda. Israel is training units guarding presidential regimes in African states. According to reports, this is happening in Cameroon, Togo and Equatorial Guinea—nondemocratic states, some of them dictatorships, that kill, plunder and oppress their citizens."

www.haaretz.com/israel-news/.premium-1.669852. Furthermore, "Israel markets its weapons as 'field tested'—which means they have been trialed using human guinea pigs—Palestinians, or other Arabs during Israel's various wars of occupation and human rights abuses. This is a part of their appeal to unethical governments around the world who buy their weapons from Israeli firms: their arms have proven to be more efficient in killing civilians, so they make an attractive investment for war criminals and torturers around the world." "The Crisis in Israel's Arms Industry," *Middle East Monitor*, November 16, 2015, www.middleeastmonitor.com/20151116-the-crisis-in-israels-arms-industry/.

105. "Israeli Doctors Accused of Collusion in Torture," *World Report* 381 (March 9, 2013), www.thelancet.com/pdfs/journals/lancet/PIIS0140–6736(13)60612–1. pdf; "Israeli Medics Collude with the Torture of Palestinians," *Middle East Monitor*, May 29, 2015.

106. Weizman, *Hollow Land*, 237–58.

107. Gil Eyal, "Dangerous Liaisons Between Military Intelligence and Middle Eastern Studies in Israel," *Theory and Society* 31, no. 5 (October 2002): 653–93. "It is a 'well-known secret' in Israel that scholars of Middle Eastern studies are heavily involved with military intelligence: they serve their reserve duty there, provide research service for it, and when they are interviewed in the media, they speak with the authority of those 'in the know.' The fact that such relations exist, therefore, is well known" (653).

108. In one study, 80 percent of primary school students thought of the Arab as someone dirty; 75 percent thought the Arab to be a murderer and terrorist; 90 percent thought that Palestinians had no right whatsoever to the "land of Israel." See Masalha, *Palestine Nakba*, 238.

109. See Masalha, 237. Another, more recent study has further shown how school textbooks used with Palestinian students in Israel between grades five and twelve are systematically geared to reinforce a narrative in which the Zionist project is legitimized whereas Palestinian history is marginalized and suppressed. "The textbooks . . . divide history into three periods: the ancient, the middle ages, and the modern. These share some commonalities: the centrality of the Jewish contribution to world history and civilization as well as a selective emphasis on history of regions, events, and historical actors related to Judaism—and the marginalization of Arab history [emphasis original]. . . . Generally the books attach Hebrew names to geographical sites that, in the Israeli narrative, are considered part of Biblical Jewish history, regardless of whether these were ever populated or controlled by ancient Israelites. Interestingly enough, the main source of knowledge used in the textbooks pertaining to ancient history is the Jewish Bible rather than more contemporary and scholarly sources. Using the Jewish Bible as a historical text not only politicizes religion, but it transcends historical events, sites, and Jewish

historical figures into a messianic sphere, untouched by scientific scrutiny and unchallenged by other . . . narratives or historical findings. As a result, the Israeli narrative is presented as a set of ideas that are universally true. It provides . . . moral, religious, and political foundations for the exclusive ethnic Jewish claims in Palestine. [The Zionist] struggle is portrayed as acts of liberation from an oppressive rule, that is from the Ottomans, the British, and the Arabs. Simultaneously, the textbooks portray Palestinian resistance to colonialism and Zionism as illegitimate acts of terror. In other words, while Jewish national aspiration for freedom and self-determination are praised, similar Palestinian aspirations are denied and, in many cases, denounced. Moreover, the textbooks criticize both Arab and Palestinian resistance to Zionism, describing Zionism (and British colonialism) as a modernizing force to the 'backward' Palestinian society [emphasis mine]. The Zionists are portrayed as seeking to live in peace with the Arabs, while the Arabs chose to fight against the Jews. . . . The textbooks fail to explain why the Zionist movement, before Palestinian resistance intensified, built exclusive Jewish settlements where only Jews can work. In addition, the textbooks explain such separatist Zionist policies and the creation of an ethno-national political entity by emphasizing the historical victimization and persecution of Jews. However, the textbooks do not discuss the Palestinian refugees, and the reasons behind the loss of their homeland. The textbooks published in the 1960s blame Palestinians for their own tragedy, arguing that Zionist leaders had urged Palestinians not to leave Palestine but stay and live in peace with them. The textbooks published in the 1980s/1990s do not discuss whether and why Palestinians were expelled or fled, nor do they explain why Palestinians have not been allowed to return following the 1948 war." Riad Nasser and Irene Nasser, "Textbooks as a Vehicle for Segregation and Domination: State Efforts to Shape Palestinian Israelis' Identities as Citizens," *Journal of Curriculum Studies* 40, no. 5 (2008): 627–50, at 642–43.

110. See, for instance, the mission statement of the Moshe Dayan Center for Middle Eastern and African Studies, an academic unit of Tel-Aviv University. "Brokering treaties between sworn enemies. Calculating the next moves of international terrorists. Forecasting a future with nuclear neighbors. Without the scholars and analysis of the Moshe Dayan Center for Middle Eastern and African Studies, global democracy would not be the same. . . . With roots stretching back to 1959, the think tank was incorporated into Tel Aviv University six years later. In 1983, friends and admirers of Israel's late military hero and government minister Moshe Dayan raised funds to endow the Center in his name. Working closely with the Israeli government and army, the Dayan Center's international board is chaired by American investment advisor Lester Pollack, who is a long-time supporter of Tel Aviv University and the State

of Israel." www.cftau.org/spotlights/moshe-dayan-center-for-middle-eastern
-and-african-studies/. An earlier incarnation of the Moshe Dayan Center, the
Shiloah Institute, was no less explicit about its political engagements. As Gil
Eyal notes, this Institute "invited military intelligence officers and state officials to become guest researchers, who reside[d] for a year at the institute, and
[made] use of its research facilities. The guest researchers were asked to participate in the institute's regular teamwork, preparing the annual publication
Middle East Contemporary Survey (MECS). They also published their independent research in the Institute's monograph series. Second, they appointed
military intelligence officers and state officials to serve on the permanent
research committee of the institute, responsible for approving research grants,
selecting guest researchers, deciding on team projects, etc." Eyal, "Dangerous
Liaisons Between Military Intelligence and Middle Eastern Studies in Israel,"
679–80.

111. Most memorable of all in my experiences as an undergraduate student of Middle Eastern studies and politics in Israel was Professor David Farhi, a colonel
in the IDF, at the time appointed to the military administration of the occupied West Bank, who used to teach courses on the history of the Ottoman
Empire, attired, often flamboyantly, in full military uniform! On Farhi's
career, see Shlomo Gazit, *Trapped Fools: Thirty Years of Isareli Policy in the Territories* (London: Frank Cass, 2003), 67.

112. Samantha Power, *"A Problem From Hell": America and the Age of Genocide* (New
York: Basic, 2002).

113. On hating the self, see discussion in chapter 2, section 4.

5. Refashioning Orientalism, Refashioning the Subject

1. As I argued in chapter 2, Shari'a in modernity has been eviscerated by both
colonialism and the modern nation-state, rendering at least the institutional
structures defunct. See also Wael Hallaq, "Can the Shari'a Be Restored?," in
Islamic Law and the Challenges of Modernity, ed. Yvonne Y. Haddad and Bar-
bara F. Stowasser (Walnut Creek, CA: Altamira, 2004), 21–53, at 21–22.

2. Whenever the reference is to the Shari'a, my use of the term "legal" connotes
a concept, phenomenon, or category that must always be taken as subservient
to the moral, this latter being an enveloping structure of norms that, conversely, both subordinates and commands the legal. In a system that did not
differentiate between the moral and the legal, but was a comingled admixture
of both (as the Shari'a was for centuries before the onset of modernity), the
segregated uses of the terms, including the "moral," must be understood as

conditioned by modernity's *inescapable* conceptual-linguistic repertoire that insists on corralling the two terms into separate spheres.

3. Any expert in the Shariʿa's history will know that by about 1850, if not somewhat earlier, a dramatic change in the very language, style, modes of reasoning, and structure of the Islamic legal text had already taken place, a change that exhibits an equally phenomenal drop in the intellectual quality of legal discourse and one remarkably alien to any preceding form. Generally on this point, see the useful work of John Walbridge, *God and Logic in Islam: The Caliphate of Reason* (Cambridge: Cambridge University Press, 2013).

4. I use this term entirely in reference to my earlier discussions of central and peripheral domains, and not in its common denotative sense.

5. For this practice, see Hallaq, *The Impossible State: Islam, Politics, and Modernity's Moral Predicament* (New York: Columbia University Press, 2013).

6. An argument advanced in my *Impossible State*, 37–97, as well as in *Shariʿa: Theory, Practice, Transformations* (Cambridge: Cambridge University Press, 2009), 125–221, and, in certain respects, developed further in "Regarding Liberty, Freedom, Representation, and the Rule of Law: How Would the Shariʿa Fare?," an unpublished lecture delivered at the School of Oriental and African Studies, London, February 4, 2014.

7. In many significant ways, the concept "Islam" as a generic category in effect represents a modern translation (often crude and reductive) of the various formations that worked together throughout time and space to produce the conditions of possibility for diverse ways of life that had their common denominator reside in a varied subscription to Islamic conceptions of ethics, morality, mysticism, law, theology, philosophy, and economy, or, at times, in as partial a conception as that of religious works (what were generally identified as ʿibadat). Yet, the *abstracted totality* of the historical interactions between all these conceptions—as well as their implementation in practice—would be claimed, for instance, by newly converted societies as their own, and inherited as a matter of course, as if those societies had always been participants in that history (observe, for example, the history of Islam in the Malay archipelago during the last five or six centuries). It is in this sense that even in hybridity and partiality, these historically claimed formations dictated the actual conditions of the social "subject and the predicate."

8. Foucault, "The Subject and Power," in *Power: Essential Works of Foucault, 1954–1984*, ed. James D. Faubion, trans. Robert Hurley et al., vol. 3 (New York: New Press, 1994), 326–48, at 336.

9. In light of the distinctions made in note 7, the rendering of the formations as an object of inquiry *also* translates into exteriorization, stripping these formations of temporal relevance and historical-teleological validity. This seems to me oppositional to the claimed legacy I have spoken of in that note.

Whereas in the native soil the discursive-cum-applied traditions would be absorbed *post eventum* into the fold as integral to communal memory, they were, at the hands of European philology, not only externalized (psychologically and epistemically) but also lodged in the world of the historical past as irrelevant, save for the scholarly curiosity that aims to "understand" that "museum-situated" culture. In due course, I will note the implications of this exteriorization for my overall argument.

10. Said's humanism is not only "a gesture of resistance and critique," but also part of a distinctly "secular intellectual tradition that sees in unafraid and unapologetic critique the path to human freedom." (See Said, "Presidential Address 1999: Humanism and Heroism," in *Publications of the Modern Language Association of America* [May 2000]: 285–91, at 290–91.) Lumping together and equating "ethnicity and sect" (read political violence) with "tradition" and "religion," Said insists these are "neither adequate as guides to nor useful as modes" for the humanist in "making sense of human history." (See also Gil Anidjar, "Secularism," *Critical Inquiry* [Autumn 2006]: 52–77, at 52–56.) Unlike Scheler and others (including Said's much-admired Vico) who allowed religion the possibility of making as much sense of the world as secular humanist dogma, Said dismissed *both* tradition and religion out of hand, in effect replicating the very biases he critiques in his celebrated book. What remains useful for us in Said's position on humanism is therefore reduced to that "gesture of resistance and critique." (That his definition here remains confined to "gesture," as Orientalist and colonialist practices were confined to a "style" of domination, betrays much about the depth of his engagement.) Humanism then is never concerned with the problems of an anthropocentric existence, as his *Humanism and Democratic Criticism* as well as other writings attest. Said, *Humanism and Democratic Criticism*, ed. Akeel Bilgrami (New York: Columbia University Press, 2004). Even when drawing on Vico, Said argues for taking seriously the philosopher's stubborn insistence that men forge their own path and make their own destiny (through resistance and critique, and perhaps through striving). Yet, Said does not appropriate, and in effect entirely excludes, Vico's idea of the central importance of religion and providence to society, a "scandalous" "detail" that would perhaps tarnish, in Said's mind, Vico's image as an advocate of "human freedom." Unlike Vico, and situating himself at the center-right of the Enlightenment, Said saw a contradiction between religion and freedom, a contradiction resolved by secular humanism. On some aspects of Vico's "scandalous" thought, see Robert C. Miner, *Vico: Genealogist of Modernity* (Notre Dame: University of Notre Dame Press, 2002), 137 and passim.

11. This is of course somewhat of a charitable allowance, since the domination of nature and environmental degradation have been noted as quasi-philosophical

problems by many of the intellectuals I have been citing, including Guénon, Scheler, the early Frankfurt School thinkers, Arendt, and several others.

12. Naomi Oreskes, "The Scientific Consensus on Climate Change: How Do We Know We Are Not Wrong?," in *Climate Change: What It Means for Us, Our Children, and Our Grandchildren*, ed. Joseph F. C. DiMento and Pamela Doughman (Cambridge, MA: MIT Press, 2007), 65–99.

13. See thesis 3 in Dipesh Chakrabarty, "The Climate of History: Four Theses," *Critical Inquiry* 35, no. 2 (2009): 197–222, at 215–17.

14. For a powerful argument in this direction, see Sanjay Seth, " 'Once Was Blind but Now Can See': Modernity and the Social Sciences," *International Political Sociology* 7 (2013): 136–51, especially at 144.

15. In fact, it is plausible to argue, as Andrew Vincent does, that it is the very values and practices of liberal justice theory that "constitute the key environmental danger." Vincent, "Liberalism and the Environment," *Environmental Values* 7 (1998): 443–59, at 443. See also Avner de-Shalit, "Is Liberalism Environment-Friendly?," in *Environmental Philosophy: From Animal Rights to Radical Ecology*, ed. Michael Zimmerman (Upper Saddle River, NJ: Prentice Hall, 1998), 386–406.

16. The minimalism here is intended to avoid entering the fray over whether or not preindustrial societies contributed to the deterioration of environment and ecology. See, in this respect, the instructive arguments made by Chakrabarty, "The Climate of History," and chapter 2, section 4. Nonetheless, these arguments may not be sufficient. Skeptics may still be unconvinced that industrialist society departed radically from earlier epochs of human degradation of the environment, this latter having been less extensive and occurring in piecemeal fashion. But the disagreement cannot be resolved just by recourse to quantitative data. The argument insisting on preindustrial degradation stands in collusion with not only a conception of history that is predeterminative but also one that squarely rests on a dogmatic doctrine of progress. This narrative insists that any society, "civilization," or culture would have done exactly what the West has in fact done had it stood in its place, the logic being that progress is inevitable and that it happens to have (or, alternatively, must have) a price. The question that, among others, is never raised is why such massive degradations didn't take place elsewhere and *before* modern Europe came along. In this narrative, it seems that the questions pertaining to the specific conditions that made destructive modernity possible are readily universalized within a trajectory that knows nothing but predetermined progress. This is not merely a historical force, but metaphysics galore. For more on these themes, see Stephen M. Gardiner, *A Perfect Moral Storm: The Ethical Tragedy of Climate Change* (Oxford: Oxford University Press, 2011).

17. David Schrader, "Living Together in an Ecological Community," *Journal of Philosophy* 7, no. 18 (Fall 2012): 42–51, at 42.

18. For more on relativism, see Thesis Sixteen in Hallaq, "Seventeen Theses on History," in *Manifestos for World Thought*, ed. Lucian Stone and Jason Bahbak Mohaghegh, (Lanham, MD: Rowman and Littlefield, 2017): 199–208.

19. Modernity appears unique in the imperial and "civilization-defined" history of mankind, at least insofar as it is a complex system (perhaps too complex) that has failed to acknowledge and articulate its own metaphysical doctrine. Indeed, any attribution to modern phenomena of a metaphysic has invariably been articulated as a critique of, rather than as an internal elaboration of, the modern project. The denial of the metaphysical doctrinal structure undergirding modernity is, needless to say, deemed both integral and indispensable to the continued justification and survival of the project as a "rational" one—the assumption being that metaphysics is a commodity of myth belonging to a primordial past. See also Jan C. Schmidt, "Defending Hans Jonas' Environmental Ethics: On the Relation Between Philosophy of Nature and Ethics," *Environmental Ethics* 35 (Winter 2013): 461–79, at 467–69.

20. On technique as technology and its determining role on modern life, see Jacques Ellul, *The Technological Society*, trans. John Wilkinson (New York: Vintage, 1964).

21. Whence another contradiction in the modern project ensues. Rationality is presumed to be the foundation of Enlightened modernity that moves in a progressive line, always toward a better future; yet, few would deny that this modernity (or our current condition, at any rate) is heavily involved in less-than-healthy ways of living, engendering a marked increase (rather than decrease) of health, economic, and environmental-ecological problems, among many others. To exonerate rationality of the outcomes of its own work (as in the claim that side effects justify the goal, or that side effects justifiably cannot be foreseen) is to embark on yet another contradiction, namely, that rationality is ipso facto deficient, is unreliable, and cannot provide solutions to the very problems that it, through human agency, creates. This is not all, however. This rationality descends furthermore into metaphysics, the same kind of traditional metaphysics that our secular world vehemently shuns. The stubborn insistence on the belief that our rationality and its resultant sciences can and will accomplish our ideals has developed into a theology, if not a myth, namely, like God, reason and rationality as conceived by modernity must be served irrespective of how punitive they are or might become. This is no different than the inquisition besetting biblical Job, who accepts God's severe punishment in the hope of salvation.

22. Max Scheler, *Problems of a Sociology of Knowledge*, trans. M. Frings (London: Routledge, 1980), 78, 118, 119; W. Stark, *The Sociology of Knowledge* (London: Routledge, 1960), 114–15.

23. A "market" (economic, cultural, and ideational) that was essential for the development of liberalism itself. On the connections between ideals of liberal thought and slavery, violence, colonialism, and horror/demonization, see Dominico Losurdo, *Liberalism: A Counter-History*, trans. Gregory Elliott (London: Verso, 2011); Sven Beckert and Seth Rockman, eds., *Slavery's Capitalism: A New History of American Economic Development* (Philadelphia: University of Pennsylvania Press, 2016); Lisa Lowe, *The Intimacies of Four Continents* (Durham: Duke University Press, 2015); the useful review essay by Panjak Mishra, "Bland Fanatics," *London Review of Books* 37, no. 23 (December 3, 2015): 37–40; and Elisabeth Anker, "The Liberalism of Horror," *Social Research* 81, no. 4 (Winter 2104): 795–823.

24. The Basques, Irish, Galicians, and Catalans being prime examples. For the connections between colonizing Celtic Ireland and the later colonization of North America, see the important work of Aziz Rana, *The Two Faces of American Freedom* (Cambridge, MA: Harvard University Press, 2014), 28–30.

25. I have in mind examples like Louis Massignon and, most notably, René Guénon (see chapter 3).

26. Although it is eminently arguable that, despite the global spread of modern technology and industry, the destructive effects have been far greater on the non-Euro-American world than the latter world was responsible for the causes of destruction.

27. Giorgio Agamben, *The Signature of All Things: On Method* (New York: Zone, 2009), 17.

28. Arran Gare, "MacIntyre, Narratives, and Environmental Ethics," *Environmental Ethics* 20 (Spring 1998): 3–21, at 14; Schmidt, "Defending Hans Jonas," 463.

29. Alasdair MacIntyre, *Whose Justice? Which Rationality?* (Notre Dame: University of Notre Dame Press, 1988), 12.

30. Patrick Joyce, "The Return of History: Postmodernism and the Politics of Academic History in Britain," *Past and Present* 158 (1998): 207–35, at 223.

31. Gare, "MacIntyre, Narratives, and Environmental Ethics," 10.

32. An account of this history may be found in Hallaq, *Shariʿa: Theory, Practice, Transformations* (Cambridge: Cambridge University Press, 2009), 357–550.

33. And in some cases much earlier, as Kaviraj shows (see next note).

34. See, for instance, Pransenjit Duara, *The Crisis of Global Modernity* (Cambridge: Cambridge University Press, 2015); Sudipta Kaviraj, "The Reversal of Orientalism: Bhudev Mukhopadhyay and the Project of Indigenist Social Theory," in *Representing Hinduism: The Construction of Religious Traditions and National Identity*, ed. Vasudha Dalmia and H. von. Stietencron (New Delhi: Sage, 1995), 253–79; Kaviraj, "The Idea of Europe: Bhudev Mukhopadhyay and the Critique of Western Modernity" (unpublished paper); Zhao Tingyang,

"A Political World Philosophy in Terms of All-Under-Heaven (Tian-xia)," *Diogenes* 56, no. 5 (2009): 5–18; Xiang Shiling, "Theory of 'Returning to the Original' and 'Recovering Nature' in Chinese Philosophy," *Frontiers of Philosophy in China* 3, no. 4 (2008): 502–19; Mukul Sharma, *Green and Saffron: Hindu Nationalism and Indian Environmental Politics* (Ranikhet: Permanent Black, 2012); Vandana Shiva, *Biopiracy: The Plunder of Nature and Knowledge* (New Delhi: Natraj, 2102).

35. See chapter 2, section 1.

36. While I take it for granted that nonmodern discourse within modernity is both an ontological and an epistemological impossibility, I draw a distinction between paradigmatic discourse (that which represents the enduring power and perpetuation of the central domains) and subversive discourse (that which is embedded in the multilayered constitution of substantive power, often but not always associated with peripheral domains). (See the discussion in chapter 2, for the distinction between the substance and the mechanics of power.) For instance, a reenchanted philosophy of the world insisting on subordinating capitalism, materialism, and secular humanism to an organicist, mildly mystical, ethico-centric, and nonfragmented/integrated view of the world is no doubt a modern creation and no more than a reenactment of a modern narrative whose authenticity cannot be validated outside of a squarely modern conception of reality. Yet, this very modern conceptualization—integral to the discourse of power—substantively militates against the paradigmatic domains, both as a discourse and as a structure of power. It does so as a substantive alternative to the dominant forms of knowledge and power, an alternative that—by virtue of its drastically different conception of the world—provides a qualitatively and (perhaps "genetically") different kinds of solutions than those produced by modernity's paradigmatic domains.

37. Jackson, "Outer Worlds: The Persistence of Race in Movement 'Beyond the Human,'" *GLQ: A Journal of Lesbian and Gay Studies* 21, nos. 2–3 (2015): 215–18, at 215.

38. Jinthana Haritaworn, "Decolonizing the Non/Human," *GLQ: A Journal of Lesbian and Gay Studies* 21, nos. 2–3 (2015): 210–13, at 212.

39. "Oriental" thus covers Africa and Amerindia as much as Asia or any other place generally outside of Europe.

40. Quoted in Timothy McCune, "The Solidarity of Life: Max Scheler on Harmony of Life with Nature," *Ethics and the Environment* 19, no. 1 (Spring 2014): 49–71, at 57. Cf. Ghazzali's discourse on *qalb*, in *Ihya' 'Ulum al-Din*, vol. 1 (Aleppo, 2004), 117–22, 209–24; Muhammad b. 'Ali al-Hakim al-Tirmidhi, *Bayan al-Farq Bayna al-Sadr wal-Qalb wal-Fu'ad wal-Lubb*, ed. Yusuf Walid Mar'i (Amman: Mu'assasat Al al-Bayt al-Malakiyya lil-Fikr al-Islami, 2009).

41. 'Ali b. Muhammad al-Sharif al-Jurjani, *Kitab al-Taʿrifat*, ed. M. Marʿashli (Beirut: Dar al-Nafaʾis, 2007), 259.

42. McCune, "Solidarity of Life," 57.

43. Boyle's own characterization. See Akeel Bilgrami, "Gandhi, Newton, and the Enlightenment," in *Values and Violence*, ed. I. A. Karawan et al. (New York: Springer, 2008), 15–29.

44. Karen Bardsley, "Mother Nature and the Mother of All Virtues: On the Rationality of Feeling Gratitude Toward Nature," *Environmental Ethics* 35, no. 1 (Spring 2013): 27–40, at 27–28.

45. Ronald Aronson as cited in Bardsley, 28.

46. Obviously, secularism and atheism are not interchangeable categories, but the secularist relegation of God and religion to the private domain makes both the secularist and the atheist, insofar as the problem of ingratitude is concerned, equally antithetical to theism.

47. This is not to privilege modern religionists, for these tend to see and live in the world in a vein similar to their secularist counterparts. What applies to art and aesthetics in the modern central domains applies to religion as well. See chapter 1, section 2.

48. Bardsley, "Mother Nature," 37–38.

49. Bardsley, 38.

50. Bardsley, 39–40.

51. A theme I have considered in *The Impossible State*, 89–93.

52. Taha Abdurrahman, *Suʾal al-Akhlaq: Musahama fi al-Naqd al-Akhlaqi lil-Hadatha al-Gharbiyya* (Casablanca: al-Markaz al-Thaqafi al-ʿArabi, 2000), 59, 78–80. For the relationship between "speech" and the question "what should I do?" see Abdurrahman, *Suʾal al-ʿAmal: Bahth ʿan al-Usul al-ʿAmaliyya fil-Fikr wal-ʿIlm* (Casablanca: al-Markaz al-Thaqafi al-ʿArabi, 2012), 13–37 and passim.

53. The same can be said of the otherwise admirable efforts of Claudia Card, who aims to show, on what she calls "the capacity interpretation," that "intolerable harm [to nonsentient nature] can consist in diminishing or destroying functional capacities central to the meaning or value of life, when that life is sufficiently complex in its capacities for realizing positive values that it has a welfare or, as some would say, 'a good of its own.' " "And if flora are included with fauna among the victims of culpable wrongs that are destructive of species and ecosystems, the evil of environmental atrocities is deeper and more extensive than many may have thought, regardless of whether species and ecosystems are living beings." See Claudia Card, "Environmental Atrocities and Non-Sentient Life," *Ethics and the Environment* 9, no. 1 (2004): 23–45, at 27 and 42. What is remarkable about Card's argument is that it illustrates discussions in environmental moral philosophy that inch toward a concept of

evil that is a secularized form of Christian concepts. This, in other words, seems to me to represent the latest installment in the transpositional relationship between Christian and secularist concepts, where the latter become a transformed version of the former, just as with political concepts. The problem with such transpositions is that they jettison much of their epistemic and ethical foregrounding, leaving them floating without a proper subjectification. Like Bardsley, Card does not attend to the subject and the necessity of its revaluation, if not reconstitution. The insertion of a secularized form of evil to the debate does little work, if any at all. See also Kathryn Norlock, "The Atrocity Paradigm Applied to Environmental Evils," *Ethics and the Environment* 9, no. 1 (Spring 2004): 85–93.

54. Foucault also sums up the entirety of the modern struggle and resistance against forms of power in such terms. "All these present struggles revolve around the question: Who are we? They are a refusal of these abstractions, of economic and ideological state violence, which ignore who we are individually, and also a refusal of a scientific or administrative inquisition that determines who one is." See Foucault "The Subject and Power," 331. In fact, this very question is declared by Foucault to be his chief, if not sole, interest in scholarship. He wrote that his work is not, properly speaking, about "the phenomenon of power," but rather about the formation of the subject, how the human is formed into a particular subject. Foucault, 326–27.

55. McCune, "Solidarity of Life," 58.

56. Scheler, "Man in the Era of Adjustment," in *Philosophical Perspectives*, trans. Oscar A. Haac (Boston: Beacon, 1958), 114.

57. Scheler, 113; McCune, "Solidarity of Life," 61.

58. Vincent, "Liberalism and the Environment."

59. The ultimate cause for the rise of the unprecedented discipline of psychoanalysis and related fields of inquiry.

60. Scheler, "Man in the Era of Adjustment," 115: "Man must again learn to grasp the great, invisible, mutual solidarity of all beings in total life, of all spirits in the eternal spirit, and, simultaneously, the solidarity of the world process with the evolution of its first cause and the solidarity of this cause with the world process. Man must accept this relatedness of the world, not only as a theory, but also live it and practice and activate it externally and internally. God's essence is no more 'lord' of the world than man is 'lord and king' of creation, but both are, above all, companions of each other's fate, enduring, overcoming, some day perhaps victorious" (his emphasis).

61. On moral benchmark, see chapter 2, section 3.

62. See, in this regard, Joseph Massad's observations in "Orientalism as Occidentalism," *History of the Present* 5, no. 1 (Spring 2015): 83–94.

63. The reemergence of *longue durée* history (particularly as exemplified in J. Guldi and D. Armitage, *The History Manifesto* [Cambridge: Cambridge University Press, 2014]) suffers from certain structural problems, on the grounds of modernist and largely Eurocentric standards, but also on the grounds that this conception of *longue durée* fails to give credit to (or even understand the significance of) circulatory history, stubbornly insisting on linear and singular historical time.

64. Not to mention the anachronistic implications of such projects, implications that have far too long escaped the standard definition of anachronism.

65. The most intellectually problematic of such research questions is the "Weberian" sort, which proceeds with an inquiry, posited as self-evident, as to why a certain concept or practice "did not develop" or "failed to develop" in Islam (or anywhere else in Asia and Africa), where the governing assumption is the success of the concept or practice in modernity.

66. Other effects are discussed in Hallaq, "Groundwork of the Moral Law: A New Look at the Qur'an and the Genesis of Shari'a," *Islamic Law and Society* 16 (2009): 239–79; Hallaq, "Qur'anic Constitutionalism and Moral Governmentality: Further Notes on the Founding Principles of Islamic Society and Polity," *Comparative Islamic Studies* 8, nos. 1–2 (2012): 1–51; Hallaq, "Quranic Magna Carta: On the Origins of the Rule of Law in Islam," in *Magna Carta, Religion and the Rule of Law*, ed. R. Griffith-Jones and Mark Hill (Cambridge: Cambridge University Press, 2014), 157–76.

67. Omar Farahat, *Between God and Society Divine Speech and Norm-Construction in Islamic Theology and Jurisprudence* (Cambridge: Cambridge University Press, forthcoming), Ms. 98–158, esp. 102–3, 146–58, and 189–99, https://search .proquest.com/docview/1851256301?accountid=15172.

68. For Western anxieties about tyranny and projection of this fear onto Islam as a form of "Oriental despotism," see Ivan Kalmar, *Early Orientalism: Imagined Islam and the Notion of Sublime Power* (London: Routledge, 2012).

69. Hallaq, *Impossible State*, 111–12. Some of my critics have rushed to the claim that I do not account for the premodern origins of the question "Why be moral?" They must have forgotten to read my three long footnotes (notes 56–58, at pp. 202–3) to the two paragraphs on this question in my book, where I explicitly say that the question was discussed in Plato's *Republic*.

70. See chapter 2, section 7, and chapter 4, section 5.

71. Hallaq, *Shari'a*, 159–221; Hallaq, *Impossible State*, 37–97; Hallaq, "Qur'anic Constitutionalism and Moral Governmentality."

72. M. Foucault, "Technologies of the Self," in *Ethics, Subjectivity and Truth*, ed. P. Rabinow (New York: New Press, 1994), 223–51, at 226.

73. The assumption being that violence extends over a wide typological spectrum, ranging from the natural violence of birth (seen, if at all, as happy and

blissful violence) to the coercive violence involved in cultivating the disciplinarian technologies of the moral self, a type that one may characterize as ethical violence.

74. Walter Mignolo, *The Darker Side of Western Modernity* (Durham: Duke University Press, 2011), 30.

75. These modernist religious convictions (like all convictions of traditional religion) also entail the derivative dogma that no modern form can be inferior to its premodern predecessor(s) or analogue(s). Thus, a claim to the effect that, say, the Islamic premodern conception of the rule of law is as robust as, if not more robust than, the Euro-American model is dismissed out of hand, without evidence whatever, as preposterous or mythical. What is not seen as preposterous is the power that this dogma exercises over modernist minds, one that is self-justifying and entirely resting on unfounded supremacist ideology.

76. See the instructive debate between A. Dirk Moses and Hayden White in *History and Theory* 44, no. 3 (October 2005): 311–32 (Moses); 333–38 (White); and 339–47 (Moses).

77. F. Nietzsche, "On the Uses and Disadvantages of History for Life," in *Untimely Meditations*, trans. R. J. Hollingdale (Cambridge: Cambridge University Press, 1997), 59–123. I am perfectly aware that Nietzsche may have changed his mind about the concept of history he outlines in this essay, but the magisterial vision and philosophical tour de force of this discursive fragment do not diminish in the least just because its author changed his view, if he indeed did. For Nietzsche's change of mind, see Thomas H. Brobjer, "The Late Nietzsche's Fundamental Critique of Historical Scholarship," in Nietzsche on Time and History, ed. M. Dries (Berlin: Walter de Gruyter, 2008), 51–60. Curiously, in the concluding paragraph (p. 59), Brobjer concedes on behalf of Nietzsche the very grounds on which the latter is alleged to have "abandoned" his essay. An insightful analysis of Nietzsche's concept of monumental history and its relevance (contra Brobjer) to his later philosophy may be found in Scott Jenkins, "Nietzsche's Use of Monumental History," *Journal of Nietzsche Studies* 45, no. 2 (Summer 2014): 169–81.

78. See note 75 of this chapter, but also the case that Dipesh Chakrabarty makes against Natalie Zemon Davis with regard to "magical" historiographical proofs, in Chakrabarty, "The Politics and Possibility of Historical Knowledge: Continuing the Conversation," *Postcolonial Studies* 14, no. 2 (2011): 243–50, at 247–50. Chakrabarty's argument for his position against Davis remains defensive, poignantly pointing to the fact that history's "success as a hegemonic knowledge-form . . . depends on the destruction of the society that made some humans history-poor to begin with" (249). Chakrabarty

does not go down the philosophical path to argue that the inescapable meta-physics that modern historiography cannot but assume (knowingly or not) as constitutive of its own foundations is no less mythical precisely because it rests on a particular conception of metaphysics, not least of which are the linear, singular, progress-based dogmas.

Index

Abbasid caliphate, 70, 286n77

Abdel-Malek, Anouar, 1, 2, 7, 285n59

Abdurrahman, Taha, 242, 290n15

academia: and collective/institutional sociopathology, 24, 186, 190, 192–93, 325n31; and the corporate world, 103–4, 186–92, 196–97, 286n73, 305n127, 321–22n9, 323n20; and the creation of sovereign knowledge and practice, 24, 277–78n43; critical thought and "thinking the world," 103, 304n124; currently undergoing self-evaluation, 243–44; departments classified into central or peripheral domains, 24, 25, 194–96; fundamental questions for scholars, 248; funding for, 102–3, 303–4n120; implicated in genocide, 24, 67; implicated in the same sovereign project as Orientalism, 23–24, 186, 194–96, 277–78n43; implicated in unethical sovereign practices, 184–87, 190–93, 324–25n27;

intertwined with colonialism, 24, 197, 223–24; Israeli academia, 223–26, 334n107, 334–35n109, 335–36n110, 336n111; and liberalism, 23, 238–39, 264, 305n127; moral and ethical education, or lack thereof, 186–87, 322n12; and the normalization of structural genocide, 214; opening critical space for scrutiny of, 25; Orientalism of a piece with, for Guénon, 177, 181; Orientalism seen by Said as anomaly/ exception within, 165, 177–78, 181–82, 319n76; Orientalism's similarity to other fields, 183–84; psychopathology and sociopathology in, 192, 197, 325n31; reasons for rise of Western academia, 69–70; Said's influence on, 173–74; scholar's ethical/moral responsibility, 264–67; single-discipline focus of, 73; and the state's sovereign will, 102–4, 303–4n120, 324n24; this book's

[349]

academia (*continued*)

place in the landscape of, 25–26. *See also* business schools; scholarship; *and specific fields or areas of study*

Actor Network Theory, 199. *See also* Latour's Stone

adab, 3, 73, 74

adat, 127–30, 132

Adeola, Francis O., 323–24n22

Adorno, Theodor W., 111, 158, 272n22

Aeschylus, 27, 28, 33, 39, 45, 50, 58–59

aesthetic appreciation, 169–70

Africa: genocides against Africans, 87; Islamic cultures in, 73, 78, 109–10, 119, 124 (*see also* Algeria, French colonialism in); Israeli arms and military training in, 333–34n104; multinational corporations and imperialism in, 189, 322n18, 323n20, 323–24n22. *See also* Nigeria

Agamben, Giorgio, 207, 240, 329n64

agency, theory of: about, 108; agency of Palestinians, in Jabotinsky's construction, 200–202; agency vs. presence, 199, 202 (*see also* Latour's Stone); colonialism and agency, 21, 108–9, 199, 215, 307n135, 327n48; and the history of the Muslim world, 107–8, 109; individual agency disallowed by Foucault and Said, 2; Said's concepts of, 307n135

Ahmad, Aijaz, 328–29n60

Algeria, French colonialism in, 17–18, 27, 116–24, 127, 162, 216. *See also* French Orientalism

Allen, Amy, 110

the Americas: Amerindians and Latour's Stone, 216; Britain's sovereign domination over North American settlers, 212; corporate exploitation in South and Central America,

189–90, 323n20, 323–24n22; Orientalism and, 105; racism in, 205; settler colonialism and genocide in, 20, 86–87, 198, 206, 217

Amerindians. *See* the Americas

the "ancient" (concept), 180–81

Andalusia, 86, 298n66

Anglo-Muhammadan Law (India), 119, 135. *See also* India, British colonialism in

Anidjar, Gil, viii, 55, 297n62

Anievas, Alexander, 276n39

Anscombe, E. M., 93

anthropocentrism, 217; benefits tied to pervasive destruction, 234; as central domain of modernity, 4, 105; classical Islam's nonanthropocentrism, 81; failure of, 4, 5, 245; of mechanical philosophy, 95–96; Scheler on, 254; of secular humanism, 5, 110, 183, 232, 314n6, 338n10 (*see also* secular humanism); shedding, 25. *See also* modernity

anthropology, 4, 6, 15, 25, 69–70, 164, 243, 289n6

Apter, Emily, 54–55, 275n33

Arabs, 70, 221, 332n93. *See also* Islam; Islam, premodern; Palestine and Palestinians

Arendt, Hannah, 154, 163, 194, 214, 330n70

Aristotle, 45, 84, 151

Armenakis, Achilles A., 325n31

the arts: capitalism and, 35, 36, 281nn21–22; located in peripheral domains, 194–96. *See also* Picasso, Pablo; literature; music

Asad, Talal, 298n64

assimilation: in French-occupied Algeria, 122; in Guénon's thought, 161–62, 167

atheism, 249–50, 343n46. *See also*
secular humanism
Auerbach, Erich, 54
Austin, J. L., 39, 45, 61–63, 283n34
the author: allowing for the author's
"determining imprint," 22; death of
(dead author), 26, 42, 44, 45, 47, 169,
173, 190–91; determining imprint
determined within a system, 39;
determining imprint of certain
Orientalists, 140; determining
imprint of some Enlightenment
authors, 37; determining imprints
and the rise of central domains,
40–41; dissenting authors, 171–75,
319n92 (*see also* Said, Edward);
Foucault's theory of, 41, 42–49, 171,
174–77, 190–91, 319n90, 320n94,
383–84n39; Hallaq's conception of
critique fundamental to theory of,
66–67; the ideological author, 45,
47–49 (*see also* Foucault, Michel:
theory of the author); importance of
a theory of, 23, 30; individual
author's intention vs. the use of their
work within in the system, 146–47,
158, 315n13, 317n49; Marx and
Freud as discursive authors, 43,
47–49, 171, 174–75, 320n94 (*see also*
Freud, Sigmund; Marx, Karl);
originality of, 32–33, 39;
relationship of authors to paradigms
and domains, 11, 14, 33–34; Said's
choice of subject authors, 10, 39, 49,
271–72n17; Said's conception of, 9,
30–33, 39, 41–42, 49, 242, 280n10
(*see also* Said, Edward: understanding
of Foucault); subversive authors, 23,
105, 138, 143, 171–72, 174–75, 176
(*see also* Guénon, René); writing in
premodern Islamic scholarship, 75.

See also discursive formation(s); *and
specific individuals*
Averroes, 194, 326n41

Bacon, Francis (painter), 35
Bacon, Francis (philosopher), 94, 153,
299n78, 301n101
Barad, Karen, 62, 63
Bardsley, Karen, 249–53, 255, 263
Barthes, Ronald, 44, 60
Bauman, Sigmund, 214
Bayt al-Hikma (Baghdad), 70, 289–90n9
Beginnings: Intention and Method (Said),
313–14n3
benchmark, ethical: central domains
and, 34, 257, 293n37; and the
concept of the rule of law in
premodern Islam, 80–84; defined,
79; and juristic personality, 79–80;
premodern power/force and, 199;
presence/absence of, and the
European model of modernity, 3,
18–20, 152, 209. *See also* ethics and
ethical conduct; morality
Benjamin, Walter, 110–11
Bentham, Jeremy, 234
Benvenisti, Meron, 333n96
Berlin, Isaiah, 151–53, 186. *See also*
negative liberty
Bessie, Adam, 305n127
Bhabha, Homi, 108–9, 307n135
Bilgrami, Akeel, 51, 285n62
biopower (biopolitical power), 16, 82,
84, 231, 295n56, 297n59. *See also*
power
Biruni, Abu Rayhan Muhammad ibn
Ahmad Al-, 61, 289n6
Bisharat, George, 222
Blake, William, 278n43
Bookchin, Murray, 85
Bowden, Brett, 306n133

Boyle, Robert, 95–96
bracketing, 169–70
Britain. *See* Great Britain
British Orientalism, and juridicality, 56,
131–36, 196, 312n180. *See also* Jones,
Sir William
Buddhism, 11, 187, 255, 257, 262
business (academic field) and business
schools: classified in central domain,
187–88; and the creation of sovereign
knowledge and practice, 24, 186,
187–88, 190–92, 321–22n9; existence
of, as academic discipline, 15, 70,
196; objectivity and detachment in,
96; Orientalism compared to,
183–84; scrutiny of, 25. *See also* the
corporation; economics
Butler, Judith, 62, 176

Cahen, Claude, 30, 42
The Cambridge History of Islam, 285n60,
319n76
capitalism: Asian cultures and,
276–77n39; as a central domain or
paradigm, 4, 11, 12, 34–35, 37, 40,
66, 92, 105, 152, 196, 236 (*see also*
modernity); and the colonial project,
118–20, 196 (*see also* Algeria, French
colonialism in); and education and
the structuring of the modern state,
100, 101; the Enlightenment and, 92,
231; and ethical precepts/moral
value, 157, 186–90, 235–36 (*see also*
ethics and ethical conduct); and the
fine arts, 36, 281nn21–22; Guénon
on, 146, 157 (*see also* materialism);
Islamic cultures and, 209, 231,
274n28; Keynes's dissenting critique
of, 173; knowledge forms governing,
266; laissez-faire system of, 48; the
market and unethical/criminal

conduct, 193–94; Marx's discourse
and, 48, 205 (*see also* Marx, Karl);
modern man as *homo capitalisticus*,
254; Ottoman Empire and the rise
of, 276n39; paradigmatic critique of,
66; and positive vs. negative liberty,
152, 157; revaluation of, 233, 244,
247, 342n36; and the rise of
modernity, 40; Said and, 160, 164,
174, 329n60; subordinate status in
Islamic and Asian traditions, 247;
subordinate to human value, 247–48.
See also the corporation; materialism
Card, Claudia, 343–44n53
Carlyle, Thomas, 277–78n43
central domain(s): academic departments
belonging to, 24, 194, 326n39
(*see also specific fields of study*);
capitalism as, 4, 11, 12, 34–35, 66, 92,
105, 152, 196 (*see also* capitalism);
changes/shifts in, 40–41; core
Enlightenment project as, 37, 282n28
(*see also* the Enlightenment); cultures
and, 12, 73; defined (Schmitt's notion
of), 34; and discursive formations,
47–48, 194–95; dominance proved
by exceptions, 11 (*see also* state of
exception); domination over nature
as, 96 (*see also* domination of nature);
domination (will to power) woven
into modernity's central domains, 91;
Enlightenment philosophy as, 184;
and ideal values, 38; modern vs.
indigenous, 313n1; opposing forces
within, 138, 313n1; Orientalism and,
105, 240 (*see also* Orientalism);
paradigmatic critique unable to issue
from within, 66; peripheral domains'
relationship to, 35–36, 37–38 (*see also*
peripheral domains); power relations
and, 38–39; of premodern Islamic

Comte, Auguste, 153–54

conquest, by premodern/non-Western cultures, 87, 206, 329n61

Constitution (U.S.), 205

contrast as epistemology, 11, 15, 16, 33, 34, 127

the corporation: and academia and economic discourse, 103–4, 186–89, 191–92, 196–97, 286n73, 305n127, 321–22n9; colonialist/imperialist role, 188–90, 322n18; company Orientalism omitted from Said's narrative, 57, 286n73; environmental injustice/damage, 189–90, 323–24n22; human rights and labor abuses, 189–90, 323nn20, 22; juristic personality, 80; multinational corporations in Africa, 189, 322n18, 323n22; opposed on moral grounds, 79–80, 192, 293–94n38; pathologies and unethical conduct, 186, 188–94, 232, 323n20, 323–24n22, 324–25n27; rise of, 79–80, 188, 212–13. See also East India Company

Council of Vienna, 28, 70, 297n62

creation (genesis), Christian conception of, 89–90. See also domination of nature

criminality, 193–94, 211, 324–25n27, 333–34n104. See also ethics and ethical conduct

critique: critical secularism, 54–55 (see also secular humanism); Hallaq's conception of, 66–67, 320n94; Said on the function of, 319n92; systemic vs. foundational, 320n94; Wacquant on critical thought, 304n124. See also specific authors, and specific subjects of critique

Cronon, William, 206

Crosby, Alfred W., 288–89n5

culture: constituted/driven by central domains/paradigms, 12, 73 [see also central domain(s); paradigm(s)]; and the existence of the "Other," 58, 286–87n80; in Said's works, 141–42, 160, 174, 277–78n43, 317–18n61, 319n92 (see also Said, Edward; and specific works). See also specific cultures and regions

Culture and Imperialism (Said): academia and "culture" elided into analytical mode of literary crisis, 277–78n43; on colonialism and "mythmaking," 68, 288–89n5; coloniality of literature exposed, 195; on cultural resistance, decolonization, and Third World nationalism, 307n135; humanization of the colonized in, 275n33; importance (monumentality) of, 13; on openings and fissures as sites of critique, 279n45; Said's literary method in, 271n16; unidirectionality from Orient to Occident within, 53

Dante, 33, 45, 50, 58–59

decolonization, Said on, 307n135

deist movement, 87, 94–95

de Lesseps, Ferdinand, 57

Descartes, René, 86

detachment, 96

determining imprint. See under the author

Deuling, Jacqueline K., 325n31

Dickens, Charles, 278n43

difference: Massignon on the difference between East and West, 180; in Said's works, 12, 51–52, 68–69, 140–43, 156, 179, 285n60. See also distance, as epistemology

dignity, human, 92–93

diplomacy, 190, 324n24

directionality (in Said), 52–57, 142, 156

discursive formation(s): Foucault on discursive authors, 42–43, 46–48, 171–72, 174 (*see also* the author: Foucault's theory of; Freud, Sigmund; Marx, Karl); Guénon on the dialectical function of Orientalism, 163–64; Orientalist project masked by "scholarly" cloud, 120; originality subject to perspectivism of, 39; performativity of, 176 (*see also* performativity); relationship to central domain, 47–48, 194–95 [*see also* central domain(s)]; Said's understanding of Foucault on, 29–30, 139. *See also* academia; the author

discursive subversivity, 39–40, 48, 140, 245, 342n36. *See also* subversive authors

dissenting authors, 171–75, 319n92. *See also* the author; Said, Edward; *and specific works*

distance, as epistemology, 50–52, 57–59. *See also* difference

the Distinction: about, 85, 297nn60–61; as dominating problem in moral thought, 92, 184; and Dutch colonialism, 125; and French colonialist policies, 121; Guénon's critique and, 149–50, 157; in Jabotinsky's "The Iron Wall," 201; and modern legal positivism, 260–61; and the modern state, 113–14; no narrative of genealogy of, 185; and Orientalism and colonialism, 105–6; primacy of, 185, 206–7; Said blind to effects of, 232; science and, 77; Shari'a legal tradition and, 292n28; and the sovereignty of human reason,

93 (*see also* sovereignty); validity of, 93; value removed from nature and humans by, 204–5

domination (generally): as ontological sovereignty, 91–93; use of term, 96–97. *See also* domination of nature; domination over the Other; domination over the self; sovereignty

domination of nature: attempts to universalize, 88, 299n72; canonization of, 96; colonialism and the environment, 97, 288–89n5 (*see also* environmental degradation); corporate exploitation of resources and environmental harm, 189 (*see also* the corporation); the Distinction as justification, 93–94, 204–5; Enlightenment concept of nature defined by sovereignty, 98; and French colonialist policies, 119 (*see also* Algeria, French colonialism in); Islam's conception of the world vs., 81; in Israel, 218, 224; in Jabotinsky's "The Iron Wall," 201; origins in European Christian dogma, 85–91, 94–95, 298nn64, 66, 299n72, 299–300n78; philosophy and science and, 184–85, 338n11 [*see also* philosophy; science(s)]; by premodern/non-Christian peoples, 88; rejected by Asian environmental voices, 244; Scheler on, 92–93, 254; transforming into attitude of harmony, 254–55; Zionism and Palestinians as example, 218 (*see also* Israel). *See also* environmental degradation; sovereignty

domination over the Other: by Islamic empires/kingdoms, 97; in

Jabotinsky's "The Iron Wall," 200–202; racial theories and, 205–6 (*see also* racism); remaking the Other in the Western image, 120, 131, 141, 159–60, 198. *See also* colonialism; genocide, colonialism and; racism; sovereignty

domination over the self, 90–91, 93–94

Dussel, Enrique, 86–87, 158–59, 185, 276n38, 298n66

Dutch colonialism in Indonesia. *See* Indonesian Archipelago, Dutch colonialism in

Dutch Orientalism, 127–30

the East. *See* the Orient

East and West (Guénon), 169. *See also* Guénon, René

East India Company (British), 188, 212–13. *See also* British Orientalism, and juridicality; India, British colonialism in

ecological crisis. *See* environmental degradation

Ecological Imperialism (Crosby), 288–89n5

economics (academic field): classified in central domain, 4, 24, 25, 187–88; and the corporate world, 187–90, 192, 286n73, 321–22n9; and the creation of sovereign knowledge and practice, 24, 103, 164, 186–92, 267, 286n73, 321–22n9, 322n12; existence of, as academic discipline, 15, 69–70, 195, 196; objectivity and detachment in, 96; scrutiny of, 25; specialization of, 183–84, 186

education, in premodern Islamic cultures, 73–78, 115, 129, 267, 290nn12, 19, 291n23, 292nn30–31. *See also* Islam, premodern

education, modern: constitution of new human subject through, 16; Dutch educational system in Indonesia, 130; and the formation of the citizen, 101; Israeli education (primary and secondary), 225, 334n108, 334–35n109; as means of Westernizing colonized peoples, 160; moral and ethical education, or lack thereof, 186–87, 322n12; and the state's sovereign will, 100–101. *See also* academia

Egypt, 69, 287n80, 312n184

Eitan, Raphael, 332n88

Eliade, Mircea, 170

Emon, Anver, 302–3n110

engineering (academic field), 4, 15, 77, 183–84, 224, 243–44

the Enlightenment: as break from preceding paradigms, 272n19; and colonialism, 282n28 (*see also* colonialism); core project of, 36–37; and domination of nature, 86, 94–96, 98 (*see also* domination of nature); individual and corporate exemplars of, 88, 299n69; Muthu's effort to pluralize, 282n28; as a paradigm, 36–37; as process of secularization, 86, 87, 298nn64, 66; rationalism, 92–93, 113, 234; and the relationship of knowledge and power, 16, 94–95, 274n29; sovereignty as the governing understanding in, 98–99 (*see also* sovereignty); sovereignty of human reason, 92–93 (*see also* rationality); values present but manifested differently in Islamic cultures, 231. *See also* liberalism; modernity; philosophy; *and specific Enlightenment thinkers* environment: Bardsley on gratitude to nature and environmental ethics, 249–53, 255; colonial exploitation of, 96–97; colonialism and ecological change, 288–89n5 (*see also* nature); environmental ethics, 184, 185, 233–34, 254–55 (*see also* Bardsley, Karen); environmentalism, 244–45, 256; Hallaq's conception of, 234. *See also* domination of nature; environmental degradation

environmental degradation: chain reactions of, 239; ecological/environmental crisis, 232–34, 240; as an evil, 343–44n53; examining all forces responsible for, 245; in Israel, 224; by multinational corporations, 189, 323–24n22; preindustrial societies and, 88–89, 339n16; as product of science, 185; as product of sovereignty, 97, 190, 206; as quasi-philosophical problem, 338n11; Said's silence on, 166; and territoriality, 206; unequal distribution of, 341n26. *See also* domination of nature

épistémès, Foucault's theory of, 44–45, 66, 139, 171–72, 174, 176–77, 313–14n3, 320n94

ethical benchmark(s). *See* benchmark, ethical

ethical order (of world/cosmos): Islamic, 262–63 (*see also* Islam, premodern); Schelerian, 156, 167, 184, 246–47. *See also* unity

ethics and ethical conduct: academia implicated in unethical sovereign practices, 184–87, 190–93, 324–25n27; corporate and institutional disregard for, 186, 188–94, 323n20, 323–24n22, 324–25n27 (*see also* the corporation);

divine-command ethics, 261–63; ethical benchmark(s), 18–19, 34, 79–84, 199; ethical violence, 346n73; Foucault on individual ethical formation, 264; individual as moral/ethical subject, in Islam, 75, 77, 79, 192, 261–63, 293n34; internal vs. externally imposed ethics (i.e., through modern law), 261; moral and ethical education, or lack thereof, 186–87, 322n12; rationality, as epistemology, lacking ethical restraints, 233; scholar's ethical/moral responsibility, 264–67. *See also* morality

ethnic cleansing, 218, 219, 221, 332nn86, 93. *See also* genocide, colonialism and; Holocaust; settler colonialism

Europe: classical Greece appropriated as "Western," 28; and the colonialist modernization of the Ottoman Empire, 116–18; disenfranchised Europeans, 237, 341n24; ethical benchmark(s) lacking, 20; and the evolution of the modern project, 18–21, 276n36; hegemony of NATO allies, 166; literature of (*see* literature); and the Ottoman Empire, 116–17, 216–17 (*see also* Ottoman Empire); rise of the corporation in, 80, 293–94n38 (*see also* the corporation); Said on Europeans as racist, imperialist, and ethnocentric, 29, 42, 70–71; Scheler on 19th-century technical progress in, 34; self-formation of, 13; unique in producing Orientalism, 68–69, 70, 72–73; universalizing of modern European problems/concepts, 299n72. *See also* colonialism; the

Enlightenment; imperialism; the modern state; modernity; progress; the West

evil, concept of, 89–90, 227, 343–44n53

exception, state of. *See* state of exception (extraordinarity)

existential threat, 220

extraordinarity, state of, 210–13. *See* state of exception (extraordinarity)

Eyal, Gil, 318n73, 334n107, 336n110

the Fall, Christian concept of, 89–90

Fanon, Frantz, 211, 330n72

Farhi, David, 336n111

felicity, conditions of: Austin's theory of, 39, 62–63, 283n34; and discursive formation, 171, 190; the Distinction as, 157, 185 (*see also* the Distinction); and Foucault's ideological author, 48–49; not explored by Said, 164; and Orientalism's performative power, 138, 148, 149; of philosophy, 92

"fixity," in Guénon's thought, 155–57

Flaubert, Gustave, 51, 59

Foucault, Michel: on beginning an analysis with a "how," 320n96; "dead author" of, 26, 42, 47; on discourses of power, 38; on discursive formation, 29–30, 139; on discursivity in science, 383–84n39; on the formation of the subject, 344n54; as founder of discursivity, 48–49; on "immediate struggles," 5; importance of Foucault's project, 118, 242–43; on the necessity of distinguishing power relations from communication, 13; the "order of things," 34, 281n15; on pastoral power, 99; points of contrast mainly

European, 15; Reformation identified as a point of beginning, 280n6; on the relationship of knowledge and power, 15, 273n25; Said's disagreement with, re individual texts/authors, 9; Said's understanding of, 2, 13, 29–30, 31, 41–42, 44–45, 139, 177, 242, 313–14n3; schematization of, 46; on sources of power, 97–98; on taking care of the self, 186–87, 257; theory not universally applicable, 85, 296–97n59; theory of *épistémès*, 44–45, 66, 139, 171–72, 174, 176–77, 313–14n3, 320n94; theory of felicity adapted to theory of power by, 62; theory of the author, 41, 42–49, 171, 174–77, 319n90, 320n94, 383–84n39; on the Western knowledge-power relationship, 94

France. *See* Algeria, French colonialism in; French conquest and colonialism; French Orientalism

freedom: Foucault on liberating the individual from the state, 176; Guénon on freedom of thought, 150; intellectual freedom and sovereign knowledge, 264–66; Kant's concept of, 301n94; as metaphysic, 235–36; modern subjectivity, freedom, and gratitude, 253; negative liberty, 152, 153, 157–58, 184, 186–87, 256; positive liberty, 151–52; Said on critique as path to, 338n10; and the self, 93; and sovereign reason, 92–93

French conquest and colonialism, 69, 216, 241. *See also* Algeria, French colonialism in

French Orientalism, 119–25, 162, 309n157. *See also* Algeria, French colonialism in; Guénon, René

Freud, Sigmund, 31, 43, 47, 49, 171, 174–75, 320n94

Frings, Manfred S., 300n81

Gare, Arran E., 280n12

Gay Science (Nietzsche), 84–85. *See also* Nietzsche, Friedrich

genocide, colonialism and: 20th century as "genocidal century," 162; Arendt on genocide, 330n70; Christian doctrine and, 90; colonialism inherently genocidal, 24, 210, 223; critiques of policies on, 226–28; the Distinction and, 206–7, 265; environmental degradation and, 97; forms of, 24–25; in French-occupied Algeria, 118, 124; Holocaust as "paradigm" of, 205, 214–15 (*see also* Holocaust); instrumentalism and, 198–99, 202–4, 206–7; Israel's settler colonialism and, 211, 217–26, 332nn86–88, 332–33n96, 334n104, 334–35n109 (*see also* Israel); knowledge, academia, and, 24, 67, 197, 223–26, 264, 265–66; in the "long sixteenth century," 86–87, 298n66 (*see also* the Americas); military technology not accountable for on its own, 125–26; modernity/ modern thought structure and, 13, 14, 18, 20, 125–26, 183; modern power and instrumentalism and, 198–99; Moses on, 154, 210; multinational corporations and, 323n22; normalization of structural genocide, 214; omitted from Said's narrative, 57, 68, 164, 183, 226, 286n73; Orientalism and (generally), vii, 14, 53, 67, 164, 197, 223, 243; Ottoman Empire, structural genocide of, 216–17 (*see also* Ottoman

Empire); positive and negative dimensions to genocide, 213–14; racial discourse and, 205–6; rearrangement of existence a goal of, 138, 214; self-hate and, 227–28, 255; sovereignty (sovereign structure of thought) and, 24–25, 97, 124, 197–99, 200, 265–66; structural genocide, 214–22, 229, 230, 234, 237, 260; structurally related to the state of exception, 208; structural relationship between colonialism and genocide, 24, 67, 183, 200, 213–15, 216, 223, 227; U.S. foreign policy and, 226–27; as weapon when other colonial efforts fail, 20; Wolfe on, 197–99, 213–15, 216, 276n36 (*see also* Wolfe, Patrick). *See also* domination of nature

German Orientalism, 7, 49, 161–63, 220, 271n15, 310n158

Ghazali, Abu Hamed Muhammad b. Muhammad al-, 186, 290nn17–18, 292n26

Gibb, H. A. R., 31

Giroux, Henry A., 305n127

global crisis, 232–34, 239, 242, 245–46, 341n26. *See also* modernity: crisis of, and needed restructuring

Goldziher, Ignaz, 49, 320n1

Gordon, Colin, 273n25

Goshgarian, Rachel, 303n110

Gramsci, Antonio, 50

gratitude, 249–53, 256–57

Gray, John, 36

Great Britain: efficiency of British colonialism, 216; and the field of economics, 188; and Indian independence, 211; North American settlers/colonizers dominated, 212 (*see also* British Orientalism); and the

Ottoman Empire, 117; rise of the corporation in, 80, 188. *See also* British Orientalism; East India Company; Europe; India, British colonialism in

Greece, ancient/classical, 27, 28, 50, 70

Grice-Hutchinson, Marjorie, 188

Grove, Richard, 88

Guénon, René, 143–64; about, 143–44, 169, 170–71; on "blindness" of Westerners, 158–60, 161, 185; critique of modernity, 145–51; critique shaped by engagement with Eastern traditions, 144–45, 171; "Easterners" contrasted with "Westerners," 151–52, 316n32; on "fixity," 155–57; full destructive forces of 20th century not seen by, 162, 178; on history, 145–46, 153–54, 158; influence and relevance of, 143–44; Massignon compared with, 179–80, 181; on materialism, 145–48, 153, 157–58, 168, 315n13; on the "moralism" commanding modernity, 233; on the need to reform the Western outlook, 167; on Orientalism, 147, 152, 160–64, 318n72; on philosophy, 149–51, 153, 157; proposed reforms of, 164–69; as refutation of Said's categorical brush, 29, 320–21n1; Said contrasted with, 22–23, 152–53, 160, 163–65; on science, 147–50, 153, 157; as subversive author, 143, 171, 174–75, 177

Guha, Ranajit, 303n111

Guyer, Paul, 301n94

Hallaq, Wael. *See The Impossible State* (Hallaq)

Hanafi, Sari, 329n63

harmony, 254–55

Harper, C. L., 323–24n22

Hastings, Warren, 131

Hastings Plan, 131. *See also* Jones, Sir William

hate of the other, 91, 197, 227. *See also* domination over the Other; racism

hate of the self, 51, 90, 91, 197, 227–28, 255

Heath, Joseph, 193–94

Heidegger, Martin, 97, 145, 147, 328n56

Herder, Johann Gottfried, 36, 37, 232, 256, 282n28

Herzl, Theodor, 333n96

heuristic historicism, 257

Hinduism, 11, 131–32, 151–52, 257, 262. *See also headings beginning with* India

history: agency theory and, 108–9; circulatory model, 244, 267; classified in central domain, 25, 194–95; and the colonial project, 194; currently undergoing self-evaluation, 243–44; existence of, as academic discipline, 70; Foucault's *épistémès* and, 176–77; Guénon's view of, 145–46, 153–54, 158; "historian" label falsely neutral, 4; historical perspective important, 46; historiography, 258–59, 264–67, 345nn63–64, 346n77, 346–47n78; linear concept of, 107–8, 110–11, 125–26, 241, 244, 266, 345n63 (*see also* progress); *longue durée*, 258, 345n63; as methodology, and the colonial project, 195–96; Nietzsche on, 267, 346n77; Said's lack of historical perspective, 45, 284n55; sovereign knowledge of, 265–66; and the theology of progress, 107–12, 194–95, 266, 306n133, 346n75

Hitler, Adolf, 206, 210, 220. *See also* Nazism

Hobbes, Thomas, 87, 94, 98, 235

Hodgson, Marshall, 42, 156

Holocaust, 208, 210, 214–15, 219–20, 226–27, 330n70

homo capitalisticus, 254. *See also* the human, concept of

homo economicus, 186. *See also* the human, concept of

homo modernus, 209, 248, 254, 257. *See also* the human, concept of

Horkheimer, Max, 158, 272n22

Hourani, Albert, 42, 49

How the West Came to Rule (Anievas and Nışancioğlu), 276n39

hubus (Fr. *habous;* also *waqf*), 116, 117, 118–20. See also *waqf*

the human, concept of, 16, 84, 118, 186, 193, 209, 251, 344n54. *See also headings beginning with* homo

human beings: capacity for violence, 126 (*see also* genocide, colonialism and; military technology); corporate violation of human rights, 189–90, 323n22; dehumanization of the Other, 95–96, 218, 220, 240; dignity of, 92–93; Said's "human" as textual human, 275n33; survival of, 232–33 (*see also* environment); value of humanity, 204–5, 247–48. *See* dignity, human; the human, concept of; the individual; the modern subject; the Muslim subject; the self; *and headings beginning with* homo

humanism. *See* secular humanism

Humanism and Democratic Criticism (Said), 308n137

Ibn Battuta, 61

Ibn Fadlan, 61

Ibn Jubayr, 61

imperialism, 266–67, 277–78n43. *See also* colonialism; *Culture and Imperialism* (Said)

The Impossible State (Hallaq), vii, viii, ix–x, 21, 112, 240, 274n28, 281n13, 309n155, 345n69

India (Biruni), 61, 289n6

India: circulatory model of history in, 267; postcolonial/independent India, 244–45; precolonial India, 68–69, 70, 88. *See also* India, British colonialism in

India, British colonialism in: British colonialism and Indian agency, 327n48; Coca-Cola's abuses in, 323n20; conventional genocide absent in British India, 198; "conversion" of, 218; date of effective colonization, 27; independence, 211; Jones and juridicality in, 56, 131–36, 196, 312n180; Latour's Stone in, 215–16; Macaulay on need to create British-like Indian subjects, 120, 131; Orientalists called upon, 127, 131; reasons for examining in this context, 17–18

the individual: Guénon on, 146–47, 150–51. *See also* human beings; the modern subject; the Muslim subject; the self

Indonesian Archipelago, Dutch colonialism in, 17–18, 125, 126–30

instrumentalism: about, 203–4; and codification, 133; and the Distinction as primary structure of thought, 206–7; and French vs. British colonialism, 216; Guénon on, 147, 148; of *homo capitalisticus*, 254; of human reason (instrumental rationality), 92, 93, 105, 122; and Orientalism, 163, 182, 231;

paradigmatic nature of, 236; power and, 198–99, 203–4, 273n25; of racial discourse, 205–6; and structural/paradigmatic critique, 66; subordinate status in Islamic and Asian traditions, 247; this book's critique of (generally), 19, 24–25

intent, and agency, 199

International Congress of Orientalists (29th), 269n1

international law, 222–23

Iqtidar, Humeira, 274n28

"The Iron Wall" (Jabotinsky), 199–202

Islam: concept "Islam" as collectivity/ category, 231, 337n7; conversion seen as desirable by, 70; cosmic unity and sacredness of life in, 247–48; gratitude as rational stance in, 256–57; Guénon's understanding of, 156–57; *hadith*, 292n30, 320n1; legacy of Said's *Orientalism* in speaking of, 12; Orientalism as rival tradition to, 241; Orientalist narrative of legal deficiency of, 122–23, 124, 310nn161–162, 311n165 (*see also* juridicality); paradigmatically contrasted with modernity, 11; perceived as existential threat by U.S., 220; "positive" representation of a cause for charges of "Orientalist" attitudes, 3; relationship to the (postcolonial) West, 238–39; Said on fundamental misrepresentation of, 59; Said's attitude toward, 321n2; Scheler's position similar to that of, 255; studying Islam and Islamic history and law (as scholar today), 246–47, 258–63. *See also* Arabs; Islam, premodern; Islamic law; Muslim world; Ottoman Empire; Shari'a; Sufism

Islam, premodern: Bayt al-Hikma (Baghdad), 70, 289–90n9; central domain(s), 73, 76–79, 83, 243–44, 274n28 (*see also* Shari'a); charity and philanthropism in, 281n23; circulatory model of history in, 244, 267; concept of the rule of law, 80–84, 112–13, 208–9, 260–63, 310n162; conversion in, 87; corporation opposed on moral/ ethical grounds, 79–80, 192; cultural similarities and variations, 73; defining characteristics of Islamic cultures, 73; ethical benchmarks in, 79–84; governance without modern sovereignty, 112; individual as moral/ ethical subject, 75, 77, 79, 192, 261–63, 293n34; *jihad* in, 295n56; juristic personality in, 79–80 (see also *waqf*s); likelihood of evolution of modern project in, 20; and medieval Christianity, 28; Muslim project and, 231; the Muslim subject produced by nonstate socioethical formations, 82, 295–96n57; no analog to Orientalism in, 68–69, 70, 72; nonanthropecentric conception of the world in, 81; Orientalists' study and epistemic transformation of, 230–32 (*see also specific individuals*); relationship of knowledge and power in, 78–79, 82–85, 295n56, 295–96n57, 296n59; rule of law, concept of, 80–84, 112–13, 310n162; rulers and Islamic scholarship/ education, 76, 289n8, 291n23; rulers and political structures subordinate to Islamic moral law, 78–79, 82–84, 112, 209, 260, 295–96n57; Saljuq system of surveillance, 296n59; status and treatment of conquered peoples,

Islam (*continued*)
129, 311n169; "transmission" of
Greek knowledge by Arab scholars,
70; travel literature, 61, 289n6; use of
as case study, 72–73; *waqfs*, 79–80,
114–24, 126, 168, 310n162. *See also*
education, in premodern Islamic
cultures; Islam; Islamic law; Muslim
world; Ottoman Empire; Shariʿa;
Sufism

Islamic law: British assault on, in India,
131–35, 196, 312n180 (*see also* Jones,
Sir William); concept of the rule of
law, 80–84, 112–13, 208–9, 260–63,
310n162 (*see also* Shariʿa); conquered
peoples subject only to "public" law,
129; diversity, flexibility, and
plurality of, 133–34; Dutch assault
on, in the Indonesian Archipelago,
126–30; economic and mercantile
spheres governed by, 76, 78;
European assaults on Shariʿa
(generally), 122–24; French assault
on, in Algeria, 118–24; *hiyal*, 292n32;
Jones's work on, in India, 131–37,
196, 312n180; judicial accountability,
293n34; judicial reforms in the
Ottoman Empire, 116–18; and juristic
personality, 79–80; the legal as
instrument of the moral, 77, 292n28;
orality of, 134–35; Orientalist
discourse on, 259–60; Orientalist
narrative of Islam's legal deficiency,
122–23, 124, 310nn161–162, 311n165;
Shariʿa as law of the land, 78–79; use
of "legal" as term in discussing,
336–37n2. *See also* Shariʿa

Islamism, 274n28

Is/Ought distinction. *See* the Distinction

Israel, 213, 222–23; academia in, 71,
223–26, 334n107, 334–35n109,

335–36n110, 336n111; anti-Arab
feeling/rhetoric in, 218, 225,
332nn86–88, 93, 334–35n109,
334n108 (*see also* Jabotinsky,
Vladimir); expulsion of Palestinians,
218, 219, 221, 332nn86, 93; founding
myth, 218; Israeli Orientalism
(*Mizrahanut*), 225–26, 318n73;
Jabotinsky's "The Iron Wall" essay,
199–202; military and military
technology, 224, 226, 333n102,
333–34n104, 334n107, 336n111;
settler colonialism and genocide, 213,
217–23, 331nn82, 84, 332nn86–88,
332–33n96, 334nn104, 108,
334–35n109. *See also* Palestine and
Palestinians; Zionism

Jabarti, ʿAbd al-Rahman al-, 69
Jabotinsky, Vladimir, 199–202, 332n86
Jackson, Zakiyyah Iman, 245
Japan, 276–77n39
Java, 125. *See also* Indonesian
Archipelago, Dutch colonialism in
Jews: anti-Arab racism, 218, 224–25,
332nn86–88, 93, 334n108 (*see also*
Jabotinsky, Vladimir); anti-Semitism,
220; constructed as existential threat
to Germany's Third Reich, 210, 220
(*see also* Holocaust); forced conversion
of Andalusian Jews, 86; Said's
Orientalism charged with ideological
bias against Judaism, 7. *See also* Israel;
Zionism
jihad, 295n56
Jones, Sir William, 3, 56, 105, 106–7,
131–36, 195–96, 312n180
journalism, 4, 15, 25, 69–70, 194
juridicality: constitution of new human
subject through, 16; defined, and use
of term, 18, 207; the Distinction and

modern legal positivism, 260–61; distinction between rule of law and rule of the state, 112–13; Dutch colonization of Indonesian Archipelago and, 126–30; Foucault's concept of, 62–63; French colonization of Algeria and, 118–24; international law, 222–23; Jones's work in British-occupied India, 56, 131–37, 196, 312n180; judicial reforms in the Ottoman Empire, 116–18; law and sovereign will, 99–100, 207, 208–9, 211, 222–23; and the marital "I do," 62; not examined by Said, 18; of Orientalism, missed by Said, 106–7; Orientalist narrative of Islam's legal deficiency, 122–23, 124, 310nn161–162, 311n165; purpose and practice of codification, 132–33; rule of law, in premodern Islam, 80–84, 112–13, 208–9, 260–63, 310n162 (*see also* Islamic law; Shari'a); and the state of exception, 123, 207–8, 209–10, 329n64. *See also* codification; law

juristic personality, 79–80

Kahn, Paul, 88, 89–90, 94–95

kalam, 3, 73

kalam al-nafs, 263

Kant, Immanuel, 31, 36, 37, 93, 170, 175–76, 282n28, 301n94

Karatani, Kojin, 36, 107, 167, 169–71

Kaviraj, Sudipta, viii, 270n10, 288n4, 326–27n48

Keynes, John Maynard, 173, 188

Kimmerling, Baruch, 221

knowledge, 233; Christian concepts of creation and the Fall and, 89–90; close proximity of fields of, in Islamic education, 74–75; ethical/

moral responsibility of the scholar re knowledge production, 264–67; and genocide, 24–25; Guénon's attitude toward, 147–48; Orientalism represented as "text" in Said's account, 56–57; outward- (European colonialist scholars) vs. inward-facing (Islamic jurists), 289n8; Scheler's "cultural knowledge," 94; sovereign knowledge, 22, 24, 98, 104, 125, 132, 211–12, 265–66 (*see also specific topics and areas of knowledge*); "systemic" knowledge of Orientalism reinforced by colonial encounter, 52. *See also* academia; knowledge and power, relationship between; scholarship; science(s)

knowledge and power, relationship between: academia as state entity, 102–3, 303–4n120 (*see also* academia); academic units involved in the creation of sovereign knowledge and power, 23–24, 277–78n43; Aristotle on, 84; British colonialism and Indian cognitive structure, 327n48; contrasting Western relationship with that in the premodern Islamic tradition, 15–16; corporatization of academia, 103–4, 305n127; dialectical nature of, 14–15; the Enlightenment and, 16, 86, 94–95; ethical problem at the root of, 191–92; Foucault on, 273n25; *jihad* doctrine and, 295n56; knowledge as weapon, 264–65, 345–46n73; modern "power" organically tied to knowledge, 16; Nietzsche on, 84–85 (*see also* Nietzsche, Friedrich); in *Orientalism*, 52–54, 55, 72; in premodern Islamic cultures, 78–79, 82–83, 84–85, 295n56, 295–96n57, 296–97n59

Schmitt, Carl; state of exception); slavery and, 341n23; structural critique impossible from within, 66; as taken-for-granted phenomenon, 164. *See also* domination of nature; the Enlightenment; freedom; libertarianism; progress; secular humanism; sovereignty; *and specific individuals*

libertarianism, 228

literature: classified in peripheral domain(s), 194–96; coloniality exhibited, 195; non-Western literature, 142; Said's focus on, in *Culture and Imperialism*, 195, 277–78n43, 314n7; Said's literary (textual) approach, 5, 9–10, 271n16, 271–72n17, 314nn6–7; Said's valuing of Western over non-Western literature, 142, 314n6

Locke, John, 95–96, 205, 228

Loi Warnier (1873), 123

"long sixteenth century," 86–87, 298n66

longue durée, 258, 345n63

Loomba, Ania, 272n21

Löwith, Karl, 195

Macaulay, Thomas Babington, 120, 131, 141

MacIntyre, Alasdair, 5, 93, 149, 241–43, 248, 252, 256

Malay people, *adat* law of, 127–30. *See also* Indonesian Archipelago, Dutch colonization of

Maldonado-Torres, Nelson, 274–75n29, 298n66

Marchand, Suzanne, 271n15

Marx, Karl: determining imprint of, 31; as discursive author, 43, 47–49, 171, 174–75, 320n94; materialism as

explicans for rise of capitalism, 205; and the modern thought system, 147

Massad, Joseph, 273n23, 279–80n5

Massignon, Louis: compared with Guénon, 179–80, 181; debate over Orientalism of, 3; exoticization of the East by, 52; Said's analysis of, 28, 31, 32, 52, 55, 139, 142, 171, 179–81, 328n48

materialism: as central paradigm, 272n19; characterizing modernity as materialist, 11; communism and, 152; the Enlightenment and, 231; Enlightenment/Western philosophy and, 95–96, 149–50, 153, 184, 248; as explicans for capitalism's rise, per Marx, 205; Guénon on, 145–48, 149, 151, 152, 153, 157–58, 167, 168, 170, 315n13; and human value, 190, 247; materialist worldview forged by capitalism, 34; and the modern subject, 254; and moral value, 236; *Orientalism* (Said) absent a critique of, 160, 164, 165–66; progress and, 150–51, 152–53, 154, 157 (*see also* progress); and racial theories, 205; revaluation of, 342n36; Scheler on, 254, 256; and territoriality, 206; Western education and, 101. *See also* capitalism

mathematics, 194, 326n39. *See also* science(s)

Mbebe, Achille, 210, 329n68

mechanical philosophers, 95–96

Mein Kampf (Hitler), 220. *See also* Hitler, Adolf; Nazism

Meir, Golda, 332n88

Mesopotamia, 287n80

metropolis (metropole), 211–12, 217–18, 331n84

Migdal, Joel, 221

Mignolo, Walter, 266, 276n38, 298n66

military technology (modern/ European): instrumentalism and, 203–4; Israeli, 224, 333n102, 333–34n104; mathematics and, 326n39; not the cause of colonialism and genocide, 125–26, 136, 204; as product of same mindset that produced modern Europe, 125–26

Mill, J. S., 188, 228, 234

miracle (concept), 262, 263

misrepresentation (in Orientalist works): Guénon on, 160–64; Orientalist text not just about, 17; Said's concerns about, 13, 22, 28, 55–61, 63, 70, 107, 140, 162–64, 226, 287–88n84; Said's legacy re, 12, 22, 140; structure of thought behind, 136, 147

Mitchell, W. J. T., 180, 308n137, 321n2

Mizrahanut (Israeli Orientalism), 225–26, 318n73. *See also* Israel

modernity: ancient tradition vs., 180–81; bringing Said to the reality of, 13; central domains of [*see* central domain(s)]; concept of history, 266, 346n75 (*see also* history); concept of sovereignty and, 98–100 (*see also* sovereignty); crisis of, and needed restructuring, 232–34, 239, 245, 341n26 (*see also* Orientalism: and the challenge of transcending modernity); critiques unable to escape/transcend epistemological framework of, 66; and culture and the "Other," 58; defined by colonialism, 54 (*see also* colonialism); and domination over nature, 85–91; and ethical conduct (*see* ethics and ethical conduct; pathology;

sociopathology); Europe and the evolution of the modern project, 18–21, 276n36 (*see also* Europe); and gratitude, 242, 249–50, 343n46 (*see also* gratitude); Guénon's critique of, 145–51, 315n13 (*see also* Guénon, René); inability of dominant discourses to transcend own categories of thought, 248–49; metaphysic(s) of, 235–36, 339n16, 340n19; openings and fissures as sites of critique, 26; Orientalism and the formation/construction of, 231–32 (*see also* Orientalism); Orientalism as another name for, 105, 305n130; overlooked/not questioned by Said, 12–13, 110, 272–73n22; positioning Orientalism within large structure of, 14; and the production of the Other, 21 (*see also* the Other); rationality as epistemology of, 233 (*see also* rationality); rationalization and justification of the modern project, 234–35; rise of, 40–41; Said on the crisis of, 165–66; Said's assumption of Western modernity as standard, 141–42; "undetermining imprints" of early modernity, 40; value and morality, modern system of, 235–36 (*see also* ethics and ethical conduct; morality); war and the modern paradigm, 274n29; and the will to power/domination, 91–92 (*see also* domination of nature; domination over the Other). *See also* the Enlightenment; Europe; the modern state; the modern subject; secular humanism; the West; *and specific topics*

modernization theory, 107–12. *See also* progress

the modern state: academia as state
entity, 102–4, 303–4n120; colonies
as structural extension of, 211
(*see also* colonialism); concept of
sovereignty and, 104–5 (*see also*
sovereignty); the Distinction and,
113–14; and existential threat, 220;
Foucault on liberating the individual
from, 176; historiography deeply
implicated in state domination, 266;
imposition of, on Muslim world, 114
(*see also specific examples, such as*
Ottoman Empire); and modern
education, 100–101; origins and rise
of, 85, 98–99, 113; rule of law
within/subordinate to the state,
112–13; sovereignty over nature and
the rise of, 98–99 (*see also*
domination of nature); sovereign
will and the formation of the state
subject, 100–102; and subjects' moral
agency, 262 (*see also* criminality;
ethics and ethical conduct)
the modern subject: in Bardsley's
account, 253, 255; at center of
Hallaq's analytical scrutiny, 8;
formation of, 234–35; placing at the
center of critique, 4; Schelerian
transformation of, 254–56;
sovereignty and the formation of the
state subject, 100–102; subjectivity of
the sovereign individual, 253;
totalizing subjectivity of, 102. *See
also* modernity
Moncrief, Lewis, 88
Mongols, 329n61
morality: of colonialism, in Jabotinsky's
view, 200–202; the corporation and,
80, 293–94n38, 294n39; critical/
rational morality of the
Enlightenment, 36; of detachment

and separation, 96, 302n108;
distinction between the citizen and
the moral individual, 303n119;
Guénon on materialism and the
West's "moral order," 146, 158, 159,
317n49; individual as moral subject,
in Islam, 75, 77, 79, 192, 261–63,
293n34; individual vs. collective
self-awareness and, 191–92; of man vs.
God, 95; modern system of, 235–36;
moral and ethical education, or lack
thereof, 186–87, 322n12; normative
anchors, 191–92; rationality, as
epistemology, lacking moral
restraints, 233; scholar's ethical/
moral responsibility, 264–67; Shari'a
as moral system, 75, 77–79, 80–84,
292n28, 293n34; sovereignty and
self-declared morality, 201;
sovereignty of human reason vs.,
92–93; subjectivity of moral value,
235–36. *See also* benchmark, ethical;
domination of nature; domination
over the Other; ethics and ethical
conduct; knowledge and power,
relationship between
Morris, Benny, 332n86
Moses, Dirk, 154, 210, 330n70
Moshe Dayan Center for Middle Eastern
and African Studies, 335–36n110
Movement for the Survival of the Ogoni
People (MOSOP), 323n22
Mulk, Nizam al-, 296n59
multinational corporations. *See* the
corporation
Mun, Thomas, 188
murder, 204
Murdoch, Iris, 303n119
music, 142, 174, 194, 195, 196
the Muslim subject, 82, 83–84, 117,
121–22, 295–96n57

Muslim world: epistemological implications of secular thought system rejected, 261–62; imposition of the modern state on (generally), 114 (*see also specific examples*); legal reform, narratives of, 107–8; literature of, 142; Mongol invasions of, 329n61; status and treatment of conquered peoples, 129, 311n169. *See also* Algeria, French colonialism in; Islam; Islam, premodern; Islamic law; Ottoman Empire; Shariʿa

Muthu, Sankar, 282n28

narcissism, 232, 325n33
Nasser, Riad and Irene, 334–35n109
nationalism, 102, 266, 307n135
Native Americans. *See* the Americas
nature: gratitude toward, 249–53, 256–57; scientific Islamic conception of, 302n103; shame of, 51, 89, 90, 197. *See also* domination of nature; environment; environmental degradation
Nazism, 162, 163, 206, 210, 214–15, 220. *See also* Holocaust
negative liberty, 152, 153, 157–58, 184, 186, 187, 256
neocolonialism, 166, 189–90, 322n18. *See also* the corporation
Nietzsche, Friedrich, 84–85, 91, 99, 145, 232, 266, 267, 346n77
Nigeria, 189, 323n22
Nisaburi (scientist, astronomer), 302n103
Nişancioğlu, Kerem, 276n39
Nugent, David, 304n120
Nussbaum, Martha, 305n127

Occident, production of, 13, 273n23. *See also* Europe; the West

ontological, as term, 300n87
orality, 117–18, 127–28, 134–35
the Orient (the East): corporate exploitation of, 189–90 (*see also* the corporation; East India Company); difference of, in Said's account, 51–52 (*see also* difference); exoticization of, 2, 3, 52, 140, 141, 163, 167, 229; "fixity" of, 155–57; Guénon on misrepresentation of, 160–64; Guénon's contrast of "Easterners" with "Westerners," 151–52, 316n32; and Guénon's proposed reforms, 168–69; life valued intrinsically, 205; Massignon on the difference between East and West, 180; misrepresentation of, in Said's account [*see* distance, as epistemology; *Orientalism* (Said)]; no analog to modern state in, 112; not valued by Said, 182; Occident included in, 17, 189 (*see also* the Americas); reengineering of, 57; Said on aspects of the Orient's difference, 140–41; silent nature of, Said on, 50–51. *See also* Islam; Islam, premodern; Muslim world; *and specific countries and regions*
Orientalism: ambiguity and classification, 1–4; and the Americas, 105 (*see also* the Americas); as another name for modernity, 105, 305n130; "bad" or "good" Orientalism/ Orientalists, 10, 30, 52; blanket condemnation unhelpful, 22; and the challenge of transcending modernity, 240–49, 257–58; critical apparatus lacking for diagnosis of bias of, 8; "determining imprint" of certain Orientalists, 140; discursive tradition and normalization of colonization,

119, 309n157 (*see also* colonialism); and the Distinction, 105–6 (*see also* the Distinction); "Eastern" Orientalists, 162; ethnic or religious background and charges of, 3; and the experience of the Other, 21; failure to see significance of Islamic thought, 263–64; and the formation of modernity, 231–32, 237 (*see also* modernity); function of structurally reformed and ethicized Orientalism, 24; global crisis, more profound critique required due to, 234; Guénon on, 147, 152, 160–64, 318n72 (*see also* Guénon, René); historical writing essential to, 153 (*see also* history); liberalism and, 144, 238–39, 241, 242 (*see also* liberalism); mainstream Orientalism as closed system, 172; "native" Orientalists, 238–39; misrepresentation in (*see* misrepresentation); "orientalism" vs. "Orientalism," 1–2; origins of, per Said, 27–29; other/rival traditions confronted, 241–42; performative nature of, 67; political framework of, 2–5; politicization of term/concept, 4, 139–40, 288n4; possibility of opposing forces within, 138–39; postcolonial stage, 237–40; reduced to political concept/enterprise, 67–72, 288n4, 288–89n5; and representations of Islam, 3 (*see also* Islam); represented as "text" in Said's account, 56–57; as ruse for production of the West/Occident, 13, 273n23; Said on who is an Orientalist, 28–30, 39, 58–59, 139–40 (*see also specific individuals*); Said's first definition of, 29; Said's premises and methods insufficient for

penetrating critique of, 234; Sardar on who is an Orientalist, 283n35; scapegoating of, 6, 8; similarity to other academic fields, 183–84; structural features of, in Said's characterization, 50–57 (*see also* difference; distance, as epistemology); as the study of the Other, 243; subversive strategies/discourse within, 140; as systemic structure, 9–10; tautological argument linking the structuring of modernity and, 21; as "text," 56–57; as a totality, in Said's narration, 22, 23–24; as a tradition of rational inquiry, 241–42; transforming, 25, 240–41, 243–44, 246–48, 257–58; why Orientalism, 69–70. *See also* British Orientalism; *Culture and Imperialism* (Said); French Orientalism; German Orientalism; *Mizrahanut*; *Orientalism* (Said); Said, Edward; *and specific authors and works*

Orientalism (Said): on the antihuman nature of Orientalism, 272–73n22; canonicity of, 8, 65, 179; Clifford's critique of, 6, 57; concerned about misrepresentation, 162–63 (*see also under* Said, Edward); critique of liberalism lacking, 160, 164, 165–66, 182, 317–18n61; critiques of (generally), 5–8; the "determining imprint" of the author in, 31–33, 41–42, 280n10; discursive strategy of, 55–56; on Europeans as racist, imperialist, and ethnocentric, 29, 42, 70–71; and Europe's self-formation, 13, 273n23; on Gibb, 139; grounds for critiques, 7; Guénon's work contrasted with, 22–23, 144, 152–53, 160, 163–65 (*see also* Guénon, René); Hallaq's approach to, 8, 13–14; on the

Orientalism (*continued*)
historical origins of Orientalism, 27–29, 70, 71–72, 297n62; importance (monumentality) of, 13; individual humanity of Orientals not expressed, 275n33; on Jabarti, 69; on Jones, 3, 56, 106–7; juridicality not examined, 18, 275n34; on language, 63; length criticized, 58; literary (textual) approach of, 9–10, 271–72n17; many questions not addressed, 183; Massignon analyzed/critiqued, 31, 32, 52, 55, 139, 142, 171, 179–81, 328n48; modernity not questioned in, 12–13; notion of (mis)representation in, 59–61, 287–88n84 (*see also* misrepresentation); on Orientalism as "a Western style" of domination, 95; Orientalism framed in political terms, 4–5, 67–72, 106, 197; Orientalism seen as anomaly within Western academia, 165, 319n76; preceded by Abdel-Malek's critique, 7, 285n59 (*see also* Abdel-Malek, Anouar); predecessors (*see* Tibawi, A. L.); and the problem of knowledge and power, and alternatives to Orientalism, 165–66; progress, science, philosophy not implicated, 160, 317–18n61; qualitative distinctions lacking, 70–72; relationship of knowledge and power in, 52–54, 55, 72; rise of non-Western apologists of Islam not addressed, 239; Said's secular humanism in, 232 (*see also under* secular humanism); on the scope of Orientalism, 14; structural features of Orientalism, as characterized in, 50–57 (*see also* difference; distance, as epistemology; knowledge and power, relationship between); on studying other cultures/peoples from a libertarian perspective, 227–28; theory of power incomplete in, 139, 313–14n3; third definition of Orientalism criticized, 109–10; Western modernity assumed as standard, 141–42. *See also* difference; knowledge and power, relationship between; Said, Edward

originality, 32, 39, 173

the Other: "aesthetic worship" of the "inferior Other," 169–70 (*see also* the Orient: exoticization of); agency of the "Oriental" Other, 21 (*see also* agency, theory of); constructed as the enemy, 219–20 (*see also* Israel); culture and the existence of, 58, 286–87n80; dehumanization of, 95–96, 218, 220, 240 (*see also* racism); "detached" separation from, 96, 302n108; Guénon on science and materialism's role in judging, 148–49; Guénon on Western "proselytizing" (remolding) of, 159–60, 317n53; hate of, 91, 197, 227 (*see also* racism; genocide, colonialism and); as ontological and epistemological necessity, 58; Orientalism as the study of, 243; and the project of transcending modernity, 239–40; and the structuring of modernity, 21. *See also* domination over the Other; *and specific countries, cultures, and peoples*

Ottoman Empire, 17–18, 114–18, 123, 198, 216–17, 276n39

Palestine and Palestinians: and Israel's settler colonialism and genocide, 211, 217–26, 332nn86–88, 332–33n96,

334n104, 334–35n109; Latour's Stone and, 199–202, 218; and *Mizrahanut* (Israeli Orientalism), 318n73; racism toward, 218, 225, 332nn86–88, 93, 334n108, 334–35n109 (*see also* Jabotinsky, Vladimir); Said's concern with, 166. *See also* Israel; Zionism

Panalba (antibiotic), 324–25n27

Pappe, Ilan, 219, 332n93

paradigm(s), 78; cultures and civilizations driven by, 73; exceptions and irregularities embodied, 78; existence of exceptions acknowledged by, 11; fields of "force relations" embodied by, 38; fissures and openings and, 26, 279n45; historical outlook essential to theory of, 46; language and performativity and, 12–13; paradigmatic instances, 153, 316n34; paradigmatic vs. subversive discourse, 245, 342n36; place of the author within central paradigms, 11, 14 (*see also* the author); Shari'a's paradigmatic status as central domain, 76–79 (*see also* Shari'a); shifts in, 40–41; situating the author within, 11; subversive discourses and resisting strategies that challenge, 39–40, 78; theory of, 11–12, 15, 33–41, 73, 102, 281n15, 281n23; use of, 11. *See also* central domain(s); *and specific paradigms*

Pascal, Blaise, 153

pathology, 211, 232, 330n72. *See also* psychopathology; sociopathology

performativity: Austin's theory of performatives, 61–62; Barad on, 63; capitalism as, 35 (*see also* capitalism); of discursive formations, 176 [*see also* discursive formation(s)]; and

Foucault's call to study discourses "according to their mode of existence," 45; of Guénon's materialism, 146–47; Hallaq's conception of, 12–13; not a license to accord language an absolute power, 22; Orientalism as performative, 67; psychoepistemic performativity of the modern/Western vision of nature, 184–85; Said's notion of representation and, 60–61, 63

peripheral domains: academic departments belonging to, 194 (*see also specific fields of study*); central domain's relationship to, 35–36, 37–38; Shari'a and, in premodern Islamic cultures, 77–78; subversive discourses and resisting strategies within, 39–40. *See also* central domain(s)

Petty, Sir William, 188

philosophy: as central academic domain, 25, 92, 153, 167, 184, 186, 194, 196, 267; currently undergoing self-evaluation, 243–44; the Distinction as dominating problem, 92, 184 (*see also* the Distinction); Enlightenment rationalism, 92–93, 113, 234; and gratitude to nature, 252 (*see also* gratitude); Guénon on, 149–51, 153, 157; mechanical philosophy, 95–96, 248; moral philosophy not taught in conjunction with business/economics, 186; rationalization and justification of the modern project, 234–35; Said's *Orientalism* on, 160, 317–18n61. *See also specific philosophers*

Picasso, Pablo, 35, 36, 281n22, 326n42

poetry, Islamic, 78, 292n31

political economists, 19, 276n36

political power, 84. *See also* knowledge and power, relationship between; power

Poo, Mu-chou, 286–87n80

poor, care for the, 80. *See also* charity and philanthropism

positive liberty, 84, 151–52. *See also* negative liberty

postcolonial Orientalism, 237–40

power: and agency, 108–9 (*see also* agency, theory of); biopower, 82, 84, 295n56, 297n59 (*see also* power); distance and, 59; Foucault on discourses of, 38; Foucault on juridical systems of, 62–63 (*see also* juridicality); in Foucault's conception, 297n59; and Foucault's theory of the author, 171, 175–76 (*see also* the author); incomplete theory of, in Said's *Orientalism,* 139; and instrumentalism, 198–99, 202–7; *jihad* doctrine and, 295n56; lack of organizing principle, 202–3; Orientalism's complicity with, in Said's account, 52–54, 65; pastoral power, 99; political power subordinate to ethical/moral precepts in premodern Islam, 78–79, 82–83; power relations and central domain(s), 38–39; rationality and, 243 (*see also* rationality); Scheler's "innate drive" for, 91, 151 (*see also* Scheler, Max); scholarship and, 65, 288n1; systems of, and Hallaq's conception of critique, 66–67; through systems of law (*see* juridicality); and tradition, 242; use of term, 97–98. *See also* central domain(s); domination of nature; domination over the Other; knowledge and

power, relationship between; sovereignty

Power, Samantha, 226–27

presence. *See* Latour's Stone

prison system(s), 100, 101, 117

progress: 19th-century European technical progress as example of central domain, 34; 19th-century technical progress as example of central domain, 34; basic features of, 306n133; Comte's Law of Three Stages and, 153–54; destructiveness as part of theology of, 88; doctrine not needed in premodern Islamic system, 209; in Guénon's thought, 150–51, 153–54, 157–58; history and the theology of, 107–12, 194–95, 266, 339n16, 346n75; infliction of, on longstanding cultures, 129; and materialism, science, and philosophy, 150–51, 153; and negative misrepresentation of the "Oriental," 152; not addressed in Said's *Orientalism,* 317–18n61; Orientalism defined by doctrine of, 240; theory of agency and, 108–9; universalization of the theology of, 107, 306n133, 339n16

property and property law/custom, 80, 115–24, 197–98. *See also* territoriality; *waqfs*

proselytizing, in Guénon's thought, 167, 317n53

psychology: classified in central domain, 103, 194; individual vs. collective self-awareness and responsibility, 191–94; in Jabotinsky's construction, 200; narcissism, 325n33; pathology, 211, 232, 330n72; psychopathology, 192, 232, 325n31; sociopathology, 24, 186, 190, 192–94, 197 psychopathology (psychopathy), 192, 232, 325n31. *See also* sociopathology

Quran, 260–61; charity and philanthropism in, 81, 115; and divine cosmic order, 247; as founding text across all Islamic traditions, 75–76; French Orientalism and colonialism and, 120–23; Orientalist discourse on Islamic law and, 259–61; Quranic studies, 74; route to understanding of, 264; "to be/do good" as dominant prescription in, 82. *See also* Islam; Islam, premodern; Shari'a

racism: anti-Arab racism, 218, 225, 332nn86–88, 93, 334n108, 334–35n109 (*see also* Jabotinsky, Vladimir); anti-Semitism, 220 (*see also* Holocaust); concept of civilization and the human and, 113–14; the Distinction and, 205; of Orientalist discourse on Islamic law, 259; racial theories and colonialism and genocide, 113–14, 205–6 (*see also* colonialism; genocide, colonialism and); Said on, 29, 42, 70–71; Zionist racism against Palestinians, 332nn87–88. *See also* domination over the Other

Rana, Aziz, 212

rationalism, Enlightenment, 92–93, 113, 234. *See also* philosophy; rationality

rationality: as central paradigm, 272n19; and the current crises, 234, 236, 340n21; as epistemology, 233; and gratitude, 249–53; and the intrinsic value of physical objects, 244–45; as metaphysic/theology, 235–36, 340n21; moral and ethical restraints lacking, 233; and power, 243

reason, sovereignty of human, 92–93. *See also* rationalism, Enlightenment; rationality

reductionism, fallacy of, 12

religion: critical secularism and, 55; divine-command ethics, 261–63; gratitude as rational stance in, 256–57; and moral benchmarks, 34 (*see also* benchmark, ethical); Said's problems with, 110, 180–81, 308n137, 321n4, 328n48, 338n10; seen as primitive, 260. *See also* Christianity; Islam; Islam, premodern; morality

Renan, Ernest, 28, 39, 56

Renoir, Pierre-Auguste, 35

representation(s): and performativity, 62–63 (*see also* performativity); purpose and effectiveness of, 60–61, 286–87n80; Said's notion of, 59–61, 63, 70–71, 287–88n84 (*see also* difference; distance, as epistemology). *See also* misrepresentation

Richter, Gerhard, 36, 37

Rome, ancient, 287n80

Rose, Deborah Bird, 199

Ruskin, John, 277–78n43

sacrifice, 255

Safi, Omid, 296–97n59

Said, Edward: Ahmad's critique of, 328–29n60; and authors' determining imprints, 31–33, 39, 280n10; bringing Said to the reality of modernity, 13; choice of subject authors, 10, 271–72n17; conception of the author, 9, 30–33, 39, 41–42, 49, 242, 280n10; concerned with misrepresentation, 13, 22, 28, 55–61, 63, 70, 107, 140, 162–63, 164, 226, 287–88n84; confusion of, 71; criticized for overlooking "good"

Said, Edward (*continued*)

Orientalists, 30, 42; critique lacking sharp boundary-definition, 29; critiques of (generally), 5–8 (*see also specific authors*); culture in Said's works and thought, 141–42, 160, 174, 317–18n61, 319n92; as dissenting author, 171–74, 178, 182, 319n92; first definition of Orientalism, 29; Guénon contrasted with, 22–23, 152–53, 160, 163–65 (*see also* Guénon, René); historical sense lacking, 45, 284n55; "human" as textual human in, 275n33; on humanist critique, 182–83; idea of Europe as superior culture seen as "never far" from the Orient, 276n36; importance of Said's work, 6, 13; juridicality not examined by, 18, 275n34; Karatani on Said's meaning of "Orientalism," 170; Kaviraj on the relation of Said's work to colonial discourse, 270n10, 326–28n48; legacy regarding misrepresentation, 12, 22, 140; legacy regarding representations of Islam, 3; liberalism of, 5, 22, 23, 71, 110, 142, 152–53, 166, 174, 182, 232, 242, 314n6, 317–18n61; literary (textual) approach of, 5, 9–10, 13, 271n16, 271–72n17; modernity overlooked/not questioned, 12–13, 110, 272–73n22; modern state taken for granted, 113; Mufti on, 277n42, 280n11, 314n6; Oldmeadow's criticism of, 1–2; Orientalism seen as anomaly/exception within academia, 165, 177–78, 319n76; political nature of Said's critique, 4–5, 67–72, 106, 197; and positive vs. negative liberty, 152–53;

preoccupied with horizontality, 30; relevance of, for Hallaq's critique, 6; and religion and tradition, 110, 180–81, 308n137, 321n4, 328n48, 338n10; secular humanism of, 6, 22, 54–55, 70, 152–53, 182–83, 232, 277n42, 338n10; starting point criticized as "without foundation," 280n12; totalization of Said's narrative, 22, 23–24, 136–37; traveling from the text to "worldliness" as preoccupation of, 275n31; understanding of Foucault, 2, 13, 29–30, 31, 41–42, 44–45, 139, 177, 242, 313–14n3; Western modernity assumed as standard by, 141–42; work preoccupied with "immediate enemy," 5. See also *Culture and Imperialism* (Said); *Orientalism* (Said)

Saljuq regime, 296n59

Sardar, Ziauddin, 283n35

Saro-Wiwa, Ken, 323n22

Schacht, Joseph, 49, 305–6n131, 320n1

Scheler, Max: disenchantment with modern condition, 232; and domination of nature, 91–92, 97, 338–39n11; on domination over the self, 93–94; on the ethical order of the world/cosmos, 156, 167, 246–47; on the need for a transformation of the modern subject, 254–56; and religion, 338n10; restructured view of world's unity called for, 256, 344n60; theory of innate drives, 91–92, 151, 236, 300n81

Schmitt, Carl, 34, 37–38, 91, 93, 207, 220, 281n15, 300n79

scholarship: European scholarship and colonialism, 69, 289n8; fundamental questions for scholars, 248; and power, 65, 288n1; premodern Islamic scholarship, 70, 73–78, 261, 289nn6, 8, 289–90n9 (*see also* education; Islam, premodern; Shariʿa); scholar's ethical/moral responsibility, 264–67; single-discipline focus of Western scholarship, 73; Western Orientalist scholarship without analog in non-Western cultures, 68–69, 70, 289nn6, 8. *See also* academia; knowledge; *and specific academic fields, including* Orientalism

School of Salamanca, Jesuit, 188

Schopenhauer, Arthur, 161–62

science(s): classified in central domain, 194, 196; crises in the natural world brought about by, 185; currently undergoing self-evaluation, 243–44; detachment and objectivity in, 96; dialectical relationship with philosophy, 184; existence of, as academic discipline, 15, 70; exploitative science rejected by Asian environmental voices, 244; Foucault on discursivity in, 383–84n39; in Guénon's thought, 147–50, 153, 156, 157; Israeli science, 224–25; and military technology, 204, 224, 326n39 (*see also* military technology); in premodern Islamic cultures, 77, 292n31, 302n103; Said's *Orientalism* on, 317–18n61; sheltered from Said's critique, 182; sovereignty of, 184–85; as taken-for-granted phenomenon, 164

secular humanism: benefits tied to pervasive destruction, 234; Europe's transformation from Christianity to domain of, 86, 298nn64, 66; gratitude a

conundrum for, 249–50, 343n46 (*see also* gratitude); incapable of appreciating/sympathizing with non-secular-humanist phenomena, 5; problematic nature of secularism, 277n42; of Said, 6, 22, 54–55, 70, 152–53, 182–83, 232, 338n10; Said's "human" as textual human, 275n33; secular system of thought judged unsatisfactory by Muslim intellectuals, 261–62; as taken-for-granted phenomenon, 164

the self: domination over, 90–91, 93–94; ethical training of, 186–87 (*see also* ethics and ethical conduct); Foucault on taking care of, 186–87, 257; freedom and, 93; hate of, 51, 90, 91, 197, 227–28, 255; Shariʿa and self-rule, 133; transformation/reengineering of, 254–55, 257

self-constitution, 212–13

settler colonialism: colonialism intensified through, 215; of Israel, 213, 217–26, 331nn82, 84 (*see also* Israel; Jabotinsky, Vladimir); natives as obstacles to, 199; in North America, 212, 213 (*see also* the Americas); relationship to genocide, 198 (*see also* genocide, colonialism and); sovereign domination over settlers/colonizers, 212; territoriality and, 206; units of, 211–12. *See also* Algeria, French colonialism in; colonialism; India, British colonialism in

"Settler Colonialism and the Elimination of the Native" (Wolfe), 197–98. *See also* Wolfe, Patrick

Shafir, Gershon, 331nn82, 84

Shalem, Avinoam, 271n15

shame of nature, 51, 89, 90, 197

Shari'a: and *adat,* in the Indonesian
Archipelago, 127, 129–30 (see also
adat); British colonialist policies
toward, 131–35 *(see also* Jones, Sir
William); as central domain, 76–79,
83, 292nn30–32; colonialist
evisceration of, 124, 129–30,
305–6n131, 336n1, 337n3; concept of
change in, 156–57; concept of the
rule of law and, 80–84, 112–13, 260
(see also under Islamic law); diversity,
flexibility, and plurality of, 133–34;
economic and mercantile spheres
governed by, 76, 78; French
colonialist policies toward, 122–24
(see also Algeria, French colonialism
in); and Islamic education/
scholarship, 75–78, 229–30,
292nn30–31; and juristic personality,
79–80; the legal as instrument of the
moral in, 77, 292n28; orality of,
134–35; and the (per)formation of
the Muslim subject, 82, 83–84; and
the production of the moral subject,
75, 77, 79, 262–63, 293n34; *shar'i*
subject as central benchmark of,
79–80; use of "legal" as term in
discussing, 336–37n2; violations of,
78, 293n34. *See also* Islam,
premodern; Islamic law
slavery, 20, 237, 274n29, 341n23
Snouck Hurgronje, Christian, 30, 127
social responsibility: corporate and
institutional disregard for, 186 (see
also the corporation); in premodern
Islamic cultures, 114–15 (see also
*waqf*s)
sociology (academic field), 25, 69–70, 103
sociopathology, 24, 186, 190, 192–94,
197, 232. *See also* psychopathology
(psychopathy)

sovereignty: academia and the state's
sovereign will, 102–4, 303–4n120;
diplomacy and, 324n24; and the
Distinction, 93, 206–7 *(see also* the
Distinction); domination as
ontological sovereignty, 91–93
(see also domination of nature);
Foucault's pastoral power and, 99;
and the four units of the colonialist
project, 211–13; in Jabotinsky's
"The Iron Wall," 200–202; and
juridicality, 99–100, 207, 208–9,
211, 222–23, 260–61 *(see also*
juridicality); and the modern state,
98–102, 104–5 *(see also* the modern
state); of multinational
corporations, 189–90, 322n18,
323n20, 323–24n22; philosophical-
scientific sovereignty, 184–85 [see
also philosophy; science(s)]; real
meaning of, over the colonized,
122; right over life and death
commanded, 124, 189–90, 210;
science and philosophy, and
sovereign will, 150; as shared
denominator of all European
colonialist projects, 124–25; and
sociopathology, 186, 190 (see also
sociopathology); sovereign
domination and sovereign
knowledge, 132; sovereign
knowledge of history, 265–66; and
the state of exception/
extraordinarity, 210–13, 222–23;
subjectivity of the sovereign
individual, 253; use of term, 96–99;
Western science as example of
epistemic sovereignty, 148. *See also*
specific states and colonized regions
Spain, 86–87. *See also* Andalusia; the
Americas

stability and change, Guénon on, 155–57

the state. *See* the modern state

state of exception (extraordinarity): colonialism and, 209–13, 329n68; corporate sovereignty and, 190; Islamic (moral) law and, 112; juridicality and, 123, 207–8, 209–10; not exceptional, 210–11; Schmittian-Agamban "miracle" and, 263

Stevens, Gregory W., 325n31

Stewart, Gordon T., 282n28

subversive authors, 23, 105, 138, 143, 171–72, 176. *See also* the author; Guénon, René

Sufism, 3, 73, 74, 75, 76–77, 79, 83–84, 292n26

surveillance, systems of, 100–101, 117, 296–97n59

Taylor, Charles, 92, 93, 149

technology: military technology, 125–26, 136, 203–4, 224, 326n39, 333n102, 333–34n104; as a way of revealing, 203, 328n56

Ter Haar, Bernard, 130

territoriality, 206, 221, 329n61

The Text, the World, and the Critic (Said), 174. *See also* Said, Edward

theism, 262. *See also* religion

Tibawi, A. L., 1, 7

torture, 15, 103, 225, 323n22

tradition(s): ancient tradition vs. modernity, 180–81; global crisis recognized by all traditions, 242; gratitude as rational stance in, 256–57; Guénon's definition of, 155–56; Orientalism as rational tradition, 241–42; and power, 242; Said's problems with religion and, 110, 180–81, 308n137, 321n4,

328n48, 338n10; Scheler's philosophical narrative compared with, 257 (*see also* Scheler, Max). *See also* Buddhism; Hinduism; Islam; Islam, premodern

Transfer Plan (Israel), 221–22, 332nn86, 93

Tyan, Émile, 29, 279n4

Udofia, O. E., 189, 322n18

United States, 166, 205, 217–18, 220, 226–27, 331n84

unity, 247–48; diversity within unity, in paradigm theory, 36, 40; Scheler on, 256, 344n60; state sovereignty and the unity of the subject, 102; of the world/cosmos, 157, 205, 244, 247–48, 254, 256 (*see also* ethics and ethical order)

the university. *See* academia

Upjohn, 324–25n27

usul al-fiqh (legal theory), 74, 82, 292n30

Valladolid Trial, 87

van den Berg, L. W. C., 129

van Vollenhoven, Cornelius, 127, 129–30

Varisco, Daniel Martin, 280n7

Veracini, Lorenzo, 212

Vico, Giambattista, 94, 186, 266, 338n10

Vincent, Andrew, 339n15

violence, human capacity for, 126. *See also* genocide, colonialism and; military technology

Volney, Comte de, 51

Wacquant, Loïc, 304n124

Wagar, W. Warren, 299–300n78

*waqf*s, 79–80, 114–24, 126, 168, 292n30, 310n162

Weizmann, Chaim, 199, 332nn86–87